NEW ESSAYS ON ZIONISM

NEW ESSAYS ON ZIONISM

Edited by

David Hazony, Yoram Hazony,
and Michael B. Oren

SHALEM PRESS

JERUSALEM AND NEW YORK

Book and cover design: Erica Halivni
Cover pictures: Copyright © GPO Israel,
Ya'akov Sa'ar, Moshe Milner, Ya'akov Green,
Avi Ohayon, Zvika Israeli, Einat Anker

Printed in Israel

ISBN 965-7052-44-0
    978-965-7052-44-0

∞ The paper used in this publication meets the minimum requirements of the American National Standard for Information Sciences—Permanence of Paper for Printed Library Materials, ANSI Z39.48-1992

CONTENTS

Foreword   vii

Part I: The Jewish State and Political Theory

Ruth Gavison   The Jewish State: A Justification   3

Yoram Hazony   The Guardian of the Jews   37

Ofir Haivry   On Zion: A Reality That Fashions
                      Imagination   65

Natan Sharansky   The Political Legacy of Theodor Herzl   101

Amnon Rubinstein   Zionism: A Deviant Nationalism?   116

Eyal Chowers   The Zionist Revolution in Time   127

David Hazony   Zion and Moral Vision   168

Part II: Zion and the Crisis of Jewish Culture

Assaf Sagiv   Dionysus in Zion   199

Anna Isakova   The Goldfish and the Jewish Problem   221

Ze'ev Maghen   Imagine: On Love and Lennon   252

Part III: Zion and History

Daniel Polisar   Making History   295

Arie Morgenstern   Dispersion and the Longing for
                      Zion, 1240-1840   304

Yoram Hazony   Did Herzl Want a Jewish State?   357

Michael B. Oren   Orde Wingate: Father of the IDF   390

Michael B. Oren   Ben-Gurion and the Return
                    to Jewish Power   405

About the Authors   416

Sources   419

Index   421

FOREWORD

THOUGH JEWS HAVE ALWAYS lived in their historical homeland, it was not until the second half of the 20th century that a large part of the Jewish people returned to settle in the land of Israel. There they built major cities—Tel Aviv, Haifa, Beersheva, and Jerusalem—a social and economic infrastructure, national institutions of culture and education, and a democratic system of government. They also built a sovereign state, the State of Israel, created in 1948 and subsequently recognized by most nations of the world. Today, Israel is home to the world's largest Jewish community. It maintains a vibrant, free press, a diverse and dynamic culture, and a powerful citizen army. After two thousand years of state-lessness, the Jewish people have achieved a vital national home.

Should this state exist? Does this small, precariously positioned Jewish state have a moral, political, or religious significance that can justify the hardship involved in maintaining it, in defending it? And if it has such significance, is this something that can speak to non-Jews as well, or is it a matter of concern only to Jews?

There was a time when such questions seemed pressing. Throughout the 19th century, the idea of a Jewish state was invoked time and again, usually by Jews whose purpose was to emphasize that their people had long ago abandoned the dream of establishing a state of their own. Jewry had become a faith, they argued, and no longer harbored political aspirations that might stand in the way of their integration into the public life of Germany, Austria, France, England, or America. Later, at century's end, the tide turned. Resurgent anti-Semitism spread across Europe, in response to which arose the Zionist Organization in 1897. Under the leadership of a Viennese journalist named Theodor Herzl, this organization set out to establish the very Jewish state that many European Jews had insisted they did not want. From that time until the German invasion of Poland in the fall of 1939, the question of the importance of the Jewish state haunted the public life of the Jews the world over. Many felt that the future of the Jewish people hinged on the answer that was given to this question. History proved them correct.

In May 1948, the Zionist leader David Ben-Gurion declared the Jewish settlement in Palestine an independent Jewish state. A tiny minority of Jews still opposed this step, but by this point their influence on Jewish opinion had become negligible. It had become clear that even a weak Jewish regime in Palestine, in the years before and during the war, would have been able to rescue hundreds of thousands of Jews who perished, perhaps even millions. The Holocaust had persuaded nearly all Jews of the necessity of a Jewish state. Even the Communists and the Haredi-Orthodox Agudat Israel, which had historically been opponents of the state, became signatories in the declaration of Israel's independence. The same was true among gentile friends of the Jews, most of who likewise came to think that the need for a Jewish state was self-evident.

The matter, it seemed, was settled. For nearly a generation Jews and those who sympathized with their cause treated ideological opposition to the idea of a Jewish state as a marginal phenomenon, the province of a few anti-Semites and cranks. When in 1975, the General Assembly of the United Nations equated Zionism (i.e., the existence of a Jewish state) with racism, the declaration was dismissed in the free world as a hypocritical maneuver on the part of Communist and Arab dictatorships to defame a democratic country and the West in general. Jews now recognized that ideological opposition to the idea of a Jewish state could be turned into an intellectual truncheon in the hands of despots and terrorists not overly troubled by what had happened in World War II.

But the possibility that such ideas could gain currency among decent people of good will remained inconceivable.

But the times have quickly changed, and what was inconceivable only yesterday has become reality. With the collapse of the Soviet Union, one can now give voice to anti-Zionist ideas without associating oneself with totalitarianism; and with the rise of a generation that has no memory of the Holocaust, the old taboos against such ideas are falling throughout the Western world and even among Jews. Controversial Israeli policies in Lebanon, in the West Bank, and in Gaza have exposed the state to widespread criticism, facilitating the task of those who question its right to exist. In Europe, overt anti-Semitism has made a feverish re-appearance, for which hostility towards Israel serves as an all too effective cover. In North America, a generation of anti-Zionist propaganda—originally fanned by the Soviets, but now a part of mainstream discourse in the mass media and on university campuses—has taken a fearsome toll, with many young Jews withdrawing their support for Zionism entirely. In Israel, too, a new generation of academics and writers has placed the criticism of Zionism and of the idea of the Jewish state at the center of their intellectual agenda, ravaging both the historical and the philosophical basis for the state.

Is it important that there be a Jewish state? It is now evident that this matter is not settled at all. The majority of Jews and their friends may still offer instinctive and unthinking support for the idea of the Jewish state. But with increasing frequency, one hears the voices of Jews and non-Jews whose answer to this question is in the negative. As Prof. Adi Ophir of Tel Aviv University has put it:

> Jewish sovereignty has turned out to be the biggest danger to Jewish cultural and moral existence.... They tell us that the only question left open, the only real question, is how to get "peace".... They fail to realize that the question lies in the very idea of national sovereignty.... We envision a state that will not be a [Jewish] nation state.[1]

There are many who seem to believe that the only answer to the accelerating delegitimization of Zionism both in Jewish and non-Jewish circles is to ignore it. No other nation in the world, it is said, is required to justify its existence. The English or the French, for example, do not have to explain to themselves or to others why they should have their sovereign states. They simply exist, leading their lives without explanation, without justification, as do all other peoples.

Perhaps there was a time when this view made sense. During the Cold War, when the United States and the Soviet Union were locked in a relentless competition for the loyalty of various peoples around the globe, self-determination and political independence seemed to be the way of the world, for the Jews as for everyone else. But the world in which one might have reached this conclusion is now gone. In its place is one in which the system of sovereign states is challenged by a quickly rising European ideology that sees the future of mankind in the dissolution of state sovereignty. The classic European national states—England, France, Holland, Italy, Germany—appear to be in the process of giving up their independence, choosing instead to lose themselves in a great European state whose ideological commitment is to something akin to world government. The fact that the French or the Germans do not seem overly concerned with justifying their continued existence as politically independent nations is thus hardly a precedent that Jews should rush to embrace. Indeed, it is the Europeans' manifest disinterest in such questions that makes it possible to imagine that these nations will no longer exist as politically independent states a few years from now.

Moreover, Israel is not watching events in Europe unfold through a telescope. We often forget that the Jewish state is, in terms of its geography, a province of Europe. Israeli cultural figures spend a great deal of time hopping planes to Paris and Berlin, moving in precisely those circles in which the dismantling of the national state is seen as a moral imperative. The extraordinary outpouring of "post-national" sentiment in Israel in the three decades since the 1973 Yom Kippur War—climaxing in the 1990s with the demands to change the national anthem, the flag, the Law of Return, and virtually every other aspect of Israeli public life that makes it a Jewish state—was thus not merely a homegrown expression of a desire to tone down the passion of Jewish national life in the hope of bringing the Arab-Israeli conflict to an end. It was at least as much an expression of a desire to "make it" in Europe by mothballing most of the old Jewish concerns and embracing what might be called the European Dream: A social-welfare system capable of guaranteeing a high standard of living for all, and assimilation into the machinery of world government. As Yossi Beilin, one of the leading architects of this new Israel, put it:

My dream is that Israel should be a kind of Denmark or Norway of the Middle East.... What I would like to see is a country with a powerful economy, whose citizens have a high standard of living.... I see Israel becoming one of the most important countries in the UN, a country involved in resolving the conflicts of others, with the ability to contribute officials to the UN, including a UN secretary-general whose focus would be on questions of human rights....[2]

Of course, the last few years have not been kind to this dream. The terrible bloodshed that has visited Israel since the resumption of warfare with the Palestinian Authority in September 2000 and with the Second Lebanon War in 2006 has, to be sure, made it implausible that the Jewish state will soon be able to spare soldiers for UN peacekeeping missions. Moreover, the international reaction to the killing of over 1,000 Jewish civilians in the streets of Tel Aviv and Jerusalem has taught us a hard lesson about post-national Europe, which is well disposed to Jews when they seem to be progressing towards the European Dream, but is also capable of shocking outbursts of anti-Semitism the moment they are seen wielding military power in an attempt to defend themselves. This, too, has played a role in sharpening Jewish skepticism concerning the virtues claimed for the new identity Europe is building for itself.

This widespread and deepening skepticism has opened the way for a revival of Jewish national sentiment—of Zionism—both in Israel and in the Jewish Diaspora.[3] The purpose of this anthology of essays is to begin a discussion whose ultimate purpose is to provide the intellectual framework for such a revival.

It is no secret that Zionism as an intellectual movement is believed by many to have spent itself. Zionist thought is typically depicted as though it came to an end with the founding of the state in 1948, or was then succeeded by the platforms of the various political parties. But this view of the history of Zionist thought is mistaken. There were always individuals who continued to contribute to the store of constructive thought concerning the nature, meaning, and purpose of the Jewish state, even as this kind of writing was marginalized in favor of ever-more aggressive "critiques" of Zionism that were, in the 1970s, to become the hallmark of high Israeli culture. The Zionist writings of Nathan Rotenstreich, Eliezer

Schweid, Eliezer Berkovits, and Yosef Dov Soloveitchik are among the significant exceptions to this trend.

It is not until the mid-1990s, however, that one can point to a real revival of the classical trend in Zionist thought. This, of course, was precisely the moment when the general distancing of Israel's intellectual culture from traditional Zionist presuppositions reached its height. Not since the 1930s had Zionism come under such systematic criticism from what could be considered the mainstream of Jewish opinion. In particular, this rupture with the Zionist political tradition was symbolized by the nearly complete delegitimization of the term "Jewish state," coined by Herzl and incorporated by Ben-Gurion into Israel's Declaration of Independence.

The revival of Zionist thought in Israel in the mid-1990s can be described as consisting of two different types of material. In the first place, there is what can be called *controversial* material, most of it written by the older generation of Labor-Zionist academics and other writers born before the establishment of the state, including the authors Aharon Meged and Moshe Shamir, historians such as Shabtai Teveth, Yehoshua Porath, Yosef Gorny, and Anita Shapira, the political scientists Shlomo Avineri and Shlomo Aharonson, and the sociologist Moshe Lissak. These responses were in effect a countercritique, whose purpose was to highlight various flaws perceived in the works of many of the prominent critics of Zionism.

In addition, there was what may be called *constructive* material, whose purpose was not so much to set up a countercritique, as to offer a philosophical and historiographic alternative capable of reviving the Zionist political tradition and serving as the basis for a renewed and deeper appreciation of Zionism and of the Jewish state. Here, the tendency was to prefer essays and larger expositions, most of them composed by younger writers who were at the time largely unknown. In this category one may include the writings of historians such as Tuvia Frieling, Tzvi Tzameret, Alex Yakobson, and Arie Morgenstern, political and legal theorists such as Amnon Rubinstein, Ruth Gavison, Eyal Chowers, Ofir Haivry, Daniel Polisar, David Hazony, and Assaf Sagiv and scholars and essayists such as Anna Isakova, Ze'ev Maghen, and Assaf Inbari.

The full inventory of controversial and constructive works that can be associated with this trend would by this point extend to many volumes. For this reason, we have decided not to include in this anthology those writings whose purpose was largely countercritique of post-national trends in Israel. Instead, we have tried to focus on constructive works that may prove to be of enduring worth. Our hope is that these new essays on Zionism will prove to be as provocative and fruitful to Jews in the Diaspora as they were when originally published in Israel.

The Editors

NOTES

1. Ariela Azoulay and Adi Ophir, "100 Years of Zionism: 50 Years of a Jewish State," *Tikkun* (March-April 1998), pp. 68-71.

2. Yossi Beilin, *Israel at Forty-Plus* (Tel Aviv: Yediot Aharonot, 1993), p. xiv. [Hebrew]

3. To a certain extent, this is already here. We all know people who have felt a strengthening of their commitment to being a Jew during these hard years. In Israel, this has expressed itself in various ways, including the Israeli president's proposal to add representatives of the Jewish Diaspora to Israel's parliament; acts of the Knesset and Education Ministry to curb some of the worst excesses of post-national historiography in the public schools; and the 2002 Kineret Declaration by a broad range of Israeli public figures re-confirming, for the first time in a generation, Israel's character as a Jewish state.

PART I

THE JEWISH STATE AND POLITICAL THEORY

THE JEWISH STATE:
A JUSTIFICATION

RUTH GAVISON

IS IT POSSIBLE to justify the existence of a Jewish state? This question, raised with increased frequency in recent years, is not just a theoretical one. Israel will endure as a Jewish state only if it can be defended, in both the physical and the moral senses. Of course, states may survive in the short term through sheer habit or the application of brute force, even when their legitimacy has been severely undermined. In the long run, however, only a state whose existence is justified by its citizens can hope to endure. The ability to provide a clear rationale for a Jewish state is, therefore, of vital importance to Israel's long-term survival.[1]

Over the many years in which I have participated in debates about Israel's constitutional foundations and the rights of its citizens, I did not generally feel this question to be particularly urgent. Indeed, I believed that there was no more need to demonstrate the legitimacy of a Jewish state than there was for any other nation state, and I did not take claims to the contrary very seriously. Those who denied the legitimacy of Israel as a Jewish state were, in my eyes, little different from the radical ideologues who dismiss all national movements as inherently immoral, or who insist that Judaism is solely a religion with no right to national self-expression; their claims seemed marginal and unworthy of systematic refutation.[2]

Today I realize that my view was wrong. The repudiation of Israel's right to exist as a Jewish state is now a commonly held position, and one that is increasingly seen as legitimate. Among Israeli Arabs, for example, it is nearly impossible to find anyone willing to endorse, at least publicly, the right of Jews to national self-determination in the land of Israel. Rejection of the Jewish state has in fact become the norm among most representatives of the Arab public—including those who have sworn allegiance as members of Knesset. As far as they are concerned, the State of Israel, inasmuch as it is a Jewish state, was born in sin and continues to live in sin. Such a state is inherently undemocratic and incapable of protecting human rights. Only when it has lost its distinctive Jewish character, they insist, will Israel's existence be justified.

More worrisome, perhaps, is the fact that many Jews in Israel agree with this view, or at least show a measure of sympathy for it. Some of the Jews committed to promoting the causes of democracy, human rights, and universal norms are, knowingly or not, assisting efforts to turn Israel into a neutral, liberal state—a "state of all its citizens," as it is commonly called. Few of them understand the broader implications of such a belief for Israel's character. Most are simply reassured by Israel's success in establishing a modern, secular, liberal-democratic state with a Jewish national language and public culture, and think these achievements are not dependent on Israel's status as the nation state of the Jews. Like many liberals in the modern era, they are suspicious of nation states, without always understanding their historical roots or the profound societal functions they serve. This suspicion often translates into a willingness to sacrifice Israel's distinct national identity—even when this sacrifice is demanded on behalf of a competing national movement.[3]

Nor, at times, have Israel's own actions made the job of justifying its unique national character an easy one. On the one hand, the government uses the state's Jewish identity to justify wrongs it perpetrates on others; on the other, it hesitates to take steps that are vital to preserving the country's national character. The use of Jewish identity as a shield to deflect claims concerning unjustifiable policies—such as discrimination against non-Jews or the Orthodox monopoly over matters of personal status—only reinforces the tendency of many Israelis to ignore the legitimate existential needs of the Jewish state, such as the preservation of a Jewish majority within its borders and the development of a vibrant Jewish cultural life.

It is against this backdrop that I write this essay. In what follows, I will argue that the idea of a Jewish nation state is justified, and that the existence of such a state is an important condition for the security of its Jewish citizens and the continuation of Jewish civilization. The establishment of Israel as a Jewish state was justified at the time of independence half a century ago, and its preservation continues to be justified today. Israel does have an obligation to protect the rights of all its citizens, to treat them fairly and with respect, and to provide equally for the security and welfare of its non-Jewish minorities. Yet these demands do not require a negation of the state's Jewish character. Nor does that character pose an inherent threat to the state's democratic nature: On the contrary, it is the duty of every democracy to reflect the basic preferences of the majority, so long as they do not infringe on the rights of others. In Israel's case, this means preserving the Jewish character of the state.

The argument I will present here is framed mainly within the discourse of human rights, including the right of peoples, under certain conditions, to self-determination. Such an argument begins by recognizing the uniqueness of peoples and by acknowledging as a universal principle their right to preserve and develop that uniqueness. This starting point may seem shallow or even offensive to some Jews, particularly those for whom the Jewish right to a state and to the land of Israel is axiomatic, flowing inexorably from Jewish faith or history. According to this view, neither the long exile of the Jews nor the fact of Arab settlement in the areas where the ancient Jewish kingdom lay undermines the Jewish claim, which is absolute and unquestionable, an elemental point of religious belief.

In my view, it is crucial to base the justification of a Jewish state on arguments that appeal to people who do not share such beliefs. We must look instead for a justification on universal moral grounds. This is the only sort of argument which will make sense to the majority of Israelis, who prefer not to base their Zionism on religious belief, or to those non-Jews who are committed to human rights but not to the Jews' biblically based claims. Moreover, such an argument may have the added benefit of encouraging Palestinians to argue in universal terms, rather than relying on claims of historical ownership or the sanctity of Muslim lands. Locating an argument within the discourse of universal rights is, therefore, the best way to avoid a pointless clash of dogmas that leaves no room for dialogue or compromise.

Justifying the principle of a Jewish nation state, however, is only part of protecting the future of Israel. No less important is demonstrating that the state in fact can uphold, and does uphold, the principles considered essential to any civilized government, including the maintenance of a democratic regime and the protection of human rights. Accordingly, after presenting the arguments that support the existence of a Jewish state in the land of Israel in principle, I will go on to discuss how such a state ought to be fashioned—that is, how its policies and institutions should be crafted so as to help preserve the country's Jewish character without violating its basic obligations to both Jews and non-Jews, in Israel and abroad.

One commonly held view of liberal democracy asserts that the state must be absolutely neutral with regard to the cultural, ethnic, and religious identity of its population and of its public sphere. I do not share this view. I believe such total neutrality is impossible, and that in the context of the region it is not desired by any group. The character of Israel as a Jewish nation state does generate some tension with the democratic principle of civic equality. Nonetheless, this tension does not prevent Israel from being a democracy. There is no inherent disagreement between the Jewish identity of the state and its liberal-democratic nature. The state I will describe would have a stable and large Jewish majority. It would respect the rights of all its citizens, irrespective of nationality and religion, and would recognize the distinct interests and cultures of its various communities. It would not, however, abandon its preference for the interests of a particular national community, nor would it need to.

The Jewish state whose existence I will justify is not, therefore, a neutral "state of all its citizens." Israel has basic obligations to democracy and human rights, but its language is Hebrew, its weekly day of rest is Saturday, and it marks Jewish religious festivals as public holidays. The public culture of this state is Jewish, although it is not a theocracy, nor does it impose a specific religious concept of Jewish identity on its citizens. No doubt this kind of state should encourage public dialogue about the relationship between its liberal-democratic nature and its commitment to the preservation of Jewish culture. In what follows, I will offer an argument for the justification of an Israel that is both proudly Jewish and strongly democratic—and that has the right, therefore, to take action to preserve both basic elements of its identity.[4]

II

I begin with the premise that peoples have a right to self-determination in their own land. Exercising this right, however, does not necessarily depend on establishing a sovereign state. Self-determination can be achieved, for example, by securing cultural autonomy within a multi-national political framework.[5] Yet a nation state—a state whose institutions and official public culture are linked to a particular national group—offers special benefits to the people with whom the state is identified. At the same time, it puts those citizens who are not members of the preferred national community at a disadvantage. Whether it is just to give the advantage to one people at the expense of another is a question that cannot be answered *a priori*. Rather, we must take into account the competing interests of the different parties, as well as their relative size and the political alternatives available to each of them. The starting point for our justification of the Jewish state, then, is an examination of the advantages of such a state for the Jewish people—in Israel and elsewhere—as compared to the disadvantages it poses for other national groups within its borders.

While a vibrant Jewish state plays a variety of roles in the lives of Jews, we must not forget the circumstances that gave rise to the Zionist dream. It is well known that Zionism emerged as a response to two interrelated problems: The persecution of the Jews on the one hand, and their widespread assimilation on the other. Of the two, the concern for the security of the Jewish people predominated: For years, the Zionist movement claimed that only a Jewish state could ensure the safety of Jews around the world. Today, however, it is fair to ask whether this claim has really stood the test of time. After all, the Jewish people survived for two millennia without a state, often in the most difficult of conditions. In recent generations, particularly in Western countries, Jews have enjoyed an unprecedented level of security and freedom of cultural expression. Perhaps this recent success stems in part from the sense of belonging Jews feel toward Israel, and the knowledge that there exists in the world a country committed to their safety. It may also be a result of lessons the world learned from the destruction of European Jewry. But these alone do not seem to justify the claim that a Jewish state is somehow essential for Jewish survival. Even the clear rise in anti-Semitism throughout the Diaspora over the last few years does not decide the issue. While some argue that this new trend is merely the emergence of previously suppressed anti-Semitic sentiments, we should not dismiss out of hand the claim that this renewed anti-Semitism is, at least in part, a response to Israel's behavior in its ongoing conflict with the Palestinians. Moreover, Israel's ability to protect its own Jewish citizens appears tragically limited—a fact made brutally clear by the murder of hundreds of Jewish civilians by Palestinian terrorists since September 2000. Nevertheless, there is one form of anti-Semitism that is inconceivable in a Jewish state: The state-sponsored, or state-endured, persecution of Jews. The trauma of systematic oppression that was the lot of every previous generation of Jews stops at the borders of the Jewish state.[6]

The problem of assimilation presents Israel with a different challenge. Israel offers the possibility of a richer Jewish life than could ever be found in the Diaspora, and not merely because Israel is the only country with a Jewish majority. The public culture of the state is Jewish, the language of the country is Hebrew, national holidays commemorate Jewish religious festivals and historical events, and the national discourse is permeated with concern for the fate of the Jews. In addition, state lands, immigration, and the defense of the civilian population are all in the hands of a Jewish government. In just half a century, Israel has become home to the strongest Jewish community in the world—a role that is likely to become even more pronounced in the years ahead, as assimilation and emigration gradually reduce the power and influence of Jewish communities in the Diaspora.[7]

For observant Jews—even those who are opposed to Zionism—the advantages of a Jewish state are obvious. Certainly anyone who has practiced an observant lifestyle in both Israel and the Diaspora knows how much easier it is in the Jewish state. In addition, Orthodox Jews in Israel fulfill the commandment of *yishuv ha'aretz*, of living in the land of Israel. While a Jewish state may not be absolutely necessary to fulfill this commandment, its absence might make it very difficult for Jews to remain here.[8]

A less obvious yet arguably greater advantage of a Jewish state is the cultural reinforcement it offers to secular Jews, whose Jewish identities are more fluid and generally lack the internal safeguards possessed by their Orthodox counterparts. For only in Israel, with its Jewish public culture, can Jewish identity be taken for granted as the default option, and the cultivation of any other identity require a special effort—the kind of effort all too familiar to Diaspora Jews, who must struggle daily to maintain their links to Judaism.

In addition to offering Jews a safe haven from the forces of assimilation, a Jewish state offers the possibility of an exceptionally vibrant secular Jewish life. Since the rise of the Zionist movement, the Jewish people has witnessed the creation, in Hebrew, of countless new works of literature, poetry, and philosophy, whose wellsprings of inspiration are Jewish beliefs, customs, and history. This immense creative activity benefits Jews everywhere, for it offers wide new possibilities for a Jewish identity that is not dependent on halacha, or Jewish law.

For Jews in both Israel and the Diaspora, then, the loss of the Jewish state would mean the loss of all these advantages. Without a Jewish state, the Jews would revert to the status of a cultural minority everywhere. And as we know from history, the return of the Jews to minority status would likely mean the constant fear of a resurgence of anti-Semitism, persecution, and even genocide—as well as the need to dedicate ever more resources to staving off assimilation. I do not feel that I am being overly dramatic, then, if I say that forgoing a state is, for the Jewish people, akin to national suicide.

The benefits of Israel for Jews are mirrored, at least in some respects, by the price it exacts from its Arab citizens. For in a Jewish state, Arab citizens lack the ability to control their own public domain. The national language and culture are not their own, and without control over immigration, their ability to increase their proportion in the overall population is limited. Furthermore, their personal and cultural security are dependent on the goodwill and competence of a regime they perceive as alien. All these are harder for Arabs to accept since they used to be a majority in the land, and have become a minority despite the fact that they remained on their land. The Jewish state is thus an enterprise in which the Arabs are not equal partners, in which their interests are placed below those of a different national group—most of whose members are newcomers to the land, and many of whom are not even living in the country. In addition, as we shall see, the establishment of Israel has had a major impact on the lot of Palestinians who are not its citizens. It follows, then, that the case for a Jewish state must weigh the advantages it brings to Jews against the burdens it imposes on its Arab citizens.

III

Balancing Jewish and Arab claims to self-determination in the land of Israel (or Palestine) is not a matter of abstract rights-talk. Rather, such claims must be addressed according to the demographic, societal, and political realities that prevail both in the Middle East and in other parts of the world. It thus follows that the degree to which a Jewish state in the land of Israel is justified does not remain constant, but instead varies over time and according to changing circumstances. Indeed, it is my contention that at the beginning of the twentieth century, when the Zionist movement was in its formative stages, the Jewish people did *not* have the right to establish a state in any part of Palestine. By the time statehood was declared in 1948, however, the existence of a thriving Jewish community with a political infrastructure justified the creation of a Jewish state. Today, Israel has not only the right to exist but also the right to promote and strengthen its Jewish character. Indeed, this dramatic shift in the validity of the Jewish claim to statehood is one of Zionism's major achievements.

This approach necessarily distinguishes between claims regarding the legitimacy of Israel's creation and claims regarding the right of Israel, once established, to maintain itself as a Jewish state. Such a dichotomy contrasts sharply with the view of most Arab leaders and intellectuals, who insist that Israel was wrongfully established and that its continued existence today is *ipso facto* unjustified. It is important to see that the two are not necessarily connected. For even if there was no justification for the creation of a Jewish state in 1948—a claim which I do not accept—it does not follow that the preservation of Israel as a Jewish state is unjustified today. Similarly, even if we accept the establishment of Israel in 1948 as justified, one would still have to show why the preservation of Israel's Jewish character is legitimate today. The point here is that changing conditions affect the balance of legitimacy, and therefore no claim to self-determination can be absolute. This approach, which may appear at first glance to weaken the case for the Jewish state by making it contingent, to my mind provides one of the strongest universal arguments in its favor.

To see why this is so, it is instructive to divide the history of modern Jewish settlement in the land of Israel into five distinct periods, and to consider the degree to which a Jewish state was justified in each of them. Relevant factors include the size of the Jewish and Arab populations in the land of Israel or in parts of it; the alternatives available to the two communities; the situation of Jewish communities in the Diaspora; the relationship of the Jewish people to the land; Jewish-Arab relations; the decisions made by those in charge of the territory prior to statehood; and the status of Arab citizens under Israeli rule.

The first period covers the end of the nineteenth and the beginning of the twentieth centuries, when the Zionist idea was first translated into concerted action. There is no disputing the fact that, at the time, the Arab population in Palestine was far greater than that of the Jews, despite the steady stream of Jewish immigration throughout the preceding generations.[9] This disparity reflected the centuries-long absence of a Jewish majority in the land of Israel, initially the result of expulsions and persecutions and later of free choice. In this period, the Jewish people did not have the right to establish a state in any part of the land of Israel, for the right of a people to establish a state in a given territory requires that it constitute a clear majority in all or part of it. The Jewish people may have longed for and prayed toward their land, but very few chose to make it their home.[10]

The important question concerning this period, however, is not the right of the Jews to sovereignty in Palestine, but rather their liberty to create a settlement infrastructure that would enable them to establish a Jewish state at a later date. From the Arab perspective, such settlement was illegitimate at its core, since it was harmful to Arab interests and limited their control over the public domain. The claim that Jewish settlement harmed Arab interests is certainly understandable, and the fears that lay at its core were no doubt warranted. But did these fears place a moral obligation on the Jewish people to refrain from returning to their homeland?

I do not believe so. To understand why this is the case, it is useful to employ the distinction between "rights" and "liberties" first introduced by the American jurist Wesley Newcomb Hohfeld. According to Hohfeld, we may speak of a *liberty* when there is no obligation to act or refrain from acting in a certain manner. A *right*, on the other hand, means that others have an obligation not to interfere with, or to grant the possibility of, my acting in a certain manner. Using this model, we may say that as long as their actions were legal and nonviolent, the Jewish settlers were at liberty to enlarge their numbers among the local population, even with the declared and specific intent of establishing the infrastructure for a future Jewish state.[11] Their liberty to create such an infrastructure was certainly greater, for example, than that of England and Spain to settle the Americas, and Palestine was certainly a more legitimate destination than Uganda or Argentina. The immigration of Jews to Palestine was vastly different from colonialism, both with respect to their situation in their countries of origin and with respect to their relationship with the land itself. Unlike colonial powers, the Jews were a people in exile, foreigners wherever they went; they were everywhere a minority, and in some places persecuted relentlessly; and they had never possessed national sovereignty over any land but the land of Israel. Add to this their profound cultural and religious bond to the land, and you have a solid basis for a unique connection between the Jews and the land of Israel—one far more compelling than the claims of a typical group of European settlers.

It was in fact precisely the power of this connection that made the local Arabs see Jewish immigration as far more threatening than any influx of English or French colonists. In light of the Jews' historical connection to the land of Israel, the Arabs correctly understood the waves of Zionist immigration as something new, unlike the conquest of the Crusaders during medieval times or the settlement of the British under the Mandate.[12] Considering the threat that Jewish settlement posed to the continued existence of a Muslim public culture in Palestine, the Arab population certainly had full liberty to take steps to resist this settlement, so long as they did not infringe on any basic human rights or violate the laws of the land. Thus, while the Arabs' success in persuading the authorities to limit immigration and land purchases was a setback to Zionism, it was in no way a violation of the Jews' rights.

When the Arabs realized that diplomatic measures alone could not prevent the creation of the infrastructure for Jewish settlement, however, they turned to violence as a means of resistance. This clearly was a violation of the rights of the Jews, and it was here that the great tragedy of Jewish-Arab relations began. The violent resistance of the Arabs ultimately lent significant weight to the Jewish claim to a sovereign state, and not merely to self-determination within a nonstate framework. From the 1920s until today, one of the strongest arguments for Jewish statehood has been the fact that the security of Jews as individuals and as a collective cannot be secured without it.

Both Jews and Arabs attach great importance to this early period, and both sides continue to ignore certain facts about it. The great majority of Arabs believe that Jewish settlement was both illegal and immoral; even those willing to accept the current regime still refuse to recognize the legitimacy of the Jewish national movement. As a result, we hear the constant repetition of the claim that Zionism is, by its very nature, a form of both colonialism and racism.[13] On the other hand, many Jews refuse to accept that Arab objections to Zionist settlement are not only legitimate, but almost inevitable. Now as then, Arab violence turns Jewish attention to the need for self-defense, and few are willing to admit that the original Zionist settlers did not come to an uninhabited land, or that they posed a real threat to local Arab interests.[14] As long as each side continues to deny the other's narratives, hopes, and needs, reconciliation and compromise over the long term are unlikely.

In the second period of the conflict, from the Arab Revolt that began in 1936 to the United Nations partition decision of November 1947, a number of attempts were made to find a solution acceptable to the international community and reflective of the reality in the Mandate territory. While the details differed, each plan suggested division of the territory into Jewish and Arab states in accordance with demographic concentrations, providing for the rights of those who remained outside their own nation state. This approach derived from the recognition of two basic facts: That a critical mass of Jews had formed in Palestine, in certain areas constituting a clear majority; and that the only hope for the region lay in a two-state solution. From the perspective of both sides to the conflict, this approach signaled both a major achievement and a serious setback. The Jews had succeeded in winning international recognition for their right to a sovereign state. The Arabs had succeeded in preventing that state from encompassing all of the territory west of the Jordan River, as was implied in the Balfour Declaration. The ultimate expression of this new approach was the partition plan ratified by the UN General Assembly on November 29, 1947. The Jewish and Arab

responses could not have been more different: The Jews accepted partition and declared independence; the Arabs categorically rejected the UN
plan and went to war.

The third period, which includes Israel's War of Independence and
its immediate aftermath, was one of decisive victory for one side and
crushing defeat for the other. When the smoke of battle had cleared in
early 1949, the new State of Israel controlled a much larger area than
had originally been allocated to it by the UN plan, and the remaining
territories were seized by Jordan and Egypt. Hundreds of thousands of
Arabs left the Jewish territory either voluntarily or under duress. Many
Arab villages were ruined or abandoned.[15] The Arab minority that remained in Israel was placed under military rule.

In the Palestinian narrative, this chain of events is known as *al-
nakba*, the "Catastrophe," the formative experience upon which the
Palestinians' dream of return and the restoration of the *status quo ante*
is founded. The official political expressions of this ambition have
changed over time: There are major differences between the language
of the Palestinian National Covenant as approved in 1968, the PLO's
declaration of 1988 accepting the UN partition plan (albeit with reservations), and the 1993 Oslo accords, which recognized Israel's existence and agreed to peaceful relations. Despite the progress implicit in
each of these declarations, however, nowhere has the Palestinian movement given up on its dream of return. The centrality of this issue is
impossible to understand without a closer look at the events of 1947
through 1949.

There is no doubt that the consequences of this period were tragic for
the local Arab population. This is not to say, however, that the exclusive
or even prime responsibility for this tragedy rests on Israel's shoulders.
Indeed, it is encouraging that a tendency has developed in recent years,
both in the academy and in the Israeli public, to examine more critically
the events that occurred both during and after the War of Independence.
There is, it seems, a growing awareness that no good can come of bad
history. Fortunately, while these examinations may shatter the myth of
moral purity that Jews have ascribed to their side in the war, they may
also reinforce the more substantive Jewish claims. The Arabs themselves
bear a great deal of responsibility for the region's miseries during this
period, which were brought on by a war which they themselves declared.
After all, the purpose of the war was to prevent the establishment of the

Jewish state. If the Arabs had won, they would not have allowed such a state to come into being. The Jews, therefore, had no alternative but to fight to defend their state.[16]

After the war, Israel signed cease-fire agreements with Jordan and Egypt that did not reflect the UN partition map. Nor could they have: The Palestinians lacked any official representation with which to reach a postwar settlement. More importantly, the war had rendered irrelevant the vision of two democratic nation states, living side by side under joint economic administration. In light of the Arab states' refusal to recognize Israel, no settlement on the issues of Palestinian statehood and refugee absorption could possibly have been reached.

In the fourth period, between 1949 and 1967, Israel had full jurisdiction over its new borders. Immigration, largely from Europe and from Arab countries, dramatically altered the country's demographic balance: Whereas the pre-1947 Jewish majority was a bare 60 percent in its territory, the State of Israel soon boasted a Jewish population nearing 80 percent.[17] During these years, the state consolidated control over its territory through widespread nationalization of land, including "public" lands that had been used by Palestinians, as well as abandoned areas. The enraged Palestinian community, now under military rule, was unable to mount an effective protest.[18]

The results of the war brought an end to the symmetry between Arabs and Jews. Palestinian Arabs did not achieve statehood, and their communities suffered a major setback, while Zionism made a critical transition from having the moral *liberty* to establish a Jewish state to having a moral *right* to maintain it and to preserve its Jewish character.

The regional war that broke out in 1967 marks the beginning of the fifth period, a period that has continued, in one form or another, until today. The Six Day War was another attempt by the Arab states to transform the political reality in the region through the destruction of the Jewish state. Once again their efforts failed, and Israel's overwhelming victory included the seizure of the Gaza Strip and the Sinai Peninsula from Egypt, the West Bank and eastern Jerusalem from Jordan, and the Golan Heights from Syria.

One important consequence of the Six Day War was the revival among Jews of a controversy that appeared to have been settled with the partition plan and the establishment of the State of Israel: The controversy regarding those territories that had once been part of the historic land of Israel but did not fall within Israel's pre-1967 borders. In the face of the Arab refusal to negotiate with Israel after the Six Day War, intensive Jewish settlement began in some of these territories. In the years that followed, important political developments continued to affect the territories' status: Israel imposed its civilian law on the whole of Jerusalem (immediately after the war) and on the Golan Heights (in 1981), yet refrained from doing so in the other areas it had seized. The Sinai Peninsula in its entirety was returned to Egypt as part of the Camp David peace accords of 1978, and Jordan waived its claims to the West Bank in 1988 and signed a peace agreement with Israel in 1994. The peace agreements with Egypt and Jordan only exacerbated the conflict between Jews and Palestinians over the fate of the strip of land between the Mediterranean and the Jordan River—what Jews call the "land of Israel" and Palestinians call "historic Palestine." On both sides there are advocates of a unified sovereignty over the entire area, with each side claiming the right to total control. Others call for division of the land into "two states for two peoples," and still others seek the creation of a single binational, democratic state for the entire area.[19] None of this, however, undermines the basic justification for having a Jewish state in that part of the land in which the Jews constitute a large and stable majority.

In the final analysis, it is impossible to ignore the profound changes that have occurred in the last hundred years with respect to the balance of Jewish and Arab interests in the land of Israel. True, both moral and practical considerations suggest that Israel should give up on maximalist claims to sovereignty over the entire area west of the Jordan River. A situation in which both Jews and Palestinians can enjoy national self-determination in part of their historic homeland is better than the present asymmetry between them.[20] At the same time, however, justification for the existence of a Jewish state in part of that land is stronger now than it was in 1947. This is not because of Jewish suffering during the Holocaust or the guilt of the nations of the world, but rather because Israel today hosts a large and diverse Jewish community with the right to national self-determination and the benefits that it can bring. The need to recognize the trauma of Palestinian refugees does not justify a massive uprooting of these Jews, nor does it justify the restoration of the demographic *status quo ante* between Jews and Arabs, or otherwise restoring the state of vulnerability which both communities endured.

While we cannot ignore the history of the conflict, neither can we ignore the reality that has taken hold in the intervening years. Nowhere is this more important than in considering one of the basic Palestinian claims, according to which hundreds of thousands of Palestinians should be allowed to relocate to Israel through recognition of what is known as the Palestinian "right of return." In evaluating this claim, one must first recall that a necessary condition for the existence of a Jewish state is the maintenance of a Jewish majority within its borders. It follows that Israel must not extend its sovereignty over a sizable Palestinian population, and that it must continue to maintain control over immigration into it. This control, and the Jewish majority in Israel, will both be undermined by recognition of a "right of return." It is therefore crucial to see that behind all the talk about rights and justice, the "right of return" necessarily means undoing the developments in the region since 1947, and undermining the existence of a Jewish state.[21]

A Palestinian state alongside Israel, however, would help address the claims of Arab Israelis to the effect that Israel must give up its national identity because only then would Arab citizens enjoy full equality within it. It is true that Arabs cannot enjoy a sense of full membership in a state whose public culture is Jewish. This is especially the case so long as there is a violent, unresolved conflict between their people and their state. At the same time, however, the sense of not being full partners in the national enterprise is the lot of national minorities in all nation states. This complaint should be distinguished from demands for civic and political nondiscrimination for Arabs as individuals, and recognition of their collective cultural, religious, and national interests, which Israel should provide.

It is undoubtedly true that in Israel a significant gap exists between the welfare and political participation of Jews on the one hand and Arabs on the other. This is, in part at least, the result of various forms of discrimination. But does this fact undermine the legitimacy of Israel as a Jewish state? Again, differences between Jews and Arabs in Israel are no greater than between majority and minority nationalities in other countries.[22] And while it is true that any comparison of the status of Israeli Arabs will principally be with that of Israeli Jews, it is worth bearing in mind that their situation is in many respects far better than it would be in an Arab state. This is most evident in the areas of education, health, and political freedom. Even their level of personal security is relatively high: Cases of physical abuse by the state authorities are quite rare.[23] It is therefore not surprising that despite the real difficulties of life in Israel, the majority of Israeli Arabs do not want their homes to become a part of an eventual Palestinian state.

The life offered Israeli Arabs by the Jewish state does indeed limit their ability to develop their culture and exercise their right to self-determination, but this is far from being sufficient grounds for abolishing the Jewish state. As we have seen, the Jewish state fulfills an important set of aims for Jews and for the Jewish people—aims that the Jews have a right to pursue, and which could not be realized without a state. It is possible, then, to justify the limited harm done to the individual and communal interests of Arabs in light of the mortal blow Israel's absence would be to the Jewish people's rights. The reasoning for this is straightforward: There is a great difference between preferring the *interests* of one group over those of another and the denial of *rights*: As human beings, we all have a right to life, security, and dignity, as well as to national self-determination. We cannot, however, demand that the government protect all our interests and preferences at all times. The state is justified in weighing the interests and preferences of different parties, and the resulting arrangements, although always to the detriment of one group or another, do not in themselves constitute a violation of rights. In a democracy, these arrangements are made primarily by elected representatives, and as a result they usually reflect the interests and preferences of the majority. It is therefore a fundamental principle of democracy that no minority has the right to prevent the majority from advancing its interests, so long as the minority's basic rights are respected.[24]

In other words, so long as the Jewish character of the state does not infringe on the basic human rights of those Arabs living within Israel, and the state is the only guarantee of certain Jewish rights—both individual and communal—then the continued existence of a Jewish state is justified. Palestinian self-determination, therefore, should be recognized if it concedes the right of Jews to self-determination. At the same time, a Palestinian nation state living in peace alongside Israel is preferable to the present situation, for this would mean that the rights of both Jews and Arabs to self-determination are honored.

In the abstract, a binational state between the Mediterranean Sea and the Jordan River might be easier for many people to justify than a two-state solution. However, the logic of partition seems only to have strengthened since 1947. Those who advocate the creation of a Palestinian nation state alongside Israel cannot in good faith argue that Israel should give up its Jewish identity.

IV

Can the Jewish state be a nation state for Jews without violating the rights of others? And if it can, have the rights of non-Jews in Israel in fact been protected? If the answers to these two questions are in the negative, we need to look again at the case for the Jewish state. In looking at both the underlying theory and the history of the Jewish state, however, we find that Israel has strived to meet these demands, and with no small measure of success. True, Israel's record on democracy and human rights is not perfect. But neither is that of any other democratic state, and Israel has been better in this regard than many others. Indeed, when compared to the available alternatives, the Jewish state seems to be the best way to protect the rights, interests, and welfare of all groups within it.

It goes without saying that Israel's status as a Jewish nation state does not exempt it from upholding the standards to which all states must be held. Like any civilized country, the Jewish state must provide for the security and welfare of all its citizens, and for the protection of their freedom and dignity. It must therefore be a democracy, for only democracy gives citizens the power to take an active role in decisions that affect their fate and ensures that the government will act in the people's interests. Contrary to what is popularly believed, however, the principles of democracy, individual rights, and equality before the law do not necessitate a rejection of the Jewish character of the state. On the contrary: The fact of Israel's democratic nature means that it must also be Jewish in character, since a stable and sizable majority of its citizens wants the state to be a Jewish one.

In addition, Israel should also be a liberal state, allowing individuals and groups to pursue their own vision of the "good life." This combination of democracy and liberalism is necessary not only because each is a good in its own right, but also because of the makeup and history of Israeli society. Because the country is deeply divided among people holding competing visions of the good life, the state must show the greatest possible degree of sensitivity to the rights, needs, and interests of all its constituent groups, Jews and non-Jews alike. Such sensitivity will go a long way toward engendering a sense of partnership and commitment to the national enterprise, even among those who are culturally or ethnically in the minority.

For these same reasons, democracy in Israel must be based on the sharing of power rather than simple majoritarianism; it should therefore rely on consensus building and negotiation rather than rule through dictates of the majority. It must on the one hand accord a significant degree of autonomy (and communal self-determination) to its diverse populations, and on the other hand work to strengthen the common civic framework. Only in such a framework would a substantive public debate over the nature of the state be possible.

Probably the thorniest issue to arise in this context is the status of Israel's Arab citizens.[25] Jews in Israel tend to downplay the price Arabs pay for the state's Jewish character. Many are hostile to Arab demands for equality, seeing in them a veiled existential threat. There is a reluctance to grant the Arabs a distinct collective status, coupled with a reluctance of the Jewish community to encourage the assimilation of non-Jews into Israeli society—a reluctance which finds its parallel in the Arab community as well. These sentiments are in part responsible for the very limited integration of Jews and Arabs in Israel. At the same time, some Jews are moved by a sense of guilt over wrongs committed by the state against its Arab population, and have chosen to join with the country's Arab citizens in advocating the abandonment of the idea of Israel as the nation state of the Jews. According to this view, true equality can be achieved only through the privatization of all particularistic affiliations. For their part, Israeli Arabs do demand full civic equality, but in addition they demand official recognition of their status as a national, cultural minority—a demand that is not consistent with their demand to "privatize" the national and cultural sentiments of the Jewish majority. A similar inconsistency obtains with respect to their attitude towards the Israeli-Palestinian conflict. They claim the right to identify politically and publicly with the national aspirations of the Palestinian people. At the same time, they claim that this open identification should have no bearing on their treatment by the state and its Jewish citizens, despite the fact that Israelis and Palestinians are locked in a violent conflict. All of these positions reflect a tendency on both sides to ignore the real conflicts of interest between the groups, which cannot be fully masked by a shared citizenship. These problems must be handled with the utmost candor, sensitivity, and creativity if they are ever to be resolved.

One should not underestimate the complexity of the problem. Many Israeli Arabs are willing, for practical purposes, to abide by the laws of the country they live in, but are not willing, under the present circumstances, to grant legitimacy to the Jewish state. They insist on justifying the Arab struggle against that state, and emphasize the price they pay for living in it. They find it difficult to pledge their civic allegiance to a state that, in their view, systematically acts against their interests and those of their people. Since Israeli citizenship was imposed upon them, they claim, they are under no obligation to uphold the duties it imposes on them.

This attitude reflects a growing, systemic alienation of Israeli Arabs from the Jewish state, and one that only perpetuates the current state of mutual distrust. Indeed, the Arabs' refusal to accept the fact of Jewish sovereignty makes it extremely difficult, if not impossible, to create a civic partnership of any kind. While it is true that the main burden of taking practical measures and allocating resources falls on the state, Israeli Arabs must play a part as well, at the least by trying to offer some account of what obligations *do* accompany their citizenship. For example, it is clear that virtually no one expects Arab Israelis to be conscripted into the military under the present circumstances. Yet the Arabs' categorical rejection of mandatory nonmilitary service is difficult to justify—as is the position held by most Arab leaders that Israeli Arabs who volunteer for the IDF should be condemned or even cut off from their communities.

For their part, the Jewish majority must recognize the state's basic responsibilities toward Israeli Arabs. This responsibility is threefold. First, Jews must recognize that the Jewish state has been and continues to be a burden for many Israeli Arabs. Again, this need not mean giving up the idea of a Jewish state, but it does require acknowledgment of the price the Arabs have paid, and will continue to pay, for its existence. This price may be justified when seen against the need of Jews for a Jewish state. But even if this need is sufficient grounds for causing Arabs to live as a minority in their land, it does not justify acting as though there were no price being paid. Second, the government should move immediately to address the most pressing needs of the Arab community, and to promote the civic equality promised in Israel's Declaration of Independence; bureaucratic foot-dragging only undercuts the affections that Arab citizens may have for the country. Third, the conflict between the aspirations of Jewish nationalism and the status of Arabs in the Jewish state must be admitted and addressed honestly, not downplayed or dismissed. We must recognize that the needs of Jewish nationalism do, in some cases, justify certain restrictions on the Arab population in Israel, particularly in areas such as security, land distribution, population dispersal, and education. These policies must be constrained, however, by the basic rights of the Arab citizens of the state. And they should be developed through a dialogue with the Arab community, such that the policies which emerge will promote not only the state's Jewish character, but also the welfare of Israeli Arabs.

The intensity of the conflict poses a serious challenge to Israeli democracy. We have a vicious circle here: Arab leaders express their anger and criticism of Israel in ways that strike some Jews as treasonous, and the latter respond by trying to limit the free speech of these leaders, who in turn become even more critical, depicting the state as undemocratic and censorial. What results is a no-win situation, in which there is no agreed-upon framework for legitimate discussion, further amplifying the frustration and anger of both sides. The ongoing violence has only deepened the Jewish belief that the only solution is full separation between Jews and Arabs. Naturally, many Arabs are afraid this may lead to an attempt to "transfer" them from their homes. Some of the blame, however, clearly belongs on the shoulders of those Arab leaders who deliberately fan the flames through their extreme rhetoric: While democracy cannot thrive without a robust debate on all issues of public interest, it is utterly unreasonable to expect even the most liberal of democracies to tolerate a situation in which, for example, a member of parliament openly celebrates the victory of the state's enemy, or appears to endorse violence against its civilians as reflecting a "right to resist the occupation." If both sides show sensitivity and restraint, we can have fruitful debate and some sense of a shared citizenship despite differences of opinion. If not, we may well lose the ability to agree on any shared framework—a potentially disastrous development.[26]

Beyond the question of non-Jewish citizens in Israel, the idea of a "state of the Jewish people" raises important questions surrounding the role of Jews who are not Israeli citizens—that is, the role of diaspora Jewry in shaping Israel's character and policies. Diaspora Jews clearly have a strong interest in preserving the Jewish character of the state. This interest, however, must not be confused with the *right* to participate in Israel's decision-making process. Surely someone who chooses to live in another country is obligated first to that country, and cannot insist on taking part in the decision making of another. Moreover, the full participation of diaspora Jewry in the Israeli political process would contradict the democratic principle according to which political involvement is granted only to those who are affected directly by a government's decisions. It should be clear, then, that neither Jews living outside of Israel nor their representatives have any political right to involvement in decisions made by Israel.

However, Israel is certainly entitled—and, I would argue, even obligated—to strengthen its ties with the Diaspora. Israel has an important role to play in the lives of all Jews, not only those who live within its borders. Israel must continue to welcome Jewish youth from around the world who want to experience life in a Jewish state. Israel must offer diaspora communities both material and cultural assistance, and participate in the restoration of Jewish cultural and historical sites worldwide. There must also be an ongoing dialogue between Israel and diaspora communities concerning the nature of Jewish life in Israel, including decisions about access to Jewish holy sites or legal questions about the definition of Jewish identity. Although the final say on such matters must rest with the elected bodies of Israel, the outcome may have far-reaching implications for Jews outside Israel. Therefore, both common sense and a feeling of common destiny dictate that Israel should consult with Diaspora representatives, formally and openly, when deciding on matters with consequences for the Jewish people as a whole.

V

As we have seen, the Jewish character of the State of Israel does not, in and of itself, mean violating basic human rights of non-Jews or the democratic character of the country. Non-Jews may not enjoy a feeling of full membership in the majority culture; this, however, is not a right but an interest—again, it is something which national or ethnic minorities almost by definition do not enjoy—and its absence does not undermine the legitimacy of Israeli democracy. Israel has a multi-party political system and a robust public debate, in which the national claims of the Arabs are fully voiced. It has regular elections, in which all adult citizens, irrespective of nationality or religion, participate. Since 1977, it has experienced a number of changes in government. Its court system enjoys a high level of independence, and has made the principle of nondiscrimination a central part of its jurisprudence. It has also developed a strong protection of freedom of speech, of association, and of the press. It is thus no surprise that it is counted by scholars among the stable democracies in the world.

Put another way, the idea that Israel cannot be a Jewish state without violating the tradition of democracy and human rights is based on a questionable understanding of democracy and the human rights tradition. This tradition also includes the right of national self-determination, the fulfillment of which will always create some kind of inequality—at least with respect to the emotions that members of the majority, on the one hand, and ethnic or national minorities, on the other, feel towards their country. An honest look at the democratic tradition will reveal that the real tension is not between Israel's "Jewish" and "democratic" aspects, but between competing ideas within democracy, which is forced to find a balance between complete civic equality and freedom for the majority to chart the country's course. Every democratic nation state is forced to strike that balance, and it is unfair to assert that respect for civil rights and recognition of individual and collective affiliations require that Israel's character be based solely on neutral, universal foundations.[27] The state and its laws should not discriminate among its citizens on the basis of religion or nationality. But within this constraint, it can—and in some cases it must—take action to safeguard the country's Jewish character.[28]

The Law of Return is a prime example. The law serves a number of crucial aims, including offering refuge for every Jew and strengthening the Jewish majority in Israel. Its most important task, however, is symbolic. After all, the right of Jews to settle in their land, and the belief that the Jewish state would offer Jews everywhere a place to call home, has always been the lifeblood of Zionism. Thus, when the Law of Return was enacted in 1950, there was a widespread sense that the right of any Jew to immigrate to Israel preceded the state itself; it was a right that the law could declare but not create. Perhaps this particular claim was a bit questionable: There is, in fact, no "natural right" of Jews to immigrate to Israel. Had a Palestinian state been established instead of a

Jewish one, it is reasonable to assume that it would not have recognized the right of Jews to move there, nor is it likely that international law would have done so. But once the idea of a Jewish national home became internationally recognized and a Jewish state was established, Israel was fully justified in including the right of all Jews to immigrate there as one of the state's core principles.

There are those who argue that the Law of Return is racist, one of the clearest proofs that Arab Israelis are the victims of state-sponsored discrimination. This claim is baseless. The law does not discriminate among citizens. It determines who may become one. The principle of repatriation in a nation state is grounded in both political morality and international law. The United Nations' 1947 resolution approving the establishment of a Jewish state was meant to enable Jews to control immigration to their country. Similar immigration policies based on a preference for people whose nationality is that of the state have been practiced in European countries, including many of the new nation states established after the fall of the Soviet Union. The need to preserve a national majority, especially in cases where the minority belongs to a nation that has its own, adjacent state, is not unique to Israel.[29]

Another example concerns the geographical distribution of Jewish settlement within Israel. The territorial integrity of a state is a legitimate national interest. In the context of the ongoing conflict, Israel is justified in establishing Jewish towns with the express purpose of preventing the contiguity of Arab settlement both within Israel and with the Arab states across the border: Such contiguous settlement invites irredentism and secessionist claims, and neutralizing the threat of secession is a legitimate goal. By contrast, the blatant discrimination against Arabs in the quality of housing and infrastructure cannot be justified.[30] The Israeli Supreme Court's declaration in *Ka'adan v. Israel Lands Administration* (2000), according to which the state must not discriminate against Arabs in these matters, is therefore welcomed. However, I do not accept the ruling's further implication that there is no basis for permitting the creation of separate communities for Jews and Arabs. In a multi-cultural society such as Israel, most individuals prefer to live within their respective communities, and they should be allowed to do so, provided that this does not severely undermine the common civic identity.[31]

A third example concerns education policy, and in particular the question of whether Israel's educational system should openly promote Jewish identity and the state's Jewish character in its Jewish public schools. In recent years, this has been the subject of a lively public debate, a fact that is itself highly commendable.[32] However, in the heat of the argument several important issues have frequently been overlooked. For example, while it is agreed that education for Jewish and Zionist identity should not take the form of mindless indoctrination, neither is it possible to reduce education to a dispassionate exercise in the comparative study of cultures. A proper education will give students the tools they need to examine their Jewish identity with a critical eye, and in some cases this education might even lead a student to disassociate himself from that identity. But even if education cannot be value-neutral—and by definition it never is—it has to be committed to both truth and a sense of perspective. Jewish education in Israel cannot ignore the history of the Israeli-Arab conflict and the disagreements about it that prevail today. Ignoring the more unpleasant parts of the historical record only weakens students' ability to address the conflict properly, and makes it harder for them to criticize Israel's actions while maintaining a sense of national loyalty. The richer and more complex the sense of identity, the stronger and more secure it will be.

Obviously a different approach must be taken in the Arab sector. The educational system for Israeli Arabs should strengthen Arab cultural identity and, as a result, alleviate fears that life in a Jewish state means weakening the bonds that have traditionally connected them with the Arab people. The Israeli-Arab educational system should also promote awareness of minority rights and emphasize the fact that Israel is a democracy committed to the principle of nondiscrimination, even if it may fall short in practice, and that it allows a variety of legal means for defending one's rights and dignity. Importantly, it must instill in Israeli Arabs an understanding that their Israeli citizenship is part of their identity, even if they find it wanting. This citizenship means, among other things, allegiance to the state and respect for its laws, and acknowledging the right of the majority to determine the basic character of the state.

From the argument that the ongoing presence of a Jewish state is justified, one should not draw the conclusion that Arab citizens unhappy with the state's character should resign themselves to it. The Arabs' political struggle to change the character of Israel is legitimate, even if I do not share their aspirations. Yet it is crucial that this struggle be conducted under two constraints: First, it should take place only within the confines of the democratic "rules of the game"; second, so long as the majority prefers to maintain Israel's Jewish character (again, without violating the basic rights of Arab citizens), this choice is legitimate. The state is justified in acting to preserve Israel's Jewish nature, and this fact should not be used to delegitimize the state at home or abroad. In recent years, the commitment of Arab citizens to these two conditions has been anything but clear-cut, further complicating Jewish-Arab relations in Israel.

VI

The need for a justification for the Jewish state is not simply a matter of self-beautification, nor is it an attempt to square the circle. It is, rather, an existential need. The Jewish state will survive over time only if the majority of Jews are convinced that its existence is justified, and that it can retain its moral compass despite the difficult conditions of today's Middle East. Unfortunately, however, many Jews prefer to ignore the question completely. As a result, our sense of justice has come to depend on our maintaining a persistent close-mindedness. As a result many of our best people—those Jews with the greatest moral sensitivity and empathy for the suffering of others—may in the end lose their will to identify with the Jewish national enterprise and begin to view its existence as indefensible. Even worse, those of us who are morally uncomfortable with Israel's current policies will have no real tools for determining whether these policies are in fact unjustified and should be opposed, or are indeed justified by the necessity of preserving the Jewish character of the state (so long as human rights are protected).

If we are to dispel the fog of pessimism that has recently settled over the Zionist enterprise, then, we will have to begin with a clearheaded approach. There is no point in denying that the State of Israel faces profound internal and external challenges. Israeli society is increasingly divided by economic disparity and conflicts between Jew and non-Jew, secular and religious, Left and Right. Yet the Jewish state is, in many respects, a major success, particularly when one considers the circumstances with which it must contend. In terms of democracy, Israel is far ahead of its neighbors, and far ahead of where it was in its early years. Israel's economy and its scientific achievements place it among the world's most developed countries. It boasts an open, self-critical society with considerable political freedom, and its rule of law and judicial independence rival those of the healthiest democracies. And these successes have come without the benefit of the rich natural resources found in other countries, including Israel's Arab neighbors. True, Israel has not yet achieved a stable peace with many of its neighbors. We should continue to make such an agreement our goal, while remembering that its achievement does not depend on Israel alone. In the meantime, we can look back with pride and forward with hope. Israel has a great deal to offer its citizens, both Jews and Arabs.

For now, Israel is the state of the Jewish people. In the present circumstances it is justified in being so, and I hope that it will take the necessary steps to preserve this status in the future. This is no small aspiration: The history of the land of Israel is strewn with the remains of many peoples and cultures. Israel's Jewish majority need not apologize for seeking to retain the Jewish identity of the state, but it must recognize the rights of Palestinians living between the Mediterranean and the Jordan. This includes their right to express their own unique identity both through an independent state of their own alongside Israel, and as a minority within the Jewish state. This issue cannot be wished away; it must be addressed in a way that is both effective and moral.

The hope that the Jews of Israel will become more culturally homogeneous is also pure fantasy. Israel will never be either wholly secular or wholly religious, wholly East or wholly West. Israel will never be a Western European country, nor will it be a typical Levantine one. But the tensions that arise from these various dualities are hardly to Israel's detriment: The strength of Israeli society is derived from the combination of its elements, and this carries an important lesson for the state's future. Israel must struggle to protect the unique combination of cultures, traditions, and identities that make up the Jewish state. Every group should feel at home, and no one group should be capable of imposing its ways on others. If we are wise enough to uphold this principle, it will not only serve the ends of the majority, but also safeguard the uniqueness of the minorities.

"It is not for us to finish the job," we are told by the rabbis of the Talmud.[33] Our generation is not responsible for establishing a Jewish state; rather, we are responsible for preserving it for future generations, and for ensuring that it is passed on to our children as a worthy inheritance.

This requires that we give them solid grounds for believing in the justice of our common enterprise—and this, in turn, means recognizing the diversity of Israel's citizenry and the complexity of our life together. Our generation needs to channel this diversity to good ends, even when different groups disagree, or when one group's aspirations do not line up perfectly with those of the state as a whole. The key to our success, then, will be our ability to preserve the delicate balance between what unites us and what makes us different.

If we will it, this too will be no dream.

NOTES

I would like to extend special thanks to Yoav Artzieli for his help in preparing this essay for publication.

1. For my purposes, there is no substantial difference between the expression "Jewish state" used in this article and others employed in public debates, including "the state of the Jews" or "the state of the Jewish people," all of which attempt to underscore the particular, unique foundation of the State of Israel. The initial appearance of the latter expression in Israeli law occurred in Clause 7a(i) of the Basic Law: The Knesset, passed in 1985, which prohibits any party that denies that Israel is "the state of the Jewish people" from standing for election. This expression was preferred over the popularly used "Jewish state," which can be seen as having an overly religious connotation. Nonetheless, when it was pointed out that the expression "the state of the Jewish people" implies that Israel is not, in fact, a state for its non-Jewish citizens, the legislature reinserted the term "Jewish state" in the Basic Laws of 1992, wherein Israel is defined as "a Jewish, democratic state." This was also the expression of choice in United Nations Resolution 181, of November 29, 1947, which speaks of "a Jewish state" in contrast to an Arab one, as well as in the Declaration of Independence, which called for establishing "a Jewish state in the land of Israel."

2. In my book *Israel as a Jewish and Democratic State: Tensions and Prospects* (Tel Aviv: Hakibbutz Hame'uhad, 1999) [Hebrew], I deal summarily with these preliminary challenges, and conclude that Israel as a Jewish and democratic state is both coherent and legitimate. I then concentrate on the tensions between these elements and on ways of mitigating them.

3. This misguided alliance between liberal Jews and Arab enemies of the Jewish state is strengthened by a tendency to equate the Jewish state with a Jewish theocracy. A Jewish theocracy is not legitimate, they argue, because by definition it cannot be a democracy, and because religions are not entitled to political self-determination. However, this is clearly a misreading of the term "Jewish" in a "Jewish state," which refers not to religion but to national identity. The confusion stems from the fact that the relationship between nationality and religion in Judaism is a unique one. No other people has its own specific religion: The Arab peoples, for example, comprise Christians, Muslims, and Druze. While there was a time when the French were mostly Catholics or former Catholics, they still waged religious wars with the Huguenots, and today a large number of Frenchmen are Muslim. At the same time, no other religion has a specific nationality of its own: Christians can be French, American, Mexican, or Arab; Muslims, too, can be Arabs, Persians, or African-Americans. This distinction is not merely the result of secularization: Judaism, at least from a historical per- spective, has never differentiated between the people and the religion. Nor was there any belated development that altered this unique fact: Social stereotyping never allowed an individual to be a part of the Jewish people while at the same time a member of another religion; nor could one be an observant Jew without belonging to the Jewish people.

This uniqueness, however, should not cloud our thinking. The Arab chal- lenge to the Jewish state rejects any claim to Jewish self-determination, be it based on nationality or religion. It is important that those secular Jews who insist that Jewish identity is not exhausted by religion do not allow their posi- tion in the internal Jewish debate over the Jewishness of Israel to obscure for them the legitimacy of a Jewish nation state. Likewise, the state must accept all interpretations of Judaism and Jewish identity put forth by its Jewish citizens, and provide a home for all Jews, irrespective of their attitude to the Jewish religion. In this essay, I use "Jewish" and "Jewishness" to incorporate all forms of Jewish culture and Jewish identity.

4. The Jewish character of the state is a source of tension not only between Jews and Arabs, but also among Jews. Some of the more extreme Orthodox leaders, who advocate a kind of Jewish theocracy, insist that a democratic Is- rael is, by definition, not Jewish. This conception of the Jewishness of Israel has been rejected by all mainstream Israeli political leaders, including Orthodox ones, and rightly so. At the other extreme, however, there are many Jews who insist that liberal democracy demands perfect neutrality with regard to religious identity, and therefore the absolute separation of religion and state. This view is misguided. A liberal political stance does not automatically mean rejecting the establishment of religion any more than it means abandoning the state's Jew- ish national character in favor of a universal one. Liberal democracy does insist on freedom of religion and from religion, as is recognized in international law, but this is not the same as disestablishment: While those who call for absolute separation generally refer to the American model, there are many European

democracies that ensure religious freedom while granting official status to one church or another.

These two kinds of tension surrounding Israel's Jewish character—arising from the Jewish-Arab and religious-secular rifts—are both addressed in my book, note 2 above. In the present essay I concentrate on the Arab challenge to Jewish self-determination. For my views on some of the issues in the internal Jewish debate, see also Ruth Gavison and Yaakov Medan, *A Basis for a New Social Contract Between Religion and State in Israel* (Jerusalem: Israel Democracy Institute and Avi Chai, 2003). [Hebrew]

5. For a detailed and well-reasoned argument on the advantages of national self-determination at the sub-state level, see the writings of Haim Gans, and especially *The Limits of Nationalism* (Cambridge: Cambridge, 2003). Self-determination of different national groups in the framework of one state can be found, for example, in Belgium, Canada, and Switzerland.

6. There are some Jews who claim that the hatred of some in the secular Left toward the Haredim is in fact a unique manifestation of anti-Semitism in Israel. This is an intriguing claim, but we should note that critical sentiments against the Haredim almost never involve violence against them, or an attempt to limit their freedom to conduct their religious life.

7. There is a dispute regarding the size of various diaspora Jewish communities as a result of methodological difficulties in collecting data. According to the World Jewish Congress, the number of Jews in the United States is estimated at between 5 and 6 million; in Israel, there are 5 million. The third-largest Jewish community is in France, home to approximately 600,000 Jews.

8. There are many religious Jews who oppose the existence of a Jewish state that is not a Jewish theocracy. From this perspective, the present State of Israel may be worse than having a non-Jewish state. Yet in a non-Jewish state, the Jewish population, including the observant and Haredi sectors, would undoubtedly not enjoy the current level of freedom to preserve and develop their way of life. Furthermore, it is a fact that Tora learning among the Jewish people has never been as widespread as it is in Israel today.

9. According to a census taken in 1922, there were 83,794 Jews in the Mandate territory out of a total population of 757,182 (approximately 11 percent). See Dan Horowitz and Moshe Lissak, *The Origins of the Israeli Polity: The Political System of the Jewish Community in Palestine Under the Mandate* (Tel Aviv: Am Oved, 1977), pp. 21-22. [Hebrew]

10. Why the Jews did not return to the land of Israel in greater numbers is a vexing and complex question. For our purposes, however, the numbers and their implications are sufficient.

11. Wesley Newcomb Hohfeld, *Fundamental Legal Conceptions as Applied in Judicial Reasoning, and Other Legal Essays* (New Haven: Yale, 1923). Using

Hohfeld's distinction, I would assert that the Jews had the liberty to settle in the land of Israel at the beginning of the Zionist movement, and that the local Arabs likewise had the liberty to oppose this settlement by means of political, economic, and other nonviolent measures. Jews did not have a *right* to settle (since the Arabs did not have a duty to allow them to do so), but Arabs did not have the *right* to prevent them from doing so (since Jews did not have a duty to refrain, and the Arabs did not themselves control the land or make its laws; if they had, they would have legislated controls over immigration that would have denied the liberty of Jews to come). Liberties may of course clash, since the agents, by definition, are under no obligation to refrain from acting. However, once a large Jewish community had taken root—and certainly after the establishment of the state, which housed a large Jewish concentration with no other home—this community had the right to self-determination and security. A corollary of this right is the obligation of the Arabs to refrain from violence in their attempts at resistance.

12. On the whole, Arabs make a point of denying the historical-cultural-religious relationship of the Jews to the land of Israel. Thus, at the Camp David summit in August 2000, PA Chairman Yasser Arafat questioned the historical relationship of the Jews to the Temple Mount (despite the fact that Muslim sources—even those that claim a Muslim hegemony in the land during the time of Napoleon—admit this historical relationship). Some Arabs go even further, comparing Israel to the Crusader kingdom in the hope that, in the long run, its fate will be the same. This consistent denial makes it difficult for Palestinians to accept that there are two justifiable yet conflicting claims, and consequently to reach a historic compromise. There is also reason to fear that this denial expresses the hope that the Jews of Israel do not in fact feel closely connected to their land, and that a sufficient combination of force and rhetoric will cause them either to leave or to forgo the state's Jewish character.

13. Regrettably, the anti-Israel majority in the United Nations General Assembly succeeded in 1975 in reaching a decision, in force for a decade and a half, according to which Zionism was considered a form of racism.

14. One thinker who understood the significance of the Arab presence in Palestine was Ahad Ha'am. See his "The Truth from Palestine," in Ahad Ha'am, *The Parting of the Ways* (Berlin: Judische Verlag, 1901), p. 25. [Hebrew] A Zionist thinker who stressed that the Arabs could not be expected to agree to a Jewish state in their native country was Ze'ev Jabotinsky. See Ze'ev Jabotinsky, "The Iron Wall," *Jewish Herald*, November 26, 1937.

15. Despite the fierce dispute surrounding the claims of the "new historians," the picture remains reasonably clear: More than half a million Arabs left Israel during the 1948 War of Independence and in the period immediately after, forming the basis of the refugee problem that continues to plague the region to this day. There was no systematic policy of expelling or uprooting them—in fact, in some places the Arabs were specifically asked to remain, while in others

they left in response to their leaders' calls. Many Arabs, however, indeed fled from the threat of hostilities, and in certain instances were expelled. See, for example, Benny Morris, *The Birth of the Palestinian Refugee Problem, 1947-1949* (Cambridge: Cambridge, 1987).

16. It should be noted that there is no corresponding soul-searching in the Arab sector. Arab analyses of the period of 1947-1949 include regrets for the consequences suffered by the Palestinians, and at times even a measure of anger against neighboring Arab countries and the local Arab leadership for their failure in preventing these consequences. Yet there is almost no recognition of the fact that it was wrong for the Arabs to reject partition.

17. Different internal growth patterns between the two peoples account for an almost constant demographic ratio, despite large waves of Jewish immigration over the last fifty years. For details, see Issam Abu Ria and Ruth Gavison, *The Jewish-Arab Rift in Israel: Characteristics and Challenges* (Jerusalem: Israel Democracy Institute, 1999), p. 16, table 1. [Hebrew]

18. For a fuller discussion of this, see David Kretzmer, *The Legal Status of Arabs in Israel* (Boulder: Westview, 1990).

19. The Oslo process, which started in 1993, seemed to have decided the issue, on the part of the representatives of both peoples, in favor of the two-state solution. There is consistent international support for this kind of solution, culminating in a UN Security Council resolution in 2001. However, the violence that erupted in the aftermath of the failed Camp David II talks in September 2000 has made this route questionable again.

20. From a moral point of view, it is preferable to give the Palestinians national sovereignty over at least part of their homeland. In this way, the Jewish people's right to exercise self-determination would not come at the expense of the corresponding rights of the Palestinians. A Palestinian state of this kind would also give Israeli Arabs the choice of living in their own sovereign state or of maintaining their citizenship in the Jewish state. If they chose the latter, their fate would be no different from that of other minorities in countries identified with another, majority nationality. Prudence dictates a two-state solution because of the demographic reality: The Jewish people is a small one, and unable to create a stable majority in the entire land of Israel. Israeli sovereignty over the whole land between the sea and the river will undermine the logic of partition and create a binational state.

21. On the one hand, it would appear that the Palestinian approach to the "right" of return is only a negotiating position, one that they will not give up until they have obtained what they consider to be an acceptable agreement on borders. Indeed, there were Palestinians who interpreted the signing of the Oslo accords in this way. On the other hand, the Palestinian position in favor of an unconditional right of return is expressed consistently not only in political statements but also in their educational doctrine. Jews should take this position just as

seriously as the Palestinians take the position of those Jews who refuse to relinquish even part of Israel's territory because of its connection to their forefathers.

22. For data on the status of Israeli Arabs, see Abu Ria and Gavison, *The Jewish-Arab Rift.* For the situation of blacks in the United States, see Jennifer L. Hochschild, *Facing Up to the American Dream* (Princeton: Princeton, 1995). Comparisons of this kind are always highly charged: Israeli Arabs object to such comparisons, arguing that they—in contrast to black Americans—are living in their homeland. Often, the fate of native minorities in countries like the United States and Australia is not very encouraging. On the other hand, African-Americans do not question the existence of the United States and are not engaged in a struggle against it.

23. In the 1956 case of Kafr Kassem, in which Israeli reservists killed 49 Arab villagers who were not aware of a curfew, those responsible were brought to justice; when 13 Israeli Arabs were killed during the Arab rioting in October 2000, a state committee was set up to investigate the matter. The only other case of Arab citizens being killed by state authorities is that of the Land Day demonstrations in 1976, which resulted in the deaths of six Arabs. It is not trivial to note that after two years of terrorism against Israeli civilians, which included a number of cases in which Israeli Arabs were involved as perpetrators or abettors, no violence against Israeli Arabs has been reported since October 2000.

24. For a detailed analysis of the compatibility between Israel's democracy and its Jewish character, see my "Jewish and Democratic: A Rejoinder to the Ethnic Democracy Debate," *Israel Studies* 4:1 (1999), pp. 44-72.

25. Issues of membership and legitimation arise for other groups in Israel, such as non-Jewish immigrants or Haredi Jews, some of whom reject the state altogether. I have dealt with some of these issues elsewhere; in this essay I concentrate on the tension generated by the Jewish-Arab conflict.

26. In May 2002, three laws were enacted to deal with these tensions. One of them forbids incitement to armed conflict with the state or support for such conflict, and the others allow for the disqualification of party lists or candidates who express such support. Israeli law also disqualifies parties or candidates that "deny that Israel is a Jewish and democratic state." The latter laws were invoked in 2003 to ban two Arab parties and their MKs. All bans were overruled by the Supreme Court. It is my hope that the criminal law will be applied as seldom as possible in this context; it is far simpler to prevent a person who makes such declarations from being on the public payroll than to send him to jail. While the disqualifying laws may raise the risk of undue limits to freedom of speech, they may also help create shared "red lines" for political activity, by forcing candidates and parties to clarify that their positions are not inconsistent with the integrity of the state and the legitimacy of its being Jewish if the majority so wishes.

In view of the importance to Jews of a Jewish state, some ask why the right of the Jewish people to a sovereign homeland should depend on the ongoing support of a majority of the public. Why not simply determine that Israel is the national home of the Jewish people, and that this fact should not be subject to change by the electorate? Why take the roundabout route of disqualifying parties who make this their explicit political platform? Why then allow them to run after all, once they mask their intentions a bit? Or, at the very least, should we not require a special majority for any change in the state's basic character, as with many constitutional premises in democratic states?

In the context of a democracy of consensus building and negotiation, it is still possible to establish Israel's Jewish character as a constitutional credo that could be changed only by the will of a special majority. This would lend the country's particularistic character a measure of constitutional stability, and even provide some small insurance against demographic changes or temporary swings in public sentiment. However, it is important to recognize the limits of such benefits. It will not be possible to preserve Israel's Jewish character if the majority of its citizens are not so inclined. After all, the great advantage of democracy is the fact that diverse groups can play a role in shaping the country's character. Thus, decisions concerning the nature of a Jewish state—decisions that will invariably affect the interests of both Jewish and Arab citizens—will always be more readily accepted if they are made in the context of an open democratic system, rather than being imposed on the public. The law may demand that challengers accept the legitimacy of the Jewish state once the majority supports it, not that they should refrain from wanting to change its character.

Finally, it is worth emphasizing that the quest for civic equality is not the same as "colorblindness." The privatization of collective identities will help neither Jews nor Arabs, and will obscure important differences between different Jewish and Arab communities. The pursuit of equality should therefore be accompanied by a careful analysis of the needs and aspirations of all communities.

27. Further evidence of immanent tension, in most democracies, between the culture of the majority and that of the minority is found in the issue of language. France stresses the use of French and French culture as a national unifying feature, and in the United States we see a re-assertion of the need to maintain the primacy of English. This preference inevitably creates difficulties, both real and symbolic, for communities which resist assimilation into the majority culture.

28. Methods of safeguarding the state's Jewish character may include policies on immigration, settlement, housing, and education, as well as decisions regarding state symbols, public culture, and national language. As regards state symbols, it is clearly difficult for an Israeli Arab to identify with the national flag (based on a Star of David) or seal (based on the *menora* of the ancient Temple). As a result, there are those who think that Israel should adopt symbols that will not alienate its non-Jewish citizens. I have serious doubts about this: Many countries use symbols that express the characteristics of the majority, and the existence of minority groups is not considered sufficient reason to change them. For example, many European nations have a cross on their flag, and the

Indian flag is based on the symbols of Hinduism. Nevertheless, we must take
into account the alienation of Israel's Arab citizens as a result of these symbols.
It seems to me that the flag is less problematic, however, because it does not
require any act of identification on the part of the minority. But the national
anthem *Hatikva* ("the hope") arguably places Arab citizens in an untenable situation. After all, it is impossible to expect an Arab to identify with the joy of
realizing "the hope of two thousand years," the dream of the Jewish people "to
be a free people in our own land." It must be remembered that this "hope" is
the Arabs' calamity. I am therefore of the opinion that a second anthem should
be considered—one with which the state's non-Jewish citizens would be able to
identify, stressing only civic shared aspects. Both anthems could be played at
official events, and individuals could participate in the singing of the anthem(s)
of their choice. It is not unreasonable, however, to expect Arab citizens to show
courtesy while *Hatikva* is played or sung.

29. Amnon Rubinstein and Alex Yakobson, *Israel and the Family of Nations: The Nation State and Human Rights in Israel and Around the World* (Tel
Aviv: Schocken, 2003).

30. The issue of housing should be handled in cooperation with representatives of both the affected villages and those communities seeking a solution
to their housing problems. It is important that there be no illegal building: This
sort of construction could be dangerous and might disrupt vital development
plans. However, in the absence of formal planning that allows for legal construction according to need, efforts to stop illegal construction would be arbitrary at
best, and almost certainly doomed to failure. The decision to demolish illegal
structures (or to "legalize" some of them) will be easier if it is accompanied by
the development of an integrated building program in Arab villages. Moreover,
plans of this nature will encourage the Arab population to adopt a variety of
housing styles, as opposed to the single-story type of construction to which
they are accustomed and that is wholly unsuitable for the population's size and
financial resources.

31. For a more detailed discussion, see Ruth Gavison, "Zionism in Israel?
A Note on Ka'adan," *Mishpat Umimshal: Law and Government in Israel* 6:1
(2001), pp. 25-51.

32. For an analysis of the debate on the teaching of history in Israel, see
Eyal Naveh and Esther Yogev, *Histories: Towards a Dialogue with the Israeli Past*
(Tel Aviv: Bavel, 2002). [Hebrew] Israel never considered a neutral public educa-
tion, since it is mainly a country with two dominant national groups. Among
Jews, there is a distinction among educational streams according to religious
attitude. Some of the Arab schools are run by churches, but they do admit
Arabs of other religions.

33. Mishna Avot 2:16.

THE GUARDIAN OF THE JEWS

YORAM HAZONY

IN A RECENT ESSAY, I argued that the institution of the national state, together with the political order based on it, is the foundation of the liberty that characterizes the free states of the West; and that this order of national states is clearly preferable to the imperial and anarchic orders that are its rivals.[1] In the pages that follow, I wish to explore the reasons that one among the order of national states should be a Jewish state.

Peoples vary greatly in their self-understanding, traditions, and laws, and at the heart of the conflict between the principle of empire and that of national sovereignty is a dispute as to how far such differences should find expression in the way in which peoples are governed. It is a hallmark of imperial states that they strive to bring the laws of all peoples under the rubric of a single will; while the principle of national sovereignty tends in the opposite direction, regarding the differences among nations as a desirable reflection of each people's efforts to advance itself in knowledge, justice, and honor in accordance with the unique tools at its disposal. Indeed, it is a premise of the order of sovereign states that each state is unique, and that states will necessarily differ in the purposes for which they are founded and, consequently, in their internal constitutions. Thus while every state bears the same obligation to care for all who are in its charge, sovereignty means independence not only with respect to the more superficial aspects of national custom, but also with respect to the deeper questions of national constitution and purpose.

It is this variation of purpose that makes the independent nation at once truly different from all others, and at the same time potentially worthy of imitation. In this regard, Montesquieu writes concerning the purpose of various states that "although all states have the same purpose in general... yet each state has a purpose that is peculiar to it: Expansion was the purpose of Rome; war that of Lacedaemonia; religion that of the Jewish laws; commerce that of Marseilles; public tranquility that of the laws of China; navigation that of the laws of Rhodians;... the independence of each individual is the purpose of the laws of Poland, and what results from this is the oppression of all. There is also one nation whose constitution has political liberty for its direct purpose"—and this last observation, of course, is the beginning of his famous inquiry into the English constitution.[2]

Israel, too, is a state founded with a unique purpose that distinguishes it from other states. This purpose is to be what Theodor Herzl called "the guardian of the Jews," the one *Judenstaat* (or "Jewish state") whose laws, institutions, and policies would be directed towards the advancement of the interests and aspirations of the Jews as a people.[3] It is this idea that stands at the center of Israel's political tradition, and it is this that brought Jews the world over, as well as the statesmen of many other nations, to give their support to the birth and consolidation of this state.

Many years have passed since the heyday of the theoretical disputes that surrounded the establishment of Israel, and some, as we know, now feel they have no further need to investigate this topic. One may, of course, love one's country as a child loves his mother, without understanding her. But such an innocent love of country is insufficient to many, both Jews and gentiles, and it is especially so in these times, in which the Jews of Israel are being called upon to devote ever more of our attention and resources to ensuring that this state will continue to exist for the generations to come. Under such circumstances, it is important to remind ourselves of the reasons why we should accept the burden of building and sustaining such a Jewish state, and even of making very real sacrifices on its behalf. To establish our loyalty to the idea of the

Jewish state on firmer foundations, it is necessary to understand the purpose of this state, and it is to such an exploration that I will devote the remainder of this essay.[4]

II

A generation ago, a good case might have been made for understatement in everything regarding the most familiar aspect of Israel's purposive character, its mission as guardian of the physical well-being of the Jewish people. To discuss it would have been to raise questions whose answers were too obvious to benefit from extended inquiry; and at the same time, there was a certain dignity to be found in discretion concerning such matters, as is always the case when civilized men speak of power. But there is a fine line between that silence which is born of quiet knowledge, and that which is born of unfamiliarity, or of an inability to address the subject coherently, or of indifference to it. In recent years, the location of this line has been lost, much that was obvious has ceased to be so, and we no longer dignify the subject of Jewish strength by our reticence. Today there is a great need for speaking of these matters plainly.

By now, however, it is not easy to reconstruct in our imagination the circumstances of Jewish life in the centuries prior to the establishment of Israel. The exile has in many ways ceased to be real for us, and this fact has made it difficult to fully comprehend the idea that the Jewish state exists to ameliorate the conditions of that exile. In this regard, it is useful to recall the views of Edmund Burke, the great eighteenth-century British philosopher and statesman. For Burke, as for many others, there was no question but that the intolerable circumstances of the Jews resulted from the lack of the diplomatic and military instruments that would be afforded by a sovereign Jewish state. The British and Dutch, he argued before Parliament in 1781, have their army, fleet, and foreign service to protect the individuals belonging to those nations. But the Jews have no such recourse:

> Having no fixed settlement in any part of the world, no kingdom nor country in which they have a government, a community and a system of laws, they are thrown on the benevolence of nations.... If Dutchmen

are injured and attacked, the Dutch have a nation, a government, and armies to redress or revenge their cause. If Britons be injured, Britons have armies and laws, the law of nations… to fly to for protection and justice. But the Jews have no such power and no such friend to depend on. Humanity, then, must become their protector and ally.[5]

It is important to notice that Burke's conception of the service rendered by the state to the members of a given nation is quite different from the "safe haven" of traditional Zionist parlance. This old catch phrase is itself a reflection of a profound insecurity, which permitted Jews to imagine that the advantage of a Jewish state would be that within its borders, at least, the Jews would finally be "safe" from harm. The British, of course, did not build up the might of their military and foreign services in order to make of their island the one place where an Englishman might hide from the dangers of the world. As is evident from the above passage, the purpose of British power was to make the *world* safer for the subjects of that nation, so that no matter where their affairs might lead them, their enemies would have to take account of the very real possibility of British intervention—and, indeed, of British vengeance. By the same token, it was the absence of such an independent Jewish power which made the existence of the Jews so terrible in every corner of the world, and which moved men such as Burke to raise the possibility that a civilized state might serve not only as the protector of its own people, but of the Jews as well.

Sympathy with the people of the Bible was to lead, not many years later, to the extension of British protection to the Jewish community in Palestine in the time of Lord Palmerston,[6] and eventually to the British alliance with the Zionist Organization that would lay the foundations for the State of Israel. But the possibility Burke foresaw—that the humane nations could take upon themselves the protection of the Jews—proved to be no more than a romantic hope. By the time Herzl wrote of the same problem a century later, he saw clearly that the circumstances of statelessness had brought the Jews to the brink of horrors believed to have been left behind in medieval times. "It was erroneous… to believe that men can be made equal by publishing an edict in the Imperial Gazette," Herzl wrote in 1895.[7] Any gains the Jews had made in Europe would eventually be called into question, and when this time came, whatever the Jews did not have the political power to protect would be destroyed: "What form this [destruction] will take, I cannot surmise. Will it be a revolutionary expropriation from below or a reactionary confiscation from above? Will they drive us out? Will they kill us?... [In] France there will come a social revolution whose first victims will be the big bankers and the Jews.... In Russia there will simply be a confiscation from above. In Germany they will make emergency laws.... In Austria people will let themselves be intimidated by the Viennese rabble.... There, you see, the mob can achieve anything."[8]

In Herzl's day, most of the leading Jewish figures could not be induced to see matters in this fashion. Only with the passage of another generation did the darkness Herzl saw on the horizon begin to fill the noonday sky so that none could miss it. In 1942, the movement for the creation of an independent Jewish state had gained a significant foothold in Palestine, but the Viennese rabble had long since seized power not only in Austria, but in Germany and much of the rest of Europe as well. There, a people that had, in Burke's words, "no such power and no such friend" was incinerated like so much unwanted refuse. The Jews, without independent state power and an army to throw into the alliance against Germany, were once again excluded from the councils of nations and left to plead for mercy, in a war in which mercy had run out long ago. When reliable information concerning the destruction of European Jewry finally reached Palestine, Ben-Gurion, speaking for nearly all of Jewry, once more asserted the need for a Jewish national state before the Jewish National Assembly in Palestine:

> We do not know exactly what goes on in the Nazi valley of death, or how many Jews have been slaughtered.... We do not know whether the victory of democracy and freedom and justice will not find Europe a vast Jewish cemetery in which the bones of our people are scattered.... We are the only people in the world whose blood, as a nation, is allowed to be shed.... Only our children, our women... and our aged are set apart for special treatment, to be buried alive in graves dug by them, to be cremated in crematoriums, to be strangled and to be murdered by machine guns... for but one sin:... Because the Jews have no political standing, no Jewish army, no Jewish independence, and no homeland.... What has happened to us in Poland, what may, God forbid, happen to us in the future, all our innocent victims, all the tens of thousands, hundreds of thousands, and perhaps millions... are the sacrifices of a people without a homeland.... We demand a homeland and independence.[9]

It has often been said that the destruction of European Jewry might have been greatly reduced in scale, and perhaps even prevented, had Israel come into existence in 1937, when Britain first proposed a partition of Palestine that would give the Jews an independent state. And it is surely right that even a relatively weak Jewish state—had it possessed the power to legislate in matters of immigration in a part of Palestine, and an armed force and diplomatic corps capable of being taken into account by the nations—might have done much to alter the fate of the Jews during the war.

But this historical hypothesis, which so easily evokes assent among us, carries within it an implication too rarely discussed. We are all aware of the failure of the United States and Britain to respond with even token efforts to relieve the plight of the Jews during the war, and yet most Jews are careful not to speak of this fact in too straightforward a fashion. The reason for this is certainly the universal esteem in which these two nations have been held by Jews, both during the war and since. Yet these nations, which we justifiably hold in such high regard, stood by in near-perfect inaction as the "crimes against humanity" they excoriated after the fact were committed. Nor is this only a matter of the failure of the Allied armed forces to take action against the machinery of extermination—action which would have required the diversion of a minuscule quantity of men and arms in a direction that might not have contributed optimally to the prosecution of the war. For in Palestine, British forces that could have been engaged in the war against Germany were instead assigned to preventing European Jews from reaching safety—and this, despite the fact that few British statesmen were more inclined to consider favorably the cause of the Jews than was Churchill, then the British prime minister.

It is difficult not to conclude from these events that Burke's supposition of a humanity capable of offering protection to the Jews was hopelessly misguided. For the truth is that those states we most admire for their humanity are those whose thoughts were elsewhere during the long years in which Jewry was being hunted down in every corner of Europe. Now the precise combination of causes which brought about this result may never be known for certain. But the more general cause is, I think, evident: Every state has its purpose, and the purposes of states have a profound effect on the manner in which national priorities are determined, whether in peacetime or in war. Thus while the Germans had seemingly excellent reasons not to divert their resources, in the midst of total war, to scouring Europe in search of Jewish children, these reasons were of secondary significance to a state whose purpose was to unite humanity under a regime of racial enslavement and purification. This overarching purpose rendered the destruction of the Jews a significant war aim for Germany, and it was pursued with consistency and determination over a period of years, even at the expense of other aims.

Had the United States and Britain regarded saving those Jews who might still be saved as one of the major aims of their war effort, just as the Germans saw murdering those Jews who might still be murdered as one of the aims of their own war effort, then the outcome of the war would certainly have been different. But the simple truth is that the Germans were prepared to make very real sacrifices to achieve the extinction of the Jews, while the Allies were not prepared to make even remotely comparable sacrifices to save them. And the reason for this is that the purpose of the English state, like that of her daughter America, is in fact what Montesquieu claimed it to be: The creation of the conditions of political liberty. This is without question one of the most noble purposes any national state has ever taken up, and in championing it, these states have immeasurably improved the condition of mankind. Moreover, it was for the sake of this cause that so many Americans and Britons gave their lives during the war against Germany. Yet there is no avoiding the fact that this purpose is exceedingly remote from a commitment to seek the salvation of endangered Jews come what may. To say this is not to deny that the British and the Americans have, on the whole, been better to the Jews than any other powers in history. Nonetheless, a state whose overriding purpose is the pursuit of political liberty cannot be counted upon to act like a state whose purpose is to pursue, with constancy and vigor, the well-being and interest of the Jewish people. For this, one must have a state whose purpose is to be the guardian of the Jews. For this, one must have a Jewish state.

Some well-educated Jews are ill at ease with this conclusion, preferring to believe that the idea of the guardian of the Jews is an anachronism, and that humanity has learned its lesson from the experience of Nazi Germany. Is it not absurd, they ask, to speak of the enemies of the Jews and of the need to defend the Jewish interest in an era in which a concern for human rights is becoming universal; in which the United Nations and the leading Western powers act on behalf of oppressed

peoples everywhere; and in which Europe's national states are dissolv-
ing themselves due to a widespread sense that such states are no longer
needed in an era of international fraternity? Does this not augur a new
age in which the Jews will no longer face enmity and danger?

It is sobering to recognize how limited is our capacity for education, if we still find these questions being asked—not only because
the destruction of Europe's Jews took place a mere fifty years ago, and
because one would have to be foolish indeed to suppose that the fundamental dangers posed by man's nature would be overturned in such
a brief time; but principally because these same arguments concerning
the imminent disappearance of hostility towards Jews and the imminent
end of politics based on national interest were already being advanced
with such great conviction, and with the most terrible consequences,
a hundred years ago. Indeed, these arguments were so common in the
decades before the Holocaust that Herzl felt he had to address them
directly in *The Jewish State*:

> It might… be said that we should not create new distinctions between
> people [by creating a Jewish state], that we ought not to raise fresh
> barriers, but make the old ones disappear instead. I say that those who
> think along these lines are loveable romantics. But the idea of the fa-
> therland will go on flourishing long after the dust of their bones will
> have been blown away without a trace…. The Jews, like every other
> nation, will always have enough enemies.[10]

Today we know that Herzl was right, and his interlocutors unequivocally mistaken, regarding the feasibility of eliminating competition and
enmity from the political life of nations. But the point that bears emphasizing is that the then-prevalent belief in such an imminent improvement
of man's condition was not without foundation. During the 1870s, for
example, when citizenship and equal rights were being granted to the
Jews throughout central Europe, a certain optimism may well have been
in place. But it is hard to forgive the lavish interpretation that many
German Jews gave to these events—a striking example of which can be
found in Hermann Cohen's 1915 essay "Germanism and Judaism," which
should perhaps stand as a warning to all of us concerning our procliv-
ity for overly sanguine readings of political conditions. Written with the
encouragement of leading members of established German Jewry, this
discourse by the foremost Jewish thinker of his age announced that the

German people had discovered and engraved upon its heart the truth of a pure universal brotherhood of man; and that, as this was none other than the eternal message of the Jews, the souls of these two peoples were in effect one, and Germany itself was the new homeland of the Jewish spirit. As he argued:

> The inner commonality between Germans and Jewishness should now be evident to everyone. The concept of humanity has its origins in the messianism of the Israelite prophets.... Now, however, the Messiah is again to be found... within the framework of the German spirit.... The Jews in France, England, and Russia are also subject to the duty of loyalty to Germany, because Germany is the motherland of their souls.... Accordingly, irrespective of common prejudices, I venture to assert that the equality of the Jews in Germany is more deeply rooted than anywhere else.[11]

In short, Cohen, and through him many of the leading Jews of Germany, assured all who were willing to follow their advice that the long history of adversity they had experienced in Europe was virtually at an end. And yet when this essay was written and the era of good feeling was at its height, a mere *eighteen years* remained before the crisis that led to the murder, at the hands of the German state, of two-thirds of the Jews in Europe.

These facts must teach us something concerning the nature of the political realm, and especially concerning the feebleness of our capacity to predict political events. For if the Jews of Germany could have erred so terribly concerning the disappearance of the anti-Semitic hostility that was shortly to consume them, it is difficult to imagine what prudence there could be in building our own politics on the assumption that we can know, better than they, what the future holds for us fifty or a hundred years from now. This tendency to mistake limited fluctuations in political fortune for permanent changes in the fabric of political reality is, as it seems, endemic to human nature. We should know this well. It was just yesterday, after all, that some among us were speaking with such eloquence and conviction of the impending arrival of the "end of history," and of a "new Middle East."[12] Yet all that is gone now as if it had never been, lost in a world reeking of war.

It is perhaps a bitter fact, but nonetheless true, that for us, having been denied prophecy, the future is a closed book. Regarding its contents, we find time and again that we know next to nothing. And this is true even where events not many years hence are concerned, not to speak of events and conditions a generation or two in the future. Reasonable men should be able to understand this, and to accept it as a political premise that those who believe otherwise can contribute little to our efforts to guide the state.

A century ago, our people inclined its ear to false prophets who encouraged them to believe that the terror was gone from the world, or would shortly disappear; and we will never know how many lives might have been saved had they kept their peace, or had their predictions at least been greeted with suitable skepticism. Today new voices bear this same message, saying that the terror is gone from the world, or will shortly disappear. The lives of our children and grandchildren depend on our ability to dismiss all such vanity without hesitation and without afterthought. For we must always bear in mind: *The future is for us a closed book, and regarding its contents we know next to nothing.* We do not know with certainty that our world is no longer that of our fathers, in which men and governments found cause to practice terror and make war against our people. And even if we did know this, we would still not know that such a world will not return in the time of our children and of our children's children. And since we cannot know these things, we also cannot know that the inheritance of a Jewish state, which our fathers bequeathed to us and which was won at such great cost, is a gift whose time has come and gone.

It is argued by some that Israel today seems hardly to possess the wherewithal to defend itself, much less the Jews of the world.[13] And indeed, amid the black winds that swirl around us now, the product of our own folly, we can see the Jewish state in all its human frailty. The existence of a state is no guarantee of wise rulers, and we certainly have it within our power, by our own errors, to transform Israel into a helpless nation. But one cannot judge an enterprise spanning centuries on the basis of the foolishness of this minister or that one. One must not forget that it was no more than a handful of years ago that Israeli security services devoted a decade of dangerous but successful work to the rescue of the Jews of Ethiopia, saving tens of thousands of lives that would otherwise have been lost. And one must not forget the triumph of the Six Day War, and of Entebbe, nor the work of Israeli officials on behalf of Jews in the lands of Islam, Russia, Argentina, and elsewhere.

Nor even the trial of Eichmann, which established for the first time the principle of worldly punishment for those who commit crimes against the Jewish people.

The Jewish state is an extraordinary instrument in the hands of those who wield it well, and no moment of weakness is an argument against the principle of guardianship of the welfare of the Jews, any more than it would be an argument against American liberty if the nerve of America should fail under pressure of one test or another. For it is the nature of all political states that even at their finest, they grant to their heirs only a great potential—the potential to protect those who depend on them, and the potential to fulfill a higher purpose. Whether the Jews redeem this opportunity or not is left to each generation, whose great deeds are visited upon its children, and whose sins are as well.

III

If Israel could do no more than offer diplomatic and military assistance to Jews in need, this would be sufficient reason to maintain it as a Jewish state. Such a purpose is one of *pikuah nefesh*, the safeguarding of life, which in Jewish tradition is a purpose that has precedence over virtually every other concern.[14] Given what we have learned in recent generations concerning life among the nations, no further motive should be necessary to persuade Jews that we must learn the arts of statecraft and war, teach them to our children, and maintain ourselves as a sovereign citizenry prepared to make use of them whenever the need should arise. Every effort in this direction is a matter of safeguarding lives, and must be understood as an imperative of the highest order.

This having been said, there is nevertheless something degraded and insufficient in the sober, businesslike manner that has crept into Jewish discourse in the years since the Holocaust, in which all discussion begins and ends with *survival*, regardless of whether the subject is education, economics, war, or peace; and no word is spoken concerning any greater end, for whose sake we Jews continue to choose survival over the other, all too realistic, option. For sixty years, it is this imperative—to survive for the sake of those who were lost—that has sustained us, whether in the struggle to establish the Jewish state, or in the effort to rescue persecuted Jewry, or in attempting to shore up communities that have been ravaged by assimilation and intermarriage and a reluctance to bear children. But though such a motivation may yet have its effect on some Jews, we must recognize that the day is fast approaching when the banner of survival will no longer suffice. Memory of the Holocaust recedes day by day, and with it the self-evidence that once clung to the need to survive. The younger generation, which did not grow up in the shadow of the death camps, is no longer moved by such an emotional mechanism. For this generation, it is only the degradation that is self-evident: The degradation of a people that once bore a great ideal, but which no longer seems to have an interest in anything beyond formulas for its own continued existence.

I am aware that there are Jews for whom any discussion of that ideal has itself become a kind of sacrilege, and who, whenever they sense that conversation is in danger of proceeding in such a direction, immediately let loose with a torrent of protest, to the effect that no people save the Jews finds need to justify its existence, and that even to admit such questions is to encourage a corrosive self-doubt. And it is of course true that there have been, and always will be, countless peoples that exist unattended by an awareness that they have any special purpose or calling among mankind. Such peoples are born constantly and disappear constantly, leaving no one to grieve for their passing.

But there also exist in history nations that do, at a certain point, awaken to a sense of the unique vantage point from which they regard mankind, and of those traditions, ideas, and virtues that make their destiny different from that of other peoples. Such nations find that they have long ago become a subject of discussion among other peoples, and that their insights and manners have touched the rest of mankind even without their desiring it, at times engendering admiration, at times anger. A truth or virtue that one possesses without knowing that others are in want of it can seem a small thing, and one may not recognize the importance of preserving or strengthening it. From the admiration and anger of other peoples, however, one begins to see with increased clarity those aspects of one's own inheritance that are of true significance. And with this awareness comes the need to articulate the unique vantage point from which the nation regards the condition of mankind.

Certainly this has been true of England and France, Italy, Germany, and Russia, and, of course, America; and it has been true of others as well. Among such nations, the struggle for survival is not a matter of raw spirit. It is conceptualized, which is to say that an intellectual order is imposed on it, so that it may be understood. I do not mean by this that the character of the nation is invented or imagined, in the sense that it did not exist beforehand and is artificially grafted on. Rather, the existing character of the people is for the first time articulated in clear terms—not in traditional, esoteric, or holy language that speaks only to the nation in question, but in general terms that can be understood by everyone. Very often it is a foreigner, in fact, who first succeeds in rendering the character of a nation in this way: In England's case, Montesquieu; in the case of America, Tocqueville.

I say this in order to set aside the pretense that other peoples do not engage in discussion of their special purpose or calling, and that it is somehow unseemly for Jews to do so. The truth is exactly the opposite: There are many peoples who have not yet reached a point where they can reasonably see themselves as being of significance to mankind as a whole, and these may well be able to dispense with such discussion; but all great nations—what used to be called the "historic nations"[15]—conduct such conversations among themselves with intensity, knowing full well that the future of humanity depends on it.

More than any other people, the Jews have understood themselves as a historic nation—that is, as the bearer of an idea, as a people with a role to play in history. It was this commitment to an idea that was the true strength of the Jews and the secret that kept us alive in the bitter sea of exile, while so many nations around us vanished into the mists of history; it was this loyalty to the ideal of Israel and to the God of Israel that moved so many generations, including a great many Jews who did not understand this ideal or believe in this God, to suffer privation and death for their sake. In other words, what brought the Jews eternal life among the nations was not a preoccupation with survival, whether individual or collective, but rather the opposite. It was the willingness to give up one's life for an idea, for a historic calling, that saved us.

The Jews are among the oldest of the existing historic nations, and in some respects the most successful, having become aware of our unique purpose more than thirty centuries ago, and having in the meantime influenced the self-understanding of mankind more than any nation. This is not only because of our people's authorship of the Bible in antiquity, but because it has throughout these centuries devoted its highest energies, often under conditions of great danger and hardship, to the cultivation of an intellectual tradition unique among the nations. This tradition, forged in light of the main currents of Western thought but in conscious and constant contradistinction to them, is for this reason unparalleled as an alternate vantage point from which to address the central questions that confront humanity.

I have already discussed the response of the Hebrew Bible to the dilemma of empire and anarchy, but one may as easily point to many other instances in which there exist independent and, to one degree or another, characteristic Jewish views. I think it is obvious, for example, that the Jewish intellectual tradition is without the towering walls erected in the last few centuries by Western thought, which separate *is* from *ought*, prudence from duty, and the ideal state from man's vision of the good. Similarly, one finds in Jewish tradition an understanding of the world in which man is inclined to evil from childhood, but free to choose the good without need of grace; in which reward and punishment are primarily a matter of this world rather than the next; in which responsibility is not only individual, but collective; in which memory is sacred, and every generation must see itself as if it had lived in the time of its forefathers; and in which love is rejected as the main wellspring of morality, in favor of justice and even honor (as in "Honor your father and your mother"[16]). This last, especially, is the reason that law is understood among Jews as the only natural discipline capable of reasonably adjudicating conflicting moral demands.

Moreover, there is in the Jewish tradition a distinct approach to epistemology, in which tradition is recognized as the mainstay of wisdom, and truth triumphs not through "pure" reasoning, but through history. There is also a distinct Jewish view of politics, in which the ways of power and worldly wisdom are not removed from the city of God, but are of it; the goodness of regimes is judged not by the procedures they have devised but by the benefits they confer on men; and no king and no public may be obeyed by the individual in the face of the demands imposed by higher moral law. And, of course, there are many specific moral principles of our tradition that constitute a proposal and a challenge to mankind: The idea that the debasement of the body is sacrilege; that books may deserve the same dignity in death as do men; that hard labor must be limited by an insuperable commandment of rest; that poverty, like celibacy, is no virtue, and achievement no vice; that the material world is not our property, but only in our care; and many others. With regard to theology, I will say only this much here—that in the Jewish tradition, God's many other perfections are of less significance than this one: That he keeps the promises he makes to man.[17]

Not long ago, Jews were still capable of speaking about such matters as though we were a match for other great nations, with much to learn from them, but also with much to teach them. As late as the early eighteenth century, the tradition of the Hebrew Bible, the Talmud, and Maimonides was still a living intellectual force in the West, borne by our people and informing the worldviews of men such as Hobbes, Grotius, Selden, Milton, Cunaeus, and Newton, in the process making a not insignificant contribution to the development of the European national state and the modern understanding of freedom.[18] Rousseau, too, inquired after the views of the rabbis, and when he published *On the Social Contract* in 1762, he well understood that it was with the political tradition of the Jews that his own ideas were most fundamentally in conflict.[19] The period of Enlightenment all but closed the door on such engagement between the Jewish tradition and the West, but even thereafter, the Jews continued to see themselves as the bearer of an idea of great importance not only to themselves, but to all humanity. One need only read Moses Hess' *Rome and Jerusalem* (1862) to catch a fleeting glimpse of the ancient Jewish message, its grandeur undiminished, still sharply distinct from the understanding of the Christian world around it, yet couched in general terms accessible to all men.[20]

Difficult as it may be to admit, it was the Holocaust that extinguished the flame of intellectual independence within the Jewish people, destroying our confidence in our tradition and ourselves, and reducing our conceptual horizon to that of a small people, overwhelmed by the day-to-day cares of its struggle to survive. That is, it was the Holocaust that destroyed our belief in ourselves as a historic nation. And while the conviction and valor of Ben-Gurion and his generation may have obscured this from view, engaging all our attention in the quest to achieve and consolidate a Jewish sovereignty, the struggle for the establishment of Israel only deferred the reckoning, whose time has now come. The signs of this can be seen everywhere: The sense of exhaustion which haunts us, while our enemies seem forever young; the inner cry that we have paid enough and deserve finally to rest; the feeling that our hope, while not yet entirely extinguished, is without any fixed object. All these cavernous hollows that now open up around us are the deep aftereffects of a life deprived of the end that once animated it, of a people no longer convinced it bears an idea, or at least one worth bearing.

Of course, there are peoples that can continue for a long time without permitting themselves to ask *why*. But ours is not among them. A historic nation, its life unnaturally extended by virtue of its ideal, loses its taste for ignorance. I do not mean by this that it is impossible for us to return to the path of a minor people, obsessed with persistence alone, and therefore utterly mortal—another Albania or Bulgaria or Montenegro, as Franz Rosenzweig once said, on the shores of the Mediterranean. We can choose this road, but we cannot prevent the devastation this choice will visit upon the next generation of Jews, the best of whom now have the option to slip away from such a people without a trace of regret. Indeed, we are already seeing this choice being made every day, not only in the Diaspora but in Israel as well.

I know our people fears this road—the road of a historic people, a people that seeks its calling before the nations and responds to it, and which, in its truer moments, breathes the air of eternity. To hear some Jews speak on the subject, one would think that to believe in any Jewish calling or purpose other than survival and benignity is of necessity to be a fanatic, a messianist, and a hater of other peoples. This is the root of the constant vituperation one hears against even the mildest efforts to understand why the Jewish people might in some sense be chosen, and of the insistence that the Israeli state must be a "neutral" state, which is to say one that is stripped clean of any overarching purpose. But the truth is that the Jews have given much to humanity and are, even today, potentially one of the great factors in civilization. And one does not have to see the hand of the divine in history to understand this. Mankind has in the last hundred years arrived at a crossroads such as it has not known since the time of Elizabeth, Shakespeare, and Bacon. The Jews are one of the few peoples with the capacity to offer significant and independent answers regarding what man has come to, and where he must now turn. In this we are not "like all the nations." At most we are like a very few other nations. And our destiny, like that of those other nations, is therefore of no mean, parochial interest.

It is this realization that brings us to the second aspect of the Jewish state's purpose as the guardian of the Jews. For the conditions of dispersion and exile that preceded the establishment of the state spelled not only physical insecurity but intellectual insecurity as well. Certainly, there were important windows of grace—not only the "golden" ages in exilic Babylonia and Spain, but other, lesser-known periods of ferment and transaction. Nonetheless, it is difficult to deny that the normative state of Jewry was one of intellectual siege, in which neither the free, internal development of Jewish ideas nor a real public airing of them was even remotely possible. Rousseau described these conditions in *Emile* (1762):

> Do you know many Christians who have taken the effort to examine with care what Judaism alleges against them? If some individuals have seen something of this, it is in the books of the Christians. A good way of informing oneself about their adversaries' arguments! But what is there to do? If someone dared to publish among us books in which Judaism were openly favored, we would punish the author, the publisher, the bookseller.... There is a pleasure in refuting people who do not dare to speak.
>
> Those who have access to conversation with Jews are not much farther advanced. These unfortunates feel themselves to be at our mercy.... What will they dare say without laying themselves open to our accusing them of blasphemy?... The most learned, the most enlightened among them are always the most circumspect....[21]

It was these conditions that stood before the eyes of early Zionist writers in their hope that an independent Jewish state could provide a suitable soil for the proper elaboration of Jewish ideas. Perhaps surprisingly, Rousseau himself came to this same conclusion, arguing that only a Jewish state would bring about a truly free development of the Jewish perspective in intellectual matters. As he concluded in the passage quoted above: "I shall never believe I have heard the arguments of the Jews until they have a free state, schools, and universities, where they can speak and dispute without risk. Only then will we know what they have to say."[22]

Now this claim is one that requires some consideration, since it is hardly the most obvious argument Rousseau might have made. One of the architects of the egalitarian state, he might easily have argued that the absence of a distinctive Jewish voice in European public discourse was the result of intolerance, and that reducing the latter would create the conditions for the free development of the ideas of the Jews. Certainly, this is what many of his admirers would say today. Rousseau, however, seems to have realized that there is a far deeper question here than can be addressed by a simple end to persecution. For the desire to which he gave voice—the desire to "know what the Jews have to say"—is a burden that the principles of equality and freedom of expression cannot possibly bear. To have a hope of achieving such a purpose one needs to seek out additional analytic principles suited to this end.

The recognition that the machinery of political equality does not necessarily lead to intellectual and cultural independence—not of the Jews, and not of anyone else—is an insight of great importance in an age in which the liberty to speak is consistently treated as though it were the sole and sufficient condition for the development of ideas worthy of being spoken. In keeping with Mill's infectious enthusiasm on the subject, we all tend to believe that given the free competition of ideas, the truth concerning every subject of importance will eventually be discovered, expressed in a persuasive fashion, and, as a consequence, heeded. And yet experience teaches something different. In public affairs, as in the life of the individual, we find that the liberty to express an opinion often does little to assure its eventual acceptance in the face of an opposite, prevailing one. The prevailing idea is defended by a great many individuals, whose desire to avoid the unpleasantness of revising their way of thinking is generally far in excess of their desire to learn the truth; and even those whose desire to know the truth is beyond question are rarely capable of investing the intellectual and emotional energies required to uproot a long-established way of understanding things. Moreover, the resistance to change is generally intransigent, poorly reasoned, and virulent in direct proportion to the importance of the subject. In the general case, it is only the young who even approach being "open-minded." The rest of humanity have their minds opened for them by a catastrophic turn of events that forces them to reconsider, or else they do not reconsider at all.

Given this reality, the price of nonconformity becomes, for most people, unbearably high. Without the shelter provided by a community of the like-minded, the dissenting individual finds himself exposed and set upon from all sides. And, unless he is made of truly extraordinary materials and has no need for encouragement or for the respect of others, capitulation and accommodation are not long in coming. In this way, disagreement is driven underground or becomes the province of eccentrics, and every original strand of thought that emerges is forced to conform to the standards generally prevailing long before it reaches its full development.[23]

It was this that caused Ahad Ha'am, himself no friend of the ghetto, to regard with such horror the fate of Judaism in the free lands of the West. As he wrote:

> It is only in the latest period, that of emancipation and assimilation, that Jewish culture has really become sterile and ceased to bear new fruit. This does not mean that our creative power has been suddenly destroyed, or that we are no longer capable of doing original work. It is the tendency to sink the national individuality, and merge it in that of other nations, that has produced [the] characteristic phenomena of this period:... The really original intellects desert their own poverty-stricken people and give their efforts to the enrichment of those who are already rich, while our literature remains a barren field for dullards and mediocrities to trample on.... Even what is good in our literature... is good only in that it resembles more or less the good products of other literatures.... We cannot feel that our national life is linked with a literature like this, which is in its essence nothing but a purveyor of foreign goods, presenting the ideas and feelings of foreign writers in a vastly inferior form.[24]

Once these considerations are taken into account, the idea that freedom of expression will lead to truth must be significantly qualified. Statements of fact pertaining to subjects both easily understandable and readily verifiable may on occasion be quickly accepted as truth, even if they overturn prevailing views. But the great issues are never of this kind. Arguments over moral, political, or religious truth are typically fought and won only over the course of generations or even centuries. Even where the falsehood is blatant, as was the case, for example, with Marxist historical and economic theories, it may be a century or more before disputes over abstract ideas begin to gravitate towards real resolution. In such protracted conceptual struggles, the truth of an idea is little guarantee of its acceptance if its advocates do not have at their disposal instruments appropriate to articulating, preserving, and advancing it over the course of long generations, and in the face of the vindictiveness that is inevitably arrayed to protect an established contrary view.

When I speak here of instruments suitable for the development of ideas over generations, and especially in the face of overwhelming opposition, I have in mind social institutions substantial enough to create a community of the like-minded, whose members can find mutual encouragement, assistance, and respect among themselves to a degree that cannot exist when the individual stands alone before society as a whole. Such institutions include universities and monasteries—and, on a far larger scale, the national state. What these institutions have in common is the recognition that *seclusion*, no less than liberty, is a precondition for the development of ideas of consequence. This insight was expressed long ago by Humboldt, the founder of the modern university,[25] and it is perhaps most immediately understood with reference to that institution (and similar ones such as yeshivot). Conditions of liberty, as we know, create a public arena in which ideas are tested against their competitors. The metaphor of the arena is apt: It is here that ideas are pitted against one another, here that they garner the applause or scorn of the public. The purpose of argument becomes, above all else, to sway the crowd, and its qualities are in accordance with this need. Arguments are chosen not because they are best but because they sound best. The prestige of the forum in which an argument is made, or of the individuals who can be induced to lend their names to it, is found to be of greater effect than the substance of what has been said. Humiliation and anger reign, careers are made and broken, everything is exaggerated and all subtlety lost. Quiet is restored only when one side reaches exhaustion and retires to the sanctuary of his study.

This is the public arena, the inevitable and wholly desirable outcome of liberty. It is the best means we have of adjudicating intellectual disputes. But it is absurd to think that weighty intellectual innovations are born or brought to maturity under such conditions. Rather, it is in the secluded society, in which like-minded individuals can work together over long years without fear of humiliation born of malice, that novel ideas appear and mature. Think of the university: There one has the benefit of a select audience comprised of individuals of like concerns, whose attention span is therefore measured not in minutes, but in years. There one has the benefit of the private criticism of one's associates, whose interest is not in swaying the crowd, but in improving the argument and bettering the common intellectual effort. There one may engage the attention of future generations of scholars and public figures who are

immersed in the complexities and difficulties of the developing idea, and
for this reason steeled against the shallow rhetoric of its detractors—as
they must necessarily be if they are to take up the work of construction
themselves. In short, it is here that one finds an environment conducive
to the articulation of an independent idea, and to the upbuilding of
an independent school of thought, even in the face of severe prejudice
and hostility on the part of the world beyond. And this is possible only
because the university consciously secludes itself—using a variety of barriers, physical, psychological, and social—from the clamor of the utterly
open society beyond its gates.

Anyone familiar with the national state will recognize in this description a model and a metaphor for such a state. For with its territorial,
linguistic, and political barriers and boundaries, the national state is itself
the greatest natural shelter under which an alternative understanding of
truth and right living can take root and flower. Of course, the national
state is an institution on an altogether different scale. And if the university is understood as a sheltered social space conducive to the development of an innovative but on the whole unitary school of thought,
then the national state—which can be home to a wide array of such
institutions—is best understood as having the potential to be a school
of such schools: A microcosm in which various schools of thought compete with one another in interpreting a people's heritage, each seeking to
influence the basis for the intellectual and moral contribution that the
national state will make to mankind. In the Jewish historical context,
one easily thinks of the competing schools of Hillel and Shamai, or of
the later schools of R. Yishmael and R. Akiva, which wrestled with one
another over the precise location of the unique Jewish vantage point and
of what might be seen from there, but which were nonetheless united in
advancing a common and unique Jewish perspective before the world. As
our tradition understood it, "These as well as the others are the words
of the living God."[26]

In our own day, a sovereign Jewish state holds out the only option for a society that is regulated in accordance with the principles of
liberty, while at the same time affording the seclusion necessary for the
development of a specific Jewish vantage point that will not be a mere
imitation of the main intellectual currents circulating in the West.[27] Like
other national states, Israel is well suited to provide just such seclusion,
which is to an important extent an inevitable result of the territorial,

linguistic, and political divisions created by virtue of its existence as an independent, Hebrew-speaking country: Differences in language in any case have the tendency to reflect (and encourage) divergences from other cultures regarding the proper understanding of reality; and the language itself, by erecting a natural barrier to communication of these ideas to the outside world, and by damping outside criticism, is in and of itself a powerful sheltering agent militating in the direction of a secure space in which such alternative understandings can take root.[28] The barriers created by geography have a similar effect, even with their attenuation by modern methods of transportation and communication. Nor is it possible to overlook the cultural differentiation that results from political division and from variations in political regime. For the heart of every civilization is its historical experience, and historical experience is principally the experience of the political. The trials, accomplishments, and catastrophes shared by a given political society form the backbone of that which the individual shares with his neighbor, and these experiences, the basis for traditions of thought and action extending far beyond the strictly political, divide men from their colleagues who are members of another polity, no matter how much they share with them a fundamental sympathy.[29]

When these factors are considered together, we see that the national state is an immensely powerful seclusionary institution, well able, in principle, to establish a sheltered cultural space in which differentiated and original ideals may find their full development for the common benefit of mankind. It was just this possibility that led Ahad Ha'am to argue that the answer to the deterioration of Judaism in the West had to be the creation of a concentrated Jewish settlement in Palestine. "The spiritual trouble of which I have spoken is fraught with danger to our people's future," he wrote, "no less than the physical trouble. A 'home of refuge' for the national spirit is therefore not less essential than a home of refuge for our homeless wanderers.... It is impossible, in my opinion, to deny that the necessary scale would be very large indeed... [if we are] to create a fixed and independent center for our national culture—for science, art, and literature."[30]

The shelter and seclusion provided by the national state cannot, of course, guarantee that it will be home to the creation of an original and worthwhile intellectual life within its boundaries, any more than the establishment of a university can guarantee it. Every institution depends on the particular men who comprise it, and if these choose to devote all their activities to mimicking the ideas of others, then no institutional structure will prevent such assimilation. But where there exists an intellectual leadership of even moderate creativity and daring, the barriers erected by language, territory, and polity assume their seclusionary role, creating the secure space in which different voices can be heard and can gain their first blush of respect, without immediately becoming the focus of withering opposition from the partisans of dominant contrary ideas. Under such circumstances, the national state becomes the ideal vessel for the development and propagation of an original intellectual climate. And if, as often happens, we find the writers and scholars of other national states jealous for the reputations of their own peoples, we may also find that the system of independent national states—with each nation devoted to the development of its own special way in life and thought—has become a great nursery for innovations and experiments, in which each people pursues its own ends, to the ultimate benefit of all.

In October 2002, exactly one hundred years will have passed since the Minsk Conference, at which Ahad Ha'am called for the establishment of an extensive and concentrated Jewish settlement in Palestine capable of serving as what he called a "spiritual center" for the Jews. In the intervening time, the work of generations has succeeded not only in making the Hebrew language one that is spoken with fluency by millions of Jews, but also in bringing it to a level of sophistication and beauty not seen in many centuries. And in this land, too, there have arisen universities and other institutions of higher learning and culture, as well as a greater number of yeshivot than the Jewish world has ever known—so that the potential for learning what the Jews have to say, to use again Rousseau's phrase, has never been greater than it is in modern Israel.

The reality, of course, has been something of a surprise and a disappointment. The spirit of the German academy, in which the works of the Jewish mind were seen as having contributed little or nothing to man's advancement, hovers over the universities of the Jewish state; and many a good mind has succumbed to this view of things. Nor do the great founders of our national intellectual life—Agnon and Bialik, Dinur, Scholem, and R. Kook, all of whom were immigrants from Europe—have much in common with the new generation of Israeli academics and authors, many of whom seem to believe that the nihilistic fads emanating from America and Germany constitute a definitive revelation as to how we must understand our world. A book published in Hebrew, as it turns out, may be as distant from making a contribution to the dream of a "home of refuge for the national spirit" as any in German or English.[31] And as might be expected when the best energies of so many of Israel's men of letters are devoted to copying foreign fashion, the nations of the world, who can more easily have the originals, tend to dismiss the entire gallery of them without so much as a footnote.

Unfortunate though the failings of many among the present generation of Israeli writers and scholars may be, these cannot be considered decisive. The establishment of the Jewish state is an enterprise of many generations, and it should always be judged from this perspective. On such a scale, perhaps only the re-establishment of the Hebrew language as a living medium can be judged to be of enduring significance. True, this is in an important sense no more than the achievement of a *formal requirement* of an independent national life, as is the establishment of a Jewish political sovereignty. After all, Jewish sovereignty will not rescue persecuted Jews in other lands if we have no public men devoted to the principle of Jewish guardianship; and by the same token, our intellectual heritage will remain a closed book to Jew and gentile alike as long as we do not have an intellectual leadership guided by a similar devotion. But this is already a matter of *character*, the third aspect of Israel's purpose, which will be the subject of the third and final section of this essay. For our purposes here, suffice it to say that an apparently formal achievement on the scale of the revival of the language of the Bible is not to be underestimated in terms of the possibilities it opens up for us as a historic nation.

NOTES

1. "On the National State, Part 1: Empire and Anarchy," *Azure* 12 (Winter 2002), pp. 27-70.

2. Charles de Secondat Montesquieu, *The Spirit of the Laws*, ed. and trans. Anne M. Cohler et al. (Cambridge: Cambridge, 1989), p. 156.

3. Theodor Herzl, *Der Judenstaat* (Vienna: Breitenstein, 1896), p. 94. [German]

4. In the Zionist political tradition that preceded the establishment of Israel, this purpose of Jewish guardianship was conceived in threefold fashion, with the hoped-for Jewish state envisioned as a polity that would: *First*, ameliorate the condition of persecution that had afflicted the Jews in their dispersion; *second*, permit the establishment of an independent Jewish national culture based on the unique perspective of the Jews; and *third*, assist the Jews in developing a character suitable for a life of self-reliance and independence. Although these three facets of the idea of Jewish guardianship can be, and in practice often were, treated as though each were an end in itself independent from the others, it is helpful to think of them as being dependent on one another in a hierarchical fashion: It being understood that the ability to maintain a Jewish state concerned with the condition of diaspora Jewry is ultimately dependent on the development of a unique Jewish vantage point or culture; and that both of these are dependent on the development of a strong Jewish character. It is in this fashion that I suggest we think about the different aspects of Jewish guardianship, each of which I will examine in turn. The present essay deals with the first and second aspects of Jewish guardianship. A discussion of the third can be found in Yoram Hazony, "On the National State, Part 3: Character," *Azure* 14 (Winter 2003), pp. 107-144.

5. Burke's speech appears in William Cobbett, *The Parliamentary History of England from the Earliest Period to the Year 1803* (London: T.C. Hansard, 1806), pp. 223-224.

6. See Leonard Stein, *The Balfour Declaration* (London: Mitchell, 1961), p. 7.

7. Herzl, *The Complete Diaries of Theodor Herzl*, ed. Raphael Patai, trans. Harry Zohn (New York: Herzl Press, 1960), p. 10.

8. Herzl, *Complete Diaries*, pp. 131-132.

9. Speech by Ben-Gurion before a special session of the National Assembly, November 30, 1942. Central Zionist Archives, J/1366. Cf. Herzl, who argued that the one thing that was needed was "Jews who carry out Jewish policies, and not cabinet policies on orders from someone else." Theodor Herzl, "Judaism," in Theodor Herzl, *Zionist Writings: Essays and Addresses*, trans. Harry Zohn (New York: Herzl Press, 1973), vol. 1, p. 55.

10. Theodor Herzl, *The Jewish State*, trans. Harry Zohn (New York: Herzl Press, 1970), pp. 107-108. The possibility that the national state would wither away and would be replaced by a world of small, independent communities was also discussed by the Zionists. As Max Nordau wrote, "I would prefer to believe that the organic evolution of human beings will bring them someday to a point where... the molecular motion of the brain will be imparted directly to other

brains by a kind of radiation or continuous transmission. I ascribe the same degree of probability to this imaginary onward evolution from the national state into the independent community." Quoted in Ben Zion Netanyahu's introduction to Max Nordau, *To His People: A Summons and a Challenge* (New York: Scopus, 1941), pp. 37-38.

11. Hermann Cohen, "Germanism and Judaism," in Hermann Cohen, *Juedische Schriften* (Berlin: Schwetschke, 1924). [German] On Cohen's relationship with the established German-Jewish leadership, see Jehuda Reinharz, *Fatherland or Promised Land: The Dilemma of the German Jew, 1893-1914* (Ann Arbor: University of Michigan, 1975), p. 84; D. Engel, "Relations Between Liberals and Zionists in Germany During World War I," *Zion* 27:4 (September 1982), p. 447 [Hebrew]; Jehuda Medler, "Hermann Cohen's Philosophy of Judaism," doctoral dissertation (Ann Arbor: University Microfilms, 1968), p. 488.

12. See Francis Fukuyama, *The End of History and the Last Man* (New York: Free Press, 1992); and Shimon Peres, *The New Middle East* (New York: Henry Holt, 1993). Today these works are even more painful to read than they were a decade ago.

13. Yossi Beilin, *The Death of the American Uncle* (Tel Aviv: Yediot Aharonot, 1999), p. 49 [Hebrew]; Moshe Zimmermann, "Anti-Semitic Imports from Europe," *Haaretz*, October 26, 2000.

14. Tosefta Shabbat 15:17; Yoma 82a.

15. My use of the term "historic nation" is not intended to imply an acceptance of any of the specific doctrines that have been appended to it and to other terms that might be thought to be similar. In particular, I have no sympathy with the idea of an *ur-nation*, or "primary nation," as this term was used by Herder and others. I mean only to refer to peoples who have for many generations been aware of a particular calling or purpose which describes and animates their place within history.

16. Exodus 20:12.

17. Such a cursory mentioning of ideas cannot ever be satisfactory, much less complete in any sense. I have not, for example, included many of the most important Jewish ideas (e.g., the one God; or the social order based principally on respect for marriage and property) out of fear that these will, in this context, appear trite. In addition, it is obvious that every way of life will be of interest only relative to what is accepted among surrounding peoples, so that every such sketch must change from one generation to the next.

For a more significant discussion of this general topic, see David Novak, *Natural Law in Judaism* (Cambridge: Cambridge, 1998); Ofir Haivry, "The Way of the World," *Azure* 5 (Autumn 1998). On the place of law in Jewish moral thought, see David Hazony, "Eliezer Berkovits and the Revival of Jewish Moral Thought," *Azure* 11 (Summer 2001); on the individual and the state, see Yoram

Hazony, "The Jewish Origins of the Western Disobedience Tradition," *Azure* 4 (Summer 1998); on the Sabbath, see Yosef Yitzhak Lifshitz, "Secret of the Sabbath," *Azure* 10 (Winter 2001). It is also possible to describe a Jewish literary aesthetic with an evident affinity for the epistemology and morality described here. See Assaf Inbari, "Towards a Hebrew Literature," *Azure* 9 (Spring 2000).

The expression "a proposal and a challenge to mankind" is borrowed, roughly, from Pierre Manent, "Democracy Without Nations?" in Daniel J. Mahoney and Paul Senton, eds., *Modern Liberty and Its Discontents* (New York: Rowman and Littlefield, 1998), p. 195.

18. See Fania Oz-Salzberger, "The Jewish Roots of Western Freedom," *Azure* 13 (Summer 2002), pp. 88-132.

19. Jean-Jacques Rousseau, *On the Social Contract*, ed. Roger D. Masters, trans. Judith R. Masters (New York: St. Martin's, 1978), pp. 125-126. Nonetheless, this controversy with the Jews did not prevent him from recognizing, for instance, in his essay on *The Government of Poland*, that his own conception of the proper founding of the nation was based to no small degree on the establishment of the Jewish polity as depicted in the Hebrew Bible. Jean-Jacques Rousseau, *The Government of Poland* (New York: Bobbs Merrill, 1972), pp. 5-6, 8.

20. Moses Hess, *The Revival of Israel: Rome and Jerusalem*, trans. Meyer Waxman (Lincoln: University of Nebraska, 1995).

21. Jean-Jacques Rousseau, *Emile*, trans. Allan Bloom (New York: Basic Books, 1979), pp. 303-304.

22. Rousseau, *Emile*, p. 304.

23. It is for this reason that the institution of tenure has done nothing to secure intellectual freedom at the universities. Proponents of this arrangement claim that by removing permanently the threat of dismissal, they permit academics to write and teach according to their true convictions. But this argument is predicated on the false premise that a learned professor will generally value his daily bread more than the comradeship and esteem of his fellows.

24. Ahad Ha'am, "The Spiritual Revival," in *Selected Essays of Ahad Ha'am*, ed. and trans. Leon Simon (Philadelphia: Jewish Publication Society, 1962), pp. 265, 286-287.

25. I am careful here to speak of *seclusion* rather than *exclusion*, whose meaning is the precise opposite of my intention. By seclusion, I mean the purposive gathering of like-minded people to advance a common aim, without any intention of excluding others. In general, I think it would be correct to say that exclusive institutions do not welcome outsiders, whereas seclusive institutions do welcome outsiders who are not opposed to the aims of the institution.

26. Eruvin 13b.

27. For over a century, those who have attempted to incite the Jews to reach for such a goal have had to contend with those who say they wish to see just such a flourishing of Jewish life in Germany, or more recently, in America. I believe that this is an impossibility, unless American Jewry concludes that it is willing to sacrifice its social status and mobility for seclusionary institutions such as only the Orthodox have generally maintained until now. It is difficult to imagine, for example, a Jewish university in the United States that would be voluntarily attended by most of the country's best Jewish students. At this point, such a vision seems fantastic, and this fact is of the first consequence. For so long as Harvard and Yale continue to draw the most gifted students—including many of the Orthodox—it is futile to speak of a Jewish renaissance that is not predicated upon and derivative of such a cultural restoration in Israel. Without seclusion, in other words, American Jewry is doomed to find itself operating to a greater or lesser extent within the same framework described by Ahad Ha'am a century ago: The most original minds leave aside the concerns of Jewish civilization and devote their best efforts to the more general advancement of things American, while Jewish literature and ideas remain largely a barren field.

28. Compare this with Mill's comment that in a multi-national regime, "One section does not know what opinions, or what instigations, are circulating in another," due to differences in language. John Stuart Mill, "On Representative Government," in H.B. Acton, ed., *Utilitarianism, On Liberty, and Considerations on Representative Government* (London: Everyman, 1984), pp. 392-394.

29. These dividing effects of geography, language, and polity are well known to those accustomed to reflecting on intellectual trends, which are for this reason consistently and usefully represented by geographic designations—such as the Frankfurt school, the Austrian school, English empiricism, the Scottish Enlightenment, German idealism, and so on. This is not just convention, but a reflection of the fact that individuals familiar with the subject matter treated by these styles of thought can and do feel the changes of intellectual climate from the moment they descend from the train to pay a visit to their colleagues.

30. Ahad Ha'am, "The Spiritual Revival," *Hashiloah* 10:60 (December 1902), pp. 481-482. [Hebrew] Cf. Ahad Ha'am, "The Spiritual Revival," pp. 287-289.

31. On the change in the character of the Hebrew language itself in recent years, see Joseph Dan, "On Post-Zionism, Modern Hebrew, and False Messianism," *Haaretz*, March 25, 1994.

ON ZION: A REALITY THAT FASHIONS IMAGINATION

OFIR HAIVRY

Content and Form

In his well-known composition *The Content of the Form*, the historical methodologist Hayden White attempted to determine the extent to which the literary structure of historical writing conditions the reader's understanding of the information conveyed in it—in other words, to what extent does the form of a composition determine its content.[1] It is widely understood and accepted that in a literary composition, such as a comedy or a tragedy, form is the main factor in the shaping of influence upon the reader. But is a historical work, which seeks to ascertain the truth, also a story in which form prevails over the importance of the information? White's answer is unequivocal: As the title of his book testifies, he is convinced that the form of a historical composition is the essence of its content. There are far-reaching implications to White's viewpoint. Is it legitimate, for example, to describe World War II as a story in which it is the German nation that is the victim? Or is it the case, quite to the contrary, that the substance of events possesses an essential and inevitable form which limits the possible configurations that one can reasonably give to those events? The issue here is not the distortion of the dry facts, but the different interpretations it is possible to ascribe to them. That is, is every formal interpretation legitimate, or is there an essential bond, of moral significance, between the substance and the form of things? There are of course those who disagree with White's conception, but this is not the place to expand upon the difficulties inherent in his theory—particularly in relation to the possibility of determining historical truths or morals if it is true that the form of a composition is indeed more important than its content. It suffices that this determination serves to open the inquiry into the relation between the content of things and their form, and the nature of their influence upon one another.

Intention and Deed

It is no coincidence that Yehuda Halevi's philosophical work *The Kuzari* opens with the question of the Khazar king as to the meaning of a sentence which returns to him repeatedly in his dream: "Your intentions are pleasing but not so your deeds."[2] For Halevi sees in this the basis of the explanation of Judaism's uniqueness—the joint importance of both intention and deed.

In *The Kuzari*, Halevi suggests that human history contains two general, divergent currents of thought as to the proper way to find truth or salvation. In the Western trend—represented by Greek and modern philosophy, and by religions such as Christianity and Islam—the revelation of truth springs from a single clear principle or abstract idea; while in the Eastern tendency—Buddhism, Confucianism, and Taoism—the illumination of truth lies in action.[3]

Thus in Western tradition salvation is found through right belief: The wicked actions of the most sinful of Christians will not be an impediment to this end; it is enough that he believe in the Holy Trinity for his soul to be saved. In other words, the essence is the unmitigated adoption of the content and intent of the one truth. In Eastern tradition, on the other hand, human salvation is achieved by virtue of proper behavior, and perpetual repetition of a mantra will pave the way to nirvana for a Tantric Buddhist. In other words, what is essential is following the path of correct action.[4]

Judaism, in contrast to both of the above, is unique in the emphasis it places on an indissoluble combination of faith and deed. As the Jewish sage explains to the Khazar king, the latter's good intentions and pure heart have no value if his deeds are incorrect; likewise, good deeds without the right intentions are merely lost labor.

Even though the foundation of Judaism is the belief in a covenant with an eternal and omnipotent God, faith cannot make a person into a Jew, and in fact the Jewish religion does not explicitly demand belief.[5] On the other hand, while Judaism consists entirely of exacting ritual and rules of behavior, this ritual and these rules are intended to express belief in the Rock of Israel. Here it is important to emphasize that this does not mean that intention and action are equally important in Judaism. The place of faith is extremely limited, and the weight of the deed is the principle that occupies the overwhelming majority of the thought and creative production of the Jewish people from Horev until our day.[6] The reason for this remarkable ascendancy of deed over intention lies embedded in the very foundations of Judaism, in the need to deal with the ramifications of the belief in one God.

Principle and Ritual

In placing the affirmation "We will act" before that of "We will comprehend" at the time of the Tora's revelation, the religion of Moses expressed, at the very moment of its birth, the supremacy of the form of ritual over the content of belief. Twice more in the book of Exodus the Israelites commit themselves merely with "We will act," without even mentioning "We will comprehend," as though to make use of this potent principle only in the smallest measure.[7] And the principle represented by the "We will comprehend" was, indeed, something new in the history of the world: The principle of generalization. Generalization, which seems to us today to be a trivial component of human culture, science, and thought, was not obvious at all in human history, and it is not even clear at precisely what point it appeared. The early civilizations of the ancient world—Sumer, Egypt, Babylon, Assyria, and Persia—did not know what generalization was. These cultures, in which writing, the wheel, and the calendar were invented, were based entirely on eclecticism—on the collection of details in order to store them—without determining any universal values or seeking any sort of general principles.[8] Even though it is clear that a certain amount of abstraction and generalization are inherent in human thought, the concept of generalization was unknown during the first few thousand years of human history.

Then, suddenly, in the thought of Greece of 2,500 years ago, we find the principle of generalization occupying a central place. Thales, considered to be the first philosopher, determined that "everything is water," and with this generalization established the nature of wisdom, truth, and knowledge as we still understand them today—that is, no longer as a mere collection of details and ideas, but as an expression of general and absolute principles.[9]

However, although generalization as a defined principle was born in ancient Greece, we find its essence appearing on the stage of history about a thousand years earlier, with the appearance at Sinai of the Is-raelite concept of God as one, unique, and all-encompassing. Just how far-reaching the influence of this concept was one can learn from the exceedingly roundabout way in which the religion of Moses carefully covered and fenced in the content of this principle by means of the form of ritual.

Orchard and Road

The enormous danger that the Jewish tradition perceives in exposure to absolute principles is underscored by the well-known talmudic figure of four sages from R. Akiva's generation who "entered the orchard"[10]—i.e., who were exposed to the secrets of hidden knowledge. One of the four looked upon the secrets and died, a second looked and went mad, a third "uprooted the saplings" (ceased to keep the Jewish faith), and only Akiva came out safely.

The Jewish tradition throughout its history emphasized the danger of direct exposure to the *shechina* (the Divine Presence), an exposure which, like looking directly into the sun, blinds the viewer and is apt to cause complete blindness. For thousands of years, this has been an important and consistent element in Judaism, from the Tora's warning that whoever looks directly upon God will die, to the strict precepts governing how close one might approach the sanctuary in the days of the Temple, up to the traditional injunctions against learning Kabbala without having first undergone the necessary training.[11]

The one truth, whether it is called right belief or pure wisdom, can be so dangerous because in its generality and absoluteness it cannot but subordinate and cancel all that surrounds it. This is the nature of an absolute principle. The clash between principle and reality is inevitable, because reality cannot ever contain the pure ideal.

When the cultures of the ancient world met with the principle of generalization, all of them—except one—collapsed, because the internal contradictions endemic to their eclecticism came to light in all their inconsistency the moment they were confronted with generalization, which is consistency itself. Not only Egypt and Babylon were incapable of coping with generalization. In both Greece and Rome, where the philosophical version of generalization developed, society and culture simply disintegrated as the customs and the gods on which they had been grounded were demonstrated, by means of the newly introduced method of philosophical generalization, to be worthless.

In other words, the tension between deed and principle was gradually revealed. It became clear that a culture or religion based on traditions and customs alone could not stand up to the test of principle. However, even when these societies attempted to base themselves on the rules of philosophical wisdom, they still could not overcome the constant undermining of every social framework or custom by abstract principles, and by the ruthlessness inherent in following one ideal through to the end.

For the last two thousand years, human culture has attempted to cope with this problem with a series of systems aimed at finding the correct balance between reality and principle. Beginning with Christianity and Islam, through rationalism and Marxism, there have been repeated attempts to find the way that will lead to the much-sought orchard.

The solution offered by Judaism is found in the emphasis on the moral importance of the path itself. That is, Judaism refuses to accept the confining of its essence to the realization of an abstract, metahistorical value in "the next world." Rather, the Jewish faith ties that essence in a consistent fashion to "this world." Thus in contrast to other worldviews in which this world is understood merely as a prelude to the main essence, or in which this world is all there is, the path in Judaism is not only a tool for arriving in the orchard, but a significant part of the orchard itself.

In Judaism, the path—the means—has an inherent, irreplaceable value, which derives from the understanding that one can reach the orchard only within the framework of a life led in a very specific historical and geographical context: A way of life which is in itself supposed to embody the historical destiny of the Jewish people, and which transpires entirely in the land of Israel. The essential connection between the people and the land needs no documenting here, and is recognized even by those who could not be suspected of excessive sympathy for Judaism.[12]

Horev and Moria

From its first representations of the Jewish connection to the land of Israel, beginning with the Tora's description of Abraham's arrival in the land and of his formal covenant with God,[13] and indeed throughout its entire length, the Bible unambiguously insists that the connection to the land is an *a priori* condition for the fulfillment of the religious commandments. In addition to the significant fact of the chronological precedence of the patriarchs in the land to the giving of the Tora, all of Jewish religious ritual is intended for inhabitants of the land, and is possible only within its borders.

National existence, religious ritual, and the land of Israel are inextricably intertwined in the Bible in the centrality of the Temple in Jerusalem, in the holidays connected to agriculture in the land, in the connection between religious and political reforms, and so forth. Perhaps the most outstandingly conspicuous sign of this is the fact that Horev, the site of the giving of the Tora, which might have been expected to become an important religious focus, has always remained remote and peripheral. Mount Moria, on the other hand, which is connected to the binding of Isaac and the promise of the land to the descendants of Abraham, is what actually became the center of worship and identification for the Israelites when the Temple was erected on it. But in the wake of the destruction of the First Temple at the hands of the Babylonians in 586 B.C.E., the relationship between the people and the land changed dramatically. Although the Second Temple was already standing less than seventy years after the destruction of the first, a significant gap had already begun to crystallize between the form of Jewish existence and the content this existence was supposed to clothe, a gap which still exists and continues to exert its influence down to our own day—namely, the dwelling of a large part of the Jewish people outside the land.

Hillel and Shamai

One can observe the destructive consequences of this gap in the talmudic homily concerning a certain Gentile who asked the two most prominent sages of Israel in their generation to teach him the entire Tora in the time one could remain standing "on one leg." Shamai simply sent the presumptuous Gentile away, while Hillel accepted the challenge and told him: "Whatever is hateful to you, do not do unto your neighbor, and all the rest is merely interpretation."[14] This episode does much to substantiate the threat posed to Judaism when the connection of the people to the land is undermined. The demand of the stranger to learn the Tora "on one leg" expresses in a clear fashion the "Greek" search for the one abstract ideal which stands as the foundation of all things. The stranger expresses well the Hellenistic idea, which by this time held sway from India to the farthest west, that the most important thing is the one, concise, and generalizing principle.

Among the Jewish people, too, there were those who were beguiled by this approach, especially those who lived outside of the land or who adopted a Hellenistic outlook. These began to downplay the importance of the fine points of ritual and the tie to the land, as opposed to the importance of the pure ideal—be it called "truth" or "peace" or "faith." The struggle against this worldview was and is an enormous challenge for Judaism: The seekers after the ideal attempted to brush aside anything that was formal and ritual, and to arrive at the foundation, the faith. The sages of Israel for their part made every effort to fend off this trend, which they understood to have a tremendous capacity to destroy.

The reactions of Hillel and Shamai reveal two different attitudes as to how to deal with this struggle, attitudes that are fundamentally divergent both in terms of their philosophical points of departure and their tactics. For Hillel and Shamai were the representatives of two distinct approaches to the traditional Jewish law of their time. Shamai, born in the land of Israel and a product of its political-cultural tradition, articulates the early

Jewish legal tradition whose source is the period of the First Temple, and which is completely immersed in life in the land of Israel, in Jewish nationalism, and in the struggle for Jewish national independence. The first premise of Beit Shamai (the Academy of Shamai) is the strict preservation of the practical rules and laws of the Tora. In the legal tradition of Beit Shamai, a prohibition is a prohibition, permission is permission, and what counts is the deed and not the intention.[15]

Hillel, on the other hand, came to Israel from Babylonia and embodied the change that had taken place in Judaism with the establishment of the exile and reconciliation to it. Since in the exile many of the laws of the Tora are difficult or impossible to perform in a literal fashion, the Jewish law which was then developing in Babylonia tried to discover the intention behind the laws of the Tora so as to be able to derive a system of observance which could be performed outside the land. The advantage to this method lies in its flexibility. But in obtaining this flexibility, it runs the risk of diminishing the political-national dimension of the connection to the land, as well as of incurring other questionable consequences that such a weakening must necessarily entail.

These differences of outlook are evidenced by the tactics which the two sages are reported to have used when confronted by the Gentile. Shamai is not even willing to discuss Judaism "on one leg" and rejects any such occupation out of hand, while Hillel attempts to deal with the stranger in a sophisticated fashion that is supposed ultimately to bring the questioner to accept Judaism in its complete and inclusive form. In the talmudic story, the stranger converts in the end, and this fact is supposed to indicate the preferability of Hillel's tolerance as opposed to Shamai's zealousness. The source of this story is, as mentioned, the Babylonian Talmud, and it symbolizes the political-cultural turn that gradually took place in Judaism after the fall of the Second Temple. As long as those living in the land comprised the majority and the core of the Jewish people, it was the older traditions, those closer to Shamai and his teachings—traditions which gave birth to the national uprisings of the Hasmoneans, the Great Revolt, and the Bar Kochba Revolt—which remained in ascendance. But when the land of Israel ceased to be the living center of the Jewish nation, the traditions of Beit Shamai succumbed as well, and it was the legal tradition of Beit Hillel which was accepted in practice, and which has guided Judaism since.

However, a second look at Hillel's answer arouses much wonder: What kind of a description of the essence of the Tora does not include any reference to the uniqueness and unity of God and his relationship with the Jewish people? It would have been reasonable to expect Hillel to choose as a concise, succinct definition—the first words of the book of Genesis, or the first commandment of the Decalogue, or "Hear O Israel." But he did not do so. Hillel, one of the outstanding Jewish sages, does not even mention the existence of God or his commandments, and instead chooses to present to the Gentile a practical, behavioral principle, rational and utilitarian, which is entirely worldly.

One certainly need not suspect Hillel of failing to understand the importance of the existence of God in the Jewish religion. One is therefore left with no alternative but to regard his reply as an attempt to confront the challenge of generalization in a manner which attempts to check the antinomian danger inherent in it. In answer to the "philosophical" question about essence, Hillel deliberately gives an answer which leads in the opposite direction, faithfully following the Jewish tradition of refraining from directly occupying oneself with the sublime and the transcendent, preferring instead to concentrate on the means, the deed. Thus Hillel's answer is indirectly close to that of Shamai: A distrust for the whole idea of doing anything "on one leg," a demurral at the danger inherent in the direct answer. For a direct answer brings one to the essence, preempting the need for the means—and this is the greatest of dangers.

In the days of Hillel and Shamai, in the third decade of the first century C.E., and perhaps even on the very same day as the conversation with the Gentile, a Jewish youth from the Galilee came to a group of Pharisee sages in Jerusalem—perhaps Hillel and Shamai were among them?—argued with them, and disparaged the importance of the means. His subsequent behavior is described by his disciples:

> And one of the scribes came up and heard them disputing with one another, and seeing that he answered them well, asked him, "Which commandment is the first of all?" Jesus answered, "The first is, 'Hear, O Israel: The Lord our God, the Lord is one; and you shall love the Lord your God with all your heart, and with all your soul, and with all your mind, and with all your strength.' The second is this, 'You shall love your neighbor as yourself.' There is no other commandment greater than these." And the scribe said to him, "You are right, Teacher;

you have truly said that he is one, and there is no other but he; and to love him with all the heart, and with all the understanding, and with all the strength, and to love one's neighbor as oneself, is much more than all whole burnt offerings and sacrifices."[16]

Here we see the danger of generalization in its full and deadly form. A direct answer is given, and is immediately followed by the logical conclusion—that this principle is more important than all sorts of customs such as burnt offerings and sacrifices. We have already reached the endpoint, so why bother with the means? Now it is clear why Shamai was angered and why Hillel gave such a cautious answer. The young Galilean Jew seemingly went just one small step further, and gave the direct answer which both Hillel and Shamai had so insistently avoided. The Galilean's answer, which could easily be given while standing "on one leg," says in effect that the essential principle and the divine identity is love. Yet we know that while one can stand on one leg, one cannot walk in this way; and he who tries, falls.

Hillel's answer to the Gentile was an oblique attempt to counter the widespread acceptance by that time, among many of the Jewish people as well, of the principle of generalization. Judaism very quickly learned how dangerous this route is, because even a cautious attempt to give an answer "on one leg" regarding its essence leads in the end to the threat of messianism.

Jesus and Bar Kochba

The nature of the challenge with which Judaism was confronted can be seen in the *Histories* of the Roman historian Cornelius Tacitus, written around the end of the first century C.E., in which he argues that "The Jewish faith is paradoxical and despicable."[17] In this period Judaism was part of the cultural, philosophical, and religious controversy of the Roman world, which was attracted by the idea of the one and unique God of Israel, but was repelled by all the incomprehensible, bothersome, and exacting rites which accompanied this faith in one God. The combination of an abstract God with ritual minutiae seemed to many, as it did to Tacitus, to be contradictory; hence his harsh conclusion.

At this time pagan beliefs were already in an advanced state of decay. The social order, based as it was on inconsistent traditions and beliefs, gradually crumbled as more and more ancient customs failed to withstand the test of practical utility; and the belief in gods such as Apollo and Jupiter was shown by the philosophers to be meaningless. The cornerstones of society—such as its moral values and common goals—were eroded, and a quest began for something to replace them.

Even philosophical rationalism itself could not withstand the corrosive power of the trend towards generalization. It became clear that the attempt to base society on philosophical principles was fruitless, since these principles are susceptible to being perpetually undermined by the very process which produced them; after all, philosophical principles were originally understood as a tool for meditating upon and challenging all things. Philosophies which settle upon the impossibility of fundamentally knowing anything (skepticism), or which argue that there is no permanent value to anything and therefore no value that can be defined as meaningful (epicureanism), of necessity led to existential despair and to a search for something unshakable.

Thus by degrees, both the ignorant masses seeking support in time of trouble, and the followers of Aristotelianism and neo-Platonism who accepted the existence of one supreme abstract source of things, became ready to adopt a monotheistic faith, but not the punctiliousness of deed and ritual which are found in Judaism. They found what they were looking for in early Christianity—the religion of pure faith.

In our own day, there persists a widespread view according to which Christianity was mainly the invention of Saul (Paul) of Tarsus, while the Nazarite himself was actually a devout Jew fundamentally loyal to the religion of Israel, no more than a Galilean carpenter who did not wish to change Judaism and whose opinions were falsified after his death. But such was not the case. It is true that the Tarsean had an overwhelmingly important role in shaping Christianity by formulating concepts such as the Holy Trinity, in which the son of Mary becomes part of God, but the root of Christianity is undoubtedly in the far-reaching religious innovation whose source is the Nazarite himself: The identification of God with "love."[18]

In this pronouncement, at first blush appearing to go only a step further than Hillel, and seeming so simple, Christianity deviates sharply from Judaism—since the identification of God with love turns love into the supreme, all-encompassing value, and one has then only to accept God's love in order to be redeemed. In such a theory, there is no more real importance to truth, justice, or morality, and certainly not to ritual, since whether or not one cleaves to these, the believing Christian and his soul will in the end be saved by God's grace.

These consequences of taking the extra step beyond Hillel were inevitable, and they illustrate the danger to Judaism that lies in responding to the wish to identify oneself with a single, generalizing principle. For the identification of God with one supreme value such as "love" necessarily involves the nullification of all other values and principles. Even if the Galilean and his followers opined that they were not abrogating Judaism or its customs in their gospel but rather strengthening them (this is why in the beginning they were called "messianic Jews"), the truth is that from the moment they decided to forgo the path, the means, what they preached was no longer Judaism but something completely different.[19]

This freeing of faith from the moorings of ritual, the magic of the pure generalization, surfaced again and again in the generations that followed, among those who wished to give one fundamental, direct, and liberating explanation to the destiny of mankind. It is interesting to note how conspicuously so many of those who broke away from the Jewish community nevertheless retained that burning desire for the orchard—individuals such as Marx, Lombroso, Freud, and Levi-Strauss. This ardent longing for the one, complete, and terminal solution to all things is also known as "messianism," the belief in "the messiah." This idea has its origins in the ancient Hebrew concept of a *mashiah* ("anointed one"), but unfortunately, even among many of the Jewish people today this original concept has been displaced by that of "the Messiah."

Mashiah is a biblical political-military-religious leader who, even if the source of his inspiration is divine, is entirely flesh and blood, and all of whose actions, powers, failures, and triumphs are carried out within the course of history. The kings of Israel, such as Saul and David, were described by the Bible as *mashiah*; but so too was Cyrus, the non-Jewish king of Persia. Similarly, after the biblical period, the leader of the Jewish revolt of 132-135 C.E., Shimon Bar-Kosiba, known as "Bar Kochba," was referred to by many as *mashiah*. Yet almost at the same time, the idea of "the Messiah" began to take root, with the hoped-for leader now being an apocalyptic figure whose powers were beyond those of men, and whose coming would herald the end of days and the end of history.

This apocalyptic "Messiah" was, and is, an entirely un-Jewish idea, which has taken root within Judaism and constantly threatens to undermine it from within. The un-Jewishness of the figure of "the Messiah" springs from his superhuman traits—he is expected to be a kind of demigod whose very existence absolutely contradicts the unity and uniqueness of God—as well as from his being a figure who is expected, at one blow, to solve all problems, alter the laws of nature, and abrogate all the importance of form in favor of the age of content. In other words, "the Messiah" is a shortcut, whereas Judaism is perfect faithfulness to the whole road, as it is.

Several of the sages of Israel—such as Maimonides, who very clearly speaks of a political-military-religious leader who acts entirely within history—tried to retain the original concept of a *mashiah*, but most traditional commentators preferred to stave off the danger of messianism by postponing the anticipated arrival of "the Messiah" to the end of days—i.e., to the farthest possible future. But despite these efforts, from time to time there would appear some who would decide that the end of days had arrived. Such was the case with Jesus' followers (known as "messianic," in Greek, *christianos*), who for many years awaited his imminent return and the end of days. Thus it was, too, in the case of Shabtai Tzvi, a seventeenth-century false messiah, whose followers believed that he would lead them on a cloud to the land of redemption. And such is the case in our own day, when the leadership of Israel is convinced and convinces others that the laws of nature have been corrected, that today the world has changed and the time has come for "the wolf to dwell with the lamb" because "this is the time for the great reckoning, in order to extract the Jewish people from its past, to give it a new future."[20]

To recognize the difference between *mashiah* and "the Messiah," it suffices to recall the unmistakable tendency of messianic movements towards a sweeping cancellation of previously accepted identities, prohibitions, and rules of behavior, on the grounds that the world has been transformed down to its very foundations, obviating the need for outworn modes of behavior and identities. Among the Christians, the laws of the Tora were abrogated because there was a "New Covenant." Among the Sabbatians, everything from fast days to the prohibition against incest was nullified because the laws of nature had supposedly changed. And in our own time, messianism manifests itself in the belief that "the world has changed, and the historical process of change requires us to modify outworn perceptions and concepts in accordance with the new reality"; that "there will come a day when man's personal consciousness, his personal identity, will be based on this new reality"; that the day is not far when Jewish identity will be abandoned in favor of "an ultranational personal identity"—in the words of Israel's recent prime minister, Shimon Peres.[21]

How different from all these is a humble candidate for *mashiah* such as "Bar Kochba," Shimon Bar-Kosiba, who, around Sukkot of 134 C.E., while under Roman siege in Beitar and on the verge of annihilation, sends a letter to his men stationed near the Dead Sea. This letter, which was found in the caves of Judea, speaks entirely of his devotion to the Jewish laws of action, even on the edge of the abyss:

> Shimon [Bar Kochba] to Yehuda Bar-Menashe of Kiryat Arbiya; I have sent you two donkeys, in order for you to send with them two men to Yehonatan Ben-Ba'aya and to Masbala, in order for them to load and send to the camp palm fronds and citrons [ritual items required for the Sukkot holiday]. And send others to bring you myrtles and willows, and put them together and send them to the camp because the army are numerous. Peace be with you.[22]

Jews and Hebrews

The danger posed to Judaism by generalization became much more serious in exile, where the distance from the land of Israel tempted (and tempts) some to try to shorten the road to the orchard. Against this desire for a shortcut—which found its extreme expression in the various messianic awakenings, but which remains a perpetual threat to the Jewish consciousness in the form of other less-pronounced, universalist, cosmopolitan tendencies—the sages of Israel toiled at all times to emphasize that "there is no Tora like that of the land of Israel."[23]

In other words, the centrality of the land of Israel in Judaism is such that the Tora has no real existence without the connection to the land. In order to maintain this connection even after the destruction of the Temple and the exile from the land, Jewish ritual was built around what one can view as a "virtual" land of Israel, in which the synagogues are a miniature reproduction of the Temple and face Jerusalem; in which holidays and festivals are determined by the calendar of the land of Israel; and in which there is a constant re-emphasis that existence in the exile is merely temporary and of peripheral importance, and is to be countenanced only until the return to Zion. In this, Judaism left geography and history for the meta-geographical and meta-chronological plane which is found in the talmudic teaching. But amid this devotion to keeping the flame of Judaism alive, a different danger, which has manifested itself more than once, lay hidden: The danger that the "virtual" land of Israel would, for more than a few Jews, become the real object, so that they would cling to it even when there was an opportunity to return to the real Zion.

This reality is already reflected in an ancient work such as the book of Esther. Although the book ends with the apparent victory of Mordechai, Hadassa, and the Jews over their enemies, it is hard to avoid noticing a feeling of disappointment which steals into the reader's heart, an inkling that this is a false dawn. Something fundamental is amiss, if the happy ending leaves the Jewess Hadassa married to a drunken, capricious Gentile, if the greatness of Mordechai is dependent on the restraint and goodwill of a tyrannical king, and if the Jews remain sitting complacently in their houses in Shushan and the rest of the empire, waiting for the next wave of hate. The happiness of the book of Esther cannot therefore be complete, and the message of the story seems barren in the end. For the story of Esther takes place in the days of a king of Persia, and even if his precise chronological identification is uncertain, he clearly must have ruled during the time of the return to Zion and the rebuilding of the Temple, or thereafter. Not only does the book not contain any evidence that Mordechai the Benjaminite and the rest of the Jews had worked for this return to Zion, there is no expression whatsoever of longing for, nor even so much as a mention of, the land of Israel.

This is surely connected to the fact that Esther is the only book of the Bible in which the nation called "the Children of Israel" or "the People Israel"—that is, the Jewish nation—is not spoken of, and even the God of this people, the God of Israel, is not mentioned. Instead, we have only references to "the Jews." This is already no longer a nation, not even a people, but rather a collection of communities, subjects, dependent on the mercy of others for their protection. There is no alternative but to recognize the connection between the severance from the land and this change in identity: Outside the land, the people of Israel become simply "Jews," and instead of being called the book of Hadassa, it is known as the book of Esther—using the heroine's Persian name. In stark contrast to all of this stand the books of Ezra and Nehemia, which tell of the return to Zion, more or less during the same time period in which the story of Esther takes place; and even though those who return are the exiles of Judea, and they return to the territory of Judea, they are described time after time in these works as the Children of Israel, not as Jews.[24]

Around 2,500 years after these events, Theodor Herzl witnessed how the Dreyfus affair exposed the Jews of France to hatred and deliberate incitement which endangered their very existence. The denouement of this episode resembles the story told in Esther—Dreyfus was cleared of all wrongdoing, and the incident contributed to an awakening of sympathy and strengthening of the rights of Jews. But the lesson Herzl learned from what he saw was the opposite of that described in the book of Esther.

Herzl reached the conclusion that any victory in the exile is only temporary, based on flimsy foundations, since the very presence of the Jews in the exile is the root of the danger to their existence. He realized that there was both a possibility of, and the need to work for, the return to Zion, and that if this effort were not successful—the fate of the Jews would be hard and bitter. But he was not the last, and certainly not the first, to reach the conclusion that the persistence of the Jews in the exile is spiritually and existentially dangerous to them. This is, indeed, the reason that Yehuda Halevi ends *The Kuzari* with the declaration by the Jewish sage of his intention to immigrate to the land of Israel (and it seems Yehuda Halevi himself actually immigrated in the end). This is also the reason for the traditions of the rabbis which say that after the events described in the book of Esther, Mordechai, too, immigrated to the land.[25]

What was unique about Herzl's activity was that instead of choosing personal immigration to Israel as a solution, he came to the conclusion that the "Jewish problem" must be solved in a political fashion. Herzl refused to accept the traditional dilemma which had persisted until then: On the one hand, the existence of the exile and its evils was an unalterable fact; but, on the other hand, a fundamental solution to the problems of the Jews would be found only at the end of days. He considered practical action for its own sake to be worthless, and spirituality for its own sake to be dangerous; instead, he preferred to blend action and intention, while strictly preserving the uneven balance of power between them—the greater emphasis was placed on Zionist action. Indeed, he deliberately postponed dealing with ideological and spiritual matters until the end of the road. Herzl chose to re-enter history, and offered a practical political, religious, and military solution to the threats confronting his nation. In other words, what was special about Herzl's outlook was that he finally returned the identity of "the Jews" back to "the Jewish people," thereby renewing their identity as a nation.[26]

The establishment of a national organization whose aim was to return the Jewish nation to its land was a result of Herzl's understanding of the political and cultural conditions of the modern world, in which he believed there was no longer room for groups standing aloof from history under the protection of a ruler or historical custom. Modern culture and the contemporary state no longer allow true autonomy to minority groups and communities, and therefore the Jewish nation must either establish its own state or be annihilated.

It is important to emphasize that Herzl and the other leaders of mainstream Zionism did not hasten to formulate a new Jewish consciousness or identity. Rather, they saw their movement above all as a tool for the practical salvation of the nation, only after which spiritual correction could come. Many of these leaders wanted to consolidate an entirely new consciousness, but viewed the establishment of a state and the process of the return to Zion as being prerequisites for this.

In the exile before Herzl, Judaism walked a narrow bridge between the danger of messianism and that of an introverted seclusion amid traditional learning, divorced from the world. Even the mainstreams in Judaism were accused, sometimes justly, of having slipped too far towards one of the extremes: Hasidism, founded by the Ba'al Shem Tov, which attempted to bring about a reawakening of faith, was (and is) frequently accused of dangerously approaching messianism. The countervailing movement of the *mitnagdim* in the Lithuanian yeshivot founded by the Vilna Gaon, placed an emphasis on the learning of Jewish law, and was (and is) often accused of having concentrated in an exaggerated fashion upon dry and alienated scholasticism in which there is no room for faith or feeling.

The uniqueness of Zionism lay in its offering a way out of the pattern of the Jews' extra-historical existence in the exile, and their return to the reality of the land of Israel, that is, their return to history as a nation. In the book of Esther—floating somewhere outside the bounds of history—"the Jews" make their first appearance, and already they are on their way out of history. Zionism is the attempt to re-enter history and to change the existence of the Jews back to the existence of the nation, Jewish and Israeli, in the land.

Consciousness and Being

But the chances of success for this, the third return to Zion, were dubious from the beginning because of the heritage of the long exile: In the words of the famous Zionist adage, "It is easier to take the Jews out of the exile than to take the exile out of the Jews."[27]

In their talk of creating a "new Jew" who would cut himself off from the existential experience of the exile and would once again put down roots in his land, the leaders of the Zionist movement were in reality referring to the "old Jew" who had once dwelled in Zion—in other words, not a Jew, but an Israeli. The Jews who were born in the exile were supposed to return to their land, there to become Israelis, as one can see from the deliberate decisions taken by the renewed Jewish settlement in the land: The old-new Hebrew language was chosen as the spoken language in the old-new land, instead of other, more widespread Jewish languages (Yiddish) or non-Jewish ones (such as German or English); foreign and even Jewish names were abandoned by many in favor of Israeli names of judges, kings, and Maccabees; and the name given to the state that was established was not Judea, but Israel.

But those who returned to Zion in our own time also knew from the start that it would be no easy task to transform the exilic Jewish consciousness into an Israeli one. They feared—with reason—that the exilic consciousness which the Jews would bring here with them would perhaps create, instead of a Jewish nation, just another community of Jews with an exilic consciousness, coincidentally living in the land of Zion, but in no sense feeling a part of it.

The Zionist mainstream, beginning with Herzl and Nordau, therefore regarded the return to Zion as a means of, and a precondition for, forming a new awareness, and it opposed the romantic, irrational, and messianic tendencies which appeared in the movement. The ultimate goal was the correction of the Jewish consciousness, which according to the Zionists was flawed and threatened in the exile; but the correction of the flaw could not be accomplished in the exile, which had been the cause of the deformity in the first place. Only the path of dwelling in the land would return to the Jewish people its vitality and its destiny, in consequence of which a new consciousness could begin to crystallize. Since this new consciousness would be fashioned in the course of existence in the land, one could not know its content in advance, but must rather wait for it to be produced naturally in the minds of future generations of the native-born. In other words, classical Zionism viewed itself expressly as a practical tool for the rehabilitation of Israeli existence in the land, a precondition of the future Israeli consciousness.

One can assume that an important factor in forming this perception among the leadership of the founding generation of Zionists was the fact that so many of them were steeped in Jewish experience and understanding (sometimes, as in Herzl's case, against their will)—which was central to their consciousness even when some of them fought against its religious aspects. Because of this background, it would have been difficult for them to imagine that there could come a generation of native-born Israelis, who would, despite the circumstances of their birth, be alienated both from Judaism and from the land in which they were born.

There were also those who argued in favor of a completely different approach, and thought that what was needed first was a spiritual center and not a physical refuge. Men such as Ahad Ha'am and Martin Buber had objected to the political and material character of the solutions suggested by Herzl. Instead, they opined that a "moral renewal" and a national Jewish cultural revival must precede any political activity. The importance of the consolidation of Jewish culture and consciousness was in their eyes a necessary preliminary to the physical efforts of building the national home. Among them were also those who did not believe in the land of Israel as a national home for the Jewish masses at all, intending rather that it should be a spiritual center only, even indefinitely.[28]

In other words, we see two different trends among those who professed a belief in the renewed connection of the Jewish people with their land: The dominant stream, which advocated directly reconnecting the fates of the people and its land, held that one must first transform Jewish existence, and that only as a result of this sea change would an old-new Israeli consciousness be possible. In opposition to this, there was a second stream, including both Zionists and non-Zionists, which sought to place the fashioning of a new Jewish culture and consciousness before the building of a new Jewish existence.

In practice the supporters of the paramountcy of a spiritual center lost, and the Zionist *yishuv* was built according to the plan of those who preferred a physical refuge. One can wonder as to what might have been the outcome if the second approach had won—whether the Jewish state would have been established at all in these circumstances—but it seems that in reality there was no option other than the path that was chosen. Since the principal human reservoir for the fulfillment of Zionism was the Jewish population of Eastern Europe, and above all the youth, who were in large part socialist-activist in inclination, it is difficult to see how it would have been possible to enlist them for the national struggle in any other way.

There are many who now argue that the entire Socialist-Zionist movement was no more than a manipulative use of socialist terminology in order to win the support of a majority of the Jewish people for the Zionist leadership's nationalistic goals, and for their efforts to establish a Jewish state. Those who identify with socialism consider this fact to be execrable—but for those for whom Zionism was always the essential component of Socialist Zionism, this attitude on the part of David Ben-Gurion and others can only be considered to have been welcome in the long term.[29]

In any case, there is no doubt that the existence of renewed Jewish settlement in the land has gradually but fundamentally changed (and is still changing) Jewish consciousness, not only in Israel but throughout the world. "Jewish" languages such as Yiddish and Ladino are disappearing, while Hebrew has been resurrected; the Israeli community is growing constantly, while the other communities are being confronted, sooner or later, with either physical or spiritual demise; and Israel is becoming the world locus of Jewish corporeality, replacing the exilic community and the question of its continuity as the chief priority, and as the chief source of identification for the Jewish people as well.

The most outstanding expression of the sea change in the nation's consciousness is to be found within that Jewish stream which has been most distant from the Zionist effort over the years—the Haredim ("ultra-

Orthodox"). The growing involvement of a substantial portion of the Haredi public in issues touching on the fate of the land and the state is an unequivocal sign of a change in national consciousness, resulting from the historical change brought about by Zionism and the Jewish experience in the land. As a consequence, Haredi Judaism finds itself increasingly drawn into active participation in history—to a large degree in spite of itself.

Yet the outcome of Zionism's battle against the exilic consciousness has been ambiguous. Despite its many successes in creating a melting-pot society with an Israeli identity, the dominant Zionist Left allowed elements in the movement to become caught up in an exaggerated struggle against religion—often a brandishing socialist fervor. The result was the alienation of large parts of the Israeli public from their recent Jewish past, without their having attained the desired degree of identification with their distant Hebrew past.

It appears that many of the leaders of Israel's founding generation were aware of these problems, but thought that they were unavoidable under the circumstances. In any case, they believed that with the passage of time, the reality of dwelling in Zion would have its effect: Sooner or later, the experience of living in the land of Israel would refashion the Hebrew consciousness. Ben-Gurion provided the most outstanding expression of this attitude during his tenure at the helm of the movement, by deliberately refraining from making rigorous determinations regarding the nature and constitution of the State of Israel, since he believed that these could only be decided once the time was ripe—that is, once the borders and the composition of the population were stabilized. In other words, Ben-Gurion was convinced that it would not be right, practically or morally, to attempt to determine the content of the new Israeli consciousness when the country's geographic and demographic nature was still unformed. And indeed, from the founding of the state, Israel continued to direct its course in the expectation of waves of immigration and territorial changes yet to come—and indeed, they did come.

But today there is need to ask why—despite the far-reaching changes in the experience of Israeli and Jewish existence—the consciousness of the Israeli public continues to be so fragmented; why such a large segment continues to be alienated from its people. Why is Israel confronted with a situation in which there are those who say—and they may constitute

a majority among us—that the road and all our expectations have basically reached their endpoint; that the Israeli existence and consciousness
have been unified, and the time has now come to say: We are done with
acting, and now we shall comprehend.

Sacred and Profane

In the opening of his *Divine Comedy*, the Italian poet Dante Alighieri
describes the losing of one's way:

> Midway in the journey of our life
> I found Myself in a dark wood,
> for the straight way was lost....[30]

One may readily recognize in these lines the loss of direction which
engulfs much of the Israeli public in our time. The diplomatic moves
as played out by the Rabin government—and especially the meaning
attributed to these moves as they affect the future nature of the Israeli
experience and consciousness—have stirred up ominous feelings regarding the future among many, and not necessarily only among political
opponents of the Oslo accords. The source of this uneasiness lies in the
special manner in which the Israeli experience and the Israeli consciousness are intertwined today.

The question of the nature of Jewish consciousness in Israel in our
time is, at the very least, problematic. On the one hand, it appears
that there persists a basic Jewish outlook and identity among Israelis:
There is no Jewish community in the world (and it is questionable if
there ever was) whose calendar and daily activities are so connected to
Jewish symbols and history. Even the life dangers and possibilities with
which it is confronted are striking expressions of the integrity of Jewish history.

On the other hand, there are various manifestations of distance from
essential Jewish symbols and frameworks: Growing hostility towards the
rabbinical establishment and religious norms of conduct, astounding
ignorance in subjects related to Jewish history and, especially, growing
alienation from regions of the land of Israel over which there is political
controversy. The causes of this condition are complex, but one can single

out from among them two main elements, both of which spring from that same timeworn cause—the desire to find a shortcut to the orchard.

The first factor, heavily influenced by both Jewish and non-Jewish foreign cultural traditions, is the re-invigoration of the familiar messianic longing for the direct approach to the essence, for "real" content, which repudiates the seemingly tiresome and petty ceremonies of the way.

Throughout the early days of the Zionist enterprise, and in spite of the dominance of the practical side of building the state, there existed a strong and continuous stream of rhetoric—as mentioned, viewed today by many as having been essentially disingenuous—glorifying idealism and spirituality (for example, the myth weaving around the figure of the supposed farmer-philosopher A.D. Gordon), which were supposed to serve as psychological reinforcement for coping with the difficulties of the way.

According to the traditional Zionist leadership, the difference between the all-important deed and pretty but meaningless rhetoric was clear; and they differentiated between the two, calling the first—that which should actually be done—"Oral Tora"; while "Written Tora" referred to official plans drawn up for public scrutiny. Thus it was possible to issue divergent and contradictory declarations in an official and public manner: The state could be committed to territorial compromise such as that promoted in the Allon Plan (the "Written Tora"); but what really counted was the so-called "Oral Tora"—the actual creation of facts on the ground and the furthering of Zionist interest.

But when the need to contend with pressing practical problems—such as the construction of the state and wars of survival—began to slacken, matters of the spirit gradually began to be perceived as the essence which obviates the value of practical things. A new generation of Israeli leadership arose which forgot the "Oral Tora," and so it was even natural that the "Written Tora" should now appear to them confused and incomprehensible. One example is that of the "New Man" that Zionism sought to create. This term was originally connected with the aspiration of renewing the ancient Israelite character, but it was at the same time unintentionally (and intentionally) tied to traditional socialist symbolism in order to enlist this symbolism as well in furthering the Zionist effort. With the uprooting of the traditional practical aspects of the Zionist path—in both its Jewish and socialist elements—it is no wonder that there are many in whose eyes the New Israeli is supposed to be nothing more than a negation of everything that is old, and the realization of the messianic idea: A man in whose eyes physical things are marginal—as opposed to the essence, the pure ideal, that holy of holies, "Peace."

The second factor is a direct product of the flawed experience of the current Israeli existence. It is true that the experience of present-day Israel has indeed formed the consciousness that exists today among the Jewish people. But the experience in question is a fragmentary Israeli experience, mainly a coastal-cities experience of places like Ashkelon and Hadera, which is cut off from any practical or emotional connection to Hebron and the rest of the ancient Jewish hinterland. For if it is true that, in the words of the poet Shaul Tchernihovsky, "Man is nothing if not the image of his native landscape," the same certainly holds true for a nation, whose consciousness is also shaped in the mold of its native landscape.[31]

The homeland of contemporary Israeli consciousness is a place like Afula, Hadera, or Rehovot, a city of the Israeli everyday, whose experience is composed of the local Burger Ranch franchise, an appearance by popular singer Avihu Medina, a Steimatzky bookstore, a protest by public-housing residents next to the main municipal office building, and, just outside the city, two moshavim and two kibbutzim, one of which is experiencing financial difficulties.

These familiar experiences are much closer to the average Israeli than the grave of the matriarch Rachel, which is found, in the best case, only on the periphery of his consciousness. As a result, the Israeli cannot conceive of a situation in which Afula and Hadera would not remain under Israeli sovereignty, while the same cannot always be said of places such as Shiloh or Bethlehem—despite the vastly superior symbolic and historical connection that these latter cities have to the Jewish people.

It seems, therefore, that the Israeli feels a place to be part of its experience not by virtue of its holy places, but above all because of secular matters which are close to him. Holy places and those who fight for them seem so removed that they become a target of hostility and contempt, while the sand of Afula and Hadera and a possible ecological threat to it are a source of identification. For this reason, it appears that the classic Zionist plan of action will be that which determines the outcome of the struggle for the heartland: The building of houses is still what determines the strength of the ties of most Israelis to their land.

In other words, the first trend suggests that the time for action ("Zionism") has passed, and that the time has arrived for the actualizing of the New Israeli; while the second trend complements the first by defining this New Man in the image of the landscape of the country as it appears today—an Israel whose geographic and spiritual heart is almost empty of Jewish population. The merging of these two tendencies is so strong as to give rise to a widespread public feeling that both the path and the profane have simply ended: We have reached a state of rest and security, and now it is possible to turn to the essence, the holy. Yet this essence is one which is derived from a fragmentary reality—a reality such as one would have by declaring the week over on Tuesday, and then trying to experience the Sabbath as though it had arrived.

Although there are without question many in the upper reaches of Israel's social and cultural hierarchy who have undergone a complete conversion to this new faith, the great majority of the Israeli public—even when it has supported unprecedented diplomatic initiatives—cannot be said to have resigned itself to this shortcut to the orchard. Government ministers may pour scorn on the meaning of historical or religious sites, and the leaders of the cultural and academic establishment depict the patriotic connection to the land as fetishist and fascist, but the people still hesitate, at a loss as to how to respond to the government's plans to cut them off from the heart of their land, and exchange the historical path on which they have traveled for the past century for something else.[32]

In spite of the failure of its political, social, and cultural leadership—and to this failure and its proportions one should dedicate a separate study—the Jewish people has not been so easily swept away by the promise of a shortcut and a "new Middle East"; and most people explicitly view pronouncements by the leadership in this spirit to be expressions of messianic delusion. It is no wonder that there are those among the leadership who feel the need to try to convince the public that their activities really do not constitute such a messianism; as the late Prime Minister Yitzhak Rabin remarked of his policies: "I believe that what we are doing reflects real Zionism and not messianic Zionism."[33]

No public can withstand continuous brainwashing by its leaders forever. And yet up until now there has been a surprising degree of popular loyalty to regions whose future is in doubt—such as the Golan and western Samaria—but in which the familiar sense of an Israeli "reality" has already been consolidated. It seems that if only there were time to turn the other politically controversial regions of the country into part of the Israeli experience, the Israeli public would demonstrate a readiness to stick by them also—as has happened on past occasions when the leadership forgot the proper path, but the people clung tenaciously to the right course. In the words of the Talmud: "Leave it to Israel; if they are not prophets, they are the descendants of prophets."[34]

A Reality That Fashions Imagination

On the way to Damascus, Saul of Tarsus experienced a mystic messianic vision. As a result of this vision he began to believe in a new covenant which had altered the natural order and canceled everything that had existed before it, and was thereby transformed from a Jew (who had even persecuted the followers of the Nazarite) into a Christian. "The road to Damascus" has since become a byword denoting direct revelation of a gospel, in the wake of which one experiences a sudden and extreme conversion from an old way of belief to a new faith.[35]

Today, the road to Damascus passes through Oslo, which represents the moment of decision with regard to the future path of Israel. It should be emphasized that no particular territorial or security arrangements constitute the essence of the process in which Israel is involved. These are merely details deriving from a deeper transformation which has taken place. The essence lies in the messianic vision which the Oslo process embodies, and according to which not the path but faith is what must stand at the center of our existence, in accordance with the outlook of the process' architect, Shimon Peres: "In my eyes Judaism is above all a faith, more even than a religion."[36]

Though the diplomatic process is to a large degree a reflection of the worldviews of former Prime Minister Peres and his adherents—as well as those of many of the political and cultural leaders of the Jewish people who have made themselves partners in the Oslo process—the unbearable lightness with which every obstacle standing in the way of the present messianic peace has simply been tossed aside requires a larger understanding of the nature of the reality that is present-day Israel. This is a reality of Israel which has for many become an end in itself, the end of the road—and this despite the fact that it is also a reality in which still only a small, and in many ways marginal, segment of the Jewish people resides in the heart of its land; in which large parts of the Jewish public lack any meaningful connection—geographical, political, or cultural—to Judaism; and in which there is no sign of Jewish immigration in significant numbers from the prosperous countries where most of world Jewry resides. It is natural that such a reality should engender a perspective as to what is normal and possible, such that the large majority of citizens have no desire to fight to preserve their heartland; that its social elite is totally alienated from Judaism; and that the country has reconciled itself to the bulk of the Jewish people remaining abroad indefinitely.

Most of the Jewish people, in Israel and worldwide, has become reconciled to the Oslo agreement because it appears to suit the reality of Israel. Even among the religious and Haredi populations, where there is traditionally a greater devotion to the symbolic connection with the land, there are not a few who are somehow willing to resign themselves to the state's political course, out of what they consider to be "accepting reality."

Most astounding of all has been the desolation that has gripped most of those who were supposed to lead the political and cultural opposition to this course. Many of the opposition leaders are themselves steeped in the concepts, perspective, and symbols of the process' promoters. And indeed, in the months following the signing of the agreement, only a very few did not give in to the atmosphere of despair, in which one heard explicit, lunatic statements about the end of the road and the hopelessness of continuing to fight. Thus it was that amid the loss of equilibrium and the confusion, there was no leadership capable of mounting an effective campaign to stop the process, and the public's reservations, lacking in appropriate spokesmen, proved unable to influence the course of events.

In a twinkling, everything that had taken root in the consciousness of the Jewish people from its inception had melted away. Four thousand years of ties to the land, two thousand years of fervent longing for the return to Zion, one hundred years of Zionist history—all these became insubstantial in a moment, and in the end only one sole barrier remained in the way of an immediate and complete retreat, and still remains: Jewish settlement. Neither values, nor beliefs, nor principles, nor perspectives are for the time being delaying the collapse, but rather the commonplace and trivial difficulties presented by visible, material things: Houses, children, dunams, and goats. The practical difficulty of uprooting settlements does surprising things to a government of the Left. And wherever there is a settlement, even in the heart of the Gaza Strip, an Israeli presence is still preserved in spite of everything.

These are not, of course, insurmountable obstacles, and one can assume that sooner or later, if the same course is maintained, the government will make attempts to uproot settlers. One cannot know whether the first such attempt will be in Netzarim or Hebron, but what is important here is how the physical reality, and the expected complications involved in any act of uprooting, constitutes a unique barrier before the flame of faith, and brings even the supporters of the establishment of a PLO state, such as former Environment Minister Yossi Sarid, to propose to the government a map in which areas populated by Jewish settlers, like Gush Etzion and western Samaria, would remain in Israeli hands.

The meaning of these observations is this: Despite the manifest helplessness of opponents of the Oslo process, and the messianic fervor of its proponents, there is still considerable difficulty in forcing imaginary conditions upon reality. There are obviously ways of changing this reality—such as ensuring the attrition of the population in the settlements by making life in them unlivable—but the need to take such measures only underscores once more the truth that deeds are what matter most, not intentions.

These facts also allow us to point the way back to the proper path. For if the present 250,000 Israelis living over the pre-1967 frontier can so greatly hamper the retreat from the Jewish heartland, then a few more residents would gradually render such an abandonment impossible. The issue here is not merely one of numerical growth, although this is also important, but first and foremost the importance of turning these places into part of the experience of Israeli existence. When, thanks to the Burger Ranch and the strike across from the municipal office building, Hebron becomes like Afula and Hadera, it will no longer be possible to even consider dismissing it from the course of our lives.

But the reality of massive settlement in the heartland would have much more far-reaching consequences than the effective closing of the road to Damascus. For it would begin to refashion the Israeli consciousness, which is still so far from mature. Hundreds of thousands of Jewish inhabitants in cities such as Hebron, Eli, and Shamir would make these places part of the Israeli everyday, like Hadera, Rehovot, and Afula. And indeed such a powerful reality would refashion the collective imagination of Israel in ways which we cannot yet fathom.

The Shortcut and the Ways of the World

Everything that has befallen the State of Israel in the last three years is the negative consequence of the necessary connection between the form of things and their content—a disordered reality creating a disordered consciousness in the minds of men. A rectification of the situation demands, before anything else, the renunciation in principle of the shortcut to the orchard. In the words of the Chinese sage Kung-Fiu (Confucius): "Who expects to be able to go out of a house except by means of the door? How is it then that no one follows this Way of ours?"[37] There is an ineluctable path which one must follow in order to reach the orchard: One must give things form, and then they will become filled with content.

This is not merely the answer to a current, pressing problem. Its central importance is as a moral solution to the question raised at the beginning of this essay regarding the nature of the connection between content and form: There is an essential and crucial link between the form of things and their content, and not every conceivable version of things is possible. Rather, one must find the correct proportion between deed and intention; and the order and measure of things are important as well. Form precedes content, and the weight of the deed is greater than that of the intention. The right way ties together intention and act, but always ascribes first importance to the political and the material before the spiritual. As Shamai used to say: "Say little and do much."[38]

Thus, just as the second, forgotten, peace agreement that the State of Israel signed with an Arab country—that with Lebanon in 1982—was not worth the paper it was written on since it lacked all connection with reality, so too in that same year the attempt to stop the dismantling of the Jewish communities of Sinai failed because those settlements had remained on the periphery of Israeli experience. Due to the reality of few settlements and few settlers, Sinai remained a peripheral place in the Israeli consciousness—a vacation site, otherwise out of sight, out of mind. And because of the marginality of the experience of this place, it was impossible to save it from the bulldozers. As one of the leading political opponents of the withdrawal from Sinai, MK Hanan Porat, pronounced shortly after the destruction of the Yamit area: "There are no shortcuts."[39]

The future of Israel therefore lies in the practical response that our generation will give to two interconnected questions: What is the land of Israel? And what is the Jewish people? We are not here speaking of absolute, moral answers to these questions, which were decided long ago; but rather of the practical garb those answers will assume in our day. Will Israelis settle only in the coastal plain between Tel Aviv and Haifa, or in other parts of the land as well? What part of the Jewish people will reside in its land?

The way in which we confront these two questions will determine our experience of the reality of Israel for generations to come. It is easy to understand that the geographical settlement of the Jewish people in the land will influence their outlook. Already, cities founded by the Romans and Philistines, such as Caesarea and Ashkelon, are closer to the Israeli psyche than traditional Jewish capitals such as Hebron or Shiloh, and a rupture has been created in this psyche between the land and its own past. If Hebron and Shiloh become faraway regions on a permanent basis, and the centers of Jewish existence remain Caesarea and Ashkelon, there will eventually be a complete divorce of the consciousness of modern Israel from Jewish history. Even graver, there will be a consequent reconciliation with the lack of significant Jewish immigration, because there will no longer be any land in urgent need of being filled with those immigrants. In other words, the Jewish people will become reconciled with a reality in which assimilation will, within one generation, shrink the numbers of world Jewry by more than half.

In contrast to this, a concerted effort on behalf of settlement and immigration would create a reality in the land which could not but establish a different awareness from that which exists today. A truncated land of Israel alongside a huge and assimilating Diaspora will create a radically different outlook from a whole country in which the majority of the Jewish people dwells.

In other words, the ideological and conceptual straying of contemporary Israel is not the source of our problems, but rather the result of our experience of a stunted reality. Any attempt to establish a new ideological and conceptual consciousness will fail if its content does not match the form that the land and the people have taken on. Only when basic deeds precede intentions can the form of our lives fill itself with meaning, which in turn is the beginning of the formation of a new consciousness. There is, then, no alternative but to postpone for now the preoccupation with meanings in favor of progress on houses, and to precede the attempt to consolidate a new consciousness with a change in the face of the country. As was said: "The ways of the world preceded the Tora."[40]

NOTES

1. Hayden White, *The Content of the Form* (Baltimore: Johns Hopkins University Press, 1987).

2. Yehuda Halevi, *The Kuzari* (c. 1140).

3. The difficulty in defining these religions, philosophies, or ways of life in an encompassing fashion is one of their essential characteristics, being a consequence of their lack of an ultimate general principle and of the eclectic nature of their various incarnations. It is important to note that the emphasis on the ceremonial and ritualistic side of faith in the East does not point to a lack of spirituality, but rather to a search for the truth in which ritual acts have a transcendent value.

Buddhism holds that about 2,500 years ago there lived in northern India a man who attained enlightenment and discovered the eternal truth (and became Buddha—"the Enlightened"). He formulated a message whose aim was to combat the three evils from which he perceived mankind to be suffering: Violence, consciousness of the self, and death. It is important to remember that Buddha did not promulgate a doctrine, religion, or defined faith; rather, his intention was to devise practical ways to overcome these evils by such means as overcoming one's inclinations, meditation, and philosophical cogitation.

Confucianism is a collection of traditions, concepts, and beliefs whose source is the thought of Kung-Fiu, known as "the Teacher" (Fu-zhi), or Confucius in the West, who lived in China about 2,500 years ago. Kung-Fiu's students promulgated a philosophy of behavior, involving the social order, in which everyone has a defined role which he must perform with fidelity and obedience. This outlook formed (and, indeed, still forms) the basis of Chinese society's values.

Taoism is composed of a plethora of traditions, beliefs, and concepts which crystallized in China from various sources, and which show the path (tao) to proper behavior. The basis of the different Taoist approaches is that the natural state is the ideal order of things and that human culture represents an aberration from it; therefore accepted viewpoints, both in morals and science, are relative and lacking. The tao is supposed to lead to the discovery of the original harmonious equilibrium described frequently by means of the symbol of the interlocking yin and yang, the two sides of everything. One of the important Taoist books, the I Ching, describes this ideal state as follows: "One time yin, next time yang—that is tao."

4. "The essence"—in Christianity, "the Holy Spirit"; in Islam, Allah; and in philosophy, Logos. On salvation through faith in Christianity see, for example: "He who believes and is baptized will be saved; but he who does not believe will be condemned." Mark 16:16.

"The True Path"—in Buddhism, dharma; in Confucianism, ran; and in Taoism, tao. On salvation in Lamaistic Buddhism, by means of repetition of the miraculous mantra *om mani padme hum* (om: the ornament that is in the Lotus, hum), see, for example, Edward Conze, *A Brief History of Buddhism* (Milan: Rusconi, 1985), p. 191. [Italian]

5. See, for example, Jerusalem Hagiga 1:1.

6. It is interesting to note the ideological similarity between the terms halacha, ran, and tao.

7. Exodus 24:7; Exodus 19:8, 24:3.

8. An excellent example is the Code of Hammurabi, a collection of the laws of the powerful Babylonian king who ruled in the eighteenth century B.C.E. This is a collection of injunctions and prohibitions, many of which have similar counterparts in the laws of the Tora; yet the difference between the two codes is fundamental: The Code of Hammurabi is a collection of traditional and technical laws, containing no attempt to present any values, justice, or moral consistency. The laws of the Tora, on the contrary, are characterized by a consistency stemming from a comprehensive, principled outlook of uniform justice and order under divine inspiration.

The eclectic style, such as that of the classical cultures of the ancient Middle East, was preserved for a much longer time in the cultures of India and China, whose late exposure to generalization caused the continuation up to the present of the tradition according to which deeds and customs are superior to general and absolute principles, which often do not even exist.

9. Thales of Miletus (c. 625-545 B.C.E.), quoted in Aristotle's *Metaphysics*, 11, 17-27. See also Jonathan Barnes, *Early Greek Philosophy* (London: Penguin, 1987), pp. 61-70. It is interesting to note that Thales' family came to Miletus from Phoenicia, the coastal strip of ancient Israel.

10. Hagiga 14b. The Hebrew word for orchard, *pardes*, is laden with additional meaning, as symbol for a garden-place of superior consciousness and knowledge. Originally describing the exotic and magical palace gardens of the great Persian kings, *pardes* became identified with that other place of knowledge and mystery, the Garden of Eden, and the meaning was carried over into various terms in other languages and cultures, including the English "paradise."

11. For example, "No man shall see me and live." Exodus 33:21.

12. Even in Islam there is ample acknowledgment of the exclusive relationship between Israel and its land. For example, the only two places in the Koran to specifically mention the holy land do so in the context of the divine promise of the land to the Israelites, and of the return to Zion: "Bear in mind the words of Moses to his people. He said: 'Remember, my people, the favor which God has bestowed upon you. He has raised prophets among you, made you kings, and given you that which he has given to no other nation. Enter, my people, the holy land which God has assigned for you. Do not turn back, or you shall be ruined.'" Koran 5:20-21.

"Then we said to the Israelites: 'Dwell in the land. When the promise of the hereafter comes to be fulfilled, we shall assemble you all together.'" Koran 17:104.

And from a much later period, for example: "Who can deny the rights of the Jews regarding the land of Israel? My God in heaven, certainly from a historical point of view it is your land." From an 1899 letter to Herzl from Yusuf Zia al-Halidi, mayor of Jerusalem and afterwards Jerusalem's representative in the Ottoman parliament, where he nevertheless opposed Zionism. In Amos Ayalon, *Herzl* (Tel Aviv: Am Oved, 1979), pp. 342-343. [Hebrew]

13. Genesis 12:1 and 16:7-11, respectively.

14. Shabbat 31a.

15. See Israel Ben-Shalom, *The School of Shamai and the Struggle of the Zealots Against Rome* (Jerusalem: Yad Ben-Zvi, 1993), pp. 84, 97-98, 185-188. [Hebrew]

16. Mark 12:28-33.

17. Cornelius Tacitus, *The Histories* (c. 120 C.E.), book 5, ch. 5.

18. E.g., "I made known to them thy name, and I will make it known, that the love with which thou hast loved me may be in them, and I in them." John 17:26. Or: "A new commandment I give to you, that you love one another; even as I have loved you, that you also love one another. By this all men will know that you are my disciples, if you have love for one another." John 13:34-35.

And yet, even Christianity could not long tolerate the internal threat posed by this principle, and was gradually forced to build practical rules and ritual around it—and furthermore, to place limitations on the unlimited "love" which stood at its heart. In the end, Christianity grew distant from this ideal, often to the point of total discrepancy from the original message. Concerning the containment of monotheism in Catholicism, see, for instance, Michael Sutton, *Nationalism, Positivism, and Catholicism* (Cambridge: Cambridge, 1982), pp. 20-21, 30.

19. E.g., "You must never suppose that I have come to destroy the Law and the Prophets; I did not come to destroy them; I came to fulfill them. This is the truth I tell you, so long as heaven and earth shall last not the smallest letter, not the smallest part of a letter of the Law, will cease to be valid, it will remain until history comes to an end." Matthew 5:17-18.

20. "...the lamb" in Isaiah 11:6; "this is the time..." in *Yediot Aharonot*, November 6, 1995, p. 18.

21. Shimon Peres, *The New Middle East* (Bnei Brak: Steimatzky, 1993), pp. 37, 78. [Hebrew]

22. Yigael Yadin, *Bar Kochba* (Tel Aviv: Masada, 1976), p. 129. [Hebrew]

23. Leviticus Rabba 13:5. It is interesting to note the disdain displayed by some of the rabbis for rabbinic teachings emanating from Babylonia. For example: "What is 'Babylon'? R. Yohanan said: 'Mixed up [Hebrew: *blula*] with the Bible, mixed up with the Mishna, mixed up with the Talmud." Sanhedrin 24a. "R. Jeremiah said: 'Stupid Babylonians! Because they sit in a place of darkness they formulate unenlightened opinions.'" Menahot 52a. "R. Zeira, when he went up to the land of Israel, fasted one hundred fasts in order that he might forget the Babylonian learning, so that it would not bother him." Bava Metzia 85a.

24. E.g., Ezra 3:1, Nehemia 9:1.

25. Mishna Shkalim 5:1.

26. On the emphasis of Herzl, Nordau, Weizmann, and other early Zionist leaders on practical questions and anti-messianism, see Amos Funkenstein, *Perceptions of Jewish History* (Berkeley: University of California, 1993), pp. 341-344. Concerning Jabotinsky, see Samuel Katz, *Lone Wolf* (New York: Barricade, 1996), vol. i, p. 170. Also of interest in this context is the comment of five rabbis who left a meeting with Herzl during the First Zionist Congress with beaming faces. They were asked if this joy was due to Herzl's having promised to keep the Shabbat and Jewish dietary laws. They answered: "On the contrary. That would have worried us tremendously. If he had suddenly become devout and religiously observant, we would not be able to join the movement, for fear that we would have to accept him as the Messiah. It is preferable this way." Ayalon, *Herzl*, p. 263.

27. It is noteworthy in this connection that an entire stream of anti-Zionist Jewish thought exists, both religious and nonreligious, which views as evil precisely

this attempt to remove the Jewish people from the exile and return them to the land. These anti-Zionists see Zionism as opposed to Judaism because, in their opinion, Judaism has already long since become a metahistorical factor, whose power lies in its detachment from any land, its being rootless and "foreign" everywhere. Among the thinkers who embraced such views are Franz Rosenzweig, Hermann Cohen, and George Steiner. Funkenstein, *Perceptions*, pp. 248, 264, 291. Regarding the efforts of the Reform movement to erase all mention of Jewish nationality and territoriality from the prayer books, see Funkenstein, *Perceptions*, pp. 222, 254-256.

28. Ayalon, *Herzl*, pp. 385-386; Funkenstein, *Perceptions*, pp. 342-343.

29. For example, Ze'ev Sternhal, "Dear Friends, the Time Has Come to Grow Up," *Haaretz* Weekend Supplement, July 7, 1995; and Ze'ev Sternhal, *The Building of a Nation or the Reform of Society?* (Jerusalem: Am Oved, 1995), passim. [Hebrew] A telling example from the opposite, pro-Zionist orientation, revealing the centrality of Jewish identity to the "socialist" leaders of the *yishuv*, can be learned from a story from the 1940s told of Enzo Sireni, founder of Kibbutz Givat Brenner and a prominent Socialist-Zionist leader. One day Sireni met the author Shlomo Gruzhinski and asked him, "What will you do if Zionism fails? Will you turn to Agudat Israel or to communism?" The author replied, without any hesitation, "I would of course turn to Agudat Israel." Sireni (whose brother was one of the leaders of Italian communism) patted Gruzhinski on the back and said, "Now I know that you are a Zionist!" Shmuel Dotan, *Adumim* (Kfar Saba: Shevna Hasofer, 1991), p. 348. [Hebrew]

30. Dante Alighieri, *The Divine Comedy*, trans. C.S. Singleton (Princeton: Princeton, 1977), p. 3, canto 1, lines 1-3.

31. "Man is nothing if not the image of his native landscape," in Shaul Tchernihovsky, *A Selection* (Tel Aviv: Dvir, 1965), p. 28. [Hebrew] Tchernihovsky is regarded by many as having been a "Hellenistic" poet, because of some of his negative remarks concerning the rabbinical world, the most notorious of them being: "and they bound him with tefillin straps" in his poem "Before the Statue of Apollo." But a truer understanding of his work regards such comments within the context of his search for the old-new Jewish people—which has had its fill of the "generations of death throes" of the Diaspora, and looks towards renewing the aesthetics and character of the biblical Jewish nation, of "the God of Canaan's storming conquerors," and of love for the land. All the while, he clearly retains his attachment to the world of traditional Judaism and its symbols, as can be seen in poems such as "The Wolf's Ballad" and "Three Mules" (also from the above selection).

32. Consider, for example, the contempt of former Culture Minister Shulamit Aloni for Jericho as "the city of Rahav the whore." Cf. Aharon Meged on the growing self-hatred among Israeli writers and historians, in "The Israeli Urge to Suicide," *Haaretz* Weekend Supplement, June 10, 1994.

33. *Yediot Aharonot,* July 31, 1995; cf. Shimon Peres, in his article "Even Without the Shortcut, It's Good Enough," *Haaretz,* April 3, 1996, p. 2b.

34. Pesahim 66a.

35. Acts 9:1-6; cf. "...like every convert that has witnessed grace, so Rabin has alighted to a doctrine that he had formerly rejected with all his being." *Haaretz,* August 18, 1995.

36. Peres in the weekly program *Hatur Hashvu'i,* Israel Television, Channel 3, April 28, 1995.

37. Confucius, *Analects* (5th century B.C.E.), book VI, 15.

38. Mishna Avot 1:15.

39. *Nekuda,* May 21, 1982, p. 23.

40. Leviticus Rabba 9:3.

THE POLITICAL LEGACY
OF THEODOR HERZL

NATAN SHARANSKY

MENACHEM BEGIN ONCE SAID, "The captain proves himself in a storm, the maestro in his music, and the statesman in his prescience."[1] By this measure, Theodor Herzl was surely one of the world's great statesmen. Half a century before the Holocaust, he alone understood the nature of the threat that anti-Semitism posed, and he alone dedicated his life's work to saving the Jewish people from its clutches. Herzl believed that the establishment of a Jewish state was the only answer. True, he did not succeed in averting disaster, and anti-Semitism did not die out. But the state that he envisaged came into being, and there is no doubt that its birth gave new meaning to Jewish identity, both in Israel and in the Diaspora.

Herzl was determined to understand anti-Semitism, he said, "without fear or hatred."[2] He concluded that modern anti-Semitism was fundamentally different from the classical religious hatred of Jews, and was not a product of the psychological fear of the unknown. Nor could modern anti-Semitism be attributed to the absence of equal rights for Jews, for indeed it was rather a product of the Emancipation itself: It had been widely believed that in exchange for receiving full equality as individuals, Jews would forfeit their collective identity and dissolve among the

nations; yet for the most part, the Jews were unable or unwilling to assimilate—a trend Herzl felt certain would only continue. As he wrote
in *The Jewish State*:

> The distinctive nationality of Jews neither can, will, nor must be de-
> stroyed. It cannot be destroyed, because external enemies consolidate
> it. It will not be destroyed; this is shown during two thousand years of
> appalling suffering. It must not be destroyed, and that, as a descendant
> of numberless Jews who refused to despair, I am trying once more to
> prove in this pamphlet.[3]

Because the Jews showed no inclination to disappear as a collective, the
nations of the world would continue to treat them as a separate people
in their midst. For this reason, the problem of anti-Semitism could not
be understood purely as a function of economics or class, nor as one that
could be resolved by treating the Jews solely as individuals in need of
equal rights. "The Jewish Question," he wrote, "is no more a social than
a religious one, notwithstanding that it sometimes takes these and other
forms. It is a national question, which can only be solved by making
it a political-world question to be discussed and settled by the civilized
nations of the world in council."[4] Only when a *national* solution was
found would the problem be solved, not because all Jews would choose
to live in Israel—Herzl never believed this would happen—but because
the root cause of anti-Semitism would finally have disappeared.

It was thus that Herzl believed that after the establishment of a Jewish state, even those Jews who remained in the Diaspora would stand
to benefit. "[They] would be able to assimilate in peace," he wrote, "because the present anti-Semitism would have been stopped forever. They
would certainly be credited with being assimilated to the very depths of
their souls, if they stayed where they were after the new Jewish state,
with its superior institutions, had become a reality."[5] In Herzl's view,
any Jew who chose not to be part of the Jewish national liberation was
in effect declaring a more profound allegiance to his host nation than
to the Jewish one; by remaining in France, for example, a Jew would
testify to believing himself more French than Jewish. For Jews like these
the establishment of a Jewish state would mean that their acceptance by
French society would finally be complete, untainted by the suspicion of
dual national loyalty.

In tune with the positivistic spirit of the age, Herzl assumed that for every problem there was a rational solution. Applied to the problem of anti-Semitism, Herzl's analysis may today seem naïve and overly ambitious, ignoring as it does the profoundly religious roots of anti-Semitism, and attempting to pinpoint a single cause for what is really a complex phenomenon spanning thousands of years. Yet even if his analysis of anti-Semitism was oversimplified, he foresaw its consequences with stunning accuracy. He was, in fact, the only Jewish leader of his time who understood the calamity that was about to befall European Jewry. As he wrote in his diary:

> I cannot imagine what appearance and form this will take. Will it be expropriation by some revolutionary force from below? Will it be proscription by some reactionary force from above? Will they banish us? Will they kill us? I expect all these forms and others.[6]

Elsewhere he put it this way: "It will overtake even Hungarian Jews with brutality, and the longer it takes to come, the worse it will be. The stronger they [the Jews] become, the more bestial will it be. There is no escaping it."[7] And indeed, catastrophe struck as Herzl predicted. Far too late, both the Jews and the world at large were persuaded that without a national home, the Jewish people could not survive.

Even after a national home was established, however, Herzl's prophecy of an end to anti-Semitism went unfulfilled. He believed that once the Jewish collective won recognition as a nation, the individual Jew would finally be able to live in peace. Yet what actually happened was quite different. Over the half century since the Jewish state was founded, it has consistently been a lightning rod of hatred and enmity. There is the obvious animosity of the Arab world, which was never prepared to accept Israel's existence. But with time, the Jewish state has become the focus of a much broader hatred. In fact, the fashionable portrayal of Israel by many Europeans as the principal threat to world peace, a "Nazi state," the archenemy of human rights—this is precisely the kind of demonization previously directed at individual Jews. And because the individual Jew living in Europe is an easier target for violence than Israel, the terror war against Israel of the last four years has awakened the specter of classical anti-Semitism throughout Europe, giving rise to a renewed wave of violence against Diaspora Jewry.

It would seem, then, that we have come full circle: The old anti-Semitism now takes the form of anti-Zionism. In fact, the present wave of anti-Semitism in Europe has proven once and for all that there *is* no difference between the two, that the perceived distinction between anti-Semitism and anti-Zionism is an illusion. As far as the world is concerned, the Jews are Israel and Israel the Jews. But this means that every Jew, in turn, must define himself with respect to the Jewish state, either for or against. No Jew may remain indifferent to Israel.

II

Why was Herzl's vision not realized? How is it that the Jewish state was established, but anti-Semitism still exists? The problem, perhaps, lay with Herzl's failure to divine the true nature of anti-Semitism—a hatred that, throughout history, has always been directed at the very core of Jewish identity.[8] In ancient times, it was the Jews' monotheistic religion; later on, it would be their sense of belonging to a unique people and tradition. Today, however, as many Jews have a weakened sense of their uniqueness on both the religious and cultural levels, the State of Israel has become one of the main factors—for many Diaspora Jews, the central factor—in defining Jewish identity. As a result, anti-Semitism now directs itself against Israel.

The process of turning Israel into the epicenter of Jewish identity is particularly evident in movements which, like Reform Judaism, were once fiercely opposed to Zionism. Some of Herzl's staunchest critics, after all, came from the Reform movement, whose leaders believed that in order to spread Judaism's loftiest principles and serve as a "light unto the nations," Jews must dwell among non-Jews. They saw in Herzl's call for statehood a betrayal of the larger Jewish purpose. Today, however, even the Reform movement has made identification with Israel a major plank of its ideology, so much so that a year of study in Israel has become *de rigueur* for ordination in the Reform rabbinate.

For those of us who came from the Soviet Union, the adoption of Israel as the basis of Jewish identity is not hypothetical, but an extremely tangible, personal reality. We were born into a Jewish identity that the Soviet steamroller had almost completely crushed. We knew nothing of our roots, only that for some reason others considered us different and inferior. We knew all too well the anti-Semitic stereotypes about greed, parasitism, and cowardice—but about what Judaism stood for, we knew nothing.

That was before 1967. In the months leading up to the war, animosity towards us reached a fever pitch. Then, in six dramatic days, everything changed for us. The call that went up from Jerusalem, "The Temple Mount is in our hands," penetrated the Iron Curtain and forged an almost mystic link with our people. And while we had no idea what the Temple Mount was, we did know that the fact that it was in our hands had won us respect. Like a cry from our distant past, it told us that we were no longer displaced and isolated. We belonged to something, even if we did not yet know what, or why. Of course, we still suffered from anti-Semitism, but even that assumed a new character. Jews were no longer cowards. Instinctively, and without any real connection to Judaism, we became Zionists. We knew that somewhere there was a country that called us its children, and this knowledge filled us with pride.

This pride, born of a newfound connection with Israel, was the source of hope to which I clung during the long years of my imprisonment. I knew without a doubt that contrary to what my interrogators said, I had not been abandoned. Nor would I be: Unlike my cellmates—Ukrainian nationalists, Protestants from Siberia, Church activists from Lithuania—I had a country that wanted me, and a people that stood behind me. It was the same country that sent its soldiers to rescue its kidnapped citizens and other Jews in Entebbe, and so would they also come, I believed, to rescue me as well. I imagined that I heard the beating hearts of my rescuers in every plane that flew through the skies of the Urals. I knew that even if it took a long time, one day I would be freed.

For Jews in the Diaspora today, identification with Israel is not as straightforward. The State of Israel has long ceased to be seen in the West as the courageous underdog, and is instead increasingly portrayed by the international media as an anachronism, an illegitimate relic of colonialism, even an enemy of humanity. Nonetheless, I realized on a recent visit to Europe that identification with Israel still imbues Diaspora Jews with a sense of empowerment. Indeed, the stronger the link with Israel, the greater the Jewish pride, even in small communities and even when Jews are subjected to harsh recrimination by those hostile to Israel. Conversely, when the connection to Israel is weak, Jews in the Diaspora are inclined to downplay their Jewish identity as well. This pattern emerges most clearly in the context of programs such as Birthright Israel, in which the strengthening of Jewish identity is directly correlated with pride in the State of Israel. With few exceptions, Israel has become a nearly universal basis for Jewish identification.

Thus, while the establishment of Herzl's Jewish state did not eliminate anti-Semitism, it did fundamentally alter the identity of the Jewish people. Israel became a source of strength and pride for world Jewry, and identification with the Jewish state became a remarkably potent weapon in the struggle against anti-Semitism.

III

But what about the Jewish identity of Israelis? What was Herzl's vision regarding the future citizens of the Jewish state? And how were they affected by the establishment of the state?

At first glance, Herzl does not seem to have been particularly concerned with this question. His principal aim was to alleviate the suffering of the Jews. The future of Jewish identity and culture was naturally subordinate to the overriding goal of averting catastrophe and establishing a state in which Jews around the world could together rebuild their lives. With what values would that new nation identify? On what foundations would its citizens be educated? In *The Jewish State* we find only the most vague of answers. Indeed, Herzl's supposed indifference to the fate of Judaism and nearly exclusive focus on improving conditions for the Jewish people had earned him the fierce opposition of Ahad Ha'am, the leader of cultural Zionism who believed that the Zionist effort should be devoted to the revival of Judaism and the establishment of a center of Jewish spirituality.

But a closer reading of Herzl's writings leads to a different conclusion. He was not indifferent, but rather offered a conservative approach to Jewish culture in the new state. He repeatedly emphasized the central role that classical Jewish identity would play in the national identity of the Jewish people. "Zionism," he declared at the First Zionist Congress in 1897, "is a return to the Jewish fold, even before it becomes a return to the Jewish land."⁹ Herzl saw the Jewish religion as the common denominator among all the prospective state's diverse Jewish communities. "We identify ourselves as a people on account of our religion," he wrote in his journal. Elsewhere he said, "Our community of race is peculiar and unique, for we are bound together only by the faith of our fathers."¹⁰

Herzl did not, in fact, overlook the nature of the future Jewish state and the culture that would come to characterize it. Rather, he sought to preserve the Jewish culture of his day. For it was from within this culture, he believed, that a new Jewish culture would emerge:

> But we will give a home to our people—not by dragging them ruthlessly out of their sustaining soil, but rather by transplanting them carefully to better ground. Just as we wish to create new political and economic relations, so we shall preserve as sacred all of the past that is dear to our people's hearts.¹¹

For this same reason, Herzl opposed the creation of a new language. "Every man can preserve the language in which his thoughts are at home," he wrote. "We shall remain in the new country what we now are here, and we shall never cease to cherish with sadness the memory of the native land out of which we have been driven."¹² So how were the citizens of this new country to communicate with each other? "The language which proves itself to be of greatest utility for general intercourse will be adopted without compulsion as our national tongue."¹³ Herzl saw no problem in transporting the best of the old world into the new land. "There are English hotels in Egypt and on the mountain-crest in Switzerland, Viennese cafés in South Africa, French theaters in Russia, German operas in America, and the best Bavarian beer in Paris.... When we journey out of Egypt again we shall not leave the fleshpots behind."¹⁴

Herzl's attitude toward Jewish culture is graphically expressed in his novel *Altneuland*, a fictional representation of the vision he described in *The Jewish State*. There he repeatedly describes how the new country would incorporate the best of what each of its citizens' lands of origin had to offer: City parks constructed in the English style, the Health Ministry headquarters built in the German manner, and the streets like those found in Belgium. The finest of the world's technology, culture, and economics would be transplanted to the new country in an effort to preserve everything worth saving.

Yet alongside these imports, Herzl also wrote about the Jewish "phe-nomena": Theatrical and operatic performances on Jewish themes, for instance, and a special nationwide atmosphere on the Sabbath. Jewish religion, too, would play a decisive role: Herzl proposes in his diary that rabbis would be a "supporting pillar" of the future state, and insists that in every neighborhood the synagogue "be visible from long distances, for it is only our ancient faith that has kept us together."[15]

Herzl, in other words, was most certainly interested in Jewish cul-ture—he simply believed that it would spring from the rich mix of al-ready existing Jewish cultures, forging what one of *Altneuland*'s heroes calls a "Mosaic mosaic," a Jewish patchwork combining old with new, the traditions and experiences of history with the vision and enterprising spirit of the modern era.[16]

Herzl was uninterested in the creation of a new Judaism or a "new Jew," or in the erasure of that which had sustained the Jewish people during thousands of years of exile. Rather, he believed that these same Jews, with the languages and cultures that molded them, would create in their new country a splendid mosaic that would, in itself, be *sui generis*. This would happen not through revolutionary force, but as the natural result of the Jews' living free and creative lives in their own state. As Herzl's hero in *Altneuland* puts it, where in the past "Jewish children were weak, pale, cowed," they would become like plants that are "saved, if they are transplanted to the right soil."[17]

IV

With time, Herzl's conservative approach would be upstaged by a more revolutionary Zionist approach, which called for a dramatic change in Judaism and the Jewish character. The great proponent of this view was David Ben-Gurion, Israel's first prime minister. He called for new, "Hebrew" forms of cultural expression and festivals; for the repudiation of European-sounding names and their replacement with Hebrew ones; and for the importance of Jewish labor, Bible study, and the connection to ancient periods of Jewish independence. All these would effect, as he put it, "the integration of Diaspora Jewry into one homogeneous Hebrew brigade."[18] In describing the early years of independence, Ben-Gurion wrote,

There has been a profound and fundamental change in the lives of hundreds of thousands of Jews here... a wholesale revolution in a Jew's image and his way of life... with their arrival in their homeland, this Jewish dust (*avak adam*), living among strangers, dependent on vagrancy and serfdom, coalesces into an independent, national brigade, attached to and rooted in its great history and sharing the end-of-days vision of national and human redemption... on the trunk of ancient Hebrew culture the prospect of a new Hebrew culture is sprouting, permeated with human and Jewish values, and it makes no division between man and Jew... it is difficult to find any other example of such a transformation of man and it happens to all who return to Zion, whether they come from European countries or America or are returning from Asian and African countries.[19]

This is not so much an account of Israel's early history as a summary of Ben-Gurion's entire worldview. He sought to create a new Jew out of the Diaspora "Jewish dust," to craft a nation rooted in the Bible and in the ancient kingdoms of Israel, its landscapes bearing witness to the return to Zion. As for the millennia that had passed between the glorious biblical period and the still-greater future, these offered very little that one could take pride in, and would be pruned from the tree of history and discarded.

Anyone mildly familiar with the development of Russian socialism in the nineteenth century will quickly recognize the source of Ben-Gurion's outlook: The revolutionary ethos, seeking to create a new world, and a new man, on the ruins of the old. In contrast to the careful replanting Herzl envisioned, Ben-Gurion sought to forge the new nation in a fiery melting pot, whose principal means would be the school system, the military, and a battery of ceremonies, myths, monuments, military parades, and army bands—all of which would turn Jews into an "Israeli nation" whose history begins with the Bible, continues through the Hasmonean and Bar Kochba revolts, and then, after a long hiatus, resumes with the First Aliya in 1882. A nation, to use Moshe Shamir's phrase, "born from the sea," without a tradition, freed from the yoke of generations. All the experience of exile would be left at sea.

Today, with our experience since the establishment of the state, we can judge Ben-Gurion's vision against Herzl's, and ask whether it was indeed prudent to try to re-create the Jewish people in a new image. I, for one, harbor a deep antipathy to any attempt to create a new man or manipulate history by forcibly halting its natural progress. My antipathy grows out of experience: I grew up in a vast laboratory of such an attempt. I was one of its guinea pigs.

At the same time, I do not deny the historical imperative to create a melting pot in the Jewish state. Maimonides taught that he who wishes to escape one form of extremism should adopt its opposite. It is possible that in order to overcome the extreme circumstance of a people scattered around the world, it was necessary to adopt a countervailing extremism—an unrelenting drive toward uniformity. Herzl's vision of diverse communities living alongside one another, without even a common language to bind them, could not have formed the basis for a citizenry capable of establishing a state, winning a war of independence, or absorbing hundreds of thousands of new immigrants in a very short period of time.

But as Maimonides also teaches, after passing from one extreme to the other, one must then return to a middle path. Even if the sabra melting pot was justified at the outset of the Zionist enterprise, I do not think it continued to be valid in the 1960s and 1970s. Why did the immigrants of those two decades need to forsake their traditional Jewish identity, assuming the posture of a Moshe Dayan, Yigal Allon, or Yitzhak Rabin in order to be accepted in Israeli society?

The results of that attempt to create a "new Jew" are well-known: Orthodox Jews, refusing to give up the religious observance that Ben-Gurion considered a vestige of exile, were removed from the centers of influence. Worse, Jews from Arab lands, asked to jettison their traditions like an old suit, felt humiliated and marginalized. The discrimination resulted in the predominance of Sephardi Jews in impoverished development towns and the creation of Sephardi movements like Shas, the Black Panthers, and Tami, which built their popularity on deep resentments. To this day, Israel continues to pay the price.

V

At the beginning of the 1990s, when the Soviet Union collapsed and a million new immigrants poured into Israel, their leaders—myself among them—looked for ways to revive Herzl's more conservative vision, even if we were unaware of its existence. We did not believe in the melting-pot model for absorbing immigrants. We did not believe in expunging everything "old," but rather in preserving everything worth preserving. This was the guiding ideology behind the establishment of those organizations that sought to represent the immigrants from the former Soviet Union, culminating in the Yisrael Ba'aliya political party. We insisted that we did not want to wait decades to be assimilated, decades in which feelings of discrimination and exclusion would be allowed to fester. We wanted our own generation of immigrant Jews to stake their claim to Israeli politics and society. This view was also the force behind our insistence on establishing Russian-language radio stations, television channels, and newspapers. We recognized that these media would be the only way for the older generation of immigrants to know what was happening in, and identify with, their new country.

This is also the story behind the Russian-language Gesher Theater, perhaps the most striking example of what we were trying to achieve. It began in 1991, when I received a call from two friends in Moscow, professional actors, who were having doubts about immigrating to Israel. Acting was their life's calling, and therefore the source of their concern about *aliya*. Did I think that they could set up a Russian-language theater in Israel? And could I, as head of the Zionist Forum, help?

I was immediately taken by what struck me as an opportunity to attract a segment of the Russian-Jewish cultural elite to Israel. I took the proposal to the Ministry of Education and to the leaders of the theater community in Israel. They rejected it out of hand. They had refused to set up theater here in Bulgarian or even Yiddish, I was told. They were trying to develop a *Hebrew* culture, and therefore certainly would not create a Russian theater. It was, they felt, an anti-Zionist idea.

Seeing that I would get no help from the Israelis, I went to New York in search of funding. I was able to raise enough funds to bring the troupe of actors for six appearances in Israel. Later, the Zionist Forum agreed to provide additional funds, and so, step by step, the Gesher Theater came together. It quickly became a success: Audiences flocked to it, and Israeli institutions were eventually compelled to support it. At first, performances were only in Russian, and the audience consisted solely of immigrants from the former Soviet Union. With time, however, its actors began performing in Hebrew as well. The Gesher Theater now features both immigrants acting in Hebrew and sabras acting in Russian, and has earned acclaim from audiences and critics alike. It is hard to argue that this is not a cultural, economic, and even Zionist success.

On the face of it, the story of the Gesher Theater—like that of the Mofet schools specializing in math and the sciences, as well as any number of other examples—is the perfect realization of the Herzlian vision of preserving a particular culture even as it gradually becomes absorbed into the general one, all the while taking care to retain its distinctiveness. But while this was clearly helping form a cultural mosaic, we may still ask whether it is a "Mosaic" mosaic—that is, not only an Israeli achievement, but also a Jewish one.

It takes stones to make a mosaic, but also cement to hold it together. Herzl believed that Judaism would be the cement. But Judaism as a binding force was rejected by Ben-Gurion and his generation of Zionist leaders, who replaced it with the "Hebrew" or "sabra" ethos. Though this newly crafted identity may have fulfilled an important role in the early years, it proved too insubstantial to hold together the very different groups that constitute Israeli society. It was gradually rejected, leaving in its wake a cultural void. As a result, the last few decades in Israel have witnessed the breakdown of the Jewish mosaic into a mere collection of stones.

Russian immigrants have sensed this keenly. For in contrast to what is generally thought, most of them, at least in the early years of the immigration, wanted to be part of the Jewish-Israeli experience as they imagined it. They came here with no knowledge of Judaism, yet they were acutely aware of what they lacked. During the collapse of the Soviet Union, its former citizens once again returned to their various ethnic-religious identities. Jews, however, knew almost nothing of their roots. They found themselves lacking any clear identity, and began searching for one. They yearned to find out about the Jewish calendar, Jewish history, Jewish heritage and culture. But when they came to Israel, they discovered that they did not have to assume a *Jewish* identity in order to be Israeli. They very quickly realized that for many Israelis, to be Jewish it was enough simply to serve in the military. A friend of mine, new to Israel, described it strikingly: "I thought I would be giving my children three thousand years of history," he told me. "After all, I was taking them from a country where history began in 1917 to one with a tradition spanning thousands of years. But I soon discovered that instead of giving them an extra three thousand years, I had taken away thirty: History began here in 1948."

Without Jewish history, and without Jewish culture, it is impossible to make a mosaic. What is being produced in Israel instead is a society made up of distinct groups that tend to keep mostly to themselves, put sectarian interests above national ones, and compete for control of the country. For a society that is still very much in its formative period, and in many ways still fighting for its survival, this does not bode well.

This trend is all the more dangerous because the cultural vacuum is increasingly being filled by a post-Zionist vision of society, in which religious and secular, Ashkenazim and Sephardim, Jews and Arabs will all live side by side—but with nothing to bind them together. Israel will be a "state of all its citizens," with no specific national identity. It will no longer consider itself responsible for the fate of Jews everywhere, nor grant Jews the unconditional right to immigrate to Israel. It will certainly not try to promote Jewish culture and heritage or the Hebrew language among Jews around the world. It will provide education, health, and social services to its taxpayers, and little else. And just as in the exile, Jewish identity will gradually be relegated to the confines of the *kehila*, detached from the affairs of state.

This dream—some would call it a nightmare—is beginning to become a reality. Although the majority of the country's leadership is not prepared to sign off on the "state of all its citizens" idea, it is clearly the ideology behind, for example, the Supreme Court's landmark Ka'adan decision of 2000, in which the court ruled that the settlement of Jews in Israel, upon which practical Zionism was based since the early twentieth century, was inherently discriminatory and therefore could not be the official policy of government institutions; or the IDF code of ethics, which makes no mention whatsoever of the army's commitment to assisting Jews in the Diaspora or building a Jewish state; or the ruling this year by the attorney general, Manny Mazuz, prohibiting JNF land from being used for the creation of specifically Jewish communities. In all these cases, the principle of absolute equality was considered to trump all considerations of the state's Jewish character. Another example is the establishment in 2003 by the prime minister and education minister of a "national task force for the promotion of education in Israel," whose conclusions were included in the Dovrat Commission Report this year. While no one would consider the members of the task force post-Zionists, a simple reading of the task force's letter of appointment will reveal that the terms "Jewish state," "Jewish people," "Jews," or "Judaism" are nowhere to be found.

Instead, it mentions only "civil society," "mature, educated citizens," and "civic duty." The task force was aimed at helping rebuild the national education system, which is the government's central means of instilling social values, fostering social unity, and connecting Israel's children with their heritage. For those who commissioned the report, however, these fundamentals seem to have little to do with Judaism, and everything to do with the secular discourse of democratic citizenship. In a truly "Jewish and democratic state," however, one would expect both sides of the equation to get a fair hearing.

To turn the State of Israel into a "state of all its citizens" is nothing less than to declare the failure of the Zionist dream, to advocate the assimilation of the State of Israel into the rest of the Middle East, and ultimately to bring into being an Arab country with a sizable Jewish minority, which itself would be just another Diaspora community—albeit a less attractive one. The only way out is to return to Herzl's vision of a state that enables its various communities to give voice to their unique heritage and culture, on the one hand, but carefully preserves their Jewish commonality on the other. It is a difficult undertaking, but Israel's future as a Jewish state cannot be ensured without it. It will be built on our common Jewish history, on our common Jewish tradition, and on an unseverable bond between Israel and the Diaspora.

A hundred years have passed since Herzl's death, but his vision seems more relevant today than ever before. It was neither simple nor easy to carry out, but given the collapse of the classic Ben-Gurionite vision and the rejection of Zionism among influential Jews and Israelis, it has never seemed more urgent.

NOTES

The author would like to thank Roman Polansky and Tehila Nachalon for their assistance in preparing the present essay.

1. Menachem Begin, quoted in Harry Zvi Hurwitz, *Begin: A Portrait* (Washington: B'nai B'rith, 1994), p. 43.

2. Theodor Herzl, *The Jewish State*, trans. and ed. Jacob M. Alkow (New York: Dover, 1988), p. 75.

3. Herzl, *The Jewish State*, pp. 79-80.

4. Herzl, *The Jewish State*, pp. 75-76.

5. Herzl, *The Jewish State*, p. 80.

6. Theodor Herzl, *Letters and Journals* (Jerusalem: Mitzpe, 1928), p. 129. [Hebrew]

7. Theodor Herzl, *Letters*, trans. Y. Yavin (Tel Aviv: Hotza'a Medinit, 1937), p. 266. [Hebrew]

8. I do not wish to enter here into a full analysis of the sources of anti-Semitism, which I have explored in depth elsewhere. See Natan Sharansky, "On Hating the Jews," *Commentary* (November 2003), pp. 26-34.

9. Theodor Herzl, welcome address at First Zionist Congress in Basel, Switzerland, August 29-31, 1897.

10. Herzl, *The Jewish State*, p. 146. For a full treatment of Herzl's vision of Israel as a Jewish state, see Yoram Hazony, "Did Herzl Want a Jewish State?" *Azure* 9 (Spring 2000), pp. 37-73.

11. Herzl, *The Jewish State*, p. 123.

12. Herzl, *The Jewish State*, p. 146.

13. Herzl, *The Jewish State*, p. 146.

14. Herzl, *The Jewish State*, p. 135.

15. Herzl, *The Jewish State*, p. 102.

16. Theodor Herzl, *Altneuland*, trans. Paula Arnold (Haifa: Haifa Publishing Company, 1960), p. 201.

17. Herzl, *Altneuland*, p. 62.

18. As per the proposed phrasing in his party's manifesto. From the Ben-Gurion Archives, Letters, January 9, 1949.

19. David Ben-Gurion, *The State of Israel Restored*, vol. 1 (Tel Aviv: Am Oved, 1969), pp. 432-433. [Hebrew]

ZIONISM:
A DEVIANT NATIONALISM?

AMNON RUBINSTEIN

FOR MANY YEARS it has been taken for granted that Zionism, as a nationalist movement, is something of an anomaly. And indeed, when Theodor Herzl declared that the Jews were a nation with the right to a state of its own, there were many who thought he had taken leave of his senses. Herzl himself recognized the audacity of his position, writing in his diary, "In Basel I founded the Jewish state," but then adding that he dare not say it aloud for fear of being ridiculed. His concern was not unwarranted: When he returned from the First Zionist Congress to his office at the *Neue Freie Presse*, his friends and colleagues mocked him, dubbing him the "future head of state."[1] Herzl's vision—that the Jews, dispersed throughout the nations without a culture, language, or land in common, would be accepted as a nation deserving of a state—was revolutionary at the time.

Nevertheless, despite Zionism's anomalous nature, or perhaps because of it, one of the movement's central objectives was to make the Jews into a nation like any other. This goal was uppermost in the minds of Zionist leaders and thinkers from a variety of political perspectives, and it resonated in the writings of Herzl, David Ben-Gurion, Ze'ev Jabotinsky, and others. From this perspective, even the appearance of the first

Jewish thief in Tel Aviv was considered an encouraging sign of a new "normalcy." So we are left with a certain paradox in Zionist thinking: The extraordinary transformation of the Jews into a unified, sovereign nation was in fact intended to achieve "normalcy"—that is, the opposite of the extraordinary.

Today, after more than a hundred years of Zionism, we can declare the effort a success. Unfortunately, however, we have still not freed ourselves of the perception that the State of Israel and the idea on which it was founded are politically, legally, and morally anomalous. This way of thinking, which has taken root both in Israel and abroad, does continuous harm to Israel's image, turning it into the black sheep of the family of enlightened nations.

This attitude, however, is in fact almost completely without foundation. For in truth, some of the most important aspects of Jewish nationalism, which at first glance appear unique, are in fact shared by many countries around the world. Moreover, Israel's similarity to other countries is only increasing with time, as the nations of the West, and particularly Europe, are taking a more positive approach to elements of nationalism that not long ago were a source of dissent and suspicion. Thus, for example, it is increasingly accepted that the connections some states maintain with their ethnic or ancestral brethren abroad are legitimate—connections that bear a striking resemblance to Israel's relations with the Jewish Diaspora. Comparisons of this sort are now not only possible, but even necessary and beneficial. They confirm, both in our own eyes and in those of the world, that Israel deserves an uncontested place among the democratic nations, one that justifies neither delusions of grandeur nor gratuitous feelings of inferiority.

II

Until just a few years ago, many people considered nationalism outdated, a party at which the Zionists had arrived too late. In the new Western world of multi- and supra-national states, immigrant states with a dominant Christian culture and an official language but no dominant nationality, the nation state appeared to be irrelevant. The United States, for example, is not a nation state. Its citizens are of different nationalities, and enjoy complete constitutional equality. Europe, too, has undergone a process of great historical importance: Countries that once made much of the fact that they were independent nation states have moved towards unification with others, and the borders between them have become increasingly blurred. Thus we saw France, which had no concept of an "unconstitutional" law, and the British Parliament, which had never agreed to put its laws to a constitutional test, suddenly required to defend themselves before the European Court of Human Rights in Strasbourg. Such developments were simply unimaginable at the beginning of the twentieth century.

Two very recent developments, however, have changed matters significantly. First, new national entities have appeared on the Western European scene. The blurring of the border between France and Spain, for example, strengthened immensely the national spirit of the Basques, who boast not only their own language and culture, but also their own region. In a similar fashion do the Catalans and the Corsicans, and now even the Scots, see themselves as separate nations. Of course, this kind of nationalist sentiment, which was born in Europe and long flourished there, has also rekindled old animosities. In Belgium, for instance, an emerging divide between the French- and Flemish-speaking populations threatens to end a long period of relative tranquility. It seems that eliminating the borders between old national entities has not only failed to suppress nationalism, but has actually given it new life.

The second development occurred as a result of the collapse of communism. The Soviet bloc was replaced by some thirty new states or regimes, which adopted—at least as far as the outside world was concerned—most of the trappings of democracy. These countries, the most prominent of which is the Russian Federation, are nation states in every sense of the term. Moreover, most of them are members of the Council of Europe, and some will soon become members of the European Union. Thus while Europe may have believed that it succeeded in ridding itself of nationalism, it has nonetheless had to accept a large number of new members that are not only democracies, but also nation states.

One of the clearest signs of the change in attitude towards nationalism is a growing recognition of the existence of national minorities. There was very little real debate on the subject before the Eastern European countries joined the Council of Europe, although Western Europe itself is home to several known national minorities (such as the Basques,

Catalans, and Corsicans mentioned above). Yet in the 1990s, the Council of Europe enacted two treaties: The Framework Convention for the Protection of National Minorities, which took effect on February 1, 1998, and granted national minorities collective rights for the first time; and the European Charter for Regional and Minority Languages, which took effect one month later. France, the longtime champion of civic nationalism, rejected the Framework Convention, but was one of just three dissenters.[2] All the other European countries—including Great Britain, which has a long tradition of denying collective rights—signed both of these agreements, and in so doing gave recognition to the principles on which they were based.

These new sentiments in Europe have also meant an increased willingness to re-evaluate the idea of a diaspora. As Israelis, we have a special stake in this re-evaluation, since the word "diaspora" tends to be associated with the Jewish people. The most authoritative dictionaries offer ample proof of this fact: One prominent dictionary, for example, gives three definitions of "diaspora," the first of which is "the dispersal of Jews outside Palestine since the sixth century A.D." In fact, at the end of the nineteenth century, when the Zionist movement was still in its infancy, the term "diaspora" was identified almost exclusively with the Jewish dispersion. Yet there are obviously other diasporas. The Irish are an outstanding example: There are about 70 million people of Irish descent in the world today, the great majority of whom live outside Ireland. Indeed, when Ireland gained its independence in 1937, its prime minister was Eamon de Valera, an American citizen born in New York. The link between a diaspora and its members' country of origin has therefore long been recognized, and while this issue did not attract much attention in the twentieth century, it has now become a focus of increased interest around the world, particularly with regard to the vital role diasporas have played in the development of modern nationalism.

The British scholar Anthony D. Smith has identified three nations whose nationhood was deeply influenced by a diaspora: The Israelis, the Armenians, and the Greeks.[3] It is worth noting that historically, only the Jews had no territorial base for their resurgent nationalism; most Greeks continued to live in Greece, and most Armenians in Armenia. Nevertheless, the responsibility of the Greek and Armenian diasporas for the emergence of their national movements was immeasurably greater than that of the indigenous population. Similarly, it was actually the diasporas of the Baltic peoples—the Lithuanians, Latvians, and Estonians—who continued to maintain "virtual" embassies while their homelands were under Soviet domination. During the entire period, these diasporas exerted enormous political and diplomatic pressure on the Soviet Union, demanding independence for their homelands. Clearly, then, the Jewish example is far from the only case of nationalism developing in the diaspora, and of a nation's struggle being waged outside the borders of its ancestral land.

These special links between a nation state and its kinsmen living abroad are of increasing concern to the European community and its new members. National minorities are generally protected by either international agreements or treaties between states, but recently their status has also been discussed by their countries of origin as an internal legal matter.[4] Nine European countries—Austria, Bulgaria, Greece, Hungary, Italy, Romania, Russia, Slovakia, and Slovenia—have even passed laws granting official status to the connection between the nation and its ethnic or national brethren living abroad. Section 108 of the Greek Constitution, for example, states that Greece will take responsibility for the "care for emigrant Greeks and for the maintenance of their ties with the fatherland." Greece is now advancing an initiative to grant dual citizenship to Albanians of Greek extraction, a group of around 300,000 people, and is involved in negotiations with both the Albanian government and other European states on this issue. The situation is slightly more complicated in Russia: Although it is a nation state, its national identity is somewhat ambiguous. For this reason, Russia calls its kinsmen, and, in fact, anyone connected to Russian culture, "compatriots." While not a complete definition, the term nonetheless carries practical legal implications: A law passed by the Russian Federation in March 1999 states that any compatriot who returns to the Federation immediately becomes a Russian citizen, with all the attendant rights and obligations.[5] So many states have already adopted policies of this kind that they have earned themselves a place in the scholarly lexicon, where they are referred to as "kin states."

Last year, a dispute on the issue of kin states that arose in Eastern Europe forced the Council of Europe to formulate an official position on the matter. The source of the trouble was the Magyar Law, passed by the Hungarian Parliament in June 2001, which granted certain rights to Hungarians living abroad. Most of these Hungarians live in adjacent countries, including Slovakia, Romania, Serbia, Slovenia, Croatia, and the Ukraine, as the result of the 1920 Treaty of Trianon, in which Hungary was forced to cede a considerable part of its territory, and with it much of its population. The Magyar Law gave descendants of these nationals the right to a Hungarian identity card, which offers privileges such as the right to work in Hungary on a temporary basis, to enjoy reduced fares on public transport, and to qualify for medical insurance. But Hungary did not stop there. It went so far as to offer to finance the education of Hungarian-born residents of neighboring countries, on condition that they study in schools where Hungarian is the language of instruction. Perhaps not surprisingly, Romania vigorously opposed the Magyar Law on the grounds that it fostered discrimination among Romanian citizens, on Romanian territory. Similarly, Slovakia accused Hungary of interfering in its internal affairs and threatening its sovereignty.

The dispute was finally taken to the Council of Europe, which passed it on to a committee of jurists known as the Venice Commission. In October 2001, the commission published its findings in the "Report on the Preferential Treatment of National Minorities by Their Kin State," which stated that relationships between a homeland and its diaspora kinsmen do not contravene international law so long as they do not undermine the territorial sovereignty of the countries involved. Accordingly, the commission outlined several guidelines for policies of kin states towards nationals living outside their borders. For example, states are required to refrain from discriminating among citizens of other states and infringing on basic human rights; to respect existing bilateral agreements; and to restrict their efforts primarily to preserving ties of culture and identity. More importantly, for our purposes, the commission stipulated that nothing in these policies invalidates either citizenship or immigration laws that express a certain preference for kinsmen returning to their homeland—thereby tacitly recognizing the legitimacy of a policy of repatriation.[6] The commission's findings were eventually adopted by the Council of Europe, which decided to welcome "assistance given by kin states to their kin-minorities in other states in order to help these kin-minorities to preserve their cultural, linguistic, and ethnic identity." The resolution adds, however, that the assistance given must also be "accepted by the states of which the members of the kin-minorities are citizens...."[7]

The importance of these developments cannot be overemphasized. They have far-reaching implications for the future of Europe and for the many national minorities living within its borders. What we are see-ing, in fact, is an attempt, or at least a multi-lateral effort, to re-establish the legitimacy of nationalism within the framework of international jurisprudence.

III

The change in European attitudes towards national identity is of particu-lar interest to Israel, which defines itself as a "Jewish and democratic" nation state. True, Israeli society is sharply divided on how this phrase, which was enshrined in the form of two Basic Laws in 1992, is to be interpreted; but almost no one questions its centrality to Israel's self-defi-nition. For this reason, Israel has struggled since its founding to find a legal formula that would strike the correct balance between its Jewish and democratic aspects. Today, however, many of the new European states are grappling with a similar problem, as they, too, try to express their national identity without compromising their democracy. This is a wholly new type of nationalism, not the kind that nurtures fanatical, insular, or patronizing tribalism, but one that recognizes human, civil, and minority rights.

Israel can learn, and even take encouragement, from the European nation states' experience of giving proper expression to relationships with their Diaspora brethren. For Israel, the very fact that such an effort is being made is a welcome development. Zionism's detractors have often pointed to the problem of "dual loyalty" unique to Jews living outside Israel. American Jews, for example, have been prone to charges of this kind. Now, however, the extension of the term "diaspora" to minorities other than Jews living outside their homeland has resolved the problem of dual loyalty once and for all: The modern, democratic, multi-cultural state not only acknowledges dual allegiances, but encourages them: You can be African-American, Italian-American, or Irish-American, just as you can be Jewish-American, Jewish-British, Jewish-French, and even Jewish-Zionist.

For Israel, the most significant development in this context is the Eu-ropean Council's legal recognition of the relationship between states and their kin who live outside their borders. In the past, Israel was portrayed as an "ethnic democracy" or "ethnocracy" because of the responsibility it assumed for the welfare and interests of the Jewish people around the world.[8] Yet the Venice Commission has now not only accepted the right of countries to maintain a connection with their diasporas, but has even confirmed the legitimacy of the principle of repatriation.[9] The determination that a country's majority has the right to defend its demographic dominance by controlling citizenship and immigration provides a certain justification for Israel's Law of Return, and for other laws espousing the same principle, such as the law that grants semi-official status to the World Zionist Organization and the Jewish Agency.

Europe's recognition of homeland-diaspora relations is of enormous importance for Israel precisely because its ability to remain a Jewish and democratic nation state depends on its ability to preserve a Jewish majority within its borders. Ze'ev Jabotinsky understood this when, in 1936, in response to the Peel Commission's question, "What is a Jewish state?" he replied that it is a state in which there is a Jewish majority. A State of Israel that does not maintain a Jewish majority can be either Jewish or democratic, but not both.

Of course, it is difficult to address Israel's status as both democracy and nation state without also discussing the problem of national minorities living within its borders. In this, Israel should follow Europe's example of setting standards for the protection of such minorities. Precisely because Israel is the Jewish nation state, it must recognize its Arab citizens as a national minority with collective, and not merely individual, equality, despite all the difficulties this recognition inevitably brings. For instance, when the state was founded, Israel acknowledged the collective rights of Arabs in the realm of education. Israeli Arabs thus have the right to educate their children in a separate framework, according to their own culture and language. This is undoubtedly an important achievement—in other countries, national minorities like the Kurds and the Macedonians are risking a great deal in their struggle to obtain the same right—but it is not enough. We should be grateful, therefore, that the Israeli legislature and judiciary have recently taken significant steps towards correcting the current situation. The Knesset passed three laws in the year 2000 recognizing Israeli Arabs as a group with collective rights: The first, an amendment to the State Education Law, defines the Arab population as a group, deserving to be treated as such, for the first time. The second is the Amendment to the Government Companies Law, which states that "in the composition of the Board of Directors of a government company, appropriate expression will be given to representation for the Arab population." The third, an amendment to the Civil Service Law, institutes the principle of affirmative action for Arabs in government jobs.

The Supreme Court has also handed down several decisions that make significant progress towards recognition of Israeli Arabs' collective rights. The court determined, for example, that there should be equality in budgetary allocations for Jewish and Arab municipalities;[10] that the Arab population should have appropriate representation on the board of the Israel Lands Authority;[11] and that in towns with a mixed population, public signs should include Arabic.[12]

These legal and jurisprudential developments bring Israel closer to the standards set by Europe in the Framework Convention for the Protection of National Minorities. There still remains one point, however, on which we have failed to keep pace: The convention recognizes both the collective rights of minorities, and the individual rights of minority members. Therefore, a national group has the right to be educated in its own language and to work to preserve its culture, but individual members of that group may choose not to belong to it. This is not yet the case in Israel, which still does not recognize the right of an individual Arab to study, if he so wishes, in the Jewish school system, or to serve in the army. These barriers create an unnecessary divide between the majority and minority populations. They also make it extremely difficult for individuals to live according to their individual preferences, as is the case in every fully democratic country.

There is certainly room for improvement in Israel where liberalism and democracy are concerned. Yet as a modern nation state, Israel is not all that exceptional when compared with other countries, especially those in Europe. In fact, one might even say that Israel is in good company. What has happened in Europe since the collapse of communism has led to a positive reappraisal of nationalism, and has granted greater political and legal legitimacy to policies that express the special relationship between a country and its diaspora. It is still too early to tell just how much Israel will benefit from this reappraisal, but it will certainly give new strength to the country's ongoing efforts on behalf of the Jewish people throughout the world.

NOTES

1. Cited in Ernst Pawel, *The Labyrinth of Exile: A Life of Theodor Herzl* (New York: Farrar, Strauss, and Giroux, 1989), p. 343.

2. Apart from France, only Turkey and Andorra refused to sign the treaty, and Belgium signed with reservations.

3. Anthony D. Smith, *Myths and Memories of the Nation* (New York: Oxford, 1999), pp. 212-215.

4. There are several examples of this: The 1969 agreement between Italy and Austria that guaranteed the rights of the German-speaking minority in south Tyrol; the compromise reached between Germany and Denmark in the 1955 Bonn-Copenhagen Declarations that guaranteed the language and cultural rights of Danes in northern Germany and of Germans in the south of Denmark; and the 1995 agreement between Hungary and Slovakia that guaranteed the rights of the Hungarian minority in Slovakia and of the Slovakian minority in Hungary.

5. In the countries we have already mentioned, the laws concerning kinsmen who are not citizens are generally somewhat vague in defining national identity. Bulgaria is the exception; a Bulgarian law passed in 2001 stipulates three conditions that must be fulfilled by anyone wishing to receive the special rights accorded to a Bulgarian who is not a citizen of the country: First, at least one of his parents must be Bulgarian; second, he himself may not be a resident of Bulgaria; and third, he must consider himself Bulgarian.

6. European Commission for Democracy Through Law (Venice Commission), *Report on the Preferential Treatment of National Minorities by Their Kin State*, Strasbourg, October 16, 2001.

7. Council of Europe Parliamentary Assembly, Resolution 1335 (2003): Preferential Treatment of National Minorities by Their Kin State: The Case of the Hungarian Law on Hungarians Living in Neighboring Countries ("Magyars"), June 19, 2001.

8. The name "ethnic democracy" was given to Israel by the sociologist Sammy Smooha in articles he published in the 1990s. See, for example, his article "The State of Israel's Government: Civil Democracy, Non-Democracy, or Ethnic Democracy?" *Israeli Sociology* 2:2 (2000), pp. 565-630. [Hebrew]

9. Several countries have nevertheless adopted this principle, and based their immigration and citizenship policies on it. Germany, for example, accepted millions of German refugees who found themselves on the other side of the Iron Curtain after World War II. In 1996, Finland passed a law allowing

it to repatriate the descendants of Karelian Finns who came under Soviet rule during the reign of Stalin. Furthermore, Article 52 of the Polish Constitution states that anyone the law determines to be of Polish extraction is entitled to settle permanently in Poland, and Clause 16 of the Irish Law of Citizenship empowers the minister of the interior to exempt anyone of Irish descent from fulfilling the normal conditions for citizenship.

10. *Committee of Heads of Arab Local Councils in Israel v. Minister of Construction and Housing* (HCJ 727/00), in *Decisions of the Israel Supreme Court*, vol. 56, section 2, pp. 79-96. [Hebrew]

11. *Association for Civil Rights in Israel v. Government of Israel* (HCJ 6924/98), in *Decisions*, vol. 55, section 5, pp. 15-42. [Hebrew]

12. *Adala v. City of Tel Aviv-Jaffa* (HCJ 4112/99), in *Decisions*, vol. 56, section 5, pp. 393-480. [Hebrew]

THE ZIONIST
REVOLUTION IN TIME

EYAL CHOWERS

Introduction

The breakdown of nineteenth-century conceptions of order and purpose in history inaugurated a new type of concern among European thinkers. Weber, for example, believed that the lack of an overarching scheme ruling human events meant that nothing could avert modernity from its destructive, dehumanizing track. The problem, to be precise, was not the amorphous nature of history *per se*, but the fact that moderns have established life orders that dominate them and are immune to change. In the past, Weber seems to suggest, the openness of history granted humans the ability to introduce radical transformations solely by the power of their beliefs and actions; prophets, in particular, were able to steer history in novel directions by addressing human spiritual and emotional needs. But the last great religious revolution in the Occident spawned unpredictable outcomes that put the human capacity for renewal in jeopardy. The Protestant worldview and its accompanying ethics helped generate social institutions, such as market capitalism and bureaucratic mass organizations, that became entrenched and uncontrollable. Instrumental rationality increasingly threatens to level individual normative commitments, functional practices work to shape people to fit external necessities, and disciplinary techniques erode their perception of themselves as independent beings responsible for their convictions and deportment. Since, in Weber's view, there was and is no meaningful, benign narrative underlying historical time, he found it unlikely that the new type of person, the narrow professional or *Fachmann*, would be able to break free of the overbearing, rationalized institutions of modernity. For Weber, history might in theory be malleable and undefined, but the reflective mind at the dawn of the twentieth century should have recognized—if this mind was courageous and mature enough—that, in practice, history was locked into course.[1]

Zionism emerged as the antipode of this "entrapment" consciousness. Weber saw Western civilization as a ship without a pilot, steered by a chance event (i.e., the spiritual sea change of Protestantism) to the womb of the iron cage, where individuals remain baffled by the effects of their own creations; a small number of Jews, noticing the same undefined quality of history and its hazardous direction, chose to glorify the human capacity for self-assertion and mastery of events, to inject their lives with meaning and passion precisely by virtue of history's formlessness. These early Zionists aimed to re-appropriate the human capacity for a novel beginning, a capacity Weber thought had been lost in the modern era. In doing this, Zionists were also rebelling against their own tradition, in which the understanding that political action could, by itself, radically alter human fate had been absent for 1,800 years, since the Diaspora. How is it that, around the turn of the twentieth century, a small but decisive number of Jews began to see human affairs as hospitable to deliberate intervention and willful rupture?

Before answering this question, let us recapitulate the scope of Zionist revolution. Zionism emerged during the last decade of the nineteenth century, mainly in Eastern and Central Europe. While originally a movement of a small minority considered outlandish by their peers, its institutional ingenuity combined with pressing external circumstances turned it into a viable option for the Jewish masses. At the most basic level, Zionism aimed to restore to the Jews a political body they could claim as their own; national independence was seen as the venue for guarding the individual against physical threats, and the collective against the menace of assimilation and disintegration. Most Zionists—seeking to legitimatize their hold on a territory and to echo the glorious, Hebraic past of self-government—thought this modern project of renewal could succeed only in *Eretz Yisrael* (Palestine). But Zionism meant more than political independence in Palestine. It promised both material and spiritual transformation: a modernized economy of and for the Jews would eliminate their currently threatened, fleeting patterns of survival, as well as their dependent occupational structure, which often left them socially backward; the revival of the Hebrew language would launch a secular, fresh cultural experiment that would introduce new substance into Jewish collective identity. Given the radical and unprecedented nature of these goals, the question then arises even more forcefully: Where did the Zionists find the audacity for such an all-engulfing experiment?

I shall argue that a sudden metamorphosis in the temporal consciousness of Jews and other Europeans made the Zionists' bold faith possible. The emergence of Zionism at the onset of the twentieth century was possible only after teleological conceptions of history began to lose their allure; Zionism was an augury, crystallizing and articulating politically what was silently working on the level of ideas. More specifically, I shall try to show that Zionism presupposes a temporal ontology that could be termed "sundered history." By this I mean a precarious, in-between stage, in which various historical narratives have disintegrated and new ones are not yet entrenched. The interrupted historical narratives may be religious or secular, linear or cyclical, eschatological or catastrophic; what matters is the undefined space established within or among them. Sundered history is an interlude during which human existence in time is seen as open and without clear course: devoid of any guidance, whether in the form of divinity, natural order, an invisible-hand-like mechanism, or unfolding reason. The events taking place at this interlude cannot be explained causally; the period is a rupture made possible only by the recognition that history is empty. The consciousness of emptiness (and unbounded freedom) may induce confusion and paralysis, but it can also generate grand, radical human action. When the latter occurs, an uneasiness emerges, since the length of this hiatus in history is uncertain: the separated poles of time may meet again; the narrative space left ajar may be slammed shut by new visions of order and meaning that would steer events. Sundered history thus inspires a mode of urgency, an impatient need for action before history again becomes impenetrable, locked within a given course.

Zionism accepts this ontology of sundered history: it exemplifies the collapse of teleology that permeated both the Enlightenment's meta-narrative of progress and expanding universal community and the meta-narrative of the nation as an organic, continuously growing body. Instead, Zionists celebrated the human capacity to begin something absolutely new, eventually constructing a demographic, political, and cultural actu-ality where none had existed before. Of course, the newness of Zionism contained elements of the old, such as the revival of an ancient language and a return to the land.[2] But this revival was conceivable only because history was seen as up for grabs, inaugurating an interval where innova-tive narratives could be consciously chosen and formed. The subsequent ethos that evolved after the founding of the State of Israel in 1948 pre-serves this spirit; it is inclined to profess that human affairs succumb to the will and imagination, to the longings of the heart. Born in urgent times, this ethos also predisposes its bearers to approach social reality urgently, since there is a mistrust of tomorrow. A certain territory might no longer be obtainable, Zionist policies might be rebuffed by unexpected political circumstances, or enemies could suddenly become overbear-ing. As we shall see below, both the Nietzschean and Marxist strands of Zionism hold these foundational beliefs in the human potential for metamorphosis and the scarcity of time. More generally, a revolutionary temporal consciousness was necessary for swift and radical changes in individual identity and socioeconomic conditions—both of which were vital for the success of Zionism.

Before we proceed, a few words of caution and clarification are in order. One should remember that early Zionist writings, which were crucial for shaping the movement (written roughly between 1896 and 1905, or from the time Herzl published *Der Judenstaat* until the end of the Uganda debate), tended to be polemical, journalistic, and public in nature—and only marginally philosophical. Consequently, commentary on Zionism has been mostly historical, sociological, political, and ideological, with a few notable exceptions.[3] Any attempt to contemplate the temporal ideas of Zionism requires interpretation and extrapolation from material that differs in character, and hence this project is admittedly somewhat experimental. Nevertheless, a philosophical-political investigation of Zi-onism and its singular features may allow a deeper understanding not only of this movement, but also of its era. In attempting to highlight aspects of this distinctiveness, I depart from the dominant inclination of current scholarship on Zionism. The latter emphasizes that the last third of the nineteenth century was marked by the dramatic rise of two political ideologies and practices, nationalism and colonialism; these scholars debate which of these phenomena was most decisive in shaping Zionism. Critics of Zionism (who in Israel are often called the New Historians) point to the colonial and imperialist elements in Zionism, such as its economic exploitation of the native Arab population, its fixation on land acquisition through dubious methods, and its perception of itself as the messenger of progress and high culture in a backward environment.[4] In contrast, those who sympathize with the movement's aims underscore its affinity with other national liberation movements that evolved during the nineteenth century, arguing that Zionism was a legitimate reaction to anti-Semitism and the exclusion of Jews from European nation states. From this perspective, Zionism sought to solve a crisis—one of physical security, economic existence, and collective identity—not to exploit and control others.[5] While these interpretations differ in their normative presuppositions, theoretical frameworks, and facts highlighted, they are similar in attempting to contextualize Zionism and see it through comparative lenses that de-emphasize its distinctiveness. I believe that both of these scholarly approaches to Zionism are illuminating and called for, given the historical environment in which this movement burgeoned, but a critical and unique facet of Zionism has been so far overlooked, in part because of these contextualizing approaches.

The Skeleton of History

"In Judaism," writes Gershom Scholem, "the Messianic idea has compelled a life lived in deferment, in which nothing can be done definitively, nothing can be irrevocably accomplished."[6] The mode of lingering and hesitation that characterized Jewish existence in the Diaspora prior to secularization originated from the division of time into two distinct categories. On one hand, the individual existed empirically in history and had to confront the collective hardships of exile in addition to the inescapable lot of humans on earth, which is colored by illness, injustice, and want. On the other hand, Judaism anticipated the coming of a Messianic Age, which is seen in a radical utopian light. When that

age comes, it is believed, the Jews will be gathered from all corners of
the world, restored to the land of Israel, and given an honored position
among the nations; the dead will be awakened and join the community;
peace and justice will permeate human relations and human interaction
with nature; scarcity will cease to exist; and the Lord will reveal himself
fully to humans, becoming transparent and knowable.

In Judaism (with notable exceptions such as Maimonides), an un-
bridgeable gap separates this world and the coming messianic one. Redemption, claims Scholem, "is in no casual sense a result of previous
history. It is precisely the lack of transition between history and the
redemption which is always stressed by the prophets and apocalyptists."[7]
Moreover, human actions and intentions have no bearing on the coming of the Messiah. "Precisely in the biblical texts which serve as the
basis for the crystallization of the messianic idea, it is nowhere made
dependent upon human activity."[8] Any radical attempt of humans to
improve their lives by collective action is condemned as futile; it is
considered dangerous to "press the end," to seek to effect what solely
God can determine. This dependency on the Messiah and the utopian
quality of redemption devalued political action. While Jewish existence
in the Diaspora was not characterized by political passivity and fatalism
(as many Zionists unfairly argued)—Jews have often been very successful
at acquiring special or equal rights and privileges, and at gaining access
to centers of power—it is nevertheless true that they did not believe in
politics as a means for restoring their unity and communal life, as well
as their return to the holy land.[9] Politics is an art of this world, but in
Judaism differences among modes of earthly existence were flattened and
contrasted with the flawlessness of the Messianic Age. Indeed, as Amos
Funkenstein observes, "[T]he traditional Jewish attitude towards time
and history was neither affirmative nor negative, but indifferent."[10] Such
theological impediments to human efforts to end the diasporic existence
were reinforced by the deep ambivalence of the rabbinical leaders toward
the return to the ancient land and the overall fulfillment of the utopia.
These cautious leaders realized that, in a holy time, the halacha (Jewish
law) would become obsolete, rendering their communal and religious
authority without foundation.

These brief observations help to explain why no Jewish revival movement could have been successful before secularization, and why the attempts at returning to the holy land that did arise were associated with

the crowning of a Messiah, as in the case of Shabtai Tzvi (1626-1676). But while Zionism required the profanization of history, the decline of the messianic ideal (and the evaporation of the expectation of the unexpected) posed a grave danger to the idea of a return. The depiction of history (since the late eighteenth century) as directed by some intrinsic mechanism that could be grasped consciously, even scientifically, fostered skepticism toward the realization of an innovative human action not in line with the predictable unfolding of events. It would be a mistake, then, to assume that any divinity-free notion of time would be congenial to Zionism: the movement needed not only a novel acknowledgment of the power inherent in human deeds, but also a recognition that these deeds could give birth to the historically unanticipated, to political phenomena that do not obey any inevitable pattern of evolution, to a semi-messianism that depends on humans alone. Zionism had to eschew the teleological visions that governed social and political thought during the nineteenth century, since they did not allow collective action outside the bounds of their predicted meta-narratives. In what follows, I shall examine two of these meta-narratives and the challenges they posed to Zionism.

The first teleological meta-narrative depicts history as propelled by an internal dynamic that gradually builds toward the formation of a single, cosmopolitan, human community. Kant in particular argues that history "allows us to hope that if we examine the play of the human will's freedom in the large, we can discover its course to conform to rules [*regelmässig*]."[11] These rules help us fathom the intrinsic progression of history and its final end; they answer the desire for order in time and ameliorate the fear that human life is a bundle of meaningless, disconnected events. The existence of rules assures us that each event is connected to those that precede and follow, that no inexplicable "gaps" exist in human chronology, and that things ultimately fall into place in a meaningful fashion. Thus, Kant declares that history proceeds according to a plan of Nature, whose gist is that it "irresistibly wills that right should finally triumph."[12] Of course, as Kant explains at length in the *Critique of Judgment*, this plan of Nature has no ontological status, and can be contemplated only with the aid of a modest, "reflective judgment" (*reflectierende Urteilskraft*).[13] Nevertheless, the interested observer of history—and we should all be such observers, according to Kant—could notice that Nature steers us toward an architectonic goal, which Kant designates as the "Highest Good."[14]

In this advancement, the Enlightenment was a decisive turning point, bringing the notion of the universal into the center of public life and championing this idea by deliberate political and critical efforts. From then on, Kant held, the human will would not only conform unconsciously to an invisible plan, but should purposely promote it in two ways, external and internal. First, membership in political institutions and the status of citizenship should be based on purely legal grounds, and individual rights should be respected and granted equally to all members of society. While each state might have distinctive features, they should all have essentially compatible civic cultures based on shared principles of positive law. Second, Kant envisions a borderless ethical community whose existence depends on the inner motivations of individuals. This community is constantly expanding; it is open to all men and women, establishing bonds between the near and the distant. Each participant must recognize the respect and dignity, the rights and freedoms, that the other deserves (in accordance with Kantian morality). But Kant does not stop here; he adds another level of universality. While historically different faiths exist, there is in fact greater spiritual homogeneity than is commonly perceived. "*Differences in religion*: an odd expression! Just as if one spoke of different *moralities*."[15] The advancement of history's architectonic goal, the Highest Good, constitutes the true purpose of Creation and is therefore the essence of all religions. "There is only a single religion valid for all men in all times," writes Kant. "Those [faiths and books] can thus be nothing more than the accidental vehicles of religion and can only thereby be different in different times and places."[16]

The Jews of the Haskala (Enlightenment) were profoundly influenced by universalizing visions such as Kant's. The notion of a predetermined scheme in history that elevates legal, ethical, and spiritual homogeneity pressed these Jews to see their distinctive religion as a secondary aspect of their identities. Even Jewish thinkers such as Mendelssohn, who did not accept Kant's notion of moral progress, anticipated the privatization of religion and the increasing incorporation of Jews into the social and political life of Europe; the Napoleonic code confirmed these aspirations in practice. But some Jews went further. The Enlightenment paved the way for the Reform movement that saw Judaism as having a unique role in modernity, since this faith no longer had national aspirations and had become the forerunner in celebrating the cosmopolitan vision. According to the Reformer Abraham Geiger, a rabbi and leading figure in the emerging *Wissenschaft des Judentums*, the Jew is the consummate *Aufklärer*; history finally vindicates this believer, its true telos and import now shining in conformity with the spirit of the Jewish faith. The dispersion of the Jews all over the world served a universal purpose, since Judaism promoted the idea that humans are equal, spiritual beings with divine-like moral capabilities.[17] "I believe," Geiger declares, "that Judaism is above any national body, since its mission is to unite and affirm all peoples and languages. Therefore, it is the primary obligation of all believers of Israel to free Judaism from any national boundaries, which do not belong to its essence and only restrict its development. Instead, Judaism should be transformed from a religion of one nation to a religion of the world."[18]

The meta-narrative of teleological, expanding cosmopolitanism has been further elaborated by Marx. He criticizes the accentuation and expansion of shared humanity envisioned by Kant and Geiger, considering it abstract, deceptive—and not ambitious enough. For Marx, the universalism of the Enlightenment is merely a necessary step in the march of historical materialism toward the establishment of a *true* unity among humans. The bourgeois state generates fellowship and partnership only at the level of public institutions and the law, while in practice its citizens are divided, estranged, and ruled by contingency. The neutral "political state"—unencumbered by the need to promote specific religions and thus enjoying the allegiance of all its citizens—fosters the atomization and enslavement of its members. "Where the political state has attained its full degree of development, man leads a double life, a life in heaven and a life on earth," writes Marx. "He lives in the political community where he regards himself as a communal being, and in civil society, where he is active as a private individual, regards other men as means, debases himself to a mean, and becomes a plaything of alien powers."[19]

This division between private and public, egoism and universalism, is the ultimate victory of Judaism, contends Marx. Following a familiar argument of anti-Semites,[20] Marx views this religion harshly, assigning it a critical role in generating and sustaining the dualistic, capitalist system. "The god of practical need and self-interest is money," he claims, and "money is the jealous god of Israel before whom no other god may stand."[21] Jews, he maintains, had an important role to play in human history: they sustained investments of capital, fostered a borderless market and furthered trade, championed abstract human relations through the use of money, and especially promoted a spirit of self-interest in relations among groups. But the emancipation of mankind and the establishment of true brotherhood anchored in material life depend on deliverance from Jewish tenets and practices; Jews have fulfilled their historical role, and their faith is doomed to crumble. "We recognize in Judaism the presence of a universal and contemporary antisocial element whose historical evolution... has arrived at its present peak, a peak at which it will inevitably disintegrate." [22] The Jew is about to be released from Judaism, from the general fate of the atomized individual in civil society as well as from his particular fate as a detested person identified with dehumanizing socioeconomic conditions. Any attempt to cling to the Jewish identity is both anachronistic and impossible; with the impending collapse of the present order, Judaism will "vanish like an insipid haze in the vital air of society." [23] While this Marxian prediction on the future of Judaism was rejected by Moses Hess, most socialist theorists of the next generation embraced it. Writers such as Otto Bauer, Karl Kautsky, and Eduard Bernstein believed that if national identity was a real problem to reckon with, the Jews were not a nation but rather a fossil, and that rather than espousing the fantasies of Zionism, Jews should cast off the aegis of chosenness and particularity, finally allowing their kernels as species-beings to shine through.

To conclude this outline of the first teleological meta-narrative, both the Kantian and the Marxian visions proclaimed that history has a clear, ineluctable path and that human action advances, consciously or unconsciously, along this path. Time is the sphere of certainty and assurance, providing us with a purposeful narrative and predefined rules for what can be done and expected. While their characterizations of the shared goal of humanity differ, both theorists anticipate the expansion of human bonds and solidarity regardless of contingent nationality, gender, or religion; as a precondition, they demand that moderns make the future their center of gravity, crafting their present actions in a way that will accelerate the progression of history. In practice, whether Jews chose to seek equal citizenship in a liberal state or to take part in a transnational proletarian revolution, they were assured that, as history progressed, the particularities of Jewish identity would become a private matter or disappear altogether; although these were significantly different options, both promised full integration into the gradually forming entity called "humanity."

The other teleological meta-narrative of the nineteenth century, which is founded on the idea of the nation, is typically seen as an inspiration to Zionism rather than an impediment to its development. In analyzing Zionism, interpreters rightly point to its European political context. The aims, ideology, and strategy of Zionism took form in the light of widespread nationalism. Zionism emerged concomitantly with national movements all over Europe, and one could argue that it simply represents the most voluntaristic expression of this political phenomenon. Yet, nationalism has its own form of cyclical teleology (or natural history) that makes it incompatible with Zionism. It often employs biological concepts such as "organism" and "organic growth," postulating a united, complete social body whose parts develop synchronistically and according to one distinctive internal principle. These ideas of a natural and overarching temporality, inscribed in nineteenth-century nationalism (especially in the German world), implied that Jews, who had been politically dead for many centuries, could hardly hope to reinspire breath in their decomposed national body. This disquieting philosophical dilemma arises, for example, from the writings of one of the first theorists of nationalism, Herder. He compared the nation to a living being or plant, a coherent unit (*genetisches Individuum*) influenced by its environment (*Klima*) but essentially driven by its own singular, inner force. For Herder, each nation is a whole, both horizontally and vertically.

First, each nation has a singular *Geist* that is expressed in and formed through the national language. This distinctive spirit pervades the nation's laws, social institutions, customs, religion, and culture; each realm echoes the others, creating a living and coherent totality. Second, the *Volk* unfolds like any living creature, whereby each stage follows naturally from the previous one and brings to fruition what was present in an undeveloped form from the start. There are no leaps or radical transformations in this process, and each moment can be explained in terms of the pregiven contents (material and spiritual elements) of the social body. Herder believes that the spiritual element is particularly important in shaping the substance and duration of nations. The laws of mechanics, economics, or statistics are of little help in elucidating change, and historical rules are for him futile efforts of the mind to impose uniform order on a unique spiritual enigma. The distinctiveness of a nation's spirit gives rise to a specific temporality. "In actuality, every changing thing has the measure of its own time within itself," Herder explains. "No two worldly things have the same measure of time.... There are therefore (one can state it properly and boldly) at any one time in the universe innumerably many times."[24] As Reinhart Koselleck argues, for Herder, time ceases to be a universal and uniform phenomenon; rather, it is conceived of in the plural form, as the expressions of singular social bodies that have their own tempos, their own paces of development and decay. Each temporal unit is secluded, unaffected by experiences and formation of other units. This biological conceptualization of national time not only insulated the community from without, but also gave a certain finality to the inner process.[25] Herder's depiction of the community as a harmonious body implied that decomposition was all-engulfing; once decay set foot in one limb, no part of collective life could escape it. And decay and death, of course, are natural, inescapable phenomena that elude the human will. While cosmopolitan and universalist teleology presented Jewish identity as a cloak about to be cast off, cyclical teleology suggested that the Jews' time had passed, that the Diaspora served as proof that their cycle had long ended.

What can be extrapolated from Herder about the fate of the Jewish nation becomes more explicit with Hegel. According to the latter, nations not only exhibit a rich heterogeneity (as Herder would have it), but are also interconnected in advancing a shared scheme—world history. The end of this history is the materialization and self-realization of the Absolute Spirit in time. Thus, for Hegel, world history is not a meaningless assortment of chaotic and tragic events, but a totality through which humans progress toward full self-consciousness and freedom. Each nation has a particular gradation and unique role in this march, adding a necessary element to the formation of the whole. "The forms which these grades of progress assume," writes Hegel, "are characteristic national spirits of history; the peculiar tenor of their moral life, of their Government, their Art, Religion, and Science. To realize these grades is the boundless impulse of the World-Spirit, the goal of its irresistible urging; for this division into organic members, and the full development of each, is its Idea."[26]

According to Hegel, each nation undergoes three stages in its life: growth, height of power, and decline. Once a nation has successfully brought a distinct idea into the world and objectified it, this nation then becomes dispensable from the point of view of world history and is consumed by the same distinct features that produced its achievements. "The life of a people ripens a certain fruit; its activity aims at the complete manifestation of the principle which it embodies. But this fruit does not fall back into the bosom of the people that produced and nurtured it; on the contrary, it becomes a poison-draught to it. That poison-draught it cannot let alone, for it has an insatiable thirst for it: the taste of the draught is its annihilation."[27] The destruction of nations, although a tragic event, is nevertheless inevitable and irresistible. Throughout history, people may have deluded themselves into believing that their glorious days could return, and that the world would once more view them with awe. But this self-delusion is extinguished in modernity with the novel, temporal self-consciousness of individuals. According to Hegel, the modern must recognize that everything that occurs in history is necessary, rational, and unidirectional; freedom, which comes with this realization, accordingly demands a desistance from futile attempts at intervention in the social and political reality and against the course of the Spirit.

The Hegelian view of history posed a serious challenge to projects of Jewish national revival, since it implied that the Jews' role in history was obsolete. The Jews, according to this view, had fulfilled their role by advancing the monotheistic and abstract notion of the divine; their revival as a modern nation with independent political institutions would be an anomaly that contributed nothing to world history. Objective conditions seemed to concur with this verdict. The Jews were scattered all over Europe (and the world) and could hardly form an organic "body." They had hardly any shared concerns or civic culture, and the daily experience of the general public where they resided was much more familiar to them than the experience of distant Jews. The Jewish "people" as an undifferentiated mass, a homogeneous whole, simply did not and could not exist.[28] Jews also lacked a territory to claim as their own; their life as a community could not be associated with an existing homeland or a folklore that evolves from such rootedness. The neglect of the Hebrew language was a token of this predicament, and this neglect in turn furthered the decline of the "nation." Given this background, even nineteenth-century meta-narratives of national revival and temporal cyclicality (which could be made congruous with Herderian natural history) were irrelevant in the Jewish case: here, after all, the *essential preconditions* necessary for the (re)evolution of a nation were missing, the substratum imperative for any organism to burgeon (a unity of people and land), nonexistent. Furthermore, in order to become a nation, the Jews

had a distinctively excruciating task: they had to rebel and discard their
Volksgeist—rather than embracing it as the foundation for their collective identity. In contrast to other peoples, the Jews cultivated a tradition
that was especially incompatible with a national-political project: rather
than valorizing self-assertion, this tradition valued messianic expectation;
rather than preaching exclusivity and enclosure, it aspired to strengthen
moral consciousness and cosmopolitanism; and rather than mooring identity to a particular space, it grounded identity in a temporal continuity
sustained by the study of the Book. In short, theories such as Hegel's
and Herder's propelled Jews to recognize that their historical experience
contraindicated a realistic expectation of "nationhood."

The challenges to Jewish national identity posed by Herderian and
Hegelian notions of teleology are evident in the work of Nachman
Krochmal (1785-1840), one of the leading Jewish philosophers of the
nineteenth century. Krochmal agrees with Herder that organic patterns
rule the fate of a nation and its *Volksgeist*, that history obeys essentially
biological categories. Human events are part of nature, progressing in the
same gradual, immanent patterns of development. In a strictly continuous fashion, latent inner forces come to fruition and, after blooming and
spending their creativity, inevitable fade away.[29] In addition, Krochmal
echoes Hegelian idealism by positing an absolute, spiritual, and divine
element (*haruhani hamuhlat*), whose full comprehension requires an
elongated historical process. Interestingly, Krochmal joins themes from
these two philosophers to combat the implications of their own teleological views for the prospect of Jewish national awakening. Other nations,
Krochmal claims, have advanced limited and particularistic notions of
the divine; they therefore remained chained within Herderian organicism,
allowed only one appearance on the world stage. But the Jews, by virtue
of their abstract monotheistic faith—which is not dependent on a place,
civic life, or any other earthly precondition—have a unique bond with
the purely spiritual and are therefore blessed with reoccurring cycles of
national revival. As Jews, Krochmal maintains, "[T]he three-period cycle...
was duplicated and triplicated with us, and... with the completion of the
period withering away and vanishing, there always emerged a new and
reviving spirit; and if we fell, we arose and were fortified, and did not
abandon our God."[30] The Jews are not outside or beyond history, not free
from the dynamic of growth and decay; but each time they go through

a cycle, a transcendental force blasts the biological rules of history and inspires them to begin a new odyssey of national life. The vulnerability of worldly, social existence and institutions is ultimately not inimical to the Jews, since their unencumbered spirit is interwoven with an eternal, universal force. Krochmal's theory is an important attempt to heed the hazards of teleology and escape its implications for the Jews. But it does so at a high price: it eschews the possibility of a humanly induced break in history, and establishes monotheistic metaphysics and heightened spirituality as the lasting and constitutive elements of the Jews as a nation. As we shall see, this refusal to admit voluntaristic leaps in time, and the equation of spirituality and nationhood, were precisely what the Zionists, as virile and natural political actors, were forced to question.[31]

The two meta-narratives of the nineteenth century—expanding universalism and organic nationalism—presented history as having a skeleton, an underlying structure that provides pregiven function and location to the flesh, the actual, flowing events. In modernity, this skeleton of history must be deciphered by the reflective mind and serve as the foundation for action or inaction; it is a tribunal that separates meaningful deeds from vain attempts to cast reality against the march of time. These meta-narratives of secular temporality were potentially more deadly for the Jews' yearning for communal revival than their former messianic belief had been, since these narratives presented (sometimes with scientific assurance) views of history as teleological and unaffected even by divine intervention. It was no accident, then, that Zionism did not appear earlier in the century, in the heyday of teleology; this political movement signifies a dawn of a new era, the rise of a novel temporal consciousness that zoomed in on the formless nature of history and that enshrined the total malleability of human affairs.

Zionism and Sundered History

> *Yes, visions alone grip the souls of men. And anyone who does not know how to begin from them, may be an excellent, worthy, sober-minded person, even a philanthropist on a large scale; but he will not be a leader of men, and no trace of him will remain.*[32]

—Theodor Herzl, *Diary* (1896)

Around the turn of the century, when Zionism first emerged as a political movement, writers of very different intellectual stripes began to reject teleological concepts and voice the notion of a rent in history. For "Nietzschean" Zionists, the rupture in history expressed itself in the dissolution of one configuration of Jewish identity and the opportunity and need for creating a new one. Zionism and the evolving Hebrew culture answered the sense of meaninglessness and morbidity that came with the decline of Jewish religion and tradition. For this school, redemption was an individual affair, calling for creative and even idiosyncratic ways of forming the self within a new, secular cultural context. Socialist Zionists, in contrast, saw the rupture in history represented by the economic and social sphere. In this reading, a specific historical stage of capitalism rendered the integration of Jews into European society impossible, since they had become a surplus population that constituted a burden to others. An amelioration of the Jewish predicament could not be achieved simply by a change of occupations, locations within Europe, or even emigration to North America; rather, what was needed was a planned, collective action that would change the territory and economic foundations of Jewish life, and consequently the totality of the community's social existence.

We may say, then, that Zionism involved a singular mixture of Nietzschean and Marxian themes; its success depended on both a metamorphosis and conscious reshaping of the self, and the inauguration of new economic and social conditions. In clarifying this dual notion of rupture, I will examine the works of two prominent Zionist writers. The first is Micha Joseph Berdyczewski (1865-1921), widely considered to be among the chief founders of contemporary Hebrew literature and the writer who gave it a modernist hue. As one commentator rightly observed, the importance of Berdyczewski's thinking "in the development of the Zionist pioneering ethos exceeds that of any other Hebrew author."[33] The second is Dov-Ber Borochov (1881-1917), one of the most important thinkers of early Socialist Zionism, whose ideological vision also significantly influenced the Labor leaders who founded the State of Israel.[34] Both writers expressed the theme of sundered history, particularly in works written around the turn of the century. As such, these works celebrate on both the individual and collective levels the themes of historical discontinuity, the openness of human reality, and the urgency for action.

"For every people," writes Berdyczewski, "nationality [or national culture] is the only treasure that contains human virtues. It is where the individual finds assurance for his actions and it is the necessary guardian of his [cultural] possessions. But with us, the individual perceives in nationality everything that opposes [the aspirations of] his heart."[35] For other nations, he explains, culture is an evolving whole, modified by circumstances and shifting needs; it is the realm in which the past is continuously reinterpreted, affirmed, and criticized, thus allowing individuals to respond to the challenges of the present. Moreover, national cultures lionize the distinct attributes and experiences of their peoples— their myths and stories, guiding values and spiritual quests, models of character and emotional fabric, attachment to landscape and environment—and tend to de-emphasize religion, especially when the latter has universalist orientation and appeal. The Jews, Berdyczewski felt, had cultivated a national culture that remained lifeless, extolling the frozen tenets of religion as its chief foundation. "For two thousand years we did not have a present at all. One long past engulfed us, a past devoid of a present or a future."[36]

For religious Jews, the talmudic texts are a point of origin with absolute priority over the present; they are wholly accessible to the contemporary mind, the only venue to illuminate the perplexities of here and now. The repetitive probing of the Talmud is performed not so much to provide new insights about the ancient texts, not even to adapt them to the present. Rather, learning allows the student to immerse himself in the text until "its words and reasoning seem to be his own." The ritualistic reading of the old truths day after day "is a crucial step towards their reaffirmation."[37] But for the modern Jew who ponders how to integrate into civil society—wondering what clothes to wear, which holidays to observe, what food to eat—this reciting of the past has become a temporal labyrinth, says Berdyczewski. "The writers of every nation and language begin their life in the present, and are gradually progressing towards the past. This is like a tower that is wide at the bottom and becomes narrow towards its head. The present is the foundation and the past is the roof. But the opposite is true for us. We will begin from the past and end in the present, and most often we will get lost and become weary midway and will not get to the present at all."[38] The authority of the past prevents adaptability and rejuvenation, excluding individuals from having an impact on tradition, whether on its contents or on its future course.

The past's authority also leads to the continuous reproduction of a certain type of self. Nietzsche famously claimed that "the Jews were a priestly nation of *ressentiment par excellence*, possessing an unparalleled genius for popular morality."[39] Berdyczewski, who read Nietzsche thoroughly, seems to agree with this statement, arguing that the Jew is still characterized by excessive morality and spirituality, a lack of earthliness and manliness, the repression of instincts and feelings, and too great a distance from nature and aesthetic values. Many Jews, asserts Berdyczewski, think that "they realize the sense of national duty that lives in their hearts by preserving what has been transmitted to them by their forebears." In this way, Jews have become "*slaves of spirituality*, people without the habit of approaching life and the world around them in a natural way."[40] Christianity may also have similar repercussions, but in the eyes of Jews like Berdyczewski, the European is at the same time a citizen with a voice, an individual exposed to a blooming national culture, an independent agent in a free economy. In all of these spheres of life, non-Jewish Europeans opened domains of individual action and development that mitigated the Judeo-Christian slave morality/mentality. The Jew, in contrast, epitomizes for Berdyczewski the European malaise of morbidity and hatred of life that Nietzsche unmasked. The modern Jew must therefore view the diasporic past as a cohesive, tainted whole—and reject it in toto. "Our soul is full of bitterness towards the past," writes Berdyczewski, "against all those who left us their own beliefs and thoughts. Our soul is burning in conjoining the past into one whole element, one that stands against our life and its foundations."[41]

In developing this consciousness of a temporal rupture, Berdyczewski was rebelling against the writer Ahad Ha'am (Asher Tzvi Ginsberg), who at the turn of the century was considered the most prominent Zionist theorist. Ahad Ha'am embraced the notion of Jewish cultural renewal, but thought that such a project would be meaningful only if the fundamental spirit of Judaism were preserved and further elaborated. A radical departure from the past would leave Jews atomized, confused, and without an anchor. Ahad Ha'am even wrote a disparaging essay ridiculing "our Nietzscheans." Certainly, he writes there, the Jews must embrace the idea of an *Übermensch*, but such an individual should be true to the Jewish tradition, embodying its ethical values in their highest form. We may be correct in speculating, he continues, that "Nietzsche himself, if he had a Hebraic taste, would have changed his moral criteria. While still presenting the overman as the end in himself, he [Nietzsche] would have ascribed to this overman very different characteristics: the strengthening of the moral faculties, the overcoming of the bestial instinct, the search for justice and truth in thought and in action, and a world war against lies and evil."[42] Giving a paradoxical twist to the *Genealogy of Morals*, Ahad Ha'am claims that the Jewish *Übermensch* is therefore the *tzadik*, the moral saint.

In Berdyczewski's view, Ahad Ha'am's judgment was off course. The latter forged an untenable concept of national identity, since it was grounded in an essentialist and monolithic depiction of the Jewish tradition as centered on an intensified moral consciousness and the rejection of self-assertion. Ahad Ha'am was unable to see that a merely secularized version of the diasporic culture would be not enough to energize a national revival, and that moral saints cannot be founders and settlers, even on a limited scale. To be sure, Berdyczewski also recognized that his generation was doomed to live with ambivalence, with "a split in the heart," as he famously coined it.[43] The tradition was too near, its allure not yet wholly overcome. The Jew was at a strange junction, a temporal vacuum where the past had ended but the future was still unknown. "We don't have a sky on an earth,"[44] says Berdyczewski, no fixed hook to pull us toward the future, no foundation to ground us in the past. The temporal experience of Zionism could therefore lead to confusion and paralysis, feelings humans encounter on realizing that history is undetermined and malleable to their wills and imaginations. The answer to these feelings, according to Berdyczewski, is not to find a middle ground, to change one's geographic location and remain the same person morally, but to overcome the trepidation and stand up for the moment.

> This hour we are facing is not like yesterday, not like what came before. All the grounds and conditions at home and outside that we lived by have collapsed. Those long nights have ended, and instead new days

and conditions have emerged. And the fear in our hearts is not for nothing, since we are no longer standing on the main road. We have arrived at a point where two worlds collide: To be or to vanish! To be the last Jews or the first Hebrews.[45]

Berdyczewski's Hebrews would display a novel combination of the ancient and the new, a union whose imprints were to become evident in the Zionist ethos. First, Berdyczewski was among the first to revive and glorify biblical legends of self-sacrifice and courage (e.g., Samson), and stories of Jewish resistance to the Romans during and after the destruction of the Second Temple (e.g., Masada).[46] The fascination of people like Ben-Gurion with Joshua, the biblical military leader who conquered the land of Israel, was a continuation of this revival.[47] Second, Berdyczewski married the heroic, ancient ethos with contemporary Nietzschean notions. For him, the creative will is the highest human attribute, and by allowing its expression we affirm life and realize our personal autonomy: "The will to live characterizes every being and is the essence of every living creature. There is no life without will, without aspiration, and without expansion."[48] Will is the wish to grow, to become something that we are not; it introduces a perpetual experience of lack and aspiration. To be sure, says Berdyczewski, the Jews have always cultivated a sound will, which allowed them to preserve their religious identity and re-enact the past. But this will measured itself by its ability to obey outer commands; it demanded the negation of the self. The new will of the Jew should be re-directed toward self-formation, and growth should be redefined according to an individually chosen principle. Berdyczewski argues that personal growth should be seen aesthetically, as the creative shaping of the emotional and spiritual material of the self. "We perceive the moral question of freedom and slavery," he writes, "not in a rational fashion, but in an artistic and poetic one. Surely, the uncarved marble that changes naturally is freer than the one that bears the imprints of an artist...; but exactly because of its shape, the latter acquires true, internal freedom. The moral power of genuine man is only the power of a creator, a creator in soul and spirit, a creator in deeds and their arrangement."[49] Zionism offers a grand and exciting opportunity for the self, since it means the formation of not only individual identity, but also a new habitat: independent political institutions and civic experience, national language and culture, reunion with the land and a bond to nature. By combining the biblical spirit of courage and dignity with aesthetic creativity, modern Jews can realize their humanity: they can introduce something heroic and novel to the world, something that "did not exist in the same shape and stamp."[50]

This sense of omnipotence allows the Zionist to welcome the rent in history. In contrast to the rule-governed notion of time—whether in line with Herderian organic development or with Kantian linearism— Berdyczewski demands the recognition of the openness of history, its responsiveness to human deeds and aspirations. "They say, if we believe in the sciences, that causal laws [in human affairs] rule similarly to natural laws, and who can therefore hope to alter them?" But this notion of historical causality is the archenemy of the Zionist, teleology his foe. Change in history is brought about by individuals, by people "working with the people and the nation, within its language, as the artist will do to the material at hand." These people, he continues, "are the heroes of deeds and thought, they are the ones who force society, who bend the direction of things."[51] Observing the dynamic of historical change, we comprehend that time has no underlying structure and necessity working within it, but rather is composed of continuity and discontinuity, including moments in which events can be grasped and molded. Accordingly, human life cannot be perceived only as a continuum of interrelated, homogeneous time units. "One moment could contain a whole life, one deed and one significant phrase could be equal to many deeds and many phrases; one great hour in life could be equivalent to a person's entire existence."[52] This view of time, we may say, fosters a consciousness of urgency, an eagerness to seize the moment. The Jews—who made patience and procrastination their national traits, who suffered from an elongated repression of instincts—must now heal themselves by allowing their inner forces to erupt freely. "The conquest of the land [of Israel] certainly did not come through patience," reminds Berdyczewski. The making of the Jew into an earthly political being involves "a complete change and radical new beginning; and it is the nature of change not to be patient, it is the nature of change to reject and conquer truly."[53] Opportunities come and go, decisive crossroads may be missed by those entangled in the dream of tradition; Zionists must illuminate the potential for radical departure hidden in the moment, cultivating a will that interposes in history swiftly and unmercifully.

The sense of Jews being at a decisive historical juncture also animates the works of Borochov, who grappled with articulating a new conception

of Marxism compatible with the temporal experience of Zionism. As a
Labor Zionist, he directed his intellectual efforts not so much at rejecting the Jewish tradition and the identity it enshrined as at confronting
social theories that could have deemed Zionism illegitimate and irrational
from a historical perspective. One of his first targets was the teleological
notion of time, especially the belief in (dialectical) progress, which most
Marxists accepted. Borochov believed that, while other nations might
hold such convictions, for the Jews progress was a dangerous chimera:
"We do not rely on progress; we know that its over-pious proponents
inflate its achievements out of all proportion. Progress is an important
factor in the rapid development of technology, science, perhaps even the
arts, but certainly [also] in the development of neurosis, hysteria, and
prostitution. It is too soon to speak about the moral progress of nations,
of the termination of that destructive, national egoism. Progress is the
double-edged sword; if the good angel within man advances, the Satan
within him advances too."[54]

For Borochov, one may say, the Jew is the best reader of omens. As
marginal and dispensable, he is the first to experience the ominous European ambience that further developed later in the twentieth century.
Jews in particular could no longer think in teleological and determin-
istic ways, aspiring to be integrated into a European nation state or to
become part of a cosmopolitan human community. Borochov believed
that anti-Semitism was unavoidable, since it served economic interests; he
understood expulsions of Jews from Western countries such as England
(1290) and France (1306) mainly in functional terms. As for modernity, Borochov heeded Marx's view that the Jewish middle class would
fulfill its historical role by enhancing cross-national trade and financing
the first stages of mechanized capitalism; but unlike Marx, he believed
in the importance of national differences and identifications, predict-
ing that the Jews would constitute a growing economic threat to the
evolving, local middle classes in Eastern Europe. Similarly, he reasoned,
as industrialization and mass production advance in countries such as
Poland and Russia, and machines replace workers, the lower strata of
the Jewish community will gradually become superfluous and the local
proletariat—their potential competitors rather than comrades—would reject them. Jews never succeeded in becoming a part of the workforce in
heavy industry, and even in light industry and unskilled jobs their position was uncertain. For Borochov, then, the advent of capitalism meant

the deterioration of the Jew as worker, trader, and banker, engendering the eruption of ethnic malice.

Borochov encouraged Jews, especially those committed to socialism, to think in national terms of their own and eschew the empty slogans of equal citizenship and universalism. In common with Austro-Marxists such as Karl Renner, Borochov argued that "the national question must be considered more deeply and honestly; it is imperative to break once and for all with unfounded prejudices. We must understand that class consciousness cannot develop normally unless the national problem, in whatever form it may exist, has been solved."[55] Political independence is a precondition for the victory of socialism in any given group, since national and ethnic divisions tend to overshadow conflicts among classes. The quest for collective identity must be answered before material concerns can take precedence; struggle over the means of production develops only in well-defined social units. To join the socialist revolution, then, the Jews must possess a territory of their own, self-governing bodies, and a distinct language and culture (all of which Borochov designates as "conditions of production"). After 1905, Borochov strove to demonstrate (in essays such as "Our Platform") that this process of forming independent conditions of production would be wholly *stychic*; that is, a spontaneous and unintended consequence of the material predicament of the Jews in the *Galut* (Diaspora). While the early Borochov also mentions the external forces driving the Jews out of Europe, his conception of historical transformation highlights the role of human volition. This conviction is epitomized in his concept of "therapeutic" change, which he contrasts with the "evolutionary" one.[56]

In the evolutionary type of change, events unfold gradually, employing forces that are immanent in a given social unit. In this notion of formation, the present contains the seeds of the future, and there is no need to "obtain assistance from any special means, but rather to shoulder the development of those forces that brought about the existing situation." In the transition to socialism, this means that "everything that supports the rapid maturation of capitalism and the opposition of class interests within it brings the problem to its ultimate resolution."[57] In such circumstances, human agency has the limited role of identifying the progressive elements in society and promoting them by intellectual critique, forging class consciousness and alliances, establishing political parties, and so on. There is no need to picture a global, detailed blueprint of action: the communist vision serves only as a regulative idea, and intervention is determined according to the internal dynamic of the existing socioeconomic order and the specific developments in society and the market. In the evolutionary model, emancipation requires the ability for acute observation of the present, not the capacity to dream and actualize the nonexistent.

The second type of social change is called for in "pathological situations," situations lacking any corrective elements in their present configurations. In such cases an anomaly exists, one that "is born not from the [natural] growth of society, but from destructive, external pressures. The solution to the impasse lies in healing, that is, in joining means aimed at a thorough extinction of the causes and forces that brought about the pain." This healing demands rapid external intervention, and "should always bring to life new forces that have not existed before and that would not have appeared by themselves."[58] Therapy (or healing) is not the art of amending the given, but a radical act that destroys what exists promptly and decisively. Here, one cannot defer to empirical facts, since the nature of correction demands a break from them; the healer is characterized not by strategic play in the present, but by the ability to enliven the imagination, master unexpected powers, and render novel images palpable. Social therapy, argues Borochov, is an "enterprise" whereby the human will successfully establishes an all-engulfing, new mode of existence based on an inspiring ideal. This ideal should "sharpen the interested will, incite it to action, and prevent it from being… aloof from anything it encounters in objective reality." The *"combative [boevovo]* value"[59] of the ideal is determined according to its ability to induce an ethos of forcefulness in individuals and to energize their confrontation with the environment. Those inspired by the combative ideal should act in concert, their actions being "organized according to a given and predetermined plan"[60] that would calculate necessary means and resources, and leave as little room as possible for actual conditions to intervene in the erection of a new social order. With Borochov, "the plan" becomes a necessary means of intervention, a weapon to be inserted in the hiatus of sundered history and to steer events to a new course.

Zionism belongs to the second, therapeutic type of social change. For Borochov, those Jews who see Zionism as a mass movement of evolutionary nature rightly conclude that "under no circumstances could Zionism become a reality, that is an absolute utopia."[61] They search in vain for a tradition of audacious political deeds among the Jews, and all they find is a people who have made adaptability into an art of living, and who are reluctant to embark on an unfamiliar course. But we live in an era where today is a poor indicator of tomorrow, argues Borochov. Zionism would be possible once the Jews realized that discontinuity in history was both possible and necessary: "*The Zionist movement is one of the clearest examples of a therapeutic movement for which the ideal is something totally new and separate from the existing orders of life.*"[62] Zionism necessitated a change of landscape and climate, of familiar vocations and careers, of language and culture, of comfort and material conditions; it would succeed only if Jews deliberately distanced themselves from the *totality* of their current ways, if they welcomed the destruction. In the movement's beginnings, only a small number of people could withstand such personal sacrifice. Consequently, according to Borochov, in Zionism, "[T]he individual element plays a huge role; for us it is not the quantity of members that is important. Rather, we desire that they should possess a high quality of consciousness and devotion. They will be the pioneering foundation of the movement."[63] This avant-garde elite must be able to envision a fictional future and give it absolute priority over adverse empirical conditions; it must methodically translate into reality a detailed political and economic plan that lacks even an anchor. Borochov thus demands that the heroic figure in Judaism, the person willing to die in preserving the integrity of his or her faith in God, be displaced by a new type of hero, one characterized by a willingness to accept "sacrifices and the danger of personal extinction"[64] for the sake of the nation's cause.

Berdyczewski and Borochov represent opposing poles of Zionist thought. The former sought redemption through the aesthetic transformation of the self, the latter through the erection of a new socioeconomic reality; Berdyczewski was concerned with identity and meaning, Borochov with material existence and social justice. Despite these differences, their visions were complementary in practice, since the success of Zionism hinged upon a novel fusion of a creative notion of the self with the quest for collective therapy, upon presenting normative metamorphosis as an individual achievement that also fosters grand collective action. In fact, even from a theoretical viewpoint, Borochov and Berdyczewski shared much more than first meets the eye. They concurred in the temporal ontology they advanced and in their celebration of similar themes of sundered history: the amorphous nature of social life, the opportunity for transfiguration offered at unique historical junctures, the inadequacy of reform and other gradual processes, the valorization of risk and discontinuity, the power of the will to begin something unprecedented, and finally, the decisive role of selected individuals in revolutionary times. To be sure, Zionism was and is a modernist movement, aspiring to erect a nation state that possesses the nexus of institutions characterizing this body since the sixteenth and seventeenth centuries. But if the Western European nation states that emerged from that period did so in piecemeal fashion, with monarchies and other central institutions gradually imposing their authority on pre-existing populations, in Zionism there existed at first neither an organizational foundation nor a geographically concentrated population to undertake such a project. Hence, in establishing political, legal, military, economic, and other institutions, as well as in bringing people to Palestine and making them citizens, the Zionist endeavor required a temporal consciousness of discontinuity and a celebration of the inaugurating "event" for its realization. The establishment of the State of Israel may have been an exemplary attempt at fulfilling a modernist dream through a post-modern historical imagination.

Conclusion

> It is here that imagination must be ruthless with reality, because what is real and now is least fit for dwelling.
>
> —Eppie Zorea, Jericho

The temporal consciousness of Zionism had important consequences, not only for the emergence of the movement, but also for its future ideology and political practice. This was already evident when the first political leaders of the country preserved the revolutionary temporal imagination of early Zionism, professing that social reality is wholly open to willful intervention and is formed according to visionary human design. "The expectation of stychic process is nothing but hypocritical apology for impotence and weakness. It is not fatalistic destiny that governs history, and life is not merely a game of blind forces. The intentional and forsighted intervention of the active, creative, and conscious will in history is one of the elements effecting the stychic process."[65] In this Ben-Gurionian vista, obstacles are either minor facts to be ignored or challenges that call for higher and more vigorous action. Indeed, Zionism became increasingly dependent on and enamored with the ability of human beings to shape the existing geographical and demographic environments according to their will, to impose new, tangible "facts" where none had existed. But Zionism could never be sure how long this transformative ability would last, and it preserves even today the dual belief that humans can craft events in light of their interests and dreams and that they must act with urgency before the window of opportunity is slammed shut by an unexpected gale. This duality, symptomatic of the consciousness of sundered history, helped Zionism become arguably the most successful revolution of this century. But it also had some less laudable effects. Patterns of thinking and acting formed during the childhood of the movement became constitutive of its ethos, functioning as an inured foundation in its approach to the world. Many Zionists have gradually discovered that their source of strength is also their source of malaise, that (as is often the case) what was crucial in the formation of the movement became problematic later on.

I would like to conclude with a few remarks on the troubling political aspects of the Zionist conception of sundered history.[66] We may begin with an almost mythic incident from a relatively recent history of Palestine, one that reflects the duality of Zionist temporal consciousness.

> On 10 December 1936, a "conquering group" [*kvutzat kibush*] came... and within one day built a wall, surrounded by a barbed wire fence, which enclosed an area (about 40 by 40 yards) that included lodging cabins, a public mess hall, and a tower with a spotlight. Thus, within a few hours, with the help of a large manpower force... an entire settlement was established, ready to defend itself against Arab attack.[67]

Between 1936 and 1939, fifty-four additional settlements were established in Palestine using this method, called in Hebrew *Homa Umigdal* (the Tower and the Wall). The operation was meant to secure the hold of Jews in areas where their claim to sovereignty was in question, before the British plan for the partition of Palestine could be implemented. (It never was.) Zionists used this strategy because they rejected limits on action (legal, political, and at times even moral), because physical edifices were believed to be incomparably more potent than words, and because of the perception that shifting political circumstances might render future

actions unfeasible. More that sixty years later (March 1997), when the
Likud government wanted to ensure Israeli control over the areas surrounding Jerusalem prior to any further implementation of the Oslo
agreement, it accepted a plan to swiftly build a neighborhood on Har
Homa (Wall Mountain). In both cases, the expansion strategy generated
a profound crisis in the relations between Jews and Arabs. In Israel the
enterprise of building is often associated with patriotism, since it is the
most tangible way to change the landscape, both physically and demo-
graphically. Building is an act of claiming ownership, not on behalf of
the individual but for the community; it marks the borders of state territory. Hence, even architecture has tended to follow political exigencies
rather than aesthetic considerations. Some may argue that conceptions
of history and architectural projects are unrelated, but in the State of
Israel a building's location, contour, materials, and hour of construction
often reveal how an urgent relationship to time begets a conquering attitude toward space.

But the theme of *binyan* (building) vibrates in Zionist thought and
practice in an even deeper and more inclusive sense. The whole project
of bringing the Israeli state into actuality and erecting social and political
institutions is described by its proponents in terms of leaving corporeal
facts behind, of granting mental pictures priority over adverse empirical conditions. The Hebrew language is very revealing in this respect,
since "to build" (*livnot*) covers a wide spectrum of human actions. "The
Land of Israel will be ours," says Ben-Gurion, "not when the Turks,
the British, or the next peace council allow this and ratify a diplomatic
agreement—but when we, the Jews, build [*nivneh*] it.... The aim of our
revival effort is the building of the Land [*binyan ha'aretz*]."[68] Building
as an activity and metaphor appealed to the Zionist imagination, partly
since it echoes and re-enacts its founding, temporal experience: building
involves a rupture in existing conditions, demands audacity in re-molding
the environment, and epitomizes the ability of humans to overcome emptiness by rendering themselves subservient to a larger, concrete goal. For
Zionism, indeed, politics is *doing*: it demands one more neighborhood,
one more factory, one more brigade; it is the art of using human and
natural resources to form and benefit the Jewish community and state.
Ben-Gurion, the architect (so to speak) of the Jewish state, formulated
this conception of politics in the second decade of this century, and it

remains the predominant view, shared by both main political movements within Israel.[69]

Zionist politics, despite its republican nature and championing of the common good, is therefore hardly Aristotelian. First, it devalues the place of words in political intercourse, and expresses a mistrust of any human reality that is founded principally on language.[70] For Zionism, language is ephemeral: it is emblematic of the entire diasporic tradition and way of life, which were founded on a Book and the layers of its interpretation, on the conviction that words can create a shared world of meanings and practices, and on the temporal continuation and stability of this world regardless of frequent dislocations. The Zionists' temporal revolution was a rejection of this linguistically based world, an attempt to replace the waning power of words by mooring identity to a re-enchanted space. Hence, the main (and debilitating) internal conversation and debate in the Israeli public sphere has focused on the borders and significance of space, and not on the meaning of contemporary Jewish identity and culture or the civic norms and concepts of justice underlying social life. In fact, the current crises of collective and moral identities in the State of Israel partly spring from a mistrust in language—without which neither a shared identity nor a consensual notion of justice could be articulated and sustained. This makes Zionism incompatible with the Aristotelian tradition in a second respect: while it may lionize the *halutz* (pioneer) and is not oblivious to moral dilemmas, the success of Zionism is measured less by the excellence and complexity of the good life it offers to individuals than by its tangible and lasting evidence of collective human action. In *The Politics*, Aristotle admonishes against conceiving greatness in numerical and spatial terms, against being beguiled by the human genius associated with augmenting the concrete. "There is nothing in common between the builder and the dwelling-house he builds; the builder's skill is simply a means and the dwelling-house is the end. On this it follows that, if states need property [as a dwelling-house needs building tools and workmen to use them], property nevertheless is not part of the state... the state is an association of equals, and only of equals; and its object is the best and highest life possible."[71] Greatness is tricky, Aristotle claims, since it should be measured by the invisible: the *eudaimonia* of individual citizens who share a plural, public life. The Zionists' longing for the tangible meant that the individual was increasingly harnessed to the urgent endeavor of state building, encouraged to cultivate the various skills of *homo faber* imperative for this collective task. This drift has diminished the capacity of individuals to achieve their personal excellence, since their identification with the state and its reason has often conflicted with their own public exercise of practical reason and their ongoing, critical reflection on the good.

Practicality, however, does not mean lack of imagination. Similarly to *homo faber*, the maker of the human artifice, the Zionist builder begins the formation of the state from abstract plans that have little to support them in social reality. As Hannah Arendt explains, for *homo faber*, "[T]he actual work of fabrication is performed under the guidance of a model in accordance with which the object is constructed."[72] By insisting on the priority (both in potency and significance) of the mind over reality, and by molding matter in a creative and complex fashion, human beings become omnipotent: they create a world in their own image. "*Homo faber* is indeed a lord and master," argues Arendt, "not only because he is the master or has set himself up as the master of all nature, but because he is master of himself and his doings."[73] The ability to generate a new environment and to live with and within our physical and social creations grounds us and establishes spaces we can claim as our own; these fabrications (buildings, social institutions, identities) boost, in turn, our self-regard as potent beings. Hence, as a fabricator of social, not merely physical, reality, *homo faber* must always be on guard against hubris. The capacity to dwell in grand, self-generated spaces stifles the consciousness of imperfection and frailty, the awareness that prods humans into opening themselves to the experiences and teachings of others.

But the self-perception of potent creators harbors another problematic aspect. According to Arendt, the "element of violation and violence is present in all fabrication, and *homo faber*, the creator of human artifice, has always been a destroyer of nature."[74] The repercussions of this violence vary according to the sphere of application. The artisan, when making a chair or a table, is subject to the qualities of the wood. The designer of a house has extensive freedom in envisioning the architectonic model and changing the landscape, but must still negotiate with existing geography. The politician, however, has few visible or fixed constraints on his pre-existing models. The limits of what can be achieved by political means are rather blurred, since humans can be coaxed, shifted, ignored, manipulated, silenced, and so on. The political model, as Borochov notes in discussing therapeutic movements, does not necessarily evolve gradually out of social reality, nor is it in dialogue with the individuals and communities inhabiting its space. And the more imaginary the character of the social model—the more focused on the novelty and beauty of its own scheme, the more driven by the urgent exigencies of the initiators—the more violence toward oneself and others it can engender. With this understanding of both the novelty and danger of translating the imagination into political praxis, it is hard to regard Herzl's confessional words as merely of biographical interest. *"Vieleicht sind es übrigens gar keine praktischen Ideen, und ich mache mich zum Gespött der Leute, mit denen ich Ernst rede. Und ich wandle nur im Roman?"*[75]

NOTES

This essay has benefited, to a very considerable extent, from the comments of the following individuals: Yoav Peled, Natalie Oman, Janet Benton, and David Mayers.

1. I have explored these issues at length in my dissertation, "The Modern Self in the Labyrinth: Theories of Entrapment in the Works of Weber, Freud, and Foucault" (McGill University, 1996). For a general overview of the changes in European historical and political consciousness around the turn of the century, see Jan Romein, *The Watershed of Two Eras: Europe in 1900* (Middletown, Conn.: Wesleyan University, 1978).

2. On the plurality of temporal ontologies in the State of Israel, see Robert Pine, "Jewish Ontologies of Time and Political Legitimation in Israel," in Henry J. Rutz, ed., *The Politics of Time* (Washington, D.C.: American Anthropological Association, 1992), pp. 150-170. My use of the term "temporal ontology" was inspired in part by Pine. In any event, the temporal element of Zionism that will be explored in this essay is "negative" in nature (i.e., pointing to the openness of human existence in time). To this one must add another positive, temporal element that has been essential to Zionism: The valorization of the distant, Hebraic past and a cyclic view of time. According to this view, the healing of the Jews demands a return to the territory they left many centuries ago, the recovery of their ancient language, and the revival of an independent and virile spirit of citizenship. The correction (*tikun*) of the diasporic predicament necessitates a move backward to the point of origin where authenticity and wholeness

reside. Without the notion of cyclicality and the redemption associated with it, Zionism would not have been conceivable as a viable ideology or successful as a mass movement. This positive, temporal aspect of Zionism complimented the first negative aspect, but throughout its history Zionism often betrays a tension between them: while the negative element cherished action unbounded by external reality or by former human experience, the second channeled human deeds to a recovery of the past and suggested that all human effort should be directed solely to this mission and evaluated accordingly. I intend to explore the cyclical, temporal element of Zionism in a future essay. For studies of the Zionists' attempt to recover the prerabbinic, Hebraic past, and to reconstruct this past according to ideological needs in heroic mythologies, see Yael Zerubavel, *Recovered Roots: Collective Memory and the Making of Israeli National Tradition* (Chicago: University of Chicago, 1995); and Charles S. Liebman and Eliezer Don-Yehiya, *Civil Religion in Israel: Traditional Judaism and Political Culture in Israel* (Berkeley: University of California, 1983).

3. See, in particular, Martin Buber, *On Zion: The History of an Idea* (New York: Schocken, 1973); Nathan Rotenstreich, *Jews and German Philosophy: The Polemics of Emancipation* (New York: Schocken, 1984); and Nathan Rotenstreich, *Jewish Philosophy in Modern Times: From Mendelssohn to Rosenzweig* (New York: Holt, Rinehart & Winston, 1968). Ze'ev Sternhell's and Shlomo Avineri's writings are probably the ones most directly concerned with examining Zionism from the perspective of political philosophy. See Ze'ev Sternhell, *The Founding Myths of Israel: Nationalism, Socialism, and the Making of the Jewish State* (Princeton: Princeton, 1998); and Shlomo Avineri, *The Making of Modern Zionism: Intellectual Origins of the Jewish State* (New York: Basic Books, 1981). One should also mention here Yael Tamir's study of nationalism, which is in part inspired by the Israeli experience. See Yael Tamir, *Liberal Nationalism* (Princeton: Princeton, 1993).

4. Revisionist works on Zionist historiography include Gershon Shafir, *Land, Labor, and the Origins of the Israeli-Palestinian Conflict, 1882-1914* (Cambridge: Cambridge, 1989); Ilan Pappe, *The Making of the Arab-Israeli Conflict, 1947-1951* (New York: T.B. Tauris, 1994); and Benny Morris, *1948 and After: Israel and the Palestinians* (Oxford: Clarendon, 1990). The new Israeli historians have benefited from the contemporary literature on nationalism, especially interpretations that emphasize the place of invention and deliberate construction of national identities. See E.J. Hobsbawm, *Nations and Nationalism Since 1780* (Cambridge: Cambridge, 1990); E. Hobsbawn and R. Terence, eds., *The Invention of Tradition* (Cambridge: Cambridge, 1983); and Ernest Gellner, *Nation and Nationalism* (Ithaca, N.Y.: Cornell, 1983).

5. This line of interpretation has been formed in Israel with historians such as Ben-Zion Dinaburg and Yitzhak Baer. The latter, for example, writes that "the *Galut* (Diaspora) has returned to its starting point. It remains what

it always was: Political servitude, which must be abolished completely." See Yitzhak Baer, *Galut* (New York: Schocken, 1988), p. 118. Other relevant works include Yitzhak Baer, *Studies and Essays on the History of the Jewish People*, 2 vols. (Jerusalem: Historical Society of Israel, 1985); Ben-Zion Dinaburg, *The Struggle of Ages over Israel: From the Fall of Beitar till the Restoration* (Jerusalem: Bialik Institute, 1975); and Ben-Zion Dinaburg, *Turning Points in Modern Jewish History* (Jerusalem: Bialik Institute, 1971-1972). More recent historians in Israel are less driven by Zionist ideology, but they are nevertheless inclined to highlight the just cause of this movement rather than its colonial elements. See, for example, David Vital, *The Origins of Zionism* (Oxford: Oxford, 1975); and Walter Laqueur, *History of Zionism* (New York: Holt, 1972).

6. Gershom Scholem, *The Messianic Idea in Judaism* (New York: Schocken, 1971), p. 35.

7. Scholem, *Messianic Idea*, p. 10.

8. Scholem, *Messianic Idea*, p. 14.

9. Throughout their existence in the Diaspora, Jews have manifested considerable political adeptness, both in the internal organization of their communities and in their external relations with the relevant centers of power. Without their ability to establish vibrant and cohesive communities, and to ensure external recognition of their special status as both a part of the larger society and a distinct element, it is doubtful that Jews could have sustained their identity for so many centuries. While Jews were not politically independent in the Diaspora and mostly remained second-class citizens, they were often able to forge alliances and take part in the exercise of power. One should note, for example, periods of the Middle Ages when the Jews achieved a considerable degree of integration into the larger community, chiefly by relying on their economic power and by utilizing the maneuvering space opened by conflicts between the Church and local rulers. As urban dwellers, they obtained the rights of burghers, sometimes taking "full part in the life of their city, sometimes occupying municipal offices and contributing to the town's armed defense. In many medieval towns of Germany, France, Spain, and Italy, they were able to obtain full and equal citizenship." See David Biale, *Power and Powerlessness in Jewish History* (New York: Schocken, 1986), p. 63. A somewhat different account of the Jewish position in that period is given by H. Ben-Sasson, ed., *A History of the Jewish People* (Cambridge: Harvard, 1976), pt. 5.

10. Amos Funkenstein, *Perceptions of Jewish History* (Berkeley: University of California, 1993), p. 254. Yerushalmi, in his seminal work *Zakhor*, suggests that this indifference to temporality lies behind the striking absence of substantive historiography in Jewish culture of the Diaspora, a predicament that changed only during the nineteenth century. See Yosef Hayim Yerushalmi, *Zakhor: Jewish History and Jewish Memory* (Seattle: University of Washington, 1982).

11. Immanuel Kant, "Idea for a Universal History with a Cosmopolitan Intent," in Immanuel Kant, *Perpetual Peace and Other Essays*, trans. Ted Humphrey (Indianapolis: Hackett, 1985), p. 29.

12. Kant, *Perpetual Peace*, p. 124. Lyotard argues that in addition to the uniform temporality characterizing the plan of Nature, Kant also holds a diachronic conception of time that celebrates the political-historical "event" (*Begebenheit*). Nevertheless, one should remember that for Kant events are leaps in a predestined route rather than the inauguration of a new one. See J.F. Lyotard, "The Sign of History," in *The Lyotard Reader* (Oxford: Blackwell, 1989), pp. 393-411.

13. Whereas the "determinate judgment" (*bestimmende Urteilskraft*) "determines under universal transcendental laws furnished by understanding," the reflective judgment "only gives as a law from and to itself." In the latter case, the principles according to which we subsume data are not transcendentally pregiven, nor can they be inferred from external reality. See Immanuel Kant, *The Critique of Judgment*, trans. J.C. Meredith (Oxford: Oxford, 1973), pp. 18-19.

14. By the Highest Good, Kant means an ideal state characterized primarily by an inclusive, borderless ethical community, an internal predicament of human beings that is complemented by civil and international peace (i.e., the "highest political good"). For a discussion of these concepts, see Yirmiahu Yovel, *Kant and the Philosophy of History* (Princeton: Princeton, 1985).

15. Kant, "Idea for a Universal History," p. 125.

16. Kant, "Idea for a Universal History," p. 125. Kant, it should be noted, was especially critical of Judaism, viewing it as a religion that habituated obedience to external rules rather than promoting the inner, moral life of the individual. In this sense, Judaism is ahistorical, preserving frozen codes of observance and conduct rather than fostering the gradual march of the human race toward autonomy and rule by reason. This Kantian critique of Judaism had immense influence in Germany, and is echoed in Bruno Bauer's famous essay *Die Judenfrage* (1843). See Kant's *Religion Within the Limits of Pure Reason Alone* (New York: Harper & Row, 1960). For discussion of these issues, see Rotenstreich, *Jews and German Philosophy*.

17. Abraham Geiger, *Judaism and Its History* (London: University Press of America, 1985), p. 211.

18. Abraham Geiger, *Nachgelassene Schriften* (Berlin, 1875-1878), letter written on April 9, 1841. Quoted here from Micha Josef Berdyczewski, *Collected Essays of Micha Josef Berdyczewski* (Tel Aviv: Am Oved, 1954), p. 95. For a contemporary discussion of the Reform movement, see Michael Mayer, *Response to Modernity: A History of the Reform Movement in Judaism* (Oxford: Oxford, 1988).

19. Karl Marx, "On the Jewish Question," in Karl Marx, *Early Writings* (London: Penguin, 1974), p. 220.

20. Liah Greenfeld, *Nationalism: Five Roads to Modernity* (Cambridge: Harvard, 1992), shows that Marx's identification of the Jew with the capitalist system in general, and with money in particular, was expressed by many other influential Germans (e.g., Fries of Heidelberg and Wagner, p. 385). This insight is significant, since it implies that in embracing socialism the early Zionists were not only confronting questions of social justice, but were also attempting to cast off traditional stereotypes of the Jew. For a comprehensive study of the intellectual context in which Marx formulated his views, see also Julius Carlebach, *Karl Marx and the Radical Critique of Judaism* (London: Routledge, 1978).

21. Marx, "On the Jewish Question," p. 239.

22. Marx, "On the Jewish Question," p. 237.

23. Marx, "On the Jewish Question," p. 237. For a theoretical study of socialist Jews in Germany and their attitudes toward assimilation, see Robert Wistrich, *Socialism and the Jews: The Dilemmas of Assimilation in Germany and Austria-Hungary* (Rutherford, N.J.: Fairleigh Dickinson University, 1982).

24. J.G. Herder, *Metakritik zur Kritik der Reinen Vernunft* (Berlin: Afbau Verlag, 1955), p. 68. Quoted here from Reinhart Koselleck, *Futures Past* (Cambridge: MIT, 1985), p. 247.

25. "*Das kein Volk lange geblieben und bleiben konnte, was es war, das Jedes, wie jede Kunst und Wissenschaft, und was in der Welt nicht? Seine periode des Wachstums, der Blüte und der Abnachme gehabt; das jedwede dieser Veränderunden nur das Minimum von Zeit gedauret, was ihr auf dem Rade des Menschlichen Schicksals gegeben werden konnte—das endlich in der Welt keine zwei Augenblicke dieselben sind.*" Johann Gottfried Herder, "Auch Eine Philosophie," in *Sämtliche Werke* V (Hildescheim: Georg Olms, 1967), p. 504. Herder draws inconsistent conclusions from this position in discussing the fate of the modern Jews; in general, however, he did not foresee a Jewish national revival, suggesting that "all that was intended to be wrought [by the Jews] has probably been accomplished." Instead, the Jews should be integrated into existing European states: "A time will come when no person in Europe will inquire whether a man be a Jew or a Christian; as the Jews will equally live according to European laws, and contribute to the welfare of the state" (translation altered). See J.G. Herder, *Outlines of a Philosophy of History of Man* (New York: Bergman, 1800), pp. 335, 486. Herder's views of Judaism and the Jews are discussed by Paul L. Rose in *Revolutionary Antisemitism in Germany, from Kant to Wagner* (Princeton: Princeton, 1990), ch. 7. My own discussion of Herder has benefited from the work of F.M. Bernard, *Herder's Social and Political Thought: From Enlightenment to Nationalism* (Oxford: Clarendon, 1965).

26. G.W.F. Hegel, *The Philosophy of History* (New York: Dover, 1956), p. 53.

27. Hegel, *Philosophy of History*, p. 79.

28. According to Liah Greenfeld, when the category of the "people" begins to have meaning and a referent, nationalism has made a decisive inroad. See her introduction to Greenfeld, *Nationalism*, pp. 1-27.

29. For discussions of the relation between Krochmal on one hand, and Herder and Hegel on the other, see Rotenstreich, *Jewish Philosophy in Modern Times*, pt. 1; and Avineri, *Making of Modern Zionism*, ch. 1.

30. Nahman Krochmal, *Guide to the Perplexed of the Time* (Waltham, Mass.: Ararat, 1961), pp. 40-41. This book was first published in 1851, after Krochmal's death in 1840.

31. The influence of Krochmal's organic concept of nationality on Zionists such as Ahad Ha'am is very telling. For the latter, Zionism indeed became chiefly a cultural-ethnic project, an attempt of an elite to revive (by establishing a spiritual center in Palestine) the distinct moral consciousness (or feelings) of the Jewish people, and to adapt the tradition to a secular age. This quest to preserve the Jewish *Volksgeist* led Ahad Ha'am to question the political-practical orientation of Zionism. The values Ahad Ha'am saw as essential to the Jewish national spirit (such as the rejection of forceful means in human interaction and the sacredness of human life) were incompatible with the willful and urgent establishment of a nation state in Palestine. In other words, Zionist, organic nationalism posed a serious challenge to the activist and revolutionary strands of the movement. Commentators such as Sternhell, who present Zionism as just another instance of Herderian nationalism because it was inspired by the ethnic definition of nationhood common in Central and Eastern Europe, are therefore only partly correct. See *Founding Myths of Israel*, pp. 11-12. On Ahad Ha'am's organic nationalism, see Gideon Shimoni, *The Zionist Ideology* (Hanover, N.H.: Brandeis, 1995), pp. 108-113.

32. "*Ja, nur das phantastische ergreift die Menschen. Und wer damit nichts anzufangen weiss, der mag ein vortrefflicher braver und nüchterner Mann sein, und selbst ein Wohlthäter [sic] im grossen Stil,—führen wird die Menschen nicht, und es wir keine Spur von ihm bleiben*" (*Tagebücher*, 1896).

33. Ehud Luz, *Parallels Meet: Religion and Nationalism in the Early Zionist Movement, 1882-1904* (New York: Jewish Publication Society, 1985), p. 170.
Berdyczewski was born in the Russian Pale of Settlement, a descendant of a respected family of Hasidic rabbis. Despite his religious education, the young Berdyczewski was an avid reader of the emerging Hebrew literature, an interest that provoked his immediate environment and led to the collapse of his first marriage. Divorced, he emigrated to Germany in 1890, and lived there for most of his adult life. His studies at German universities exposed him to Western philosophy in general, and to Schopenhauer and Nietzsche in particular. Berdyczewski displays in his writings (and life story) the ambiguities of the Jewish life at the time, shifting from Yiddish to Hebrew and back, lionizing the creative

and autonomous individual while concomitantly expressing anguish over the collapse of the *shtetl*. During his life, Berdyczewski was well known as a gifted writer and an uncompromising critic of all the accepted schools and leading individuals: rabbinical Judaism, Haskala, Hibat Zion, Ahad Ha'am, Herzl, and so on. He became well known when he published (concomitantly) nine books of stories and essays near the turn of the century, expressing in these works modernist themes such as passion, longing for aesthetic experience, willpower, and ambivalence. But Berdyczewski's importance is only now recognized fully. Not only was his vast literary project a landmark in modern Hebrew literature, but the themes of his stories and essays seem to have been critical in articulating and shaping the emerging Zionist ethos (although he was not politically involved in that movement). For secondary literature on Berdyczewski, see Avner Holtzman, *Hakarat Panim: Essays of Micha Josef Berdyczewski* (Holon: Reshapim, 1993); Alan Mintz, *Banished from Their Father's Table: Loss of Faith and Hebrew Autobiography* (Bloomington: Indiana University, 1988); and David Ohana, "Zarathustra in Jerusalem," in D. Ohana and R. Wistrich, eds., *The Shaping of Israeli Identity: Myth, Memory, and Trauma* (London: Frank Cass, 1995), pp. 268-289. [Hebrew]

34. Dov-Ber Borochov was born in the Ukraine and grew up in Poltava. He was mostly self-educated, since like most Jews of his time he could not be admitted to a Russian university. His importance to the Zionist movement lay in his work as a politician and theoretician. In the former role, he was the founder of the Poalei Tzion party, which had a major role in shaping the Jewish Labor movement in Palestine (see note 51). He participated in a few Zionist congresses and lectured throughout Russia, Central Europe, and the United States. As a theorist, he not only introduced the marriage of socialism and Jewish nationalism, but also insisted on seeing the Jewish problem as fundamentally economic, and anti-Semitism as chiefly a symptom of material dependency and a distorted occupational structure. His many interests included philosophy, economics, linguistics, and statistics, all of which he examined from his particular position as a Zionist and a Jew. Between 1907 and 1917, Borochov lived in Central Europe and the United States. He returned to Russia at the start of the Bolshevik Revolution, but died soon after. For secondary literature, see Matityahu Mintz, *Modern Times, Modern Song: Ber Borochov 1914-1917* (Tel Aviv: Am Oved & Tel Aviv University, 1988); Allon Gal, *Socialist-Zionism: Theory and Issues in Contemporary Jewish Nationalism* (Cambridge, Mass.: Schenkman, 1973); Wistrich, *Socialism and the Jews*; Avineri, *Making of Modern Zionism*; and Jonathan Frankel, *Prophecy and Politics: Socialism, Nationalism, and the Russian Jews, 1862-1917* (Cambridge: Cambridge, 1981).

35. Berdyczewski, *Collected Essays*, p. 41 (my translation).

36. Berdyczewski, *Collected Essays*, p. 47.

37. Samuel C. Heilman, *The People of the Book* (Chicago: University of Chicago, 1983), pp. 65, 72. See also Pine, "Jewish Ontologies of Time," pp. 153-154.

38. Berdyczewski, *Collected Essays*, p. 37.

39. Friedrich Nietzsche, *On the Genealogy of Morals* (Cambridge: Cambridge, 1994), First Essay, sec. 16. For a general discussion about Nietzsche's place in modern Hebrew literature, see Menachem Brinker, "Nietzsche's Influence on Hebrew Writers of the Russian Empire," in B.G. Rosenthal, ed., *Nietzsche and Soviet Culture: Ally and Adversary* (Cambridge: Cambridge, 1994), pp. 393-413. For Nietzsche's influence on German Jewish writers, such as Stefan Zweig, Franz Werfel, Jakob Wessermann, and others, see Jacob Golomb, "Nietzsche and the Marginal Jews," in Jacob Golomb, ed., *Nietzsche and Jewish Culture*, Jacob Golomb, ed. (London: Routledge, 1997), pp. 158-192.

40. Berdyczewski, *Collected Essays*, p. 30. The idea that Zionists should regain their naturalness and manly strength was of course most pronounced in the writings of Max Nordau, the popular author of *Degeneration* (1892). George Mosse examined these aspects of Nordau's writings in George Mosse, *Confronting the Nation: Jewish and Western Nationalism* (Hanover, N.H.: Brandeis, 1993).

41. Berdyczewski, *Collected Essays*, p. 41.

42. Ahad Ha'am, *Collected Essays of Ahad Ha'am* (Tel Aviv: Dvir, 1947), p. 155. For a recent study of Ahad Ha'am, see Steven Zipperstein, *Elusive Prophet: Ahad Ha'am and the Origins of Zionism* (Berkeley: University of California, 1993).

43. Berdyczewski, *Collected Essays*, p. 63.

44. Berdyczewski, *Collected Essays*, p. 41.

45. Berdyczewski, *Collected Essays*, p. 29.

46. For a discussion of these themes in Berdyczewski, and of their significance for the Zionist attitude toward the use of force, see Anita Shapira, *Land and Power: The Zionist Resort to Force, 1881-1948* (New York: Oxford, 1992), ch. 1.

47. Ben-Gurion's preoccupation with biblical heroes and his special relationship with biblical scholars fostered the popularization of biblical studies in Israel. Michael Keren discusses this phenomenon in his *Ben-Gurion and the Intellectuals: Power, Knowledge, and Charisma* (Dekalb, Ill.: Northern Illinois University, 1983).

48. Berdyczewski, *Collected Essays*, p. 17.

49. Berdyczewski, *Collected Essays*, p. 349.

50. Berdyczewski, *Collected Essays*, p. 41.

51. Berdyczewski, *Collected Essays*, p. 61.

52. Berdyczewski, *Collected Essays*, p. 344.

53. Berdyczewski, *Collected Essays*, p. 87.

54. Dov-Ber Borochov, *Class Struggle and the Jewish Nation* (New Brunswick, N.J.: Transaction, 1984), p. 36.

55. Borochov, *Class Struggle*, p. 69.

56. Borochov's main influence on Socialist Zionism was his overall conceptual scheme presented above, which saw nationalism and socialism as compatible and emphasized the importance of developing an independent Jewish economy and a large working class. Yet, Borochov's legacy is varied. Groups on the Left of the Labor movement, such as *Hashomer Hatzair*, embraced the Marxist strand of his thought, as epitomized by "Our Platform." But Borochov was also espoused by those who ennobled the national cause and had little interest in class war and a universal revolution of the proletariat. In the context of this essay, of particular importance is Borochov's influence on the young Ben-Gurion, who was a member of the Palestinian branch of the Poalei Tzion party. As Ben-Gurion's biographer Shabtai Teveth notes, Ben-Gurion "was attracted by Borochov's idea that a pioneering movement to Palestine of young men and women was a prerequisite for rebuilding *Eretz Israel*," but he rejected "out of hand Borochov's fundamental maxim that historical necessity would in itself ensure a Jewish flight from exile to Palestine." In other words, Ben-Gurion embraced Borochov's early voluntaristic conception of Zionism, and eschewed the later wholly stychic, one of "Our Platform." See Shabtai Teveth, *Ben-Gurion: The Burning Ground, 1886-1948* (Boston: Houghton, 1987), p. 29. It should also be noted that, toward the end of his life, Borochov seemed to have come full circle, championing his early ideas of 1903-1905. See Frankel, *Prophecy and Politics*, ch. 7.

57. This essay has not been translated into English, and my references here are to the Hebrew edition and to the original Russian publication. See Dov-Ber Borochov, "On the Question of Zion and Territory," in Borochov, *Selected Writings*, vol. 1 (Tel Aviv: Am Oved, 1944), p. 46 [Hebrew]; "On the Question of Zion and Territory," *Evreiskaia zhizn* (*Jewish Life*), 7 (July 1905), p. 70. I would like to thank Ms. Bella Barmak for making the translations from Russian to English.

58. Borochov, "On the Question of Zion and Territory," p. 46; *Jewish Life* 7, p. 70.

59. Borochov, "On the Question of Zion and Territory," p. 78; *Jewish Life* 8, p. 40 (my emphasis).

60. Borochov, "On the Question of Zion and Territory," p. 46; *Jewish Life* 7, p. 70.

61. Borochov, "On the Question of Zion and Territory," p. 51; *Jewish Life* 7, p. 76.

62. Borochov, "On the Question of Zion and Territory," p. 52; *Jewish Life* 7, p. 78 (my emphasis). Borochov anticipates that, after Zionism has successfully established its own independent conditions of production, it will become an evolutionary movement.

63. Borochov, "On the Question of Zion and Territory," p. 52; *Jewish Life* 7, p. 78.

64. Borochov, "On the Question of Zion and Territory," p. 60; *Jewish Life* 7, p. 87. [Hebrew]

65. David Ben-Gurion, *From Class to People* (Tel Aviv: Ayanot, 1955), p. 24.

66. As this essay addresses more contemporary political issues, I should probably digress for a moment from the scholarly protocol and admit that, as someone who affirms the historic main goals of Zionism, and who has lived with its legacy, I believe that the present calls for a critical and uncompromising look at the Zionist ethos in general and the lasting effects of its temporal revolution in particular.

67. Baruch Kimmerling, *Zionism and Territory: The Socio-Territorial Dimensions of Zionist Politics* (Berkeley: University of California, Institute of International Studies, 1983), p. 88.

68. Ben-Gurion, *From Class to People*, p. 24.

69. The development of Zionism in Palestine is distinguished by the ability of its leaders to devise, in just a few decades, a complex set of institutions that organized labor, provided welfare services, orchestrated land acquisition and settlement, collected funds from Jews overseas and transferred them for local investment, recruited and trained underground fighters, served as legitimate and representative political bodies, and more. Ben-Gurion was among the most prominent advocates of this institutional approach, and his plans and actions in this sphere were characterized by decisiveness and a great sense of urgency. As his biographer writes, "History seems to have arranged a conjuncture that permitted the advent of Zionism but restricted the time span for its accomplishment. Ben-Gurion... more than all his colleagues in the Labor movement... was driven by an enduring sense that the ground was burning beneath the feet of the Jews, especially in Europe. Therefore, in his view, time was of the essence." See Teveth, *Burning Ground*, p. xiv.

70. The Zionists' mistrust of language is evident both in the international and internal spheres. Ben-Gurion is famous for saying that it is not important what other nations say but, rather, what the Jews do, and for announcing *Um Shemum*, which means that the United Nations is rubbish and insignificant. But

this difficulty with taking words seriously and understanding them as constituting the political world is also manifested in the Israeli public sphere. The deterioration of this sphere prior to Rabin's assassination was marked by the revival and distortion of concepts from Jewish religious discourse, ones that allowed the execution of a so-called traitor (*mored*). While the calls for Rabin's assassination were loud and clear before his death, very few saw them as dangerous or as having any practical significance.

71. Aristotle, *The Politics*, trans. Ernest Barker (Oxford: Oxford, 1946), 1328a30. See also 1324b and 1326a.

72. Hannah Arendt, *The Human Condition* (Chicago: University of Chicago, 1958), p. 140.

73. Ibid., p. 144.

74 Ibid., p. 139.

75. Theodor Herzl, *Theodor Herzl Zionistisches Tagebücher II* (Berlin: Verlag Ullstein, 1983), p. 52; *The Complete Diaries of Theodor Herzl*, vol. i (New York: Thomas Yoseloff, 1960), p. 13. "Perhaps these ideas are not practical ones at all and I am only making myself the laughingstock of the people to whom I talk about it seriously. Could I be merely walking within my novel?" (*Diaries*, 1896).

ZION AND MORAL VISION

DAVID HAZONY

MANY JEWS ARE ACTIVE, even vocal advocates of a Jewish state. Yet their support for Israel is rarely identified as deriving from their Judaism. Zionism is often considered to follow not from any specific religious belief, but from a concern for the well-being of one's fellow Jews. The Jews were persecuted for centuries, it is said, and the State of Israel is the remedy. But whether such a Zionism is an aspect of one's Judaism, understood as a faith, remains unclear.

This ambiguous relationship between Judaism and political Zionism is most in evidence when one considers the attitude of the great Jewish theologians writing after the emergence of the Zionist movement at the end of the nineteenth century. Most Reform thinkers, for example, opposed the idea of a Jewish nation state, its theologians arguing for decades that Zionism contradicted Judaism's universalist ethic.[1] For leading Orthodox thinkers as well, Zionism was taken to be an affront to the messianic ideal, according to which it is God—and not secular Zionists—who will redeem the Jews in the end of days. While there were noteworthy exceptions, it is fair to say that the energies Jews brought to the Zionist enterprise in the pre-state period were largely despite, rather than because of, Jewish theological reflection.

A great deal changed, of course, with the rise of Nazism, the Holocaust, and the establishment of the State of Israel. The Reform movement abandoned its opposition to Zionism, as did the great majority
of Orthodox Jews. Jewish theologians of virtually all persuasions began
to speak of the Jewish state mainly in positive terms. Yet it would be a
mistake to conclude that the idea of sovereignty came to play in Jewish
thought anything like the central role that it assumed in Jewish communal life. Joseph B. Soloveitchik, the leading interpreter of Judaism
within modern Orthodoxy in North America, endorsed the Jewish state
in 1956 as a divine "knock on the door," a wake-up call for Jews to
the possibility of redemption and repentance;[2] yet Soloveitchik himself
chose to remain in the Diaspora, and the thrust of his philosophical
efforts continued to be the ethos of the individual living under Jewish
law, or halacha. Similarly, the Reform theologian Eugene B. Borowitz,
whose enthusiasm for Israel is reflected in his hope that the Jewish state
will help Jews "sanctify social existence" in a manner impossible under
conditions of exile, nonetheless continues to place the pursuit of the
ethical and the development of the "Jewish self" at the center of his
theology—a challenge that in his view is best met in the Diaspora.[3] In
his landmark work *Renewing the Covenant* (1991), Borowitz distanced
himself from the biblical ideal of Jewish sovereignty, emphasizing the
failure of ancient Israelite rulers to meet the ethical standards established
at Sinai:

> Being human, the [Israelite] kings demonstrate the will-to-do-evil; being
> rulers, they do so on a grand scale.... The incongruity of Israel's politi-
> cal behavior in the light of its covenant ideals prompts the theological
> wonder that God did not choose another social form for them rather
> than subject them to the awesome risks of collective power.... God
> makes Abraham's family a nation in history in order to show that col-
> lective power can be sanctified through subordination to God's rule. This
> does not, however, require Israel to fulfill its covenantal responsibilities
> through political autonomy or any other given social structure.[4]

What emerges from all this is a remarkable disjuncture between Jewish philosophy and Jewish communal life. While the Jewish people has
collectively placed Israel at the center of its public agenda, to the point
that it has become one of the few causes that unite the great majority of
Jews, Orthodox and liberal Jewish thinkers alike have remained occupied

principally with the faith and works of the individual. Jews continue to love Israel, but when asked whether Judaism *needs* Zionism, most will simply shrug their shoulders or speak of the needs and history of the Jewish people.

In this light we may attach special significance to the understanding of Jewish nationhood put forward by the theologian Eliezer Berkovits (1908-1992), who wrote extensively on the meaning of sovereignty and nationhood in Judaism. According to Berkovits, modern philosophers of Judaism have misunderstood the importance of nationhood—and in particular its expression in the form of an independent state—in interpreting the biblical faith and its talmudic expansion. While most Jewish thinkers, under the influence of Kant, tended to view the classic Jewish affirmation of nationhood and sovereignty as at best secondary to Judaism's ethical or legal core, Berkovits offered an approach to morality and nationhood that understood the creation and maintenance of a sovereign Jewish polity to be essential to the fulfillment of Judaism.

In Berkovits' view, the exile of the Jewish people at the dawn of the Christian era represented more than a physical and political tragedy for Jews. It was a calamity for Judaism itself, which would henceforth be incapable of fulfilling its central mission, that of creating an exemplary people in its own sovereign state. Following the eradication of Jewish national life in the second century C.E., Judaism entered a period of preservation, during which its wellsprings of creativity grew dry and its adaptive capacity withered, until the modern era arrived, offering Jews an alternative vision for which the keepers of the tradition were largely unprepared. The opportunity to re-establish the Jewish state in our own era, therefore, signified for Berkovits not only the protection of Jewish lives from the arbitrariness of nations—a tremendous achievement in its own right—but also the reconstitution of Judaism under sovereign conditions. "The creation of an autonomous Jewish body corporate," Berkovits wrote in 1943, five years before Israel's independence, "is the *sine qua non* for the regeneration of Jewish religion and culture. Without it, further development of Judaism is impossible; without it Judaism can hardly be saved in the present circumstances."[5]

According to Berkovits, therefore, Judaism *does* need Zionism, and emphatically so. This fact places him among a handful of major Jewish theologians of the past century for whom Judaism and Zionism are effectively inseparable, forming a unified whole. Of these, however,

Berkovits' exposition is probably the most developed philosophically, and the most compelling in its refutation of competing approaches in both general and Jewish thought.

In what follows, I will explore Berkovits' philosophical Zionism, with particular attention to three of his claims: First, that the Jewish collective identity is not merely a fact of history, but a prerequisite for the fulfillment of the Jewish moral vision; second, that the centrality of the collective translates into a demand for national sovereignty, not only today but as a permanent requirement of Judaism; and finally, that the resultant understanding of Jewish history, the predicament of exile, and the problem of enlightenment makes the Jewish state a precondition for the success and even survival of Judaism in the modern era. Together, these arguments offer a coherent and powerful account of the Jewish state as an integral aspect of Jewish faith.

II

There are good reasons why Jewish philosophy has tended to view morality and collective identity as subjects that are better off addressed under separate cover. The realm of ethics, which has been perceived in Western thought as a product of reason and therefore universal, has always seemed at odds with the needs and aspirations of human collectives. The latter have often been seen as reflecting particular interests and sustained by irrational sentiments. For Berkovits, however, morality and community are philosophically linked. Not only is there a moral demand placed on human communities and not just individuals; but morality itself is dependent on the concept of the collective. According to this view, the Jewish people is a central component of Jewish morality.

To understand why this is so, it is important to consider Berkovits' approach to the nature of morality in Judaism. In a previous essay in AZURE, I argued that he developed an approach to Jewish morality that may be seen as an alternative to the main threads of Western reasoning.[6] While many of the leading philosophers of that tradition emphasized adherence to abstract ethical rules and the purity of human intentions, Judaism is seen by Berkovits as emphasizing the effectiveness of one's actions in history. As he wrote in *God, Man and History*:

Judaism is not an "idealistic" or "spiritual" religion, but a human one. It is a religion for the whole of man. It aims at relating life in its entirety to God. It is not, therefore, so much a religion of creed as it is the religion of the deed on earth. The intellect or the soul may be satisfied with the creed; the whole man, however, may serve God only through the deed.... However, in order to be, the deed must be effective; and it must be so in the place where it belongs—in the external world, in history.[7]

Thus the yardstick of morality in Judaism, according to Berkovits, is not our adherence to a set of ideas or beliefs, but the results of our actions—and, by extension, the kind of society we help create.

Two important consequences follow from this view. The first, which was discussed more thoroughly in the previous essay, has to do with our own moral education: If morality is fundamentally about results rather than rules, then the way we learn how to behave morally will more closely resemble the way other result-oriented skills are learned, through models of emulation rather than doctrine. Because morality is learned from the example of others, a significant part of transmitting morality to others consists in dedicating the totality of one's life to the creation and implementation of a higher moral order, and thereby making oneself into a moral example.[8]

The second, which will be our main concern here, is that if morality is principally about results rather than intentions or adherence to rules, then the radical individualism upon which most modern ethical thought is based must be reconsidered. Since Kant, the question of whether an act is considered to be ethical in the view of most modern philosophers has turned on the quality of the autonomous decision of the individual actor: Whether it is taken in purity of intention, and according to the appropriate abstract principles of right. But the moment results, rather than intentions and principles, are the focus, it becomes evident that *collectives* are also the cause of good or ill effects in history. While it is obviously true that any collective is made up of individuals, it is also the case that the conditions created by the character of communities, peoples, and nations have an impact on people that is far more real and powerful than can be accounted for by looking purely at the deeds of individuals acting alone.[9] If morality has to do with the establishment of a good society, then our moral thinking must take into account human behavior at the level of communities, alongside our consideration of the individual.

These consequences led Berkovits to conclude that if we are to hope for the moral advancement of mankind, such hope will rest not on the emergence of a new moral doctrine, but on a moral exemplar on the level of the human community. "For the deed to be effective," he writes in *God, Man and History*, "it must not remain the act of an individual, but must become that of a community. The deed makes history if it is the materialization of the desire and will of a community of people joined together in a common cause.... Even the purely religious aspects of the Jewish deed are most intimately interwoven with community existence."[10] Man's moral achievements are, more than anything else, the realities he creates on the interpersonal and collective level—that is, the quality of the community's norms, and its success or failure in establishing a code of behavior, caring for the poor, and educating healthy and righteous individuals and families.

For this reason, Berkovits argues, Judaism has always understood its central mission to be the creation of an exemplary community, and not just exemplary individuals. Such a community dedicates its entire public existence, as well as the efforts of the individuals who live in it, towards a higher, divinely guided order. In the biblical view, the life of the Jews as a people is to play a central role in the establishment of human morality. Man's improvement requires a living example. But "man" as we find him is not a detached individual, but part of a society, with its own distinct habits, values, and cultural dynamic. Not the education of holy individuals, but the existence of a holy people, constitutes Judaism's central contribution to establishing morality in the world.

This understanding of Judaism finds expression throughout Berkovits' writings. In his extensive works on Jewish law, for example, he argues that the law must be understood not just as a code for individual piety, but also as a system which seamlessly combines the devotional with the political, and is addressed to the life of the community no less than that of the individual. The Talmud is not merely an ethical code, but the constitutive document for a living people—"the most successful experiment in the history of national constitutions," which alone "preserved a whole nation against the continuously stupid and wicked enmity of the entire world."[11] Accordingly, Jewish law resembles far more closely the code of conduct governing a living community than the regimen for piety which is offered by most religions.

One example is Judaism's approach to economic affairs. While the idea of individual property rights is deeply embedded in Jewish law and tradition—perhaps even constituting a fundamental element of the Jewish concept of man in the world—the halacha considered the proper functioning of the economy *as a whole* to be of decisive importance, justifying the enactment of a "market regulation" (*takanat hashuk*) which overrode the strict application of individual rights. Berkovits cites a ruling of the Mishna in a case in which goods are stolen and then sold to a third party. When the original owner confronts the purchaser, demanding that his belongings be returned, there emerges a clear conflict between individual rights and the economic good: If the concept of property rights were to be strictly applied, the original owner should be allowed to reclaim his property without having to compensate the buyer. The former had never given up his rights to the object, whereas the latter had incorrectly believed he was purchasing rights that the seller (i.e., the thief) never possessed in the first place. However, the rabbis ruled that while the original owner does have a right to the property, he may only exercise that right by compensating the buyer for the amount he paid for it. Berkovits cites a rabbinic explanation for this: "Since the buyer bought in the open market... if the original owner would not return to him the price he paid, no one would dare buy anything for fear that it was stolen. Thus, all business would come to a standstill."[12] Such a regulation may seem perfectly ordinary when dealing with a system of laws intended for a living community. What is interesting, however, is the fact that Judaism is such a system: Not a faith alone, but a normative system which embraces the political and legal spheres—because one cannot understand the moral good without reference to a vision of a moral society.

This recognition of the collective, societal realm extends in Berkovits' view even to the way Jews pray. In his 1962 monograph *Prayer*, Berkovits emphasizes the significance Judaism always attached to communal prayer, above and beyond the free expression of the individual. The very fact that Jewish prayer has traditionally been centered on the recital of obligatory texts is, in his view, a direct consequence of this approach. "Free prayer is always individual prayer, even when practiced in a congregational assembly...," he writes. "Obligatory prayer, being independent of any

contingent individual occasion, is based on the existential situation of
the Jew in relationship to God. It is not the prayer of one Jew in one
situation; it is the prayer for all Jews at all times. Therefore, even when
prayed by an individual in solitude, it remains in its essence communal
prayer."[13] For prayer to have meaning, it must be a true reflection of
the Jewish community's standing with respect to God. Individual prayer,
though not without its place, is nonetheless "problematic because of the
insufficiency of the subjective experience of the individual alone."[14] Though
he does not deny the value of the words of an individual pouring out his
heart to God, Berkovits argues that in focusing a person's energies purely
on self-expression, individual prayer "may amount to outright selfishness"
and as such it can even become "unethical." Berkovits cites numerous
laws and principles from the Jewish tradition to support his claim—such
as the idea that "the prayer of the community is never despised," or the
suggestion that if one has to pray alone, it is best to do so at the time
when the community is praying.[15] He concludes:

> The concept [of communal prayer] derives directly from the specific
> nature of Judaism. Judaism is not a religion of individual souls but that
> of a people.... In Judaism it is not only the individual who confronts
> God; the people as a people is committed to living in such confronta-
> tion. As it lives as a people in the presence of God, so it turns to God
> in prayer as a people.[16]

In an age so conscious of the "self," Berkovits' words strike an unusual note. Prayer is first a representation of the community's relationship
with God, and only secondarily a means of addressing the spiritual needs
of the individual. Thus even the most intimate moment of contact between man and God is framed in the context of the larger community;
it is the community that prays to God for redemption, just as it is the
community that is ultimately redeemed. "Judaism's concern," he wrote
in *Unity in Judaism* (1986), "is not primarily the salvation of individual
souls but the comprehensive spiritual, socio-ethical, economic, and political reality of human existence. Thus Judaism is best characterized not as
a religion, but as the covenantal civilization of a people."[17]

This approach, while well grounded in the biblical and rabbinic texts,
nonetheless represents a striking rejoinder to the major streams of Jewish philosophy in the first half of the twentieth century. While thinkers like Hermann Cohen, Martin Buber, and Franz Rosenzweig did not

reject the biblical vision of the moral improvement of all peoples, they nonetheless followed the Kantian tradition in pinning their hopes on the thoughts, intentions, or emotions of the individual as the starting point for serious moral discussion. In their view, this emphasis was the natural outcome of Judaism's universal spirit. If the world is to be redeemed through a universal morality, then we must begin with that which unites mankind, namely, the capacity of individuals for reason or compassion. It was through the individual—at the expense of communities, peoples, or nations—that mankind as a whole would find redemption.

This sentiment is found most vividly in the writings of Hermann Cohen. "What, after all, is social morality, if it is not founded upon the individual?" he wrote in his great work, *Religion of Reason Out of the Sources of Judaism.* "Is not individual morality the precondition for social morality, without which the latter remains an abstraction, from which it cannot be freed even through the relation of man to the state?"[18] In Cohen's view, morality begins with the individual's recognition that he is part of a single mankind, united under the rubric of ethics guided by reason—a recognition which must ultimately result in the dissolution of peoples into a collective, universal ideal:

> Finally it is a consequence of the ethical rigor that *national* limitations are abandoned for the sake of messianism.... If one disregards the fundamental historical meaning, that through the election the national consciousness was to be substituted for the religious calling, then the election of Israel has only a symbolic significance. From the very outset this higher symbolism presaged Israel's messianic call, its *elevation into one mankind.*[19]

Cohen's vision of the unification of humanity through the individual's "ethical rigor," leading to the dissolution of distinct communities, had a profound impact on the way Jewish philosophy developed in the twentieth century. This effect has been described by Eugene Borowitz, who writes in *Renewing the Covenant,* "All modernist theories of Judaism uphold the principle of autonomy, that authority ultimately is vested in the individual mind and will." This view, according to Borowitz, was even more pronounced among existentialist thinkers, such as Martin Buber and Franz Rosenzweig, for whom the individual experience was the starting point for all religious or ethical experience. "Buber and Rosenzweig both considered the [individual's] relationship with God to be the unchanging core of Judaism.... Like any love, it commanded one only when the self willingly responded to it...." According to Borowitz, for all that thinkers such as these may have disagreed with the rationalism of Cohen, "the existentialists nonetheless shared an important precept of modernity: That all authority, whether exercised in terms of one's rationality, ethnicity, or relationships, finally resides in the individual self." [20]

Such a view, Berkovits countered, misunderstands the nature of human morals. For if the goal of morality is not just to fashion righteous teachings but to bring into being a better human reality, morality must begin with man as he really is: Both an individual and part of a larger collective. And any reasonable evaluation of history will show that for most people most of the time, it is the collective which establishes and reinforces the norms that govern the ethical behavior of individuals. Therefore, if Jewish morality contains within it a vision for mankind—a position Berkovits embraces wholeheartedly—then its realization will depend not on the hope that people will abandon their particular allegiances, but rather on the emergence of a living people that may be "history-making" in its representation of a moral ideal. "The goal of Judaism is accomplished when it is reached by all mankind," he wrote. "Since, however, the goal is not essentially the teaching of noble ideals—which would indeed be rather easy, and ineffective—but rather their realization in history, one has to start with the smallest unit of living reality within which the deed of Judaism may become history-making; and such a unit is the nation. Individuals may teach; a people is needed in order to *do* effectively." [21]

III

How would such a holy community be constituted? In Berkovits' view, the limited autonomy granted Jewish communities in foreign lands cannot meet the fundamental demands that the Bible places on the Jews. The effectiveness of the model community requires not simply congregations, or an international association joined by a common religion, but rather the creation of a "holy nation."

Basing himself on the verse in Exodus, "And you shall be to me a kingdom of priests and a holy nation," [22] Berkovits articulates a philosophy of Judaism according to which only on the national level does man possess sufficient independence of spirit and action to have the possibility of representing the divine on earth in the fullest way possible. This idea is expressed by the very term "holy nation." Holiness (*kedusha*) means, literally, *dedication*; Judaism's concern cannot be restricted to the home, synagogue, house of study, or community center. Holiness means dedicating the whole of our lives to God. But if this is the case, then any Jewish community which is dependent on others in crucial areas of life is forever prevented from fulfilling its task. An exemplary people must first be an independent, fully responsible people. It must have that which distinguishes independent nations from other forms of community. That is, it must be sovereign.

At this stage a crucial distinction must be drawn. While Berkovits insisted on sovereignty as a minimal condition for the fulfillment of Judaism, he did not advocate any sort of totalist ideal, in which every aspect of life is given over to the authority of human rulers. "This kingdom of priests is not a society in which a priestly caste rules over an unpriestly populace in the name of some god," Berkovits writes. "A holy nation is a realm in which all are priests. But where all are priests, all are servants—and God alone rules." The point of sovereignty is not to fashion a state that will become the principal conduit of sanctity, but to give the nation sufficient responsibility for its own affairs as to allow it to constitute a viable example for other nations. "A 'kingdom of priests and a holy nation,'" he writes, "is thus not a theocracy, but a God-centered republic."[23]

Berkovits expands on the question of sovereignty in a variety of contexts. In *Faith After the Holocaust* (1973), he concludes his major statement on the destruction of European Jewry with a discussion of Jewish statehood. While most Zionist writers based their arguments for statehood on a plea for justice or for the necessity of self-defense after centuries of persecution, Berkovits depicts sovereignty as a permanent need, inherent in Judaism's moral outlook:

> While by faith alone a soul may be saved, perhaps, the deed's *raison d'être* is to be effective in the world. For the sake of its effectiveness, the deed will seek for its realization a group that is motivated by a common faith and united by a common cause. The extent of the group depends on the area within which the deed is to be enacted....

But what if the fruition of the idea as the deed encompasses the whole of human existence? If the faith seeks realization in economics, morals, politics, in every manifestation of human life? In that case, the group ought to be all-comprehensive. Such a group should be mankind. But mankind is not a group; it is not a historical entity. Mankind itself is an idea, an ideal. The comprehensive group to be created to suit the comprehensive deed as a historical reality is a people *in sovereign control of the major areas of its life*. The faith of Judaism requires such a comprehensive deed. Realization through and within the all-comprehensive collective, mankind, is the ideal; the instrument of its realization in history is the people.[24]

The fallacy of political universalism, according to Berkovits, is not its wish for the improvement of mankind, but its belief that mankind as such exists at all, as a human association capable of acting in history. Collectives can be real things, inasmuch as they are made up of individuals acting in concert and united in a common cause; "humanity" may be a useful mental construct, but it does not exist as an actual human collective, so long as all mankind has not united under a common identity or goal. Universal brotherhood is at best a dream; only extant human associations can actually move history, and the form of association most suited to the aims of Judaism is the sovereign nation, which alone contains within it the full contents of human life.

The centrality of sovereignty to Judaism according to Berkovits can thus be explained in two ways. First, it is a necessary product of Judaism's insistence on re-orienting the length and breadth of human life towards a divine order. If an exilic Jewish community is without control over such far-reaching, genuinely existential concerns as defense and economics, it has assuredly been rendered flatter, less representative of the human condition, and therefore less capable of fulfilling the central aims of a holy nation. It is, literally, less holy.

Many Jews, of course, may see this as a good thing, arguing that it is precisely by delegating to others the "lower" aspects of public life, filled with power and violence, that Jews have been able to offer a superior kind of community. And yet the problem is revealed the moment one takes the argument further. One may choose to live in a monastery, in which wide areas of "profane" concern are removed from the monk's immediate attention, and call this holiness. Yet by hiding wealth and war and procreation from the monk, one does not make them disappear.

The viability of monastic life continues to depend on such questions as before—just that these areas are now left to others. Holiness is not achieved, in Berkovits' view, by ignoring profanity and celebrating its absence, but by focusing all the areas of public and private life on that which is "right and good in the eyes of the Eternal." And what holds for the monastery is no less true for exilic Judaism: It has not removed the need for righteousness in crucial areas such as security and economics; it has merely delegated them to others, and its own holiness is thereby made limited, even superficial.

Second, sovereignty is central to Judaism's aspiration to create an exemplary community. For it seems clear that few nations will look to the Jews for moral wisdom so long as they are exempt from addressing the hardest questions that come with sovereignty—questions upon which all communal life ultimately depends. Sovereign peoples are certainly capable of learning a great deal from the successes and failures of other nations, for they often face similar challenges. But how is any nation, daily charged with the task of attending to its defense and prosperity, to learn about morality from a people in exile? Put another way, if moral dilemmas increase in proportion to the power wielded by the actor, why would the powerful ever have cause to learn from the powerless, who simply do not face the same kinds of questions? A weaker country will have little to teach stronger ones about how and when to use overwhelming force to achieve just ends, for example, for it has little comparable experience; how much more so for a people with no means of self-defense at all?

To understand just how unusual was Berkovits' approach in modern Jewish thinking, it is instructive to contrast it with the ideas advanced by other major religious-Zionist thinkers. Among these, two themes are heard most frequently. On the one hand, redemptive determinists like Abraham Isaac Kook and his son, Tzvi Yehuda Kook, identified the rise of Zionism with the messianic era, brought about by divine command through the instrumentality of the Zionist movement. For these thinkers, the end of days was everywhere in evidence, and the only question was whether the Jewish people understood and acted on its implications. As the elder Kook wrote in 1920:

> From the lowliest level we are recreated as in days past.... We are invited to a new world full of supernal splendor, to a new era that will

surpass in strength all the great eras that preceded it. The entire people believes that there will be no more exile after the redemption that is presently commencing, and this profound belief is itself the secret of its existence, the mystery of God revealed in its historical saga, and the ancient tradition attests to the light of its soul that recognizes itself and the entire genealogy of events until the last generation, a generation longing for imminent salvation.[25]

Kook's son, who became the preeminent leader of the religious-Zionist community in Israel in the period following the Six Day War, put it more directly. "How is it that some religious spokesmen even withheld their support for Zionism and the movement for redemption?" he asked. "They failed to recognize that it was not that we mortals were forcing the end, but rather that the Master of the House, the Lord of the Universe, was forcing our hand...."[26]

On the other hand, pragmatic nationalists like Isaac Jacob Reines, and the religious-Zionist Mizrahi movement he helped found in the early twentieth century, advocated statehood primarily as a remedy for the tragic conditions of exile. The greatest threats to the Jewish people, they argued, are assimilation and persecution, and only Jewish nationalism, and ultimately statehood, could save the Jews. According to this approach, redemption and the improvement of mankind were irrelevant to the Zionist enterprise, and any effort to connect it with eternal Jewish ideals, rather than simply the pragmatic improvement of the condition of the Jews, was in error. "Zionist ideology is devoid of any trace of the idea of redemption...," he wrote approvingly in 1899. "In none of the Zionists' acts or aspirations is there the slightest allusion to future redemption. *Their sole intention is to improve Israel's situation*, to raise their stature and accustom them to a life of happiness.... How can one compare this idea with the idea of redemption?"[27]

Berkovits did not deny the philosophical legitimacy of these approaches.[28] In the wake of the Holocaust and the Israeli victories in 1948 and 1967, he joined many Jews in interpreting these events as revealing some kind of "messianic moment, in which the unexpected fruits of human endeavor reveal themselves as the mysterious expression of a divine guidance which the heart always knew would come."[29] Nor could he gainsay the pragmatic value of the state in defending Jewish lives and stemming assimilation. At the same time, these approaches share the weakness of being constructed on what is effectively a historical contingency: Reluctant to take upon themselves the critique of centuries of traditional Judaism in exile which such a position implied, these thinkers depicted the need for sovereignty not as fundamental to the central aims of Judaism, but rather as reflecting a specific need in our time. Berkovits, by contrast, presents sovereignty as an inherent and unchanging need, a minimum condition for the fulfillment of Judaism itself.

Moreover, Berkovits' aim in writing is different from that of other religious Zionist thinkers. The latter were directing their discourse primarily to the Orthodox rabbinic leadership, steeped in the idiom and assumptions of Tora learning; their principal ideological opponent was the anti-Zionist rabbinic establishment. Their hopes lay not in convincing a secular Zionist establishment to recognize the religious value of the moment, but in convincing Orthodox Jews to recognize the religious merits in a pre-existing, but hitherto secular, Zionist enterprise. Berkovits, on the other hand, lay aside the rabbinic rhetorical training of his youth and crafted a philosophical argument for a nationally based Judaism derived from his understanding of the unique Jewish approach to morality, thereby creating a coherent system which could serve as an alternative to the central ideas of modern moral philosophy and of those philosophies of Judaism that drew upon European thought for their inspiration.

The importance of these differences becomes apparent when we consider the fact that the most powerful intellectual opposition to Jewish sovereignty in the first half of the twentieth century came from the world of philosophical argument, and in the name of eternal, not historically contingent, Jewish ideas. Thinkers like Cohen, Rosenzweig, and Buber insisted that the idea of sovereignty violated the true spirit of Judaism, which affirmed the powerlessness of exile. Cohen, for example, argued in 1916 that the exile of the Jews two thousand years ago was a major step forward in messianic history, enabling the Jews to represent an "entirely universal religion" among the nations:

> We interpret our entire history as pointing to this messianic goal. Thus, we see the destruction of the Jewish state [i.e., of the ancient Jewish commonwealth] as an exemplification of the theodicy of history. The same Micah who said that God requires man to do justly also conceived of the providential metaphor: "And the remnant of Jacob shall be in the midst of many peoples, as dew from the Lord."[30] We are proudly aware of the fact that we continue to live as divine dew among the nations; we wish to remain among them and be a creative force for them. All

our prophets have us living among the nations, and all view "Israel's remnant" from the perspective of its world mission.[31]

Jewish history, in Cohen's view, represents the progress of the Jews from a provincial, national entity during its ancient, sovereign period to a higher state of exile and dispersion, in which they may serve as "divine dew among the nations." This position, upon which Cohen based his opposition to the emerging Zionist movement, was developed further by Franz Rosenzweig. In *The Star of Redemption* (1919), Rosenzweig posits a role for the Jewish people in the redemption of mankind, a role that has emerged precisely because of the Jews' rejection of sovereign power and their attainment of an ahistorical life in exile:

> The Jewish people has already reached the goal toward which the na-
> tions are still moving.... Its soul, replete with the vistas afforded by
> hope, grows numb to the concerns, the doing, and the struggling of
> the world. The consecration poured over it as over a priestly people
> renders its life "unproductive." Its holiness hinders it from devoting its
> soul to a still unhallowed world.... In order to keep unharmed the vi-
> sion of the ultimate community it must deny itself the satisfaction the
> peoples of the world constantly enjoy in the functioning of their state.
> For the state is the ever-changing guise under which time moves step
> by step toward eternity. So far as God's people is concerned, eternity
> has already come—even in the midst of time![32]

By rejecting statehood, and its attendant involvement in "the concerns, the doing, and the struggling of the world," the Jews as an exilic people have succeeded in achieving the same eternal status which every nation seeks. The nations of the world, however, have sought eternity through the state, which employs law, coercion, and war to create an illusion of the eternal. "The state symbolizes the attempt to give nations eternity within the confines of time," a fact which puts it forever at odds with the Jewish people, who have already discovered eternity through the exilic model. The state, in Rosenzweig's view, is nothing less than "the imitator and rival of the people which is in itself eternal, a people which would cease to have a claim to its own eternity if the state were able to attain what it is striving for."[33]

The views of Cohen and Rosenzweig, it must be emphasized, had a powerful influence on Jewish intellectual life, including in Israel. While their arguments were well developed from a philosophical standpoint, it

is fair to say that their success was no less the result of a fear that the
Jewish people, who had witnessed centuries of racist persecution in Europe, would now themselves come under the influence of that romantic
nationalism that had become popular in Europe in the nineteenth and
early twentieth centuries—a fear which to this day continues to charge
the debate over the application of sovereign power in the Jewish state. As
a young rabbi in Berlin at the time of National Socialism's ascendancy in
Germany and until the eve of the war, Berkovits understood Germany's
radicalization to be the natural outcome of the state-worship which had
swept Central Europe, and was concerned about what the renewed affection for sovereign power could mean for the Zionist movement. "Woe
unto us," he wrote in *Towards Historic Judaism* (1943), "if the degeneration of the exile should lead us to a Hebrew nationalism along the
European pattern.... Not every form of *eretz yisrael* is worth the trouble,
and many a form could be unworthy of Judaism."[34]

At the same time, for the Jews to reject worldly, history-making
power when the opportunity presented itself would mean shirking the
responsibility they had taken upon themselves at Sinai. Sovereignty was
central to Judaism, and could not be written out of it simply because
romantic Europeans had put the state at the center of their worldview.
How, then, was a Jewish state to avoid the perils of European nationalism? Berkovits' answer is clear. Sovereignty and nationhood are themselves
preconditions, not the end goal, of Judaism. A Jewish state would avoid
the dangers of idolizing the state by keeping before its eyes the higher
moral purpose for which the Jewish people was founded; by preserving
the state's dependence on Jewish tradition, through which the idea of
the "holy nation" would be continuously reinforced and the risks which
accompany empowerment kept in check. "The idea of a holy nation is
not to be confused with that of nationalism," he wrote a decade after the
establishment of Israel. "The goal of nationalism is to serve the nation; a
holy nation serves God. The law of nationalism is national self-interest;
the law of a kingdom of priests is the will of God. From the point of
view of a nationalistic ideology, the nation is an end in itself; the holy
nation is a means to an end."[35]

Thus, whereas Cohen and Rosenzweig offered a defense of exile in
the name of an ethical vision, Berkovits' emphasis on morality in Judaism
led precisely to the opposite conclusion. The idea of the improvement
of mankind, which lies at the heart of the prophetic vision, demands

not exile but sovereign empowerment, for without it Judaism cannot offer a true example of how the entire life of man may be dedicated to a higher, divine order. That national sovereignty could avoid the pitfalls of state-worship was acutely evident to Berkovits, who escaped totalitarian Germany and found in the English-speaking democracies a far more successful model. These nations understood sovereignty as the only means to vouchsafe the liberty necessary for human happiness, and their dedication to this higher ideal enabled them to write constitutions and laws which have succeeded in furthering that ideal over centuries. In Berkovits' view, the idea of the holy nation can serve as precisely such a higher vision for the Jewish state, and in fact must do so if Judaism is to establish itself as a moral force in history.

IV

If sovereignty is central, however, the Jews' history of exile and return takes on new significance. Exile is a tragedy not only for Jews deprived of a homeland, but also for a Judaism deprived of the conditions for the fulfillment of its purpose. Exile for Berkovits represents not an improvement that should be balanced against the human suffering it entails, not an "exemplification of the theodicy of history," as Cohen put it. Rather, it represents nothing less than the derailment of Judaism itself, which no amount of congregational action or individual piety can make good. "The great spiritual tragedy of the exile," Berkovits wrote in 1943, "consists in the breach between Tora and life, for exile means the loss of a Jewish-controlled environment."[36] Without sovereignty, Judaism itself is deprived of its creative capacity, its original inner vitality, and is doomed to paralysis and, ultimately, decline.

Why must this be the case? The answer, according to Berkovits, stems from the essential difference between the life of the holy nation in its land and that of a people in exile. As a sovereign people, the holy nation is not a static thing, but a living, creating entity. Faced with new challenges and possessing the power to address them, such a nation constantly struggles to improve its life and laws according to a higher vision. As such, it will of necessity be dynamic and evolving. Because it has the capacity for far greater moral effectiveness than a people in exile, it will dedicate its resources to the articulation, interpretation, and enforcement of just laws and right customs. And its best minds and spirits will be continually directed toward understanding just what it means for a sovereign nation to live in righteousness.

For many centuries, Berkovits writes, Israel enjoyed the conditions necessary for pursuing such a vision. While the Jewish kingdoms of antiquity did not always meet the standards of conduct they had set for themselves, sovereignty nonetheless meant that the idea of the holy nation was a possibility, a dream to pursue. This powerful sovereign dynamic enabled a small people to produce the most influential work of moral teaching in human history—the Hebrew Bible, which depicts, through a variety of genres, the successes and failures of a nation attempting to fulfill the purpose given to it by God. It also enabled the creation of a rich oral tradition, encompassing both law and legend. These great works, in Berkovits' mind, were produced by a living nation grappling with all the realities of human life, from warfare to public worship to education and economics, and struggling to imbue the fullness of life with sanctity. Even in the first few centuries after the Temple's destruction in 70 C.E. and the final loss of Jewish sovereignty in the second century, the intellectual habits which had been the product of sovereignty enabled the rabbinic leaders of Judaism to produce the monumental works of the Talmud and Midrash, which possessed such creativity and insight as to become the basis not only of Judaism for centuries on end, but of continued study and reverence throughout the Western world.[37]

But this momentum could carry Judaism only so far. In the centuries following the destruction of the Jewish commonwealth, the enormity of the exile began to make itself felt. Stripped of sovereignty, the Tora ceased to be "history-making." The Talmud itself gives voice to this understanding, when it asserts that "since the destruction of the Temple, God has nothing in this world other than the four cubits of halacha."[38] Judaism in exile, Berkovits writes, became at once distracted and distorted, unable to apply the divine ideal to the totality of life, while at the same time forced to modify its laws and institutions to ensure Jewish religious survival against the double threat of assimilation and persecution. "With the loss of national sovereignty," he wrote in *Crisis and Faith* (1976), "there were no more political problems with a bearing on national survival to confront the Tora.... Judaism was forced out of the public domain into the limitations of the private one. Broad layers of the Tora were thus pried away from the comprehensive life of a normal people, for which they were originally intended. The vital link between Tora and reality was severed in the exile of the people."[39] If Judaism requires sovereignty for its fulfillment, then exile is not merely a historical disaster, but a cosmic one as well, for God's teaching is deprived of its central field of application, and the presence of the divine in history becomes restricted to the "four cubits" of law in exile.

Exile meant that to survive, Judaism had to be transformed and re-tooled. Beginning with the decrees of R. Yohanan ben Zakai during the first century C.E. and continuing over a thousand years, the rabbis struggled to preserve the Jews' basic commitments to Tora study and observance in increasingly difficult conditions. The elimination of broad areas of life from the Tora's rubric meant the Jews' mission as an exemplary people would have to be put on hold; and the extreme conditions of exile posed such a threat to the survival of the Tora that preservation became an overriding existential need. Pursuing the ancient dream was no longer an option, and Jewish leaders now turned their efforts to merely keeping the dream alive.

This meant, first and foremost, a palpable constriction in the freedom of rabbinic scholars to innovate or interpret the law creatively in light of its inner meaning. Most strikingly, this was expressed in the emergence of written codes of law as the preeminent source of Jewish authority, displacing the judgment of living individuals, who in Berkovits' view were more capable of capturing the depth of the Tora's meaning and applying it to ever-changing reality. "Living authority is always built upon tradition, but as it is alive it can exist only when there is a possibility of an organic evolution in the application of tradition," he wrote. "When, owing to the hard facts of Jewish history, owing to the insecurity of Jewish life, living authority was no longer practicable, and authority had to be transferred to the book, the Talmud, the records of a once-living authority, Judaism had to sacrifice the possibility of organic development; it renounced the great principle of the evolution of traditional teachings. The structure of Judaism became rigid, for it had lost its evolutionary strength."[40]

For the preservation of their national law in conditions of exile, the Jews paid in the hard currency of the Tora's original vitality. Cut off from the hardest questions of public life, the Tora was relegated almost entirely to the purely theoretical or the purely individual. In *Crisis and Faith*, Berkovits put the problem in perhaps its harshest light:

> With the people, the Tora, too, went into exile…. The living Tora needs the dialectical tension of the confrontation with a total reality that asks questions and presents problems. Tora is alive when it meets the challenge, struggles with the problems, seeks for solutions by a continuous deepening of its self-understanding, thus forever discovering new levels of meaningfulness in the depth of its inexhaustible eternity. Tora in exile lacks the life-sustaining challenge of the confrontation. It is stunted in its vitality and, for lack of possibilities of Tora-realization, it is greatly impaired in its wisdom of Tora-application.[41]

Exile necessitates taking extreme measures just to preserve Jewish identity and to maintain the Jews' fidelity to the original dream of the holy nation. For this reason, even as the application of the law became increasingly constricted, the ideal of Tora study continued to include those areas of the law which were devoid of practical application—such as the sacrifices in the Temple in Jerusalem, the governance of the Sanhedrin, or agricultural restrictions in the Sabbatical year, which apply only in the land of Israel.[42] For this reason, moreover, Judaism throughout the centuries maintained a powerful dedication to the messianic idea, based on the hope that the Jews would re-establish sovereignty and regain their former glory—an idea which attained the status of cardinal belief in the writings of Maimonides, and which even found practical expression throughout the medieval period in efforts to return to the land of Israel and re-establish Jewish sovereignty.[43]

But these measures, while helpful for preservation, could not correct the immense "breach between Tora and life" that had resulted from exile. Over time, Judaism turned increasingly inward and attended primarily to its spiritual self-defense. It erected firm walls of law and custom, in the process becoming progressively less flexible. Judaism and Jewish life were able to continue this way for many centuries, preserving the integrity of the Jewish nation and its dedication to the Tora as a theological framework and a source of political authority. But the same rigidity and insularity which helped Judaism survive through the medieval period left it unprepared for the modern era.

The modern period in Europe presented so powerful an assault on the traditional exilic model of Judaism as to leave the Jewish people in a state of crisis from which it has yet to emerge. Politically, the emancipation of European Jewry meant that the individual Jew was suddenly offered a national affiliation that could compete openly with that of the Jewish polity-in-exile. Philosophically, enlightenment meant that reason, which always had a special appeal for Jews raised on talmudic discourse, was now turned against the foundations of biblical faith. As Berkovits writes in *Towards Historic Judaism*:

> When, through Jewish emancipation, European Jews entered the circle of modern civilization and experienced the conflict between that new world and their own Jewish world of old, the rigidity which they had taken upon themselves resulted in an inability to adapt, rendering all the important problems arising out of that conflict insoluble. Jews began to share more and more in a life that was rapidly changing, while at the same time they remained in a spiritual and religious world that had lost its capacity to develop. In such a situation, all attempts at reconciliation were doomed to failure.[44]

The result was that the majority of Jews broke with the traditional framework, abandoning the political component of Judaism as well as the four cubits of law—and in the process abandoning the ancient dream of creating a holy nation. Judaism became a realm of private belief which every Jew was supposed to interpret on his own. But in the realm of human history, where the Tora had originally sought to have its most important effect, the Jew was now a proud Frenchman, American, or German. "We German adherents of Jewish monotheism," Hermann Cohen wrote typically in 1917, "place our trust in history, confident that our innermost kinship to the German ethos will be acknowledged ever more willingly and frankly. Sustained by this confidence, we shall thus go on as German men and German citizens and at the same time remain unshakably loyal to our Jewish religion."[45]

In Berkovits' view, therefore, the central crisis facing the Jew in modern times is not his physical survival but the collapse of the system that had preserved the idea of the holy nation. The liberal forms of Judaism, which looked to a universalizing Jewish "ethics" and Jewish "religion" to replace the law and the political commitment it implied, were to him not a modernization of the ancient faith, but its material abandonment. "The biblical conception of the Jewish state is the kingdom of God on earth," he wrote. "The basic demands of Judaism compel this outlook…. Whoever breaks with it breaks with Judaism."[46] At the same time, Orthodoxy, which for a thousand years had managed to fight off every major challenge to Jewish nationhood, stood now like a castle of sand against the incoming waves—powerless to stop the erosion, yet oblivious to the failure of its own material.

The only solution to the crisis would be a radical move, one that would reconnect Jews with the creative, sovereign spirit which had earlier defined their national experience. Preservation was no longer an option, since the methods of preserving no longer worked for the great majority of Jews. Instead, Judaism must forgo the exilic model, in which evolution and creativity are all but precluded, and reconstitute itself as a national state. "Any further development of Judaism is possible only by the creation, somewhere on this earth, of a complete Jewish environment, one wide enough to embrace the whole existence of a Jewish national entity," Berkovits wrote half a decade before the advent of Israel. "Only by the creation of such a Jewish environment can we give back to Tora the great partnership of life which alone is capable of freeing Judaism from its present exilic rigidity, and create the circumstances in which evolution will again be possible."[47] Thus the Jewish state, which played so central a role in Berkovits' understanding of the ideal Jewish community, becomes the centerpiece of his approach to Jewish life in the modern era.

Berkovits, it should be stressed, was under no illusions about the realities of Jewish and Israeli history. He did not advocate "liquidating" the Diaspora, and dedicated an entire chapter of *Towards Historic Judaism* to Diaspora life and his prescription for its success. Nor did he believe that the State of Israel, as it developed over nearly half a century, had lived up to its potential as a source of creative Jewish thinking; indeed, his *Crisis of Judaism in the Jewish State* (1987), which was written following his immigration to Israel in 1975, catalogues the failure of his adoptive countrymen to recognize the potential inherent in a Jewish state, and offers a warning that without a more significant re-connection to the ancient Jewish ideal, Zionism itself may not survive.

Despite these criticisms, however, Eliezer Berkovits never abandoned his belief that in the absence of statehood, Judaism is doomed to search for ever-newer stratagems for survival, pushing the ancient dream ever further into the people's collective memory. Only with a Jewish state might the breach between the divine teaching and human history again be healed, and might Judaism reclaim its role in history as a powerful, creative, and developing source of human wisdom, a living example of holiness in national existence.

V

Religious Zionism in the twentieth century offered the Jewish people two competing images of statehood, which gained a dedicated following among a small number of adherents, but did not succeed in capturing the imagination of Jews on a broad scale. On the one hand, followers of the Mizrahi movement advocated statehood for the Jews principally as a means of protecting Jewish lives and material interests. A traditionalist offshoot of Theodor Herzl's Zionist Organization, Mizrahi built institutions along the lines of the other Zionist movements, establishing youth groups, sports clubs, kibbutzim, and a political party. Its aim was to translate modern Zionism into religious terms and to provide an environment in which Jews committed to a life according to halacha could take part in the Zionist enterprise. Although it certainly did not shun religious symbolism and terminology, the Mizrahi movement emphasized pragmatism over theology, and did not offer a coherent philosophy of Judaism in which sovereignty played the central role.[48]

By mid-century a second movement had emerged as well, around the teachings of Abraham Isaac Kook, and amplified by his son, Tzvi Yehuda Kook. This movement read the events of the late nineteenth and twentieth centuries through a messianic lens. The success of Zionism and the emergence of the State of Israel (and, after 1967, the return of the Jews to the holy places of Jerusalem, Judea, and Samaria) were interpreted as *at'halta digeula*, the beginning of the redemption, and Jews were enjoined to build and settle the land of Israel in order to hasten the messianic process. While this movement offered a more profound theoretical basis than did the Mizrahi, its overt messianism, eschatological vocabulary, and intensive settlement activism at a time when the majority of Jews and Israelis had already ceased to find in settlement a central source of Zionist fulfillment, all served to prevent it from reaching the great majority of Jews.

Eliezer Berkovits offered a very different vision, which grants Jewish nationhood and Jewish sovereignty a vital role in Judaism while avoiding the determinism and exaggerated expectations that come with messianism. According to his vision, Judaism offers an understanding of morality which takes cognizance of the importance of nations in determining man's moral fate, and which insists on the necessity of a moral exemplar in the form of a living, sovereign nation. The Jewish people was created with the singular aim of serving this vision—to be a "kingdom of priests and a holy nation." This is the challenge put forth in the biblical writings, and its centrality to Judaism is in evidence throughout the length and breadth of traditional Jewish teaching, even after two thousand years of exile. In our own era, the promise of Zion, in Berkovits' view, is the hope of rediscovering the Tora's own creative essence after centuries of suspended animation—a hope which requires the security and continuous creative exploration which only sovereignty can offer.

NOTES

1. A striking example of this appears in the 1885 Pittsburgh Platform, which delineated the core beliefs of the Reform movement at the time: "We consider ourselves no longer a nation, but a religious community, and, therefore, expect neither a return to Palestine… nor the restoration of any of the laws concerning the Jewish state."

2. Joseph B. Soloveitchik, *Fate and Destiny: From the Holocaust to the State of Israel* (Hoboken, N.J.: Ktav, 2000).

3. Eugene B. Borowitz, *Renewing the Covenant: A Theology for the Postmodern Jew* (Philadelphia: Jewish Publication Society, 1991), pp. 216, 290.

4. Borowitz, *Renewing the Covenant*, p. 231.

5. Eliezer Berkovits, *Essential Essays on Judaism*, ed. David Hazony (Jerusalem: Shalem, 2002), p. 164.

6. David Hazony, "Eliezer Berkovits and the Revival of Jewish Moral Thought," *Azure* 11 (Summer 2001), pp. 23-65.

7. Eliezer Berkovits, *God, Man and History*, ed. David Hazony (Jerusalem: Shalem, 2004), pp. 137-138.

8. Cf. Hazony, "Eliezer Berkovits," pp. 45-52.

9. In a sermon he delivered in Leeds in September 1942, Berkovits put the point as follows: "A man may be a perfect *tzadik* with nothing but good deeds to his credit, yet he cannot but share in the fate of the nation to which he belongs. And if the nation as such lives foolishly and is unable to manage its affairs competently and well, all will suffer within the nation, even the innocent; as all will benefit—even those whom you may think that they do not deserve it—from a just and honorable administration of the group or the state." Eliezer Berkovits, *Between Yesterday and Tomorrow* (Oxford: East and West Library, 1945), p. 142.

10. Berkovits, *God, Man and History*, p. 137.

11. Berkovits, *Essential Essays*, p. 157.

12. Eliezer Berkovits, *Not in Heaven: The Nature and Function of Halacha* (New York: Ktav, 1983), p. 16.

13. Eliezer Berkovits, *Prayer* (New York: Yeshiva University, 1962), p. 51.

14. Berkovits, *Prayer*, p. 59.

15. Berkovits, *Prayer*, pp. 53-54.

16. Berkovits, *Prayer*, p. 55.

17. Eliezer Berkovits, *Unity in Judaism* (New York: American Jewish Committee, 1986), p. 2.

18. Hermann Cohen, *Religion of Reason Out of the Sources of Judaism* (Atlanta: Scholars, 1995), p. 179.

19. Cohen, *Religion of Reason*, pp. 259-260, emphasis in original.

20. Borowitz, *Renewing the Covenant*, pp. 16-17.

21. Berkovits, *God, Man and History*, p. 142, emphasis added.

22. Exodus 19:6.

23. Berkovits, *God, Man and History*, pp. 140-141.

24. Eliezer Berkovits, *Faith after the Holocaust* (New York: Ktav, 1973), p. 149, emphasis added.

25. Abraham I. Kook, *Orot*, trans. Bezalel Naor (Northvale, N.J.: Jason Aronson, 1993), p. 185.

26. Quoted in Yosef Bramson, ed., *The Public Campaign* (Jerusalem, 1986), pp. 24-25 [Hebrew]; cited in Aviezer Ravitzky, *Messianism, Zionism, and Jewish*

Religious Radicalism, trans. Michael Swirsky and Jonathan Chipman (Chicago: University of Chicago, 1996), p. 79.

27. Isaac Jacob Reines, *Gates of Light and Happiness* (Vilna, 1899), pp. 12-13 [Hebrew], emphasis added; cited in Ravitzky, *Messianism*, pp. 33-34. Ravitzky also cites a letter published in 1900 by a number of rabbis under Reines' leadership, in support of the Zionist movement. They write:

> Anyone who thinks the Zionist idea is somehow associated with future redemption and the coming of the Messiah and who therefore regards it as undermining our holy faith is clearly in error. [Zionism] has nothing whatsoever to do with the question of redemption. The entire point of this idea is merely the improvement of the condition of our wretched brethren. In recent years our situation has deteriorated disastrously, and many of our brethren are scattered in every direction, to the seven seas, in places where the fear of assimilation is hardly remote. [The Zionists] saw that the only fitting place for our brethren to settle would be in the Holy Land.... And if some preachers, while speaking of Zion, also mention redemption and the coming of the Messiah and thus let the abominable thought enter people's minds that this idea encroaches upon the territory of true redemption, only they themselves are to blame, for it is their own wrong opinion they express.

Letter in *Hamelitz* 78 (1900); cited in Ravitzky, *Messianism*, p. 34.

28. It is important to note that the thinkers of religious Zionism tended to offer a range of justifications for their support of the movement, of which the above-mentioned themes are merely the central thrust of their arguments. For example, both Kook and the more pragmatic Rabbi Hayyim Hirschensohn declared "nationalism" to be central to the Jewish idea, in which that term is meant to denote the centrality of political sovereignty to the Tora's application. Cf. David Zohar, *Jewish Commitment in a Modern World: R. Hayyim Hirschensohn and His Attitude Towards the Modern Era* (Jerusalem: Shalom Hartman Institute, 2003), p. 93.

29. Berkovits, *Essential Essays*, p. 188.

30. Micah 5:6.

31. Eva Jospe, ed. and trans., *Reason and Hope: Selections from the Jewish Writings of Hermann Cohen* (Cincinnati: Hebrew Union College, 1971), p. 168.

32. Franz Rosenzweig, *The Star of Redemption*, trans. William W. Hallo (London: University of Notre Dame, 1985), pp. 331-332.

33. Rosenzweig, *Star of Redemption*, p. 332.

34. Berkovits, *Essential Essays*, p. 171.

35. Berkovits, *God, Man and History*, p. 141.

36. Berkovits, *Essential Essays*, pp. 161-162.

37. For an important example of the influence of rabbinic thought on modern philosophical discourse, cf. Fania Oz-Salzberger, "The Jewish Roots of Western Freedom," *Azure* 13 (Summer 2002), pp. 88-132.

38. Brachot 8a.

39. Eliezer Berkovits, *Crisis and Faith* (New York: Sanhedrin, 1976), pp. 142-143.

40. Berkovits, *Essential Essays*, pp. 157-158.

41. Berkovits, *Crisis and Faith*, pp. 141-143.

42. This was felt acutely, for example, in the curriculum of study in the leading European yeshivot in the nineteenth century. Cf. Norman Lamm, *Tora Lishmah: Tora for Tora's Sake in the Works of Hayyim of Volozhin and His Contemporaries* (Hoboken, N.J.: Ktav, 1989), p. 240.

43. Cf. Arie Morgenstern, "Dispersion and the Longing for Zion, 1240-1840," *Azure* 12 (Winter 2002), pp. 71-132.

44. Berkovits, *Essential Essays*, p. 158.

45. Jospe, *Reason and Hope*, p. 220.

46. Berkovits, *Essential Essays*, p. 168.

47. Berkovits, *Essential Essays*, p. 163.

48. See note 27 above.

PART II

ZION AND THE CRISIS
OF JEWISH CULTURE

DIONYSUS IN ZION

ASSAF SAGIV

IN EARLY OCTOBER of last year, the modern city of Tel Aviv became the scene of a colorful pagan spectacle. On the boardwalk overlooking the Mediterranean Sea, about 150,000 young people gathered together to take part in what the organizers called the "Love Parade." As dozens of scantily clad performers danced atop a procession of slowly moving floats, huge crowds under the influence of Ecstasy and other drugs throbbed and swayed to deafening electronic music.[1] The participants, who included not only people in their teens and twenties but also children, surrendered willingly to the intoxicating mix of sound, sight, and smell, a combination which elicited what one account described as a feeling of "pure, simple, tribal joy."[2] The daily *Maariv* reported that the mass event, whose purpose was to celebrate the "spirit of openness and freedom of the end of the millennium," proved conclusively that Tel Aviv "can look like Berlin, New York, or Amsterdam, or even more so," when it brings together "all that love, the people, the noise, the crowds, the heat, the loud music, the traffic, the colorful clothing, and the variety of naked bodies of men and women, children and adults."[3]

Indeed, the Love Parade vividly expressed the permissive spirit of the millennium's end. Yet it recalled a much older spirit as well, one whose roots are to be found not in contemporary Amsterdam, Berlin, or New York, but in a distant era that predates Western civilization itself. Thousands of years before the advent of "trance" parties, similar celebrations were held throughout the ancient world, involving the same combination of wild music, sensuous dancing, and chemical intoxicants. In ancient Greece, for example, ecstatic festivals were held for the god Dionysus (known also by the name Bacchus). In these "Bacchanalia," the deity's devotees, men and women of all classes, gathered in remote locations to give themselves over completely to the god of wine and fertility.[4] Wearing satyr masks, half- or wholly naked, they cast off their inhibitions and worshipped in dance and song the god whom Ovid described as "the deliverer from sorrow, sun of the thunder,... god of the wine-press, the night-hallooed...."[5]

To the Greeks, Dionysus represented the demonic, chaotic side of nature, which can be neither tamed nor restrained by civilization.[6] In the wild cultic celebrations held in his honor, all borders were dissolved—between the sexes, between classes, between nature and culture, and between man and the gods. "The participators in these dance festivals intentionally induced in themselves a sort of mania, an extraordinary exaltation of their being," wrote the philologist Erwin Rohde. "This excessive stimulation of the senses, going even as far as hallucination, was brought about, in those who were susceptible to their influence, by the delirious whirl of the dance, the music and the darkness, and all the other circumstances of this tumultuous worship."[7] At the climax of the event, devoted followers of Dionysus entered a kind of trance in which they lost all sense of self, becoming "empty vessels" into which the essence of the god could enter.[8] Having attained a mystical union with the god, in body and spirit, they experienced a state they called *eudaemonia*—a joy of the divine, an indescribable feeling of grace and elevation. The "sacred insanity" of Dionysus spread among the celebrants like wildfire, turning them into a single body, swaying, turbulent, possessed by an ecstatic spirit.[9]

An outsider watching the drug-and-dance festivals held today, of which the Love Parade was but one example, cannot help but sense their Dionysian intensity. After a period of dormancy that lasted for centuries, the Bacchanalia have returned with a vengeance, giving birth to an entire cultural movement that has attracted millions of young followers around the world. The last decade has witnessed the rise of a new culture of ecstasy, a resurrection of the pagan intoxication via electronic "trance" music and the widespread use of mind-altering drugs. Contemporary Israel is a vital center of this new international movement, a hothouse of permissiveness in the conservative Middle East. In this riven, embattled country, the ancient fertility cults which the zealous followers of the Hebrew God sought to extirpate three thousand years ago have come to life again in the land of Israel, in mass festivals held in the heart of nature and in crowded city nightclubs. Fueled by the frenetic energies of Israel's youth, the Dionysian spirit has cast its spell on large portions of the younger generation of the Jewish state, and they devote themselves to it with alarming enthusiasm.

II

To understand the link between the wild fertility rituals of Dionysus in ancient times and the mass trance parties taking place today in Goa, India, on the island of Ibiza off the coast of Spain, or along the beach in Tel Aviv, one must examine the underlying psychic forces from which both derive their power and vitality. As Friedrich Nietzsche wrote in *The Birth of Tragedy*, the Dionysian impulse has never been restricted to Greek culture. It is a fixed element of human nature that expresses itself through a longing to dismantle "the ordinary bounds and limits of existence" and to reach a state so intense that "everything subjective vanishes into complete self-forgetfulness"[10]—a type of ecstasy (in Greek *ekstasis*, or "standing outside of oneself"), an intense experience of elevation beyond sensual pleasure, even beyond the sensation of space and time. In the ecstatic state, the individual consciousness dissolves into an unbounded sense of the absolute. Georges Bataille described the experience as follows: "The totality of what is (the universe) swallows me... nothing remains, except this or that, which are less meaningful than this nothing.... It is at this cost, no doubt, that I am no longer myself, but an infinity in which I am lost...."[11]

The Dionysian longing for ecstasy contains within it a deep yearning for self-annihilation, for the negation of one's separate individual existence. The historian of religion Mircea Eliade described this impulse as the universal desire, manifest in religious and cultic practices around the world, to "return to the womb" as a prelude to being born again.[12]

This view of the ecstatic urge as motivated, like other states of mystical union, by the yearning for a protective fetal state devoid of worries is shared by other scholars as well. Shlomo Giora Shoham, for example, posits the existence of a deep psychological force which works against the normal development of the personality. Unlike Eliade, however, Shoham claims that this force tends not toward rebirth, but toward the negation of existence as such: "The longing not to be…," he writes, "is constantly present and active, whether openly or in secret. I am inclined to agree with the proposition that if man were to have a switch in his body, by means of which he could end his life by simply pressing a button or pulling a lever, everyone would do so sooner or later."[13]

As a primal force embedded deep within the human soul, the expressions of this longing for oblivion have accompanied human civilization from its beginnings. The ecstatic impulse played an important role, for example, in tribal societies from Siberia to southern Africa, where it was exploited for spiritual and ritual purposes. The detachment from physical reality served (and continues to serve in certain parts of the world) tribal magicians and other mediums in their communication with the world of spirits, a task requiring mastery of various ecstatic techniques. The shamanistic cultures did not see ecstasy as a type of pathological behavior, but as a heightened state of consciousness in which man touches a higher, invisible reality. The debauchery that at times characterized shamanistic rituals or ancient fertility rites was not simply a casting off of inhibitions; it expressed the terrible sense of beauty that pagans saw in nature, and the fear and awe they felt in its presence.[14]

Though many ancient pagan societies adopted a positive attitude towards ecstatic cults, not all did. Classical Greek culture, for example, was characterized by a more ambivalent approach, reflecting an appreciation for the danger that such phenomena posed to the social and political order. The Greek fertility religions were, for the most part, more inhibited than those developed by many of their neighbors. Widespread displays of public licentiousness were replaced by secret, mysterious rituals intended for only the select few.[15] The popular cult of Dionysus was the striking exception, and the Greeks—who cultivated an entire civilization based on self-control—generally responded to it with revulsion and fear (as is expressed powerfully in Euripides' tragedy, *The Bacchae*). The ecstatic religion of the god of wine was not suited for life in the polis, and its devotees therefore preferred to worship Dionysus outside the city walls.

Likewise, when certain Greek city-states adopted this cult formally, they imposed restrictions on the ceremonies.[16] But the tension between the Bacchic ecstasy and the cultural ethos of the Hellenic world did not generally result in violent campaigns of suppression. On the contrary: If we accept Nietzsche's argument in *The Birth of Tragedy*, this very tension may have brought about some of the most sublime expressions of classical culture. Thanks to the refined, reasoned "Apollonian" element in Greek society, which served as a counterweight to the Dionysian spirit, this culture gave birth to the heights of tragic drama. As Nietzsche describes it, the power of Greek culture was rooted in the synthesis it created between these two elements—in its weaving together of Dionysian passion with Apollonian restraint.[17]

Western civilization, which drew heavily on the culture of Hellenic Greece, nonetheless rejected the Greeks' relatively permissive attitude towards the Dionysian. The Romans, who saw themselves as heirs of the Greek tradition, were far less tolerant of the Bacchanalia, and in 186 B.C.E. the Senate banned them altogether.[18] But it was Christianity—which inherited its enmity towards the ancient fertility religions from Judaism—that declared all-out war on the Dionysian spirit. It launched continual and bloody persecutions which did not reach their peak until the fifteenth and sixteenth centuries, when intensive witch-hunts almost completely eradicated the shamanistic culture that had survived in Europe for nearly two thousand years.[19]

The secular religion of reason, which in later centuries sought to displace the doctrines of the Catholic Church, nevertheless shared the latter's revulsion towards the ecstatic. That which had been seen by the Catholic inquisitors as the worship of Satan came to be seen by the devotees of reason as a psychopathology that had to be expunged from civilized society. Yet the revulsion harbored by the Western intellect toward the institutionalized expressions of the ecstatic impulse did not make Western culture impervious to the seductive power of the longing for self-obliteration. A century ago, Nietzsche foresaw the end of reason's hegemony and the resurrection of the Dionysian spirit.[20] As he wrote, "The disaster slumbering in the womb of theoretical culture gradually begins to frighten modern man.... The most certain auspices guarantee... *the gradual awakening of the Dionysian spirit* in our modern world!"[21] And indeed, that same Western civilization, which for centuries had denied the Dionysian urge, has, in the second half of the twentieth century, witnessed the eruption of the enormous energies associated with this primal force. Today the Dionysian has returned with an intensity unknown since the end of the classical period—and it is directed against the cultural and social order that had suppressed it for so long.

The vanguard of the Dionysian revival was of course the youth counterculture of the 1960s, which again raised the triple banner of sexual license, mind-altering drugs, and powerful, rhythmic music—"sex, drugs, and rock 'n roll." This movement was inspired by an overtly neo-pagan vision: The liberation of man from the moralistic shackles in which the Judeo-Christian tradition had chained him, and the return of mankind to a blessed, primordial state of unity with nature. In the attempt to achieve harmony with the cosmos, psychedelic drugs played a decisive role in removing the barriers between individual consciousness and absolute reality. Timothy Leary, one of the central figures in the drug culture of the 1960s, was among the first to preach the ecstatic gospel as the path toward individual and collective redemption: "All the harsh, dry, brittle angularity of game life is melted," he reported enthusiastically concerning his experiments with LSD. "You drift off—soft, rounded, moist, warm. Merged with all life…. Your control is surrendered to the total organism. Blissful passivity. Ecstatic, orgiastic, undulating unity…. All is gained as everything is given up."[22]

In their rediscovery of the Dionysian impulse, the hippies and flower children were drawn towards shamanistic cultures and their millennia-old ecstatic rites. At the same time, however, this movement adopted a very modern mission, one quite alien to the Dionysian spirit. It saw itself as a revolutionary force, bringing about the creation of a wondrous new world. Its worldview was idealistic, optimistic, and naive. In many respects, the flower children embodied the same romantic ideal cultivated within Western culture since the eighteenth century—that of youth revolting against the rigid social arrangements and injustice prevalent in the world. As Martin Buber, one of the foremost spokesmen of this ideal in the first decades of the twentieth century, put it: "Youth is the eternal opportunity of mankind. There is constantly emerging on the scene a new generation of twenty-year-olds, filled with passionate longings for the absolute, unlimited devotion to an ideal, and the will to break the locked gate of Paradise."[23] But the real audacity of the 1960s counterculture was in its ambitious aims: In many respects, it opposed Western civilization itself, with its political, social, cultural, and psychological traditions. For many

of those who participated, the results were disastrous. In the words of
Camille Paglia:

> We put the myth of Dionysus into action, and we hit the wall of real-
> ity. The sixties revolutionized consciousness, but on the road of excess
> by which we sought the palace of wisdom, many of us lost our minds,
> lives, or careers through drugs, sexual orgy, or... constant challenges
> to authority.[24]

Today's ecstatic youth culture is in many ways a direct consequence
of the revolution of the 1960s and the new legitimacy it afforded the
Dionysian impulse. The innovation of the new movement is found in
what might be called the technologizing of Dionysus: The transfiguration
of the ecstatic craze into a pre-packaged, commercially available product,
involving a now-standard combination of frenetic lighting, overwhelming electronic sound, and the proper dose of mind-bending chemicals. It
was the discovery of this formula that spawned the new Dionysian wave
of the global youth culture in the late 1980s. The "revolution" began
in the summer of 1988 on the Spanish island of Ibiza, a center of the
world nightclub scene, when a number of young socialites from Britain
discovered the overpowering effect of combining the new generation of
synthesized music with the influence of the drug Ecstasy. The result, according to Yaron Tan-Brink of the weekly *Tel Aviv*, was nothing less than
the "great cultural explosion of the end of the twentieth century":

> The synchronicity between the new drug and the new music was per-
> fect. The music sounded so good under the influence that it was simply
> impossible to stop dancing. And this did not stop with a few good
> parties. The Summer of Love of 1988 hearkened, for the first time
> since the hippies swallowed their psychedelic sugar cubes, the birth of
> a new youth culture....[25]

The drug that gave birth to this "new youth culture" did not get
its name for nothing. Ecstasy (or methyl-endioxy-methamphetamine, as
it has been known to the scientific community for eighty years) is a
stimulant that causes feelings of elevation and euphoria.[26] At the parties
where it is taken, its effects are amplified by electronic music (of which
the popular trance music is the most prominent example), based on
rapid, pounding rhythms played at high volume. According to *Tel Aviv*'s
description of the drug's effect:

It begins in the stomach, and from there it slowly spreads through the entire body, like a bursting stream of energy. Every region reached by this stream immediately feels a greater vitality. At first everything is confused. "Undefined" is the only word people manage to utter under its growing influence. The dancing sweeps you up more. The beat too. The more you are drawn into the music, the more you forget—everything. The ecstasy reaches higher and higher, becomes more intense. The feeling of time is lost, together with all inhibitions.[27]

The pagan element of the ecstasy movement has been pronounced from the beginning, finding its most explicit expression in the stupefying mass parties—"raves"—that are held in remote locations under open skies, on the beach, in the forest or desert. The religious aspect of "raves" has been noted by Russell Newcombe, who has studied the phenomenon in detail: "The DJs are the priests of the rave ceremony, responding to the mood of the crowd, with their mixing desks symbolizing the altar.... Dancing at raves may be constructed as the method by which ravers 'worship' the god of altered consciousness."[28] Indeed, the feelings expressed by participants in the raves carry a decidedly spiritual and mystical overtone. As Ronald Tzvi Trotush relates in *Tel Aviv*:

You connect to the life energy of the galaxy and become a part of it. You feel, you love, you are open, liberated, and happy—this is the peak.... [Ecstasy] definitely causes everybody to become attached to everyone else without regard to religion, race, and sex, and it definitely causes you to love until death.[29]

The total experience of ecstasy, the feeling of union with nature, the effacement of individual identity, and the sensation of overwhelming love constitute the most important parallel between the "raves" and trance parties of today on the one hand, and the ancient Bacchanalia on the other. As Nietzsche put it when describing the latter: "Under the charm of the Dionysian, not only is the union between man and man reaffirmed, but nature, which has become alienated, hostile, or subjugated, celebrates once more her reconciliation with her lost son, man.... Now all the rigid, hostile barriers that necessity, caprice, or 'impudent convention' have fixed between man and man are broken. Now, with the gospel of universal harmony, each one feels himself not only united, reconciled, and fused with his neighbor, but as one with him...."[30]

Yet despite the supposed spirituality of the "rave" experience, it has remained devoid of anything that can be called an ideology or a vision. The ecstatic state for which it strives is not indicative of a "higher" consciousness, and serves no end other than itself. It is entirely private, and suggests no connection with the concerns of public life.[31] Thirty years after the emergence of the idealistic counterculture of the 1960s, that movement's most striking features—license, drugs, and music—have been harnessed to a diametrically opposed ideal: That of *disengagement* from society. Unlike the revolutionary fervor of the 1960s, the youth culture of the last decade is gripped by the same emotional alienation characteristic of post-modern culture. Generation X—as the phrase coined by author Douglas Coupland implies[32]—has long given up on any hopes of effecting real change in the world, and hides instead behind a hardened pose of apathy and cynicism. "Nothing can be sacred," writes sociologist Ryan Moore of the prevailing mood. "All styles are exhausted the moment they are born, and, all other things being equal, one does, says, and feels nothing."[33]

This feeling of despair and apathy is not only the product of disillusionment, of disappointment with fantasies of changing the world. Paradoxically, it is also the result of material satisfaction. Today's Western youth live for the most part in a world of plenty which caters endlessly to their needs. Today's capitalist society has identified the young as the ideal consumer class—possessing an abundance of leisure time, an insatiable thirst for new stimuli, and money to burn—and has learned to attend to their tastes and preferences, to cultivate them doggedly, and to respond quickly and expertly to their demands. The market not only provides a constant flow of new products and services but also works tirelessly to create the need for these products and services. Encouragement of the young consumer's desire for immediate and boundless gratification has become a necessary condition for the system's own survival—and the youths have played the role of willing accomplice. Never has there been a generation so aware of its own "needs"; nor has the satisfaction of those needs ever been so readily available.

In his 1843 work *Either/Or*, Sören Kierkegaard described the results of such excess, in his depiction of the "aesthetic" type whose life is geared solely to the satisfaction of his appetites.[34] Such a person, contends Kierkegaard, lives his life in an "unmediated" way in the present, always enjoying the moment. The categories which form his world are

not those of good and evil, but of satisfaction and frustration, pleasure
and pain, happiness and suffering. The most immediate threat he can
sense is that of boredom, which he seeks to escape through the pursuit
of new experiences. But in the end, after he has become aware of the
unbearable monotony of his existence, he is no longer able to escape
from despair—"Despair over himself, because he no longer believes in
himself.... Despair over his human nature, because he no longer believes
that any sort of self is possible for him.... Despair over life, because all
his tomorrows will be the same as today."[35] More than a century after
Kierkegaard, the same idea was voiced by the rock artist Iggy Pop, in
a manner representative of the prevailing sentiment of our day: "They
say that death kills you, but death doesn't kill you. Boredom and indifference kill you."[36]

According to Kierkegaard, the way out of despair lies in pursuing
a life of ethical commitment. Post-modern youth culture has chosen a
different solution: Addiction to the ecstatic experience. The feelings of
alienation and disconnection that Gen-Xers have developed in response
to a reality they feel has no room for them have led them to channel
their energies into the passive euphoria of the trance. As Yaron Tan-
Brink describes it:

> For youth in Thatcheristic Britain, Reaganistic America, materialistic
> Japan, and even in Intifadistic Israel, there were no longer any Sixties
> dreams about struggling against a corrupt establishment and changing
> the world.... All they wanted at this stage was to change their own
> impossible personal lives. Naivete gave way to cynicism, hope to despair.
> Probably the only thing the world's youth collectively decided to do
> was to cut out and dance until all the crazy people got sick of their
> money and their wars.[37]

This tragic element gives the new movement its authentic Dionysian
hue, which was absent from the utopian dreams of the 1960s. Like the
ancient devotees of the god of wine and fertility, today's youth display a
fundamental lack of faith in man's ability to shape his own future. The
Dionysian impulse, as Nietzsche wrote long ago, flourishes and feeds
upon the sense of nothingness:

> The Dionysian man resembles Hamlet: Both have once looked truly into
> the essence of things, they have *gained knowledge*, and nausea inhibits

action; for their action could not change anything in the eternal nature of things; they feel it to be ridiculous or humiliating that they should be asked to set right a world that is out of joint.[38]

III

The new Dionysian revolution, which was born in Ibiza and quickly spread throughout the Western world, found fertile soil in the Jewish state. The speed with which it caught hold, and the enthusiasm with which it was received among Israeli youth, were phenomenal. The ecstatic gospel was brought to Israel by backpackers who had been caught in its spell at the wild beach parties in Goa or on islands off Thailand, and immediately found a waiting audience among Israeli fifteen- to twenty-five-year-olds.

One expression of this wave was the sudden popularity in Israel of the drug Ecstasy. "A very intensive drug culture has developed in Israel in recent years, even by world standards," claims Yoav Ben-Dov of the Institute for History and Philosophy of Science at Tel Aviv University. "We are talking not only about a tremendous growth in the number of users.... Drug abuse is connected with widespread societal phenomena, and appears today as a unifying and identity-defining factor among different groups of the youth population, and not only in a criminal context."[39] Unlike heroin or cocaine, Ecstasy is perceived as a "soft" drug, and this has allowed it to reach a growing market and to become the "lifeblood" of nightclubs throughout the country.[40] "The pills are a hit with the youth, and are given out primarily at schools and parties," noted Yaron Tan-Brink and Tal Ariel-Amir in *Tel Aviv*.[41] Similarly, Itzik Nini of the Allenby 58 club in Tel Aviv reports that the drugs have "come on strong over the past five or six years, and every year they get stronger.... Sometimes it really seems like someone poured large quantities of Ecstasy into the country's water supply and made everybody happy."[42]

Today's Dionysian youth culture finds its fullest expression, however, at the "raves," enormous trance gatherings held out in the midst of nature. "Mass trance parties... are the form of recreation preferred by Israelis of all walks of life and of all ages," writes journalist Felix Frisch in *Maariv*.[43] Whereas the influence of Israel's flower children in the 1960s was limited to a relatively small, if vocal, group of Tel Aviv bohemians, the current trance culture has captured a far wider audience, drawing clientele from across the spectrum of ages and social backgrounds, bringing together people from widely divergent sectors of the Israeli public who previously had little or nothing in common culturally.[44] As the Tel Aviv weekly *Ha'ir* reports:

> Trance cuts across ethnic and economic classes. Whoever took part in one of the raves last summer surely noticed an amazing thing: That everyone was there. Druggies from India and greasers from the suburbs, girls from development towns with their tank tops and platform shoes dancing alongside buttoned-up BA students. This is the true power of the rave: It creates an unstoppable surge of humanity. At the raves there is no fighting, no arguments; the atmosphere is saturated with love. Trance helps people to erase their brains, to lose their ability to think—that is its purpose.[45]

It would be hard to overstate the extent of the "trance" phenomenon in Israel. In the last few years, this country of six million has become a major focus of the global rave culture, in certain respects surpassing even Britain, Holland, and Germany. Trance music has become a major Israeli export—a fact expressed in the number of Israeli recording artists who have gained worldwide recognition in this area, including names such as Astral Projection, Indoor, Sandman (Itzik Levi), Chakra, and Oforia (Ofer Dikovsky). "It seems we got the biggest trance scene in the world (per population)," enthuses Amit Eshel in one of the Internet sites devoted to the subject, a claim confirmed by a survey of world media.[46] "Trance Casts a Spell over the Youth of a Worried Israel," proclaimed a *New York Times* headline last October,[47] while the French television channel arte reported that trance in Israel has become "a mass movement" and aired an interview with the head of a British record company specializing in trance music who reports better sales in Israel than in his own country.[48]

"The phenomenon exists in other countries as well, but it seems to be particularly well developed in Israel," says Yoav Ben-Dov of Tel Aviv University. "The quasi-tribal organization of the crowds at the parties... has led to a situation in which the vast extent of the trance culture's popularity in Israel is difficult to measure. Nevertheless, even in the city streets and along the highways of Israel, there are numerous signs of trance culture which are clear to anyone who knows the language (music heard from cars and stores, clothing and record outlets, announcements of parties, graffiti, the manner of dress of young people and so on), and are indicative of its penetration into various social strata and its widespread geographic appeal."[49]

The rapid growth of the trance movement in Israel has been met with a surprising degree of acceptance, of which the most striking example has been the public outcry in response to police efforts to put a stop to it.[50] Leading the protest are a number of politicians and media figures who have railed against what they see as brutal intervention in the right of Israeli youth to cultural self-definition. MK Avraham Poraz of the liberal Shinui party protested the "demeaning" treatment trance devotees have received from the police. In Poraz's opinion, "drugs were never the reason for having the parties," and therefore "we cannot tolerate having the police forbid parties at which this type of music is played."[51] "This is a battle for a person's right to enjoy himself and to have a good time as he sees fit,"[52] said then MK Dedi Zucker of Meretz, who also appraised the trance approach as "the most universal way of thinking, post-Zionist and individualistic."[53] High-profile encouragement of this sort has led trance advocates to mount a mass campaign against police pressure—exactly the type of public involvement they had sought to avoid—which reached its height in a massive "Give Trance a Chance" rally in Tel Aviv's Rabin Square in August 1998. According to reports, nearly thirty thousand protesters attended.[54]

Intensive law-enforcement efforts have succeeded in driving much of the trance movement underground in the last year, and the massive Bacchanalia have given way to events of a more limited nature. Yet this has not meant a significant setback for the Dionysian revival. If anything, the return to nightclubs, where the movement first developed in Israel, has given it an even more intense character. The club culture, which in the last decade has expanded beyond Tel Aviv to all parts of Israel, has none of the dreamy innocence of the public raves. Nightclub operators have raised the precise and nuanced manipulation of the ecstatic experience to the level of a science. Many of these clubs are designed to foster a stunning audio-visual experience, triggering a state of physical excitement and cognitive confusion. The *Jerusalem Post*'s Leora Eren-Frucht offers the following account of the Tel Aviv nightclub scene: "The flashing strobe lights are blinding. A spooky-sounding tone—like a violin note held indefinitely—is soon overtaken by a frenetic thumping beat. The pounding electronic music either wears on your nerves or whips you into a frenzy—it's hard to remain apathetic. The partyers... are jumping and gyrating, leaping and lurching in all directions."[55]

The result is a kind of sensory overload, which charges the night-clubs with an overwhelming sensual energy that unites the participants into a single, pulsating mass, orchestrated by the DJ from his high altar. Sharon Freundlich, a disc jockey who goes by the name of DJ Choopy, describes the disc jockey's achievement with pride:

> The entire club is like a ball of fire. Like an atom bomb.... It's as if you touched a thousand people all over their bodies, and you see all the blood flowing through them, and the sweat pouring from them, and they are completely yours.[56]

IV

How did Israel become a hothouse of Dionysian youth culture? To begin with, it is not too difficult to find among Israelis under the age of thirty the same pessimism and dark apathy that characterize their American and European counterparts. In 1997, the young Israeli cultural critic Gadi Taub published *A Dispirited Rebellion: Essays on Contemporary Israeli Culture*, in which he analyzed the world of what he called Israel's "dispirited generation." He discerned in his contemporaries a feeling of "rootlessness and meaninglessness," an anguish that derives from the fact that "we have no influence on all of the truly important things, that which will determine our destiny, in the most literal sense. They are above us and beyond us, and we can only sit here quietly, go about our business, and wait for the knock on the door, the announcement on the radio, the signing ceremony on television, or the emergency draft call-up."[57]

The depression and frustration that Taub attributes to Israelis in their twenties is felt no less by adolescents. "We are a screwed generation"—the battle cry of rock singer and teen idol Aviv Gefen—has been embraced enthusiastically by many younger people who, even as they enjoy a de-gree of prosperity and security unknown to their forebears, continue to show ever-greater manifestations of nihilistic despair. Although some of this is a matter of bowing to the current international fashion, which has been promoted by a global, media-driven popular youth culture, there is nonetheless an element of genuine distress as well. Like their counterparts in London, Amsterdam, and Berlin, Israeli youth feel the malaise characteristic of "late capitalism": In a prosperous society which responds to all their material needs, they are condemned to live under the perpetual threat of apathy and ennui.

Still, the Bacchanalian impulses of Israeli youth are not solely the result of global trends. They are also the product of Israel's own past, of unique historical elements which today act as a powerful catalyst for the Dionysian spirit. It is among young people that these forces most fiercely are felt, due to the intensity with which young people experience the current dissolution of traditional Israeli norms—a process in which youth themselves have played no small role. It was, after all, youth who always took the lead in shaping Israeli culture: The Zionist revolution itself was a rebellion of youth against the older, "exilic" norms, and it is the youth who have been at the forefront of every cultural development since then. In a society that adopted the modernist cult of youth from its very founding, young people serve as the heart which—to paraphrase Pascal—the head has trouble comprehending. At the same time, no other group is more sensitive to the most profound changes taking place in society, or is more capable of formulating a response to them.

This fact was particularly striking in the last two decades, when Israel's cultural and political leadership underwent a series of demoralizing collective crises—including the war in Lebanon and the protracted deployment there, the Intifada, the Scud attacks during the Gulf War, and the suicide terror bombings in the mid-1990s. It was under the pressure of these traumas that a sense of impotence began to take hold, a disbelief in the possibility of having an impact on political and societal realities. These sentiments left deep scars, especially among veterans of combat units. The fighters who had played cat-and-mouse with Intifada rioters in the territories and with Hezbollah guerillas in Lebanon felt that they had personally suffered the consequences of the weakness of spirit demonstrated by the political leadership, and by the public in general. One result was the steady withdrawal of young adults from engagement in national concerns, and their retreat into the sphere of the exclusively private. The only two cases in recent years in which young people have turned out in substantial numbers for any cause—the mourning following the Rabin assassination, and the students' strike in 1998—are remembered, in the final analysis, as efforts that produced no tangible results, and as such contributed even further to feelings of impotence. "My idea is that I have no ideas," writes the young journalist Yair Lapid. "The trouble is that somehow or other, we have become convinced that no matter what we do, someone will always be there to stop us."[58]

For the Israeli youth whose world has been taken over by a sense of chronic passivity the Dionysian promise of ecstatic self-abandonment offers a powerful temptation. The habits of Israelis between the ages of twenty and thirty—the often reckless search for adventure overseas, the attraction to Eastern mystical cults, the steady rise in the consumption of recreational drugs—are all examples. The fact that these symptoms are most frequently the province of recently discharged soldiers may well point to the central role played by the experience of military service. The conventional wisdom holds that the army matures the young Israeli, but the truth may well be the opposite: In many respects, the military framework forces upon the young Israeli just about all the discipline, order, and duty he can handle. Once he escapes into civilian life, he feels an immense need for release, an overwhelming desire to "let go." At times, one gets the impression that the typical freshly discharged soldier views his new civilian status not as representative of new obligations, but as a license for anarchy.

The intense pressure of Israeli life, felt especially by a youth grown increasingly resentful of the heavy burden of responsibilities to society, has fed the Dionysian impulse. The eagerness with which they cast off their inhibitions is evident at the clubs and outdoor parties: "Your people celebrate as if every party might be their last," commented a Dutch disc jockey on the unusual intensity of the Israeli scene.[59] "The public here has an enormous need for this," DJ Choopy concurs, offering his own explanation: "Maybe because of the wars, the pressure, maybe because of the sea. The weather. The atmospherics here. But what is certain is that the Israeli audience has an amazing hunger that no other audience in the world has—a totally indescribable hunger—and so it just runs with it. All the way."[60] A similar sentiment is expressed by journalist Assaf Gefen of *Maariv*:

> Trance is fundamentally an extreme genre: From the style of dress
> down to the pace of the beat. Its emergence as the most popular kind

of music in Israel, far more than in the Western world, is apparently due to the fact that we are no less extreme. There must be some total experience—like army service, for example—to make people want to free themselves by throwing themselves into a similarly intense Eastern experience, only from a different direction. Japan is considered our most serious rival for the title of "superpower of trance," and it too is not exactly a normal Western country.[61]

V

There is nothing new about moralizing over the state of Israeli youth. As early as 1960, the novelist S. Yizhar coined the term "the espresso generation" to express his scorn for what he saw as the hedonistic mentality of the youth of his day, and for their pursuit of things "fast, sweet, and cheap."[62] A similar ring can be heard in the frequent complaints voiced today about young people by society's older members. But most of this criticism fails to capture what has truly gone wrong in Israeli youth culture over the past decade. The real problem is not the hedonism, materialism, and egocentrism that are characteristic of any bourgeois society. It is the culture's deep Dionysian tendencies.

The force that motivates post-modern youth is not egoistic. On the contrary, it tends in the opposite direction—towards the death of the ego, the dissolution of the individual in favor of ecstatic self-abandonment.[63] "First and foremost they are saying something in the somewhat desperate effort they are making here," writes the respected journalist Ari Shavit in *Haaretz*, "in the attempt to arrive, on the dance floor, in the bathrooms, and in the dark places, at some sort of epileptic authenticity, in a time and place that offer them no other kind of authenticity—and in their half-innocent surrender to the totality."[64] Pessimism, passivity, and disengagement from everyday life have become the most prominent features of Israeli youth, who prefer to lose themselves in psychedelic festivals rather than come to terms directly with the complex realities of personal and public life in a country in conflict.

The burden Israeli society places upon its youth has played, no doubt, a decisive role in the Dionysian outburst of the past decade. The political, social, and economic realities that surround the young Israeli have made him particularly vulnerable to the charms of the god of wine and fertility. However, the response to his call would not have been so overwhelming had Israeli society not failed to provide its young with a viable alternative ethos. The neo-pagan ecstatic revival has filled the vacuum left by the demise of the old Zionism, and has been fueled by a mistrust felt by many youth towards anything reminiscent of the grandiose slogans and utopian promises of an earlier day. Given this state of affairs, it seems that the only hope for those who are troubled by the rise of Dionysus in Zion is to nurture the same kind of countervailing cultural force which allowed past societies to ward off similar threats—not new technologies, but a new faith.

NOTES

1. *Maariv*, October 3, 1999.

2. *Z'man Tel Aviv*, October 8, 1999.

3. *Maariv*, October 3, 1999.

4. Pierre Brunel, ed., *Companion to Literary Myths, Heroes, and Archetypes*, trans. W. Allatson, J. Hayword, and T. Selous (London: Routledge, 1992), pp. 303-304.

5. Ovid, *Metamorphoses*, trans. Rolfe Humphries (Bloomington: Indiana University, 1967), book iv, lines 15-18, p. 81.

6. Most of the festivals in honor of Dionysus were conducted outside of the city limits, in the forests or mountains, after nightfall. Some of the festivals involved only women—the Bacchantes or Maenades ("the wild ones")—whose unrestrained behavior is preserved in Euripides' *The Bacchae*.

7. Erwin Rohde, *Psyche: The Cult of Souls and Belief in Immortality Among the Ancient Greeks*, trans. W.B. Hills (Chicago: Ares, 1987), p. 258.

8. Erik Lund, Mogens Pihl, and Johannes Slok, *A History of European Ideas*, trans. W. Glyn Jones (London: C. Hurst, 1971), p. 22.

9. The merging of the believer and the god turns the person into one who is *en-theos*—"including the god"; thus the term *enthusiasmus*, i.e., "enthusiasm."

10. Friedrich Nietzsche, *The Birth of Tragedy Out of the Spirit of Music*, in *Basic Writings of Nietzsche*, trans. Walter Kaufmann (New York: Modern Library, 1992), pp. 36, 59.

11. Georges Bataille, *The Accursed Share: An Essay on General Economy*, trans. Robert Hurley (New York: Zone, 1993), vol. ii, p. 115.

12. Mircea Eliade, *The Myth of the Eternal Return, or Cosmos and History* (Princeton: Princeton, 1959).

13. Shlomo Giora Shoham, *Rebellion, Creativity, and Revelation* (Tel Aviv: Urian, 1986), pp. 16-17. [Hebrew]

14. See Ioan M. Lewis, *Ecstatic Religion* (New York: Penguin, 1971). For an excellent survey of contemporary shamanistic culture, see Nahum Megged, *Gates of Hope and Gates of Fear* (Tel Aviv: Modan, 1998). [Hebrew]

15. The outstanding examples are the rituals of Demeter in Eleusis, Attica, and Arcadia.

16. Among other things, the Dionysian cult enjoyed official status in Corinth in the days of Periandros, in Sikyon in the days of Kleisthenes, and in Athens in the days of Peisistratos. Cf. Michael Avi Yonah and Israel Shatzman, *Illustrated Encyclopedia of the Classical World* (New York: Harper and Row, 1981), pp. 164-165.

17. Nietzsche argued that the refined, rational, Apollonian element protected Greek culture from the expressions of barbarism and licentiousness that characterized Dionysian outbursts in other cultures. "For some time, however, the Greeks were apparently perfectly insulated and guarded against the feverish excitements of these festivals, though knowledge of them must have come to Greece on all the routes of land and sea; for the figure of Apollo, rising full of pride, held out the Gorgon's head to this grotesquely uncouth Dionysian power—and really could not have countered any more dangerous force." Nietzsche, *The Birth of Tragedy*, p. 39. These two cultural forces, argues Nietzsche, "run parallel to each other, for the most part openly at variance," and they "continually incite each other to new and more powerful births...." Nietzsche, *The Birth of Tragedy*, p. 33.

18. It must be emphasized that ecstatic phenomena continued to exist in the framework of the great monotheistic religions, and can be seen in the activities of biblical prophets, certain Christian saints and mystics (such as Julian of Norwitch, Francis of Assisi, Teresa of Avila, Catherine of Siena, and others), the Hasidic masters, or the Muslim dervishes. Nevertheless, these are lacking in the frenzied element that is an inseparable part of Dionysian ecstasy. Regarding this, Abraham Joshua Heschel drew a distinction between the state of ecstasy of "the wild and fervid type,... a state of frenzy arising from overstimulation and emotional tension," and "the sober and contemplative type, which is a rapture

of the soul in a state of complete calmness, enabling a person to rise beyond the confines of consciousness." Abraham J. Heschel, *The Prophets*, part 2 (New York: Harper, 1962), p. 105. Even if such "complete calmness" is not always characteristic of the ecstatic practice to be found in Judaism, Christianity, or Islam, it is still obvious that these religions are constrained by a strict moral ethos that distinguishes them from the Dionysian craze of the senses. For a discussion of mystical ecstasy, see Evelyn Underhill, *Mysticism: A Study in the Nature and Development of Man's Spiritual Consciousness* (New York: Noonday, 1955); Ben-Ami Sharfstein, *The Mystical Experience* (Tel Aviv: Am Oved, 1972). [Hebrew]

19. Carlo Ginzburg, *Ecstasies: Deciphering the Witches' Sabbath*, trans. R. Rosenthal (New York: Pantheon, 1991).

20. In *The Birth of Tragedy* Nietzsche expressed his hope that German culture, and especially Wagnerian music, would be the bearer of the Dionysian message. Later on in his writings he abandoned these hopes, and focused his longing on the return of Dionysus in the figure of the Superman.

21. Nietzsche, *The Birth of Tragedy*, pp. 112, 119 (emphasis in original).

22. Timothy Leary, Ralph Metzner, and Richard Alpert, *The Psychedelic Experience: A Manual Based on the Tibetan Book of the Dead* (New Hyde Park, N.Y.: University Books, 1970), p. 59.

23. Martin Buber, "Zion and Youth," in *Selected Writings on Judaism and Jewish Affairs* (Jerusalem: Zionist Library, 1961), vol. 2, p. 105. [Hebrew]

24. Camille Paglia, *Sex, Art, and American Culture: Essays* (New York: Vintage, 1992), p. 212. Paglia argues that the flower children, in giving a Rousseauian spin on the Dionysian spirit, mistakenly identified it with the Freudian pleasure principle while ignoring the cruel and destructive aspect that is an inseparable part of its essence. This distortion, according to Paglia, is shared by the nineteenth-century Romantics' understanding of the god of wine and fertility.

25. *Tel Aviv*, July 17, 1998.

26. Unlike such psychedelic drugs as LSD, which change the user's state of consciousness and give him intense experiences, but of a type that it is difficult to express or to assimilate within everyday life, Ecstasy is said to leave the user in a normal but intensified state of consciousness, thereby enabling him to remember and absorb his experiences while under the influence. The result is a gradual change in the person's lifestyle. *Guardian*, July 22, 1995.

27. *Tel Aviv*, July 17, 1998.

28. *Guardian*, July 22, 1995.

29. *Tel Aviv*, July 17, 1998.

30. Nietzsche, *The Birth of Tragedy*, p. 37.

31. This is the significant difference between the escapist Dionysian trance culture and the spiritual pretensions of the "New Age." Whereas the New Age movement consciously attempts to reconstruct some of the mystical elements of the pagan era, the world of raves and clubs revives the wild ecstasy of the Dionysian cult without ascribing to them any deeper significance.

32. Douglas Coupland, *Generation X: Tales for an Accelerated Culture* (New York: St. Martin's, 1991).

33. Ryan Moore, "'... And Tomorrow Is Just Another Crazy Scam': Post-Modernity, Youth, and the Downward Mobility of the Middle Class," in Joe Austin and Michael Nerin Willard, eds., *Generations of Youth: Youth Cultures and History in Twentieth-Century America* (New York: New York University, 1998), p. 254.

34. Sören Kierkegaard, *Either/Or*, trans. Walter Lowrie (Princeton: Princeton, 1985), vol. 2.

35. Francis J. Lescoe, *Existentialism: With or Without God* (New York: Alba House, 1974), p. 36.

36. Irvine Welsh, *Ecstasy: Three Tales of Chemical Romance* (London: Vintage, 1997).

37. *Tel Aviv*, July 17, 1998.

38. Nietzsche, *The Birth of Tragedy*, p. 60 (emphasis in original).

39. Yoav Ben-Dov, "Waiting for Ben-Ami," in *Newzeek*, August 1999, pp. 58-59. [Hebrew]

40. "Ecstasy—illegal and problematic as it may be—has benefited Tel Aviv nightlife. It opened up and liberated the scene, for when people are turned on, they desperately need a dance floor, like air to breathe. And there's always someone ready to provide it." *Tel Aviv*, July 17, 1998.

41. *Tel Aviv*, September 25, 1997.

42. *Haaretz*, November 26, 1999.

43. *Maariv*, June 28, 1998.

44. Moreover, "The ages used to be above twenty-one. Today it has gone down drastically. Fourteen-year-olds," says DJ Miko, "are among the leading figures of the nightclub scene." *Newzeek*, August 1999, p. 29.

45. *Ha'ir*, June 5, 1998.

46. Chaishop Internet site.

47. *New York Times*, October 24, 1999.

48. arte, July 9, 1999; *Haaretz*, June 6, 1997.

49. Yoav Ben-Dov, "The Trance Culture in Israel: Aspects and Contexts," in *Makom L'mahshava* 2, November 1998, pp. 26-32.

50. *Haaretz*, September 11, 1998.

51. *Ha'ir*, June 19, 1998.

52. *Maariv*, June 28, 1998.

53. *New York Times*, October 24, 1999.

54. Associated Press Internet site, July 10, 1998.

55. Leora Eren-Frucht, "A Night on the Town," in *The Jerusalem Post* Magazine, August 9, 1996, p. 15.

56. *Haaretz* Supplement, November 26, 1999.

57. Gadi Taub, *A Dispirited Rebellion: Essays on Contemporary Israeli Culture* (Tel Aviv: Hakibbutz Hame'uhad, 1997), p. 16. [Hebrew]

58. Yair Lapid, "Mug Shot," *Politika* 23 (October 1988), pp. 22-23. [Hebrew]

59. *Ha'ir*, October 15, 1999.

60. *Haaretz*, November 26, 1999.

61. *Maariv*, September 4, 1998.

62. S. Yizhar, "The Espresso Generation," speech before the Mapai Central Committee, June 30, 1960.

63. Mordechai Rotenberg argues that the abandonment of the soul in ecstasy is a kind of immunization against the fear of death. See Mordechai Rotenberg, *Dio-Logo Therapy: Psychonarration and Pardes* (New York: Praeger, 1991), pp. 80-82.

64. *Haaretz*, November 26, 1999.

THE GOLDFISH AND
THE JEWISH PROBLEM

ANNA ISAKOVA

Introduction

Some of my best friends are Israeli liberals. Although we don't disagree on basics, there are three things we always argue about: the first is my goldfish, its aggressive behavior, and my right to mete out punishment; the second is the tendency to ostracize smokers in modern society, their conversion into a minority, and the ways this minority defends itself against the majority; and the third is cultural discrimination in Israel.

The episode of the goldfish began when I was given a present of two goldfish in a bowl and four guppies in a plastic bag and was asked to wait twenty-four hours before releasing the guppies from their sealed quarters. The next day, I discovered floating in the bowl the remains of one goldfish and four thoroughly terrified guppies, one of them in an advanced stage of pregnancy. The remaining goldfish was swimming around in the bowl looking like a shark in disguise. When it turned its attention on the pregnant guppy, I grasped the warrior firmly, removed it from the bowl, and flushed it down the toilet. That same evening, my liberal friends came to visit the goldfish they had given me as a present. Ever since, we have engaged in occasional analyses of this hair-raising story.

My friends insist that I had no right to impose the death penalty, since the goldfish had acted according to an entirely different set of values from my own, and because it was a living being and not an inanimate piece of property—it was my responsibility to care for its needs until its death from natural causes. In short, my behavior was most emphatically not politically correct.

In actual fact, when I consider the affair in retrospect, in defending the pregnant guppy I behaved according to *my* ethical principles. I have no idea if my guppy, with deference to its set of values, appreciated my coming to its aid. I am quite certain that the goldfish saw me as an enemy of the goldfish nation. I gave it a responsibility that it abused, to the detriment of the guppies, and it paid with its life when a higher power—myself—intervened. The fish had tangled with a superior power. End of story.

My liberal friends will have no truck with this. They are good people and they want good to prevail in all cases and evil to do as little harm as possible. For my part, I do not share their belief in the existence of such a possibility. Common sense tells me that it is an impossibility, and so I have excluded myself from the liberal community, and this distresses me greatly, since I am at a loss to know where I can still belong.

The subject of smoking tends to be more hotly disputed. As a smoker myself, I have no objection to the allocation of separate areas for smokers and nonsmokers. I simply have considerable difficulty in finding these special places, which, for the most part, are unaesthetic and tucked away out of sight in emergency stairwells, gloomy corners, and run-down balconies—a kind of smoker's Harlem, and this is something I am staunchly opposed to.

I know that smoking is a public health hazard, but the exhaust fumes belched out by passing cars are far more damaging. At the Check Post Junction in Haifa, for example, you could choke on the smell of chemicals in the air. So either let justice be all-encompassing—i.e., either prohibit the use of motor vehicles and chemical products until a way is found to protect the public from their by-products—or leave me and my cigarette alone. That is, if we look at things from the point of view of the common good. From the point of view of my own personal benefit, the matter would appear to be a tad more complicated. The Ministry of Health is obliged to warn me, and I stand warned. Beyond that, it's up to me, and that is insofar as the society in which I live is a liberal one.

If it is not so, and assumes the right to interfere in personal decision making, then that's a horse of quite a different color.

I do not recognize the right of the nonsmoking public to impose restrictions on smoking intended to force the smoker to desist from poisoning himself or herself. I would really like to give up smoking, but as long as I am constantly hounded and the decision is not mine alone to make, I will continue to smoke. That is my way of defending my rights as an individual.

My liberal friends tell me that this is a ridiculous attitude to take. I quite agree. Every stand on principles is ridiculous, since it is not based on the principle of pragmatism. Pragmatism is out of step with modern liberalism and is most certainly out of step with Israeli liberalism. So maybe I'm a liberal after all. If I were convinced of that, I would have a problem.

The third topic is the toughest one of all. The majority of the state's population, myself included, do not feel that the dominant Hebrew culture represents their own, and have no desire to create within it or to actively be consumers of it alone. Most of my Israeli liberal friends do in fact belong to this culture, and they have absolutely no desire to take me to task on the subject. They agree that our culture should be a mixed salad of all the cultural produce of the country. Thus far I am in agreement with them. But they also see nothing wrong in a chef preparing this salad, and this is a task that they have taken upon themselves. From this point on we go our separate ways. The moment a chef comes into sight, that's the end of the argument and when I become the goldfish. That is the reason why I am writing this article. I want to express everything I have to say, and perhaps then we can finally get the argument out into the open.

About the Writer

My life in Israel began with smuggling. In December 1971, an Israeli clerk in patched trousers was waiting for us at Vienna International Airport. He shoved us behind a makeshift screen and ordered us not to budge from there. In the Soviet Union, I had already grown accustomed to the ways of a free spirit and had no intention of backing down. I immediately moved the screen aside and went up to a counter to buy chocolates for my young daughter. The clerk began to shout: "You belong to the State of Israel now, so if I tell you not to move, be so kind as not to move! No one here intends to feed you chocolates! You'd best get used to the idea right now!" At Schönau Castle, where emigrants from the Soviet Union assembled before being sent to the country to which they would henceforth belong, it was extremely cold. Hundreds of people were crowded together in the main hall where the Joint Distribution Committee had set up a table. Those who filled out an application there were immediately whisked away to a more comfortable hotel and from there directly to the United States.

To this day I have no idea who devised this test of devotion to Zionism, but at the time everyone resisted the temptation. The crowd skirted round the table without approaching it.

There were far more people billeted in Schönau Castle than it could hold and, true to the laws of bureaucracy, no one was assigned a room. I was invited into an office where I was presented with the key to a single room as a token of appreciation for promoting *aliya*. "There's a woman out there with a baby," I said. "She needs a room more than me." "It's not up to you to decide who needs what!" snapped the clerk. Not long after this conversation, I was back in the same office, this time for a chat with an American Zionist who asked how I was doing. "How are they treating you?" he asked, apparently *au fait* with close encounters of the first kind with the Zionist dream. "Great," I lied. The clerk, who had been listening to what I had to say with a certain trepidation, nodded his head and smiled.

I hadn't lied to curry favor with him. That was a time when anyone who said anything to me against Israel or Israelis would suffer a fate worse than death. Back then I still wanted to be able to say, "Israel is me!"

Before we boarded the airplane, the selfsame clerk put a magnificent guitar into my hands and asked me to take it to Ben-Gurion Airport and give it to a young lady whose name I no longer remember. My late father was a lawyer. Moreover, unlike my mother, who was a Zionist, he was a Dubnov hasid and was therefore of the opinion that self-determination and Jews were unlikely bedfellows. "We are reduced to smuggling," he said at the time. "The guitar is almost certainly liable for tax and we are temporarily exempt. Not only that, but a state that sends a corrupt and impertinent clerk in patched clothes to meet its new citizens hardly seems worthy to me of permanent residence. Let's go to Boston!"

"No way," I said.

We had an aunt waiting for us in Boston, dying to show us her unending gratitude if we would just settle down near her. I possessed a solid command of English from my youth and I loved English literature no less than Russian literature. In contrast, I did not have the slightest knowledge of Hebrew. So what made me act the way I acted? To understand, you have to go back in time, to Russia, or more accurately, to Lithuania. We were "Litvaks," born and bred. There had been Jews in Lithuania for nearly a thousand years, and in human terms, that's an eternity. I have no idea if Lithuania is a beautiful country objectively, but it is my measure of beauty: whatever is like it is beautiful by virtue of its similarity; what is unlike it is beautiful by contrast.

The only pogrom visited on Lithuanian Jews had not been perpetrated by locals but by the Ukrainian Cossack Bogdan Khmelnitsky. To this day, old scores have not been settled between the Lithuanians and the Ukrainians, the Russians and the Poles. The Jews were not party to these disputes. They were the ones who had built the Lithuanian economy, the traders who dwelt around the walls of Gediminas Castle, named after the Lithuanian prince who had invited them to his country. This was how Vilnius became a major Jewish center, the Jerusalem of Lithuania. The Lithuanians were not opposed to this process, at least not openly.

After a thousand years of relatively untroubled coexistence, something quite inexplicable suddenly happened. Of some 270,000 Lithuanian Jews, a mere 10 percent remained after the Holocaust (some would say even less), and it was not the Germans but the Lithuanians themselves who had murdered them.

I was born at the end of the war. My parents had escaped from Lithuania on the very day that the Germans invaded. My father had managed to get hold of a bus that he filled with his closest friends and family, and he set out for the town where his sister lived. Not far from the town, the bus was stopped by a local Lithuanian who knew my father well. "Don't go there," he warned. "Your sister and her husband are hanging on trees, and their child has been spitted on a piece of wood."

My father couldn't believe his ears. This was happening in the middle of the twentieth century, when the cult of the individual was at its peak. My father was a Lithuanian intellectual of Jewish extraction, a collector of Lithuanian Impressionist and Expressionist art, a best friend to local intellectuals, and an acolyte of Nietzsche. The spectacle of human beings hanging on trees and children impaled on wooden sticks was a grim regression to medieval times. The light had been eclipsed. The bus turned around and headed toward the Russian border.

When my parents returned to Lithuania at the end of the war, the tally of those murdered appeared to be even greater than they had imagined, and they therefore decided to bring me up within Russian culture. A few Lithuanians who were known with certainty not to have murdered Jews still visited us at home. However, my parents absolutely forbade me to have any social contact with Lithuanians. This was not a problem at the Russian school. There were no Lithuanians studying there, as the Russians despised them, and the Russians made little attempt to learn their language. My father nevertheless took pains to teach me Lithuanian, mainly because he could not bear to lose the definitive part of his personality and his culture.

I came of age and was accepted into medical school at the University of Vilnius. Our anatomy lecturer was rumored to have collaborated with the Germans. When we began to study the anatomy of the human head, this lecturer asked us to acquire and bring a genuine human skull to class. One of my classmates found just such a skull for both of us. I had committed to memory the names of all the bones, the parts, and the openings in the skull with the exception of one small, round hole in the occipital bone. I was anxious to get a good grade and went through all the literature, but for some reason could find no mention of this little hole.

"It's a bullet hole," said the lecturer and burst out laughing. He wasn't particularly inclined to give good grades to Jews.

"Where did you get the skull?" I asked my friend. "From the Ponary Forest. Everybody gets them there," he answered scornfully. They had killed Jews in Ponary, hundreds and thousands of Jews. Sixty-four members of my own family were among the missing.

When the State of Israel, through the Knesset, decided to forgive publicly the Lithuanians (in the person of their prime minister) for the sins they had committed against the Jews, the Lithuanian Jewish community that had immigrated almost en masse to Israel during the seventies was not consulted. Neither did the media go to the trouble to explain to Israeli citizens who was having the slate wiped clean at the time and why.

The entirety of the world's guilty conscience and what remains of Jewish memories is squeezed into the modestly proportioned building of Yad Vashem. Its budget is cut as a matter of tradition from year to year, apparently because we don't have the money for memories. Precisely because of these memories, I had found shelter under the wing of Russian culture, even though I never forgot the fact that I was Jewish. And even if I did forget, there would always be someone who would be quick to remind me.

When I lived in the Soviet Union, anti-Semitism was as much political as it was social. Universities had a quota for Jewish students. (It's not so long ago that I read that there was talk of imposing a quota for Russian immigrant students in Israeli universities. I am unable to come to terms with this idea—for me it is completely incomprehensible.) The Jewish quota in Russian universities was usually set at around 10 percent of the entire student body. Although, for obvious reasons, such quotas did not officially exist, in practical terms everyone knew that they did, and it was an open enough secret to act as a deterrent, even if university authorities never used nationality as an excuse for rejecting applications from Jews. The various ways to refuse Jews admission were like something out of the novels of Dumas the Elder. They would mention nonexistent errors in their examination corrections, or they would spill ink on the written pages, or alternatively, they would deliberately misplace them. In oral examinations, they set special questions for Jews—questions to which the teachers themselves did not know the correct answers. (Doctors and nurses who emigrated from the Soviet Union during the nineties tell of the same methods being applied to them in medical examinations in Israel. Could this represent their projection of past memories on the present, or is what they are saying true? It would be good to conduct a serious investigation of the matter, if for no other reason than to refute these claims.) Despite this, the number of Jewish students at Russian universities exceeded the permitted 10 percent. Jewish youth were educated to excel in order to survive, and to be fair, there was also not an inconsiderable number of honest teachers. Non-Jewish teachers occasionally put their jobs at risk by defending a talented young Jew, and we owe them a debt of gratitude.

Yet, even after they had been accepted as students and had successfully coped with the extra difficulties, and after they had gotten their
long-awaited degrees, life did not become any easier for them. As Jews,
we encountered a glass ceiling that made it impossible for us to advance
socially and professionally beyond certain limits.

It is certainly true that Jews were sought after in intellectual circles,
particularly among dissident groups, just as in years gone by it had been
possible to find many Jews in communist revolutionary circles. Every regime
that has held sway in Russia at one time or another has tried to restrict
the rights of Jews, and the Jews have been, for their part, the opposition
to every regime. It is perhaps for this reason that the Jews aligned themselves with the most enlightened forces in the Russian intelligentsia, with
one exception: during the period of the Russian communist terror, when
a shameful number of Jews were involved in that despicable event.

In Soviet Russia there had been a civil war between Jews which had
lasted for many years. A Jewish communist might betray a religious Jew to
the authorities. A Jewish interrogator might torture another Jew in prison.
One Jew would build gulags in Siberia, while another Jew would send
thousands of Jews to be imprisoned there. Among those who fabricated
the charges against the Jewish Anti-Fascist Committee were numerous
Jews. Even the trial of the famous "Doctor's Plot" did not proceed without the assistance of Jews. We had to deal with this unpleasant reality,
as well as with the feeling of inferiority that the Jewish culture had in
the face of Russian culture.

Many prominent personalities were active within the framework of
Soviet counterculture. There, great humanists could find a home, including
many Jews. What the Zionist circle had to offer by comparison looked
paltry. Moreover, the goal which this circle set before Jews—to leave the
Soviet Union—looked superficial and somewhat arbitrary. It lacked the
power and appeal to effectively compete with the stated objective of the
dissident community: the overthrow of the Soviet regime. Nonetheless,
I chose Zionism.

This decision-making process was long and complicated. One could
say that, thanks to the Soviet regime and my hatred of it, I had a long
preparation in anti-Soviet activism. All that one had to do was to resist
the authorities. In other words, one only needed to read, write, or distribute whatever was forbidden to read, write, or distribute—to scrutinize
where scrutiny was forbidden and to refuse to carry out whatever was

obligatory. One might be punished for such activities, but this was a cause for which it was worth being punished.

Zionist activism was not the natural consequence of a particular way of life, although this activism was apparently the result of certain circumstances, such as life in the shadow of the Holocaust and the open anti-Semitism of the Soviet regime, which revived Russian chauvinism. Even so, every one of those elements which were supposed to, and in fact did, lead to Zionist activism could have found expression in the adoption of a different direction.

After the Holocaust one would have expected to hear a cry for a change in the global agenda which would have made racism unfeasible. The existence of a small state with a high concentration of Jews did not appear to guarantee the security of these Jews or of any others. There were no strong rational arguments in favor of Zionism—indeed, most of the points in favor of it were emotional in nature. The State of Israel, founded on the ruins of Nazi doctrine, was my own private revenge, but emotional considerations were in my mind inferior to rational ones. Anti-Semitism, as far as I was concerned, was a kind of touchstone by which humanity could be divided into enlightened individuals and barbarians. It compelled me to carry the banner of my own Jewish identity, and supplied me with the necessary amount of adrenaline. It required me to know more, to work harder, and to act with greater dignity than the members of other nationalities. Metaphysically speaking, this concurred with what was at the time my understanding of the historical role of the Jewish people: anti-Semitism enabled us to function as the yeast cells in the leavening process of human advancement.

I remember that sometime before I made *aliya*, I had a series of conversations with a close friend who remained to fight against the Soviet regime. "What will I do among the Jews?" I asked. "How will the tensions be created that are so necessary for creative activity? Is this not just a certain recipe for being sucked into a bland and lackluster life?" My friend was amused to hear my misgivings and tried to convince me that real life goes on beyond the limits of the impossible; that the life of the free spirit can be lived only when freedom is unlimited. His response betrayed a certain confusion: neither of us knew what life without limits on freedom would be like and how it would be lived.

Even Russian chauvinism was not what drove me directly to Israel. Within the anti-Soviet circle, which became my natural place of habitation, they were particularly fond of the subject of nationality. The matter of the rights of oppressed nationalities in the Soviet Union occupied pride of place in the dissident agenda. Israeli liberals have difficulty understanding the source of this clear sense of nationalism among those who were portrayed as fighters for human rights and emancipation in the Soviet Union. In fact, nationalism was inherent in Russian liberal doctrine, and this shows quite emphatically to what extent liberalism as a value is dependent on a given state and the pragmatic approach.

Yet the nationalistic idea was not what made me choose *aliya*. Nationalist Jews in Russia were divided into those who believed with all their heart that a national life is unsustainable beyond the boundaries of the Jewish state and those who believed in the possibility of reviving the Jewish community in a united and free Russia. The latter spoke of the unique road that Russian Jewry had taken, its characteristic culture, and its specific role in Jewish history as a whole. There were some who thought even then that all this would be diminished in the multi-ethnicity of Israel and would eventually be consigned to oblivion. At the end of the sixties, I heard words that have disturbed me until this very day: "Modern Jewish culture as a whole is dependent on a revival of Russian Jewry and the existence of Jewish culture in Russia itself. If we stand in front of world Jewry with empty hands, we will vanish from the earth, and our creative-cultural potential will be lost. We are the largest and almost sole remnant of secular Jewish culture." There were many who did not believe that they could realize their full cultural potential in Israel. At the time, we had no understanding whatsoever of what was happening culturally in the Jewish state. Our pessimism derived from the belief that when we left Russia we would have to tear up all our roots, including our Jewish ones in their historical sense. Eventually, the die was cast, and my family made the decision to emigrate because of a succinct remark my mother made. "Only in Israel," she said, "can your son become prime minister." This was a point for which I had no answer. Although I didn't have a son at the time, the possibility of founding a new dynasty that would be free of any external restrictions whatsoever and could aspire to achieve any goal—became an *idée fixe*. So one impertinent clerk with his stupid guitar was not about to make me change my mind. It made absolutely no sense to leave the Soviet Union simply to get to the United States.

The voyage to Israel began in 1968. One could say that it ended on December 12, 1971, when the inebriating smell of oranges caused my air passages to contract. From that day on I have been allergic to orange blossoms, and consequently I anticipate that sweet suffering every year. The thought that really troubles me, however, is that I have yet to set foot in Zion. For a long time I had taken consolation in the thought that those who live in the country, like the spies of Joshua, son of Nun, have to lie to themselves and say that the country is good, for if they were to behave differently it would remain uninhabited.

Nowadays I am of the opinion that we live an unnecessary lie. I still have faith in the country's enormous potential but wonder if the ongoing lie preserves that potential or destroys it.

I had wanted to be able to say, "Israel is me." The truth as it is today is different: Israel is all that I am not.

My life in Israel, which began with the smuggling of a guitar, continued along the same lie-strewn path, with all its twists and turns. I was forced to do things I didn't like for the sake of future generations, and little by little I began to hate myself. I came here after working for five years as a doctor, during which time I had completed several specialist residencies. I was all of twenty-six years old. I wanted to advance in my profession, but I couldn't find a hospital willing to give me the time even for a short introductory meeting. At Tel Hashomer Hospital they laid it on the line: "We don't employ Russian immigrants." The other hospitals had lied.

Despite all the restrictions imposed on Jews in the Soviet Union, professional advancement there was guaranteed (within certain limits, of course). My career there had already begun to take off. Here, all doors were closed to me. I was perplexed. The state I now belonged to sent me as a *locum tenens* to a Bedouin tribe in the Negev. I didn't see that as being much help to the Bedouin or to myself. I was unfamiliar with local methods of treatment and the local names for medicines. I should have been working in a hospital to learn all that, which, as I have said, was impossible.

A friend of mine suggested that we buy a house together in Rosh Pina and grow strawberries there to sell. That sounded more reasonable to me than carrying out medical experiments on Bedouin who had done me no harm. Houses in Rosh Pina were particularly cheap at the time and were sold with yard space. We had begun to look for professional literature on the cultivation of strawberries when I was invited to the Russian department of Kol Yisrael to talk about the status of refuseniks in the Soviet Union. I took an extreme position in the discussion: The success of the refuseniks' struggle against the authorities in the Soviet Union depended on assistance from the Western media. While we were still there, even if we had resorted to every imaginable strike and protest, these measures would never have been of any avail without some parallel expression of them on the outside. At best, we would have been ejected from all official institutions and, at worst, we would all have been arrested.

There were several radio stations broadcasting to the Soviet Union at the time: Voice of America and the Freedom Station, which were broadcast from Germany, the BBC from London, and Kol Yisrael from Jerusalem. In Russia, these stations were known affectionately as "the voices." The Israeli voice was the worst. The information we sent Kol Yisrael about various protest activities was not broadcast on time, there was constant confusion about names and places, and occasionally, they were demonstrably unwilling to broadcast our letters at all. If it hadn't been for the "voices" from Germany and Great Britain, the Zionist movement in Russia would probably have been a total fiasco.

I tried to explain these facts to the people at the station. They answered that the government was not interested in making relations with Russia any worse, and they offered me a job with Kol Yisrael there and then. I had worked in journalism in Russia. I hadn't worked in radio but I understood what the job entailed and, to make a long story short, I had a lot more experience in the field than I had in growing strawberries.

One of the reasons I was inclined to accept their proposal was that I could be more active and effective in helping my friends who were still in Russia. I was grateful to fate for having intervened so unexpectedly in my affairs. It seemed as if things were beginning to brighten up, but a dour expression came over the face of my father, who didn't have to give in to circumstance. "Prove to me that you've got what it takes to be a journalist," he said slyly. "Try to get an interview with the director of some hospital." "Get me the name of someone famous in local medicine," I responded. My father had challenged me and I had picked up the gauntlet. The name which he supplied me with—the secret password, so to speak—was "Kaplinski," the dean of Tel Aviv University's medical school at the time. I never met him face-to-face, before or after the fact. Now equipped with his name, I decided to get in touch with the very place that had rejected me so openly—Tel Hashomer.

"This is Professor Kaplinski's niece," I said. "My uncle recommended that I call you about a job." This time they didn't ask where I was from or where I was going. The only thing they wanted to know was when it would be convenient for me to come for an interview.

On the way to the hospital, I constructed a scenario. They would obviously contact Professor Kaplinski immediately, and then I would go into my Hollywood mode. I'd put my hand on the telephone cradle, switch on my tape recorder, and ask why they were not prepared to accept doctors from Russia, even to an introductory meeting. This was going to be my first interview as a journalist.

Nobody asked me anything and I got the job I wanted.

"Our troubles are over," rejoiced my father, but he was mistaken. Our troubles were only just beginning.

I quickly settled into a job that had cost me many times the effort of someone born in the country. There really wasn't much to get used to. The border between the possible and the impossible moved, so it seemed, from place to place with me, like the horizon. In fact, I found myself in an even more extreme state of exile than I had been in the USSR. Socially and professionally, I didn't think I would advance any further than I had, and culturally (as a writer, for instance), I was still destitute. I had even lost the right to turn to the enlightened powers in Israel and the rest of the world. World opinion was certainly very much sympathetic to complaints about the denial of our cultural needs in the Soviet Union, but it would be ridiculous to complain against the State of Israel from the inside. Israeli liberals did not want to understand just which human rights were in question. All cultural rights were reserved for them alone. We, on the other hand, were defined in advance as "the lost generation," whose task was to produce children for the Hebrew culture and vacate the world. Since it did not seem as if that reality was about to change, the only thing left to do was to invent different rationalizations justifying this situation and to start to believe in them. The most elegant and commonly used rationalization went like this: "Creativity, after all, is the height of solitude—pure individualism. The creator is nothing other than an immigrant who immigrates into himself, so why shouldn't we consider immigration to be a literary tactic? Many great artists have done this in the past: Joyce, for example, or Hemingway."

This attitude justified a life spent on the fringes, preserved one's sense of pride, and helped to prevent breakdowns. Many did, however, break down: they left for Europe or the United States, or simply became clerks or teachers and gave up creating.

And there was another way: to give in to the demands, to disconnect oneself from previous notions of culture, to learn Hebrew, and to try to fit into Israeli culture. I knew about a handful of such attempts, none of which was successful. For the artist, language is the wellspring of his thinking, and the culture in which the language is rooted is its raw material. The Muses will not be fooled. We can fool ourselves, of course, but this rarely leads to real creativity.

In some respects, it was easier for me than it was for others. I continued to work as a doctor. When I felt the need to write, I wrote, but I made no effort to publish my stories. I did not consider immigration to be a "literary tactic." For me it had been a personal tragedy (or, if you prefer, a unique variation on the sacrifice of Isaac, in which the one who ordered the sacrifice, the one who performed it, and the sacrificial victim are all the same. I demanded it, I carried it out, and in the end I was granted choice cuts from my own burnt flesh for sustenance. Case closed). Ironically, my current situation was very similar to my previous one. Many creative artists in the Soviet Union had worked with no possibility of presenting their creations to the public at large. There too I had had no hope of being published. The choice was mine, and it was for me alone to bear the consequences.

In this way I put the matter to rest, at least as far as I was concerned personally, and I set about resolving the cluster of problems that had meanwhile accumulated in my family. My daughter had come with me from "back there" when she was four and a half years old. She had some tough days which stretched into tough years. It seemed as if she was going through here what I had gone through back there when I was young. In the Diaspora we had called this kind of harassment anti-Semitism, but since no suitable name had been found for it here, they called it "the inevitable symptoms of building the country." Nowadays, I really do have a more appropriate name for it: xenophobia, the fear of strangers.

When I was young, I suffered because I was Jewish. The suffering was unjustified but was at least the result of an existential reality. My daughter suffered because she was "Russian," and that was not only unjustified but also factually inaccurate. I did not know what to do or how to help her cope. At the time, I did not appreciate the depth and extent of the problem. I thought that it was nothing more than difficulties in settling in. I thought that there would be some children who would defend my daughter and that it would all turn out for the best. Then something happened that gave me the chance to see things from up close.

My daughter wanted to invite the whole class to her thirteenth birthday party. I was less than enthusiastic about this form of collectivism. It was my opinion that associations between people should be personal and based on the right to choose, since those kinds of associations solved the problem of foreignness relatively easily. In an individualistic society, everything depends on the individual. The masses, on the other hand, are always cruel. However, when in Rome, do as the Romans do. It was not only my daughter who wanted to belong to Israeli society, but also me.

So we invited the whole class to our house. Our guests were relatively older children. At their age, I had had a complex system of relationships with the world around me. My daughter's life was complicated, because she had to behave at home according to one set of cultural customs and outside according to a different set. She somehow was able to do this. It was by no means easy for her, but she managed.

I was amazed by the naivete of her school friends and by their simplistic approach to everything—a regular collection of Candides. Indeed, I had already realized that the educational system was actually responsible for nurturing this kind of attitude. My daughter's teachers never failed to bring up the subject of my demands that she excel. "Children need to be happy and satisfied with their lot," they said. "The acquisition of knowledge is not all that important. What is important is for them to be happy."

"What will you do with such an abundance of happy simpletons?" I once asked angrily.

"If you abuse your daughter, we will take her away from you. This is not a totalitarian state," they warned me in response.

This approach seemed to me to be incredibly totalitarian in itself. I had certainly never raised a hand to my daughter, just as my parents had never struck me, but who knows what they meant by abuse? Maybe they meant not allowing her to go out to play in the yard until she'd finished her homework. Having received that warning, I stopped having discussions with the teachers. I agreed with everything they said and went ahead and did whatever I believed to be right.

And now, faced with the results of this pedagogical system, I was less than impressed. You could say that I was amazed. Before my daughter's birthday party, I hadn't had a chance to see this society from so close up. My daughter had been embarrassed to bring her peers to our house because we spoke Russian at home, because it looked different from other homes, and because different rules applied in it. I had asked her a number of times to invite over at least her best friends. "I don't have any," she would answer, and so I decided to make her this birthday party exactly the way that she wanted it. Within half an hour of the arrival of the first guests, I regretted my decision. The children giggled at everything in the house, openly mocked the way I spoke Hebrew, threw statuettes on the floor, and even tore up newspapers and magazines which they found in a language foreign to them. Then somebody laughed and said, "That's a funny picture on the wall. Is it from Russia?" and threw a chocolate cookie at the picture. The room became a shooting gallery, and cookies became grenades, with the pictures as targets.

My daughter took no part in the game. Her eyes welled up with tears. I began to remove the children from the room one by one. I knew that I was harming my daughter's chances of being accepted, but to be honest, I no longer cared. I couldn't stand to see her being part of that zoo. That moment was the closest I ever came to packing my bags for Boston. I had had enough.

The children's behavior and the derision with which they pronounced "from Russia," with all the mockery and contempt that it implied, was echoed in the voices of many adults: neighbors, acquaintances, fellow workers, and passersby. I couldn't stand it any longer.

My daughter burst out crying bitterly. "You would do well to remember that you come from Russia!" I yelled at her. "Remember that and never, ever deny it. At your age I was a dirty Jew, but that never prevented me from living a normal life and enjoying it, and you will be a Russian. That will be your 'Judaism,' what sets you apart, your 'mark of Cain'! Learn now how to live with it, and don't you ever dare kiss up to those who reject you. Get yourself some normal friends and have a proper relationship with them!"

She walked over and touched me. That was when I understood that my child had been defending me all the time. She had wanted to keep me away from contact with the outside world so that I wouldn't be hurt. It was awful, and I could see no way out of the situation.

From then on she never came home crying. The insults she suffered outside became her own private secrets. I saw one of her schoolbooks "decorated" with scribbles like "Dirty Russian—go back to Russia."

"What can we do?" I asked.

"Nothing," she replied. I blushed.

I didn't see her cry again until she was in eleventh grade; something affected her so deeply then that she didn't have the strength to hide it. It appeared that in spite of her outstanding command of the English language and possession of all the necessary qualifications, she was rejected as a candidate to travel to the United States and represent Israeli youth at a series of lectures to American young people. The reason given—the official one, according to her—was that she was too Jewish-looking.

I did not believe her. It was true that she looked Jewish—refined, the kind of person that artists adopted in the past as a model when they wished to paint "cultured Jews"—but it was simply not possible that her application to represent the Jewish state should be rejected because of that. I made up my mind to clarify the matter with the teaching staff. Perhaps my daughter had not understood something, or perhaps she was disruptive in class, or perhaps she hadn't done her homework and was being justifiably punished.

To my amazement, their answer to me was the same. It was true that my daughter was too Jewish looking for their tastes. "We want the young people who are chosen to represent the country to be cosmopolitan-looking, so as not to stand out from the environment in which they will be lecturing." In that instant I understood many things, and I was forced to see the country in which I was living in a completely different light.

The State

A Jewish writers' and poets' circle was formed in Lithuania after the war. A folk dancing group was organized. Nehama Lifshitz and Khayatauskas sang in Yiddish. During that same period, the first story about the Holocaust was written and published in the Soviet Union. An old friend of mine, Yitzhak Meras, had written it.

At the time, all that cultural activity was unimportant to me. I was interested in émigré Jewish artists from a Russian cultural background: Babel, Mandelstam, Mikhoels, Erenburg, Chagall, Falk, and many others. There were those among them who rejected their Jewishness and those for whom their Jewishness became pivotal to their creativity—whether willingly or by force of circumstance. Both groups expressed a Jewish experience of exceptional power.

It seemed to me that the Jewish experience was at the center of cultural activity in the State of Israel. I was of the opinion that the state was founded in order to preserve Judaism in its cultural and national manifestations which would receive legitimacy through the approval of the state. How could I possibly have imagined that here in Israel, of all places, there would be no demand for or expressions of Jewish culture or content? How would I have known that here in the Jewish state, Babel, Mandelstam, Erenburg, and Falk would be unknown and considered foreign, that if the Museum of Mikhoels should ever open its doors, it would be in Moscow, and that in Israel Yitzhak Meras would be transformed from a well-known Jewish writer to a forgotten Jewish teacher?

It has to be asked if it was worth destroying the entire Jewish community in Lithuania only for all of its previous cultural efforts to be subsequently forgotten in Israel? And who are better—the Jews who remained in Russia and built the Jewish University in Moscow, where a great deal of effort has gone into collecting, preserving, and breathing new life into the remnants of Jewish-Russian culture, or the intellectual elite of Russian Judaism, who came to Israel and became bank clerks?

I think that the mass immigration to Israel by the intellectual strata of Russian Jewry was a mistake, as was the *aliya* of the intellectual elite from every other Diaspora region. Israel has no intention of creating an all-encompassing modern Jewish culture. It is trying to create something else—and, in my estimation, in vain. It is creating an independent Israeli culture in the straitjacket of a discriminatory cultural doctrine. This Jewish-Israeli culture starts by removing all Jewish content from within its boundaries. There has been an attempt to leap straight from Tanach to Palmah, from biblical times to the creation of the State of Israel, bypassing two thousand years of cultural activity in the Diaspora. It was decided to remove all traces of the Diaspora Jew and to put in his place—in what they believed was an empty space but in reality was replete with a wonderful creative energy—the Israeli.

This kind of experiment has been conducted in three places in the world: Germany tried to create a new breed of Germans, Russia invented the "Homo Sovieticus," and Israel created "the new Jew." Today, only the Israeli line of production is still in operation, even if its performance is erratic and ineffective.

If we can return to where we began, before the appearance of the "new model" of the Jew on the shelves of stores, it would be necessary to decide what look he will have. Since this phenomenon does not exist in nature, there was a real need to sketch him out on paper first. Ideological inventions are frequently unimaginative. Mostly there are dissonant combinations of whatever is at hand. The image of the new Jew was composed from the negatives of anti-Semitic stereotypes. Those elements which had characterized the Jew in anti-Semitic jokes and caricatures were removed and replaced with their complete opposites. Thus was born the new Jewish Aryan, that is to say, the Israeli. Jewish culture was for him not only superfluous, it actually came to be taboo.

The new Jew, the "Aryan," had no liking for his past or for his appearance. North African and Middle Eastern Jews, with all their traditional Jewish culture and their striking Jewish appearance, were a constant, living reminder to him of his historical origins, and he did not like that.

In time, as the new American liberalism became the overriding model for the Israeli intelligentsia, there was a re-appraisal of which external traits should be considered desirable. The American liberal suffered from a guilty conscience with regard to the black man, and thus dark pigmentation became "in." American liberal doctrine was taken literally in Israel. The role of the African-American was taken by the Arab and, to a lesser degree, the North African or Middle Eastern Jew. The Semitic look replaced the Aryan one, but the cultural and xenophobic doctrine that accompanied it remained in place.

The Israeli came to terms with his "Jewish appearance," but he wanted nothing to do with Jewish cultural content. (Those who feel uncomfortable with that definition should replace the words "Jewish cultural" in the last sentence with "Diaspora," and then everything should make sense.) When I was working as a journalist, I once met a young "Russian" boy whose hair had been dyed black. My curiosity was aroused, and his mother explained that the boy, a natural blond, was having a hard time at school because of his fair hair and his "Russian" appearance. His social status improved to a certain extent as soon as he dyed his hair black.

As long as the xenophobic basis of the society's system of values endures, white can easily be substituted for black, and vice versa. It all depends on passing trends. After all, it's not the color that is the problem, but the xenophobia. This and this alone is what determines our attitudes towards Sephardim, Ashkenazim, Arabs, Bedouin, or Druze—towards anyone considered "different."

In polls conducted in the not-too-distant past, it was discovered that Israeli children are openly hostile toward Arabs. Newspapers reported that 30 percent of those same children defined themselves as "racists." I would dearly like to see a similar poll carried out to gauge the attitude of the Israeli student toward "Russians." I suspect that the numbers would not be all that different. The Israeli child is simply a xenophobe, and it is difficult for him to be anything else when he is, intentionally or unintentionally, the product of a concept according to which the "right kind of Jew" is one born in Israel, who speaks Hebrew fluently, who creates a unique culture in Hebrew, and who knows intimately all the subtleties and heroes of that culture. All other Jews, and other human beings for that matter, belong to a lesser species.

The Israeli media are a hotbed of xenophobia, where a person's origins are mentioned so often that one has to ask why this information is of such interest to journalists. Articles dealing with various ethnic groups are written from the remote point of view of the ethnographer (as if they were about strange tribes from the Andes and not about Israelis from Petah Tikva or Beit Shemesh) or from a paternalistic point of view reminiscent of the journals of Christian missionaries in pagan lands.

Even when the subject is politics, there is a certain tinge of the same xenophobia. It is said that the Russian-language press turned Yisrael Beiteinu (Israel Our Home) party leader Avigdor Lieberman into the "hero of the Russian man in the street." I remain doggedly convinced that a certain puppet by the name of Vladimir had more to do with it. On the satirical television show, *Hahartzufim*, Dan Meridor is represented by a puppet named Dan Meridor and Benny Begin by a puppet named Benny Begin. But for some reason, only Lieberman was transformed into Vladimir, a character made up of all the stereotypical traits of "the Russian"—and it is not the caricature of a particular individual but of an ethnic group that he apparently represents. The group accepted this xenophobic personification as a collective image and decided to identify itself with the character.

Defamatory claims that "Russians" have a "ghetto fixation" are often heard. It should be borne in mind that a ghetto is always built by both sides of the cultural divide. This brings me to describe another trait of Israeli culture, anti-Jewish in essence.

The Hebrew culture value system is unique in that it has created its framework in such a way that "good" is what is considered to be such by one particular cultural group among all those that exist in Israel—the Hebrew culture itself, whose creators and consumers account for only one-third of the country's overall population. Newspaper coverage, television debates, and academic treatment of cultural subjects all deal with the activities of this group exclusively, as if other groups simply did not exist.

The historical roots of this situation are patently obvious. Hebrew culture was created as a foil to the culture of Diaspora Jewry and was announced as the dominant culture in Israel even before it was fully developed. It had to serve as an example to those Jews who already lived in the country or who were likely to immigrate. Anyone aspiring to be a consumer of culture would have to imbibe Hebrew culture and that culture alone. I am aware that this situation was dictated by special circumstances—there was a real need to make Hebrew the common language of the entire population. If the content of Hebrew culture had only remained Jewish, and if there had only been an attempt to include in it the finest achievements of the various Diaspora cultures, then perhaps most of the country's population and even some of the Jews living in the Diaspora could have identified with it. But because it was fundamentally different from the other Jewish cultures, it was not adopted by Diaspora Jews, and not even by the general public in Israel.

"Ethnic cultures" are not a concern of Hebrew culture. The range of cultures belonging to most of the country's population has been consigned to the periphery of institutionalized cultural activity and is not made accessible to the public. These cultures survive on minuscule budgets and are in a parlous state. Whereas every irrelevant and meaningless event in Hebrew culture is blown out of all proportion and made the subject of exaggerated attention, far more interesting events in the marginalized ethnic cultures fail to reach the public at large.

The doctrine of the melting pot was ostensibly democratic in origin. At its core was the notion that every person, whatever his culture, should be able to make his individual contribution to the wider culture, and thus a common, contemporary culture was supposed to have been created for the Jewish people. Because the dominant Hebrew paradigm culture already existed, however, the rules of the game were altered. Those who wanted to break into the arena of Hebrew culture were obliged to shed their old culture and assume a vestment of values, programs, and styles belonging to the Hebrew paradigm. The melting pot became an instrument for processing raw material.

It may be acceptable to treat paper, rags, and metal in this way, but not people. The melting pot was an experiment imported directly from the United States, and it didn't actually work there either. Now there is talk in Western countries of creating a "triangular melting pot." We would each enter the cultural "bubble" most suited to us, all the cultural bubbles would be melted down in the "general melting pot," and the result would be a common culture. The initial stage of this plan, when each culture still maintains its own separate identity and the process of bringing them all together or of ethnic cross-fertilization is still in its infancy, is known as "multi-culturalism." I am doubtful that the experiment will succeed, but the doctrine of multi-culturalism is a thousand times more acceptable than any other doctrine, because it is careful to supply air for minority cultures to breathe. I am skeptical about the chances of this doctrine succeeding in Israel for the following reasons:

1. There is no one dominant culture that the general public can agree upon. The Hebrew culture that is trying to appropriate this role for itself is not strong or firmly established enough in comparison with the great cultural traditions on which Diaspora Judaism was bred. The Hebrew culture is therefore on the defensive and has difficulty allowing other cultures to flourish.

2. Most of the authentic cultures (i.e., with a solid Jewish basis) in the Diaspora were destroyed either during the Holocaust, through the processes of assimilation, or here, at the hands of the Israeli cultural doctrine. The possibility of resuscitating them remains a question that cannot be answered. The present state of Jewish culture in all its different aspects cannot be perpetuated, because there is no common medium that deals with the various Jewish groups in the Diaspora. While it is currently fashionable to speak of a Jewish cultural renaissance in the countries of Eastern Europe that were freed from the yoke of Communism and in other countries that champion the cause of multi-culturalism, there is still no basis for it within our own cultural reality.

The only cultural group whose status I can evaluate on the basis of personal knowledge is that of the Jews of the former Soviet Union. This group is certainly culturally active, but it is not yet clear in which direction it is going. The split in the forces of Russian Jewry resulting from the *aliya* of intellectuals and artists to Israel, the immigration of a few to Europe and the United States, and the fact that a considerable number remained behind in the CIS, produced a vast cultural presence dispersed over a number of continents. Although the links between these groups are strong, each of them operates independently as dictated by local conditions.

Only time will tell if the links will endure or if each group will go its separate way. None of the countries in which these cultural activities are going on has any real interest in them, and this includes Israel. I would therefore expect the groups to become disconnected rather than more closely bound together. The Israeli group can lead the way, because of its strong foundations, but the temptation to join the culture of metropolitan Russia continues to gain ground against the need to become involved in Jewish culture. If, by some miracle, the Israeli doctrine should change, the flight into the arms of Russian culture will be arrested. If it does not change, then this flight will be unstoppable.

In the early nineties, I spent a most enjoyable evening in the company of well-educated Israeli friends. On the TV screen we saw the startled face of the 200,000th Russian immigrant, who obviously had not the slightest notion of what all the fuss was about. The lady of the house and her guests were full of admiration. "What do you think of that?" she said to me. "Isn't this the answer to all our prayers? Is this not the beginning of a secular Israel and the end of Levantization?"

"In my opinion," I answered her in all seriousness, "it is the beginning of the destruction of Israel as it is currently constituted." I was almost thrown out of the house. Our hostess and her friends collected used clothing and utensils to give to the poor immigrants. The immigrants were happy to receive them and sent most of these rags to a Russia that was crumbling and starving at the time. Hardship alters people's behavior. For those who had come out of Russia, it was shameful to accept hand-me-downs. It is almost certain that the words of gratitude that the newly arrived immigrants uttered to their hosts disguised their embarrassment and shame.

"Finally we'll be able to get cheap house cleaners," one of the guests groaned in relief. No one thought it prudent to comment.

And the household help did come. A fair number of them had university degrees. My argument here is against the "Russians" and not necessarily against the Israelis. The Russian immigrants of the seventies had not been a cheap source of household help. They did everything they could and even more to return to their previous social status, and thereby helped to develop the Israeli economy. The wave of immigration in the nineties quickly collapsed and created a thick layer of economic hardship, the results of which we will feel for many years to come.

Why did this happen during the wave of the nineties and not during the previous one? There are many answers to this question. One of the principal reasons was the breakup of Soviet society and the immediate impact that this had on people's sense of self-worth.

Many Israelis enjoy pointing out the differences between the older group, the Zionists who came in the seventies, and the new and materialistic immigrants who arrived in the last few years. This perspective is indicative of a basic lack of understanding.

If we examine the numbers in proportion to the wave of immigration as a whole, the percentage of Zionists among those who came in the seventies does not differ much from the percentage of Zionists among those who came more recently. Israeli society itself was much more Zionistic in those days, and so the identification the immigrants felt with the society was expressed through declarations of Zionism. What really separates the immigrants from the former Soviet Union from those who came in the seventies is not their relationship to Zionism, but their relationship to the Soviet regime. Between the supporters of the regime and its detractors there is a gaping abyss, whereas between the more Zionistic immigrants and the less Zionistic ones at most there is a slight coolness.

In the seventies, those who left the Soviet Union were the regime's most outspoken opponents. Among those who left that disintegrating superpower in the nineties there were also people who had strong bonds with the Soviet regime. There was tension at the time between the latter and the earlier immigrants, which gradually dissipated. The Soviet Union no longer exists and the ideological differences between the two factions are going the same way. Anyone who still believes that there are two separate communities of veterans and new immigrants is making a serious mistake. The community has been united for a long time now. The venues for cultural events are filled with both veterans and new immigrants. A similar situation exists in the inner circles of social relationships and family groups.

The same Russian-language books, newspapers, and magazines can be found in the homes of new immigrants, those who have been here for some time, and those who have been here for a long time (perhaps from the fifties or sixties). Both the veterans and the new arrivals watch Russian television broadcasts (and I don't mean the programs broadcast in Russian by the Israeli stations). When the Israeli media permit themselves to attack "Russians" verbally, the veterans respond every bit as vehemently as the new arrivals. Many veterans are active in the leadership as well as in the institutions of the "Immigrant Party," and they even make up a part of its constituency. It is an ethnic party, and the ethnicity is a common one.

The worst error is almost certainly to call that ethnicity "Russian." What unites the new immigrants and the veterans, the Georgians and the Ukrainians, the academics and the *hoi polloi*, is a Soviet ethnicity.

The "Soviet" is a person with characteristic and unifying traits—social, cultural, and even personal ones—conditioned by the unique features of the Soviet regime. The characteristic traits of "Homo Sovieticus" can be found even among the most outspoken critics of the regime. The difference between them and the regime's supporters is only in a value definition of these traits on a positive or negative scale. The regime's detractors spend much more of their time in self-contemplation.

One level below "Soviet man" is ethnic man. The Soviet ingredient is a unifying force, whereas the cultural one is divisive. Geography is of no significance. Large groups came from the Asian republics as well as from the Caucasus and the Baltic states which were staunch supporters of Russian culture. From those same places there also came distinct ethnic groups, preserving whichever Jewish cultural tradition was indigenous to their country of origin. All of them are equally inclined to vote for the "Immigrant Party" and to take part in joint demonstrations, but there is very little chance that they would attend the same seminars on cultural subjects. Members of both groups, however, feel a much stronger affinity with Russian culture than with any other cultures in the world, even if those cultures may be considered closer to them historically. For example, a well-educated person from Uzbekistan will be much more interested in what is going on in Russia than in what is happening culturally in

Islamic countries. This phenomenon derives from the character of the Soviet bloc, which inherited its cultural associations from the Russian empire that preceded it.

I was surprised to discover that among the readers of the Russian-language cultural supplement that I edited there was a significant number of ex-Bulgarians, Poles, and Romanians. In spite of the fundamentally negative relationship of those living in the Soviet satellite states to the dominant and chauvinistic Russian culture, a long period of living within a common culture had created a certain linkage, not with the Russian language, but with the writing style, the variety of topics dealt with, and their presentation. This phenomenon has nothing whatsoever to do with being Ashkenazi. It's about a Soviet cultural tradition, not a Jewish one.

Incidentally, the inability to differentiate between the Russian and the Soviet cultures makes it difficult for Israelis to make a serious study of their roots. The intellectuals of Soviet-Russian extraction are frequently amazed by the impossible blend of concepts, poetry, books, and authorities presented by Hebrew culture as a Russian legacy. Most of the time these are clear instances of Soviet culture that have not been common currency for quite some time, even in the official Soviet culture of the seventies and eighties. As for the authentic Russian cultural basis that exists in the Hebrew culture thanks to the efforts of the founding Zionist fathers, even it has undergone change as a result of a re-assessment of these phenomena in a process that occurred in the Soviet Union and in the Russian intellectual diaspora of Western countries.

The point of meeting has become a point of weakness. Russian and Israeli intellectuals are on two sides of a divide. This has nothing to do with the way each of them relates to subjects such as the Arabs, the occupied territories, or the peace process. It has to do with totally different outlooks on social and cultural processes. Both these groups have in common a way of resolving disagreements that came to be known in the Soviet Union as "whoever is not with us must be against us." This common basis for the worldview of both these groups has created an almost total split between them. When two differing parties are both equally convinced of their own monopoly on the truth, and that there are only two points of view in the world—our view and the wrong view—then there can be no meaningful dialogue.

The Russian-Soviet intellectual generally belongs to the species of anti-Soviet. Nowadays he has a Western cultural orientation, and at the same time is looking inward, into the depths of Russian culture. He is infected with the virus of Russian imperialist chauvinism, but nonetheless admits to that fact. The great majority of immigrants from the CIS is genuinely convinced of the superiority of the Russian culture over most of the world's other cultures. On the whole, the immigrants from the nineties, and even some of the intellectuals from that wave, would prefer for their own cultural domain to be completely autonomous. Some of them have no interest in the Hebrew-Israeli cultural domain—the reasons for which have been previously detailed—and some of them simply have no interest in an additional domain aside from their own. This autonomy is almost complete. Anything that it lacks in order to satisfy internal creative and intellectual needs is imported from Mother Russia at the lowest possible prices.

However, something interesting and unusual happened here. Since the seventies, a special kind of Russian-language culture has developed among the veterans. This culture includes the Israeli experience and is the result of a way of thinking that is not based solely on Russian culture but has Jewish and Jewish-Russian origins. The adherents of this culture were well connected within the dissident cultural circles that developed in the centers of immigration in the West. The creative artists who came with the *aliya* of the nineties were strongly attracted to this group, since they had already been exposed to their activities in Russia through dissident literature. Nowadays, in fact, they make up one single group. Cultural activity in this domain is extremely lively in both directions.

The cultural bubble made up of the immigrants from the seventies failed to gain recognition by the Israeli cultural establishment and was on the verge of bankruptcy by the end of the eighties. Many left for the West for purely economic reasons. Those who remained succumbed to an ever-increasing apathy. The *aliya* of the nineties breathed new life into their activities and virtually restored several established figures to the center stage. New immigrants were drawn into the existing cultural frameworks and expanded them. So it happened that in parallel with the Russian culture option (both that which was actively creative and that which was imported), there was a large group trying to create a special kind of Israeli-Russian-Jewish culture.

Nevertheless, one shouldn't get too carried away with these developments. The Israeli establishment continues to renounce this group, its sources of funding are nonexistent, and its energies are limited. The local market for culture is small in comparison with that in Russia itself, and Mother Russia has no interest in Israeli content. The Jewish community in Russia provides stiff competition in everything connected with the development of Jewish-Russian subjects. It is supported by the generosity of Jews in the West and well-established Russian Jews, and it is setting up educational and cultural institutions. At this stage, the temptation to return to Russia is still relatively slight, but the process of returning has already begun. A significant number of veteran immigrants are among those returning "home." The relocation is always for the sake of coming back "sometime later," but I am doubtful that day will ever come. Russia gives prizes to writers living in Zion. That is where they publish books, take part in cinema and theater—one goes there to give lectures and to show off one's achievements.

I am fearful of what is going on, for I am still a Zionist at heart, even if, rationally speaking, I welcome this process. It is better for Jewish-Russian culture to be preserved in Russia than to perish in Israel.

In the prevailing circumstances this cultural association with the mother-tongue country seems to me to be best for all ethnic communities. Unfortunately for those communities that made *aliya* lock, stock, and barrel, they have nowhere left to turn to in their countries of origin in order to fulfill their cultural needs. If we consider the State of Israel itself for a moment, these solutions are not in its best interests. The Jewish state is gradually filling up with a population whose body is here and whose soul is wandering around somewhere else, in the East or in the West. This situation can be rectified only if the State of Israel is willing to change its cultural doctrine.

Israel today is one of a small number of countries in the West that practices cultural indoctrination and open cultural discrimination. Will this situation ever change? It seems as if it is the stuff that dreams are made of.

I Have a Dream

They say that the State of Israel was founded as the result of one man's dream.

I am not one for romanticizing history, but one can find examples of cultures that arose out of the deliberate activity of a group of people who decided to establish them. Dreaming has its own historical place, and that's an exciting thought in such a rational and commercial age as our own.

When we examine the current state of affairs in Israel, we can see that change is unavoidable. Our economic situation is tolerable, yet people are not getting all they need out of life spiritually. The threshold of cultural consumption is rising, but supply is lagging behind demand. Geysers of ethnic steam are bursting out from the depths of society and enveloping us in a thick mist that obscures the path before us. Since the foundations for a revolution have already been laid, every dream can help to move us in a new direction, and stagnation is dangerous. A nation can suffer, fight, be victorious, or make peace only when it has a goal greater than its day-to-day needs. The new Middle East is not the dream itself, but merely the ground on which it can be achieved. Nowadays in many countries across the globe it is easier for a Jew to attain personal and financial security than it is in Israel. It follows that Israel has no alternative but to offer spiritual content. The State of Israel currently provides the potential immigrant with only three possibilities:

1. Assimilation into an undefined culture
2. Life on the fringes of the official culture
3. Cultural emigration

This is obviously only the case for a secular Jew, because the religious Jew is spared these inner conflicts.

Perhaps we should be holding a dream competition, but before we do, let me offer you my dream for consideration:

The State of Israel will change its cultural doctrine and will exchange it for Jewish multi-culturalism. This will not rob the Arabs, the Bedouin, or the Druze of any rights they have, for the simple reason that they do not have any such rights at present. On the contrary, since I see in my dream a flourishing of all the ethnic cultures, the national minorities in

Israel are likely only to benefit from the change, since the budgetary and organizational frameworks will, for once, contain them as well.

So, in the first stage, organizational and budgetary frameworks will be established to nurture ethnic cultures, or more accurately, to develop the cultures of the Diaspora, with an emphasis on their Jewish elements. At the same time, as many forums as possible will be devoted to the need to create interaction between these cultures—a television and radio station in Hebrew spoken with an accent and simultaneous translation or subtitles, a multi-language newspaper, self-managed cultural centers, and so on. There will be no key roles in these organizations, newspapers, or channels allocated to representatives of the current cultural establishment. The extended dialogue must be conducted with complete freedom, with no preference for style, no supervision from above, and no overseeing deity. The more the voices raised in the discussion are different from each other, the better it will be.

There must be a place set aside in all these activities for representatives from the Diaspora. The Jewish nation, whether it lives in the Diaspora or in Israel, is one nation.

In the second stage, a contemporary cultural center will be established in Israel to provide an umbrella organization for all the existing cultural centers. Such a center will be a collection point for examples of Jewish culture past and present and a place of scientific and creative activity.

I would like, for example, to delve deeply into the realms of Jewish music. I would like to learn from films and from lectures by experts on the history of that music, about the outstanding figures in the field, and about what is happening in Jewish musical circles today. I would like to be able to listen to this music by electronic means or directly. Similarly for Jewish literature, theater, philosophy, and so forth. I would like to be able to read everything written in all the Jewish newspapers published anywhere in the world. I would like to be able to read any good book written by a Jew wherever he lives in the world. I would also like to see the publication of such a book become a more important event in Israel than the travails of Princess Diana, for example. (On this particular subject, I would like to make it clear that I do not believe in national insularity—quite the opposite. But I do have easy access to world news through a variety of channels, whereas when it comes to news from the Jewish world, I do not even know where to begin to look.)

I have another wish, if I may be permitted: it can be defined as a relatively minor one, like Herzl's wish to reach Altneuland and then to spend an evening attending a classical opera performance. I would like for a Jewish Disneyland to be opened in Israel. It would be a reconstruction of the streets of Vilna, Warsaw, Vitebsk, Marrakech, Sana'a, Salonika, Baghdad, Berlin, and the wild Jewish west. I would like to see all the landmark events in the history of Jews in the Diaspora properly represented. A colorful Jewish market should be opened—theatrical but also authentic—and in the reconstructed home of Franz Kafka there should be regular literary seminars. I should like to see dozens of ethnic restaurants and stages for singers to sing, actors to act, dancers to dance, and klezmer bands to play.

I would like to achieve a true renaissance of Jewish culture.

I would like to see xenophobia in Israeli society finally laid to rest.

I would like Israel to become an attractive place for the world's creative forces—Jews and non-Jews alike—that it should be a magnet for them, whether they come for a few months or for good.

I would like to see ties with the Diaspora strengthened.

And I would also like to see an all-encompassing Israeli-Hebrew culture created that would be attractive to all the ethnic groups living in it, and in fact to all Jews wherever they live in the world.

IMAGINE: ON LOVE
AND LENNON

ZE'EV MAGHEN

ABOUT THREE YEARS AGO, I interrupted a perfectly enjoyable pilgrimage to the Old Country (the USA) in order to fly out and visit some friends in Los Angeles, that seaside sanctum of higher culture, clean air, and tasteful architecture. So there I was at LAX on a balmy Friday morning, sitting in this nondescript bar nursing a black-and-white shake, and waiting for my ride. Out of the corner of my eye, I absent-mindedly surveyed the vigorous maneuverings of a small but dedicated cadre of neophyte Hare Krishnas, who had deployed themselves in full court press formation across the central concourse of the airport. These mantra-chanting devotees of the swami-whose-name-I-never-could-pronounce—festooned in full-fledged religious regalia—were scurrying up and down the thoroughfare like human Ping-Pong balls, energetically hawking illustrated copies of Vedic texts to the few passersby who didn't ignore them, shove them aside, or spit in their general direction. This was, of course, a familiar scene to me, jet-setter that I am.

I finished my shake (such as it was—they've never heard the phrase "black-and-white milk shake" on the West Coast, and my numerous attempts to explain this simple concept to the natives were invariably futile)—and made a beeline for the exit. I guess the old quadriceps ain't quite what they used to be, though, because within seconds, I perceived a pair of dainty, be-moccasined footsteps easily gaining on me from behind. A young feminine voice inquired politely: "Excuse me, sirrr, but—ehh—maybe you vould like to take a loook at zis boook?"

I froze. Stopped dead in my tracks. I knew that accent. I'd know it anywhere. My heart plummeted into my duodenum. I put my suitcase down. I turned around slowly. She was petite and pretty in her saffron sari and multitudinous bangles. She must have had auburn hair, once, judging from the stubble on her scalp. And her eyes were a deep, feline green, amplified by the dab of yellow mustard smeared ever so artfully between them. She held a tiny tambourine in one hand, and with the other extended, was sweetly offering me a psychedelic version of the *Upanishads*. We stood there smack in the middle of that broad, bustling promenade and stared at each other for a few seconds, and when I saw she was about to repeat her practiced pitch about the book, I hastened to preempt and queried quietly: "*Me'eifo at?*" (Where are you from?)

"*Merramat Asharrron*," she answered, naturally, effortlessly, gurgling her "r" and eliding the "h" sound as people from her neck of the coastal plains are wont to do (Ramat Hasharon is a suburb of Tel Aviv). Apparently excited by this rare opportunity to spread the Good Word in her mother tongue, and undeterred by the intense suffering that must have been seared like a cattle brand all over my face, she warmed to her subject, and launched into a series of sound bites concerning the benefits of Krishna consciousness, including especially the need to realize... to actualize... to visualize... to harmonize... to get in touch with... to remove the walls... to blend into... to meld... to merge... to coalesce... to become one....

I never even started listening (I know the lines by rote: I'm a frequent flyer *and* an erstwhile deprogrammer). "*Eich kor'im lach?*" (What's your name?) I asked her, still trying to get my mind and heart around this.

"*Shira*," she responded, displaying no such curiosity in return. In the meantime, the other two appropriately attired and dapperly depilated members of her Maha squad had drifted over, no doubt intrigued by the seldom encountered phenomenon of someone actually stopping to converse, and lured by the heady scent of fresh, missionizable meat. Well, and wouldn't you know it: The *whole gang* is from Ramat Hasharon. Meet Ofer ("*Shalom!*") and Doron ("*Ma nishma!*").

So the four of us stand there, chatting like old friends. We reminisce
about the army like good Israelis do, talk about who served where and
who spent more time "in the mud" and who hated it most; Shira, as it
turns out, is a first lieutenant and outranks all of us, and I snap to attention and she laughs; Doron was a medic like myself, and we make a
date to give each other ice-water infusions and joke about how the first
thing we look at on a woman is her veins; I remind them of this kiosk
on Herzl Boulevard in Ramat Hasharon where they fry up the *biggest* and
juiciest falafel balls in the entire country, and all three nod their heads
in vehement agreement and lick their lips in almost Pavlovian recollection: They know *exactly* the place I'm talking about (I've never been to
Ramat Hasharon, but every town in Israel has a Herzl Boulevard, and
every Israeli citizen from Dan to Beersheva is convinced that there is
this one falafel stand in his neighborhood that makes the *biggest* and
juiciest falafel balls in the entire country. I saw Hawkeye do this trick
on *M*A*S*H* once, with French fries).

So we're shootin' the breeze, the three Hebrew Hare Krishnas and
I, discoursing in the recently resurrected and unsurpassably gorgeous
idiom of the biblical prophets and kings, and finally, well, I just lose it.
"What the hell are you *doing* here?" I blurt out, diverging slightly from
the pleasantly banterish tone which has informed the conversation thus
far. "You are Jews! You are *Israelis*, for God's sake! What the hell are you
doing here, in this place, on a Friday morning, wearing *these* clothes,
chanting *those* words, and selling *that* book?!" Now in those pious days
I used to read the Tora from the pulpit every week in synagogue, and
since one has to rehearse continually, I never left home without the
Pentateuch in my pack. At this moment, then, amazed at the extent
of my own coolness, I reached back over my shoulder into my knap-
sack—the way I'm positive Robin Hood used to extract an arrow from
his quiver—and just basically whipped out the Five Books of Moses.
(Thwack!) "*That's* not your book," I cried, indicating the decorative and
abridged *Bhagavad-Gita* Ofer was clutching like it was a newborn infant.
"*This*"—and I resoundingly slapped the raggedy, worn-and-torn volume
in my own hands—"*This* is your book!"

They all looked at me sadly, with genuine pity, the way one might
look at an animal caught in a trap or at someone who had just been
diagnosed with a terminal illness. "No, no. You don't *understand*," purred
Shira, her tone managing to be both soothing and patronizing at the

same time. "This isn't a contest! We're not choosing one book over an-other, or one religion over another, we're not expressing a preference for one culture, one nation, or one ethnic or social group over another. That would mean creating *hierarchical relationships* between human beings. That would mean erecting false barriers between people, barriers which have been responsible for so much misery and bloodshed throughout history, barriers which have prevented human beings from reaching their true potential and destiny, from achieving inner peace—and *world* peace. You and I, and everyone else in this airport, and everything that lives and breathes in every corner of this planet of ours, we are all of us part of a great and wonderful unity, we are all brothers and sisters, we are all linked by the same network of indissoluble bonds—we just don't *know* it yet. Krishna consciousness is about spreading that knowledge."

Zoinks! What do you get when you combine a young socialist ideo-logue educated in the best Israeli schools with a hefty dose of ancient Sanskrit esotericism plus a dash of the Diggers? I tried to imagine Shira haranguing conscripts in boot camp. That must have been some show.

"Look around you, *habibi*," Doron chimed in, seemingly on cue. "The world is constantly imploding, getting smaller all the time. The distances between societies are diminishing everywhere, and the borders that divide us from one another are being erased, like a thousand Berlin Walls tumbling down. The world is *progressing*, moving forward, toward oneness, toward mutual tolerance and understanding, away from the petty, archaic differences that have forever pitted us against each other. As the Lord says" (and here, astonished to the point of giddiness that he had actually gotten far enough with someone to be able to quote Scripture, he flipped open his large-print, polychrome edition of the *Rig-Veda* to a pre-marked page, and reverently recited a passage highlighted in red): "*Let your hearts be as one heart, let the minds of all be as one mind, so that through the spirit of oneness you may heal the sickness of a divided community.*"

"Open your eyes!" he preached on, the already rosy cheeks of this juggernauted Jew turning increasingly sanguine with Eastern religious ardor. "These words are coming true! We are building a new reality for humankind today, and you—you are stuck, *habibi*, stuck in a past of self-isolation and limitation, hemmed in by an anachronism you refuse to let go of. But the Supreme Lord Sri Krishna can help you let go of it, can help you be *truly* free. If you'll just concentrate and chant...."

I wondered if these guys were this good in English. Just my luck
to meet up with the three most articulate initiates in the entire ashram
(that they hadn't read the books they were so zealously peddling, and
were in large degree misrepresenting Vaishnava philosophy, was clear as
glass. But so what? They were declaiming the world according to themselves—and no doubt according to their Israeli parents' liberal-leaning
"post-Zionist" progressivism—and that was more interesting to me, in
any case. I wondered what their parents thought now).

"Yes, you have an antiquated attitude, my friend—a *dangerous* attitude." This was Ofer, who was so tall that I found myself mourning his
loss not just to the Jewish people as a whole, but to the Maccabee Tel
Aviv basketball team in particular. He had managed to jettison pretty
much every Israeli trapping that would have given him away, except
the telltale Nimrod sandals and that really annoying hand gesture that
means "wait" nowhere else on the planet except in our little corner of
the Middle East. He used it on me now, as I tried to butt in and protest my general benignity.

"You Are A Fascist," he proclaimed, enunciating each word with
conviction and solemnity, as if he were a judge pronouncing a death
sentence (that was it: No more Mr. Nice Guy. Yoga and Karma and
Krishna and Swami-what's-his-name were long gone. For the moment,
anyway, I was talking to pure Israeli leftist). "What you're preaching—it's
exclusivism, it's discrimination, it's segregation, it's elitism... it is *l'umanut*,"
he declared, employing for his *coup de grâce* a subtle nuance in Hebrew
semantics which essentially distinguishes chauvinist from liberal nationalism (I doubted whether he found the latter any more palatable than
the former).

"Why should people identify themselves according to this outmoded
and flagrantly racist conception of yours?" he continued, "And how dare
you define *others* based on such artificial and reactionary criteria?" (I'm
translating freely here.) "Human beings should be judged by their individual characters, not by their national or religious affiliations! Why
are you so *prejudiced*? Why do you play favorites? What, because I was
born a Jew, and that man standing over there by the telephone was not,
you should interact with me in a different way than with him? Maybe
he's the most upright, moral person in the entire city of LA, maybe
he's calling up some charity right now to donate a million dollars!" (I
glanced over at the guy. He was unquestionably Jewish, and judging

from his contorted visage and wild gesticulations, was probably talking to his broker.) "And because I had the 'luck' to be born of a Jewish mother, and *he* didn't, because I got snipped a week after coming into the world, and *he* didn't, for these reasons you should prefer me to him? You should *care* about me more than you do about him? Why, that's SICK! It's downright *disgusting!*"

I was glad he was done so I could stop craning my neck. He might very well have been arguing as much with his own internal inclinations as he was with me—I hadn't managed to say very much, after all—but at any rate, Shira quickly laid a hand on his waist (you couldn't really reach his shoulder) and led him aside. I wasn't getting any closer to Krishna consciousness this way. The not-so-gentle giant inhaled half the oxygen in the arrivals lounge and rattled off three mantras at breakneck speed, all in one breath (not unlike the way we intone the names of Haman's sons in the Purim Megilla). Then he was back, calm and cool, all smiles and ready to Rama.

Shira placed a hand on my shoulder (you can reach my shoulder) and spoke to me softly. "Don't you see? All that His Divine Grace Swami Prah... is saying comes down to this: *We must strive with all our inner strength to love all people equally.* That is what these books we're distributing teach as well, and, in the last analysis, isn't that also the central message of *that* book, the one you're carrying?" (she pointed to the Tora).

I stood there engulfed in frustration. What could I possibly answer "on one foot" (as we say in Hebrew), in the few seconds remaining to us, that would even begin to make a dent in *all that*? I heaved a long sigh of resignation. "When was the last time you read *this* book?" was the best I could come up with under the circumstances, appealing in all directions to imaginary back-up units.

"That's not what *this* book says."

My ride showed up, and was of course parked in the red zone, which as you know is for the loading and unloading of passengers only. There was a genuinely poignant parting scene—during which, among other unexpected events, Doron pressed my hand and slipped me a surreptitious "*Shabbat shalom, ahi!*" (Good Sabbath, my brother!)—and the tantric trio from Tel Aviv went off in search of easier prey. I don't know where my three semi-brainwashed but far from benighted Brahmins are now—whether they've since managed to achieve supreme bovinity, or whether they have fallen from grace and are currently putting their

considerable mercantile talents to lucrative use fencing CD players on
Olympic Boulevard. Either way, I sure hope I get to meet up with them
again someday (yes, even if it means going back to Los Angeles). The
ensuing pages contain the gist of what I would say to them, if I did.

II

You don't have to be a disciple of Eastern mysticism or philosophy to
be struck by the apparent anomaly of being a committed, involved, or
practicing Jew today. You just have to be pre-lobotomy. Whatever doubts
I may harbor regarding their idea of a fun Friday activity or their strange
notion of musical rhythm, the objections raised by my airport interlocutors are not to be sneezed, coughed, hiccupped, or spat at. Stripped of
their atavistic, pseudo-Aryan trappings and Utopian-socialist rhetoric, the
positions propounded by Shira, Doron, and Ofer collectively represent
far and away *the foremost issue and dilemma* facing the current generation of up-and-coming Jews, as they decide just how Jewish they want
to be, as they debate how much space and how much importance to
give Judaism and Jewishness in their lives.

For the vast majority of us, after all, the poser is not "Should I
be Christian or Jewish?" or "Should I be Buddhist or Jewish?" or even
"Should I be Druid or Jewish?" No. The real quandary, the fundamental
inner conflict affecting and preoccupying most of today's Jewish young
people—whether formulated in this manner or otherwise—is without
doubt:

> Should I be a *modern, progressive, secular, nondenominationally affiliated
> American, or Canadian, or Citizen of the World* (or just "Me" with no
> strings attached whatsoever)… or should I be *actively and deeply and
> connectedly and unabashedly Jewish*—and how much of each, or where
> in-between, and which elements (if any) of these two available alter-
> egos can be reconciled?

Put in even more concise fashion, the puzzle of the hour for most of
us is simply this:

> *Why on earth be a Jew in the (post-) modern world?*

(An immediate qualifier: I am well aware that for a whole slew of young Jews, this issue burns inside them at about the level of a Bic lighter, if not lower. Such folks are complete strangers to the gut-wrenching inner turmoil associated with this question, and they are of two kinds.

The first group doesn't think about this question because, to put it simply, *they've already made their decision*. Indeed, their decision was to a large extent made *for* them, long ago, by parents who for whatever reason did not expose their children adequately to one or the other of the two worldviews described above. Either the kids had religion shoved down their throats from age one—no doubts allowed (let alone culti-vated)—and never really had the opportunity to observe the truly com-pelling aspects of life on the other side of the overly protective fence; or—what is far more common—they grew up with no exposure worth mentioning to Judaism or the Jewish people, save perhaps a few years in Hebrew school, which in the majority of cases simply furnishes the poor pupil with enduring reasons to get as far away from his cultural heritage as humanly possible. So, to you "already resolved that issue, don't bother me" types, I say: Continuous self-re-examination, even after having arrived at what appear to be immutable conclusions, is the *con-ditio sine qua non* of wisdom, humanity, meaningfulness, relationships, progress, success, and pretty much everything else worthwhile in life. So I encourage you to read on.

The second group doesn't think about the question in question, pri-marily because (how do I put this delicately?) they don't *think*. Ladies and gentlemen of this mold aren't really inclined to ponder or deliber-ate any subjects more abstract than, say, the optimal head-height of a properly poured Heineken, the relative righteousness of the NCAA versus the NBA three-point line, how fat Oprah is this month, or what T-bills are going to do over the next quarter. Issues and ideas of identity, beauty, freedom, love, art, fantasy, justice, morality, mysticism, change, history, philosophy—such irrelevancies simply do not disturb or exercise such individuals as they pragmatically plod their way through incurably superficial lives. This piece has nothing for such folks.)

The points proffered by my three Israeli amigos are of the most profound relevance and legitimacy; they are also, of course, in no sense novel. When universities were what they should be (and could be again, I remain convinced), long before any of us were born, our collegiate predecessors were *rarely known to do anything else* but stay up all night in meeting halls, public parks, drinking establishments, abandoned buildings, forests, caves, dormitories, and even houses of ill repute, incessantly and passionately debating questions related to the epic conflict between universalism on the one hand, and particularism or nationalism on the other. Here, in these feverishly fought nocturnal battles of the intellect and spirit, both sides would not hesitate to haul out the big guns: Mazzini, Marinetti, and Garibaldi; Kant, Hegel, Herder, Croce, and Fichte; Feuerbach, Lassalle, Marx, Engels, Plekhanov, and Lenin; Rousseau, Diderot, Jefferson, Adam Smith; Nietzsche and Kierkegaard, Spinoza and Hume, Russell and Rand, all going at it simultaneously in a massive, tumultuous, WWF tag-team free-for-all slug-match of the mind.

Those were the days.

Not to say that the debate is dead. Over the years, I have heard the arguments of Shira, Doron, and Ofer—against attaching oneself to particularist sociocultural cliques which split humankind—advanced with conviction and passion in a whole gamut of guises by hundreds if not thousands of young Jews (not excluding, by the way, yours truly). For that matter, I suspect that a whole smorgasbord of people perusing these lines right now could easily cite more than a few reasons why the notion of making the fact of their being Jewish into this big deal in their daily lives, or into one of the defining characteristics of their personal identity—why this notion might be far from compelling to them, or why it ranks rather low on their priority list, or why it is entirely ideologically untenable in their view, or why it's just downright stupid. I know I can.

Ever since my childhood, when I was dragged to High Holiday services once a year—where my boredom was of such magnitude that it could only be alleviated by continually conjuring up the vision of myself leaping headlong from the balcony to my death by impalement on the spikes of the menora below—ever since then, I remember wondering what the point of all this was. My budding bewilderment was in no way mitigated by the edifying and intensely spiritual experience of my bar mitzva, in the course of which I learned by rote for six months how to chant flawlessly the words (although without having so much as an inkling as to their meaning) of what turned out to be the wrong haftora (I kid you not). After this I took to imbibing mass quantities of Jolt soda to help me stay up all night every night for the final month, and just barely learn the right one.

I rode a souped-up, Harley chopper right out of that neo-fundamentalist nightmare and into my carefree, suburban, red-white-and-blue American teenage dream (okay, it was a Honda). I drank, smoked, won Frisbee-golf tournaments, and lost my innocence. Got a girl, named Sue (really), she was terrific and a Methodist. I couldn't see one reason in the whole wide world why we shouldn't be together forever (she turned out to be a staunch Republican and solved my problem). I was—and remain to this day—a full-blown child of Western philosophy, intent on participating in every facet of the modern universe of discourse, no holds barred, no parameters set. I never believed Jews were any better than anybody else (now I live smack in the middle of five million of them: I can *assure* you they're not). I'm still not buying a whole heck of a lot of what organized religion is selling, and probably never will. My personal nature is such that prescriptions and proscriptions and restraints—in short, any system or institution that aspires to tell me what to do—immediately sends me fleeing for the hills, the better to organize active rebellion.

None of the above circumstances, convictions, or character traits (and there's a *lot* more where they came from) would appear at first glance to make living a full, fervent Jewish life a sensible option—let alone an attractive one—for your humble servant here. And I presume I'm not the only one in that boat.

Nor has my confusion on this score left me since moving to Israel in 1992. A few months ago some pals and I were patrolling the Syrian border at 3:30 in the morning (really). I was intensely exhausted, and kept nodding off and banging my chin on the safety switch of this weapon comparable in size and firepower to the Guns of Navarone. Not happy with this situation, I forced our driver off the road—by repeatedly slamming my rifle butt into the back of his helmet (we had an excellent rapport, "Dudu" and I)—so that we could finally have some coffee. As I stood there—for maybe the fifteenth night in a row—bushed beyond belief, freezing my family jewels off, feeling achy and unshowered and not a little bit exposed, and marshaling the courage to quaff this ipecac-like mixture of offal and lukewarm water which the Israelis themselves refer to as "mud," I conjured up in my mind the two activities in which I had generally been engaged at this hour of the night during the overwhelming majority of my diaspora existence: (1) *Shluffing soundly* under my extra-fluffy, one 100 percent bona fide down quilt with the pictures of Rocky and Bullwinkle all over it; or, alternately, (2) *at Denny's*, after a full night of furious and paroxysmal partying, wolfing down some delectable pancakes with an equally scrumptious side of bacon. Let me confess to you that at that moment, right there on the threshold of a Golan Heights minefield (where there are no pancakes), I rained down a hailstorm of execrations—individually and collectively—on Abraham, Sarah, Isaac, Rebecca, Jacob, Leah, Rachel, Moses, King David, the Maccabees and everyone else and their mother who had a hand in sustaining us, keeping us in life, and allowing us to reach this season.

WHO NEEDS THIS?

That is the question. Why be a Jew, a committed Jew, an involved Jew, today, under current circumstances, even if this doesn't mean trudging through northern Israel in the middle of a frigid winter night? Why bother? Everything logical, indeed, everything *ideo*logical in the modern, Western worldview, would appear to be solidly stacked against such a foolish stance. Inertia itself is beating us, hands and feet tied behind its back: Like their gentile counterparts, most Jewish young people of this relatively placid and malleable generation (the sixties it ain't) are more or less going with the increasingly coordinated and egregiously conformist global flow, streaming away from everything the Jewish people once were, away from everything we could yet be together. Now that just darkens my eyes and blackens my soul, and I won't stand for it. So what comes now is basically me throwing everything I've got into one mighty attempt to convince you… to be a salmon.

(One last point before we embark. I am not going to advocate that we stay Jewish because Doron's dispensationalist vision of a new world order where there is no hatred of Jews or anybody else is pure Hindu hallucination, whereas in fact anti-Semitism will always force us to stick together in the necessary defensive formation of a persecuted clan. This may very well be the case—it has been more often than not in the past—but as a motivation, this particular claim has never been enough to get my personal motor running. *I am not now and never will be a Jew and a Zionist out of fear, or because I have no choice.* To hell with that.

Here's what else I am not going to do. I am not going to reveal to you for the first time how if you read the last six odd-numbered verses of the tenth chapter of the biblical book of Deuteronomy, backwards and diagonally, while simultaneously skipping over all personal pronouns and omitting every third, fifth, and twenty-seventh bilabial fricative, it will spell out: "Read Ze'ev Maghen's treatise in 1999 and send him a generous donation" (i.e., no "Bible codes," I promise). No exposés on how Darwin was strung out on methadone when he wrote *Origin of the Species*, no Genesis–Big Bang bull, no impartial studies on how keeping kosher increases your sexual potency and effectively prevents colon cancer, no portrayals of Semitic religion as the true fount of feminism or the real source of science or any other such puerile bunk currently making the rounds. What I have to say—and the manner in which I say it—might very well offend a broad assortment of readers in a wide variety of ways (you may have already noticed this), but there's one thing I guarantee not to insult: your intelligence.)

Shall we dance?

III

I was in junior high school when John Lennon died, and I was an absolute wreck. I grew up on my Mom's old Beatles albums, and by the time I reached adolescence, my personal classification system went: Billy Joel–John Lennon–God. So after that fruitcake son-of-a-bitch emptied his revolver into this consummate musician's chest on the corner of Seventy-Second and Central Park West on the eighth of December, 1980, I wore black to school for a month. I traveled all the way to New York and waved a candle till my arm fell off and sang "All we are saying, is give peace a chance" so many times that it really was *all* I was saying. Meanwhile, back home, I was suspended by the principal due to an unrelated bum rap (it was Aaron Mittleman, not me, who locked our French teacher in the closet and evacuated the class), and so was conveniently able to initiate "Stay in Bed and Grow Your Hair" week—soon joined, to the principal's (and my mother's) chagrin, by some fifteen classmates—at my house in John's honor. I even went out and spent good allowance money on two Yoko albums, where she intermittently shrieks and imitates whale sounds for some eighty-five minutes straight. Now *that's* a true fan.

I tell you all this in order to establish my credentials as a veteran, fanatic, and peerlessly loyal Lennon lover, because now I'm going to kill him all over again.

John was at his best as a team player, but there's no question that his preeminent *pièce de résistance*, the composition that will be for all time immediately associated with his name, is "Imagine." And justifiably so: I don't care what the idiot editors of *Rolling Stone* think, it's a great song. Gives me gargantuan goose bumps from the introductory adagio. The man was a genius, and this was his masterpiece. Even the words themselves are enough to make you weak in the knees:

> Imagine there's no heaven
> It's easy if you try
> No hell below us
> Above us only sky
> Imagine all the people
> Living for today
>
> Imagine there's no countries
> It isn't hard to do
> Nothing to kill or die for
> And no religion too
>
> Imagine all the people
> Living life in peace
> You may say that I'm a dreamer
> But I'm not the only one
> I hope someday you'll join us
> And the world will live as one

(Tell me you didn't at least hum the melody while you were reading just now. If not, you're a freak.)

Those words, those words! They're so beautiful, so encompassing, so *right*. We agree with them viscerally, adopt them instinctively. They strike some of our deepest, most primal chords, they produce (at least for a moment) a kind of nebulous but heartfelt longing, a yearning for something better, for something perfect, for something beautiful. Everything we've been taught—indeed, a decent amount of what we human beings are *made* of—is passionately stirred by the simple yet incredibly compelling message of John's poetry (actually, the words were originally inspired by Yoko's verse, if you can believe *that*).

I know what you're thinking: Oh, how *predictable*! Now he's going to explain how "Imagine" is just a pipe dream, an unfeasible, quixotic, idyllic fantasy that's nice to sing about but has no place in our individual or collective practical planning for the future. Well, if that's what you think I'm up to... you're *dead wrong*.

I am not challenging the wisdom of John's enterprise because I think it has no chance of succeeding (fact is, many aspects of it are coming truer every day). If I believed in his vision, if I truly desired that it be realized speedily and in our days, I would join up regardless, and struggle against all odds toward our common goal with all my heart, with all my soul, and with all my might.

But I *don't* want John's vision to be fulfilled speedily and in our days. I don't want it to be fulfilled—*ever*. John's beautiful ballad is a death march, a requiem mass for the human race. His seemingly lovely lyrics constitute in truth the single most hideous and most unfortunate combination of syllables ever to be put to music. The realization of his dream, or even just a large part of it, would perforce entail the wholesale and irreversible destruction of the dreams, hopes, happinesses, and very reason for living of yourself and every single person you know. If we, who for so long have unthinkingly admired and warbled Lennon's words, were to live to see his wish come true, the result would be more staggeringly horrific and more devastatingly ruinous than you could ever possibly—*imagine*.

Although some readers have no doubt long ago reached their own conclusions on this score, permit me to share with you my own personal take on this exceedingly crucial matter.

IV

Why do you get up in the morning?

Please stop and think very seriously for a moment about this matchlessly significant and yet for some reason rarely broached question. What is the juice that gets you going every day? What motivates you to pursue... anything? Why, ultimately, do you do... pretty much *everything* you do? What are you really looking for? What have you *always* really been looking for—just between you, me, and the page?

What is the *end* goal, direct or indirect, of the vast majority of your activities in life? What is the one thing you need more than anything else, the one thing you just couldn't live without, the one thing you probably wouldn't *want* to live without? What do you live for? What do you work for? What would you *die* for? In the immortal words of the Spice Girls: *Tell me what you want, what you really, really want....*

You'll agree it's not any of the basic necessities—food, shelter, clothing, Hewlett-Packard Office-Jet-Pro 1150C multi-function scanner-printer-copier-fax—you already have these. Know how I know? Because you wouldn't be reading this if you didn't. You'd be out somewhere purloining bread like Jean Valjean.

You think maybe it's your *health*? Look, I know that when two old Jewish men pass each other in the locker room on the way to or from the *schvitz*, it's a biblical precept that at least one of them has to rasp, "If you don't have your health, you don't have *nothing*." Granted. But we don't live *for* our health. Our health is only one of the things which allow us to pursue our true desires in life. So once again: What is it, that deepest, most powerful, most true desire of ours?

"Success," you say, or "fulfillment." Okay, what on earth are *those*? Of what elements are they comprised, and which are their *most important and indispensable* component parts?

"All right—happiness!" There you go again! You've managed once more to beg the question: What is it, more than anything else, that *makes* you happy?

All right, here's the final clue, a Beatles clue: All you need is…

LOVE.

And if you think this is a cliché, then it is the single most powerful cliché ever known to humankind, the one that pervades our thoughts, directs our actions, makes us move, runs our lives. *We live for love.* Love of parents, love of children, love of husband, love of wife, love of sisters, love of brothers, love of girlfriend, love of boyfriend, love of family, love of friends. *That's* what we want and need most of all, and such a vast percentage of the things we do throughout our entire lives is ultimately connected with and geared toward achieving, maintaining, and increasing that one incomparably precious treasure: *Love.*

Sure, there are other objectives and experiences we may strive to attain—the fascination of scholarship, the rush of artistic creation or scientific discovery, the thrill of the fight or the game, the various hedonistic pleasures—but tell me you wouldn't give up any of these before you'd give up love, tell me you wouldn't give up the entire kit-and-caboodle of them for the sake of love, and I'll say it again: You're a freak. "*Without love*" (to enlist the Doobie Brothers), "*where would you be now?*"

Okay, so we're agreed: No one with enough brains to read this piece will deny that love is at least one of the primary motivating factors informing human endeavor.

So let's talk just a little bit about love, shall we?

V

They asked Jesus and R. Akiva—on different occasions (they lived almost a hundred years apart)—what their favorite verse was in the entire Bible. And wouldn't you know it, both of them picked the exact same one: *V'ahavta l'rei'acha kamocha* ("Love your neighbor as yourself," Leviticus 19:18).

Now there is a fairly famous anecdote in the Talmud (Bava Metzia 62b) which describes the following situation: You and this other chap are out for a stroll in the desert. While you are both busy admiring the various lizard species and rock formations in your vicinity, *he* suddenly exclaims: "#@$%&! I forgot my friggin' *canteen!*"

You quickly assess your options. There is only enough water in *your* canteen for *one* human being to make it back to civilization alive (and no, you do not have your cellphone). So you could split the water—and you'd both perish. You could give your flask altruistically to your fellow traveler, and die a hideous death under the merciless, take-no-prisoners, desert sun. Or you could keep the canteen for yourself, and abandon him to the same fate (this is a slightly tougher decision than what shoes to wear to work in the morning). *What do you do?*

Two opinions, two legal rulings, are recorded in the Talmud regarding this matter. One of them comes straight from the mouth of the aforementioned R. Akiva. The other one emanates from an individual with a very strange name, who is never mentioned anywhere else in rabbinic literature: Ben-Petura. Now, I don't want to go into all the speculative etymology (Ben-Petura—Ben-Pintura—Ben-Pindura: The always fickle letter "nun" creeps in and we have the common, somewhat derogatory talmudic appellation for Jesus), but it is at least possible that the second jurisprudent whose expertise is consulted in this passage is none other than the Christian Savior himself. We'll never know for sure whether this is so, and it doesn't really matter for our purposes today. I am only interested in utilizing this dichotomy of views as a paradigm, and the two men who espouse them as archetypes. So let's assume, for the moment, that Ben-Petura is in fact Jesus; if he isn't, he's sure read a lot of the Nazarene's sermons, as we shall see.

Let's go back to the desert. The scorching rays of the noonday sun are cauterizing your corpuscles, your throat is so dry you could bake a matza in it, and you have quite a decision to make. Fast. Ben-Petura–Jesus advises you as follows: Share the water, and die together, because you are no better than your friend. R. Akiva rules differently: *You take the flask.*

Now this is fascinating because, if you will recall, both Jesus and Akiva chose "Love your neighbor as yourself" as their all-time favorite Tora verse. Well, what in the name of Jehosaphat is going on here? I understand Jesus' position: It is entirely consistent with genuinely loving your neighbor *as much* as you love yourself, which certainly appears to be exactly what the biblical commandment requires. Jesus' verdict makes perfect sense in this light.

But R. Akiva? What was *he* thinking? Did he *forget* that he had once put the same verse way up high on a pedestal as "the premier principle of the Tora"? His judgment—keep the canteen, share none of its contents, leave your buddy to expire miserably in the desert like a dog—seems to contradict everything that that hallowed Pentateuchal principle of mutual, equal love demands.

What we have here is a clear-cut case of diametrically opposed interpretations of scriptural intention (a common enough phenomenon in our sources). Jesus understands the Levitical injunction to "love your neighbor as yourself" just exactly the way it sounds (*pshuto k'mashma'o,* as we say in the holy tongue). We would know this even without the whole speculative business about his possible Ben-Petura alias. Because you see, the entire New Testament is simply riddled with examples which leave not a shadow of a doubt that the ideal in Jesus'—and eventually Christianity's—eyes is at least *to strive to love all human beings equally.*

One day Jesus was in the middle of preaching to the multitudes—as was his wont—when all of a sudden (every Jewish child's nightmare) his mom showed up:

> Then one said unto him: "Behold, thy mother and thy brethren stand without, desiring to speak with thee." But he answered and said unto him that told him: "Who is my mother? And who are my brethren?" And he stretched forth his hand toward his disciples, and said: "Behold my mother and my brethren." (Matthew 12:46-49)

This and more: Jesus wished there to be no misunderstanding regarding this matter:

> Think not that I am come to send peace on earth. I came not to send peace, but a sword. For I am come to set a man at variance against his father, and the daughter against her mother, and the daughter-in-law against her mother-in-law. (Matthew 10:34-35)

And in case it has yet to sink in:

> If any man come to me, and hate not his father, and mother, and wife, and children, and brethrens, and sisters, yea, and his own life also, he cannot be my disciple. (Luke 14:26)

We have not quoted verses out of context here. Christianity is a system concerned with belief, with faith, and as such it recognizes no separate national entities, no tribal affiliations, not even, in the final analysis, the significance of blood kinship. It is, at least theoretically, the world's largest equal-opportunity employer, viewing as it does all human beings as similarly deserving (more accurately: similarly *un*deserving) potential recipients of salvation. Christianity is a thoroughly universalist—and at the same time a thoroughly individualist—religious creed, and Jesus of Nazareth was without a doubt the foremost prophet of universal love (although nowhere *near* the only one).

Okay, that's settled. Now, let's get married. Uh-huh, right this minute—you and me. I'm your beau of the ball, we've been having the most awesome time getting to know each other for months, and I just can't possibly wait another second. It's time to propose. Down I go on one knee. I look dreamily up into your eyes. I reach deftly into the pocket of my Giorgio Armani blazer and pull out a rock the size of a canteloupe. I take your two hands in mine, and, gently caressing them, I coo: "My darling, I love you. I love you *so* much. I love you as much as I love... as much as I love... as much as I love that *other* woman, the one walking down the street over there. See her? Oh, and *that* one, too, riding her bike past the newspaper stand. I love you *exactly* as much as I love all my previous girlfriends, as well, and I love you as much as all the girls who *weren't* ever my girlfriends. I love you as much as I love everybody else on this planet, and for that matter, I love you as much as I love the animals, too, and the weeds, and the plankton and—Oh *God*! What's that searing, indescribable pain in my groin? Hey, where are you going, my *daaaaarliiiing*?"

No one gets turned on by "universal" love. It doesn't get you up in the morning, it doesn't give you goose bumps or make you feel all warm and tingly inside, it doesn't send you traipsing through copses picking wildflowers and singing songs about birds, it doesn't provoke heroism, or sacrifice, or creativity, or loyalty, or anything. In short, "universal love" isn't love at all.

Because love means preference. The kind of love that means anything, the kind of love we all really want and need and live for, the kind of love that is *worth* anything to anyone—that is worth *every*thing to *every*one—is love that by its very nature, by its very definition, distinguishes and prefers. Show me a guy who tells you that he loves your kids as much as he loves his own, and I'll show you someone who *should never and under no circumstances be your babysitter.* Stay away from such people. Head for the hills. He who aspires to love everybody the same *has no idea what love means*, indeed, is really advocating—and may be entirely unaware of this—*the removal of all love worthy of the name from the planet Earth.*

R. Akiva—and most of Judaism along with him—views the matter a bit differently. The kind of love (romantic or otherwise) that he unabashedly recognizes and unreservedly encourages, is 100 percent biased, hopelessly *un*equal, deeply discriminatory, and incorrigibly preferential *distinguishing* love: The kind of love that plays favorites, that chooses sides, that confers *specialness*. As a Jewish luminary, R. Akiva only understood that type of love that blossoms from the ubiquitous Hebrew root "k-d-sh," which is probably most accurately rendered into English as "to declare special, to *set apart* as unique."

When a man marries a woman in Judaism, the institution is called *kidushin*, because they *set one another apart* from the rest of humanity, because they (ideally) love each other *more* than they love anybody else (this is a far cry from the fully internally consistent Pauline-Christian doctrine of marriage, which is: "Try your best to avoid it"). When Jews bless the wine on a Friday night, this is called *kidush*, because we are *setting apart*, we are *distinguishing* the Sabbath day from what surrounds it, and saying: I love this day more than any other day of the week. When Jews do that weird, Wizard-of-Oz, "there's no place like home" thing three times with their heels, and declaim the words *kadosh, kadosh, kadosh* in the Amida, this means: "There is none like unto you among the gods, O Lord." We single you out, we love you best.

This is not a Jewish secret. It's a human secret. It's the way we all work, all of us, deep down inside. We all love *preferentially*, and that's the only kind of love we value, the only kind of love we want back from the people we love. All those perpetually smiling, lovey-dovey, touchy-feely, Swami-from-Miami types who appear at first glance to be all about love, and nothing else but love, toward every single thing that lives and breathes, *are in reality all about stealing this absolutely essential human emotion away from you* (they've already lost it themselves). It is no coincidence that the first and most indispensable step one takes in order to successfully "deprogram" a Hare Krishna (or member of any other cult) is to rekindle his *particular* love for a *particular* someone who was once very special to him.

And this means something else that everybody already knows, but is for various reasons only occasionally acknowledged: *Because* love is such a major deal in all of our existences, and because the love we're talking about is invariably distinguishing and preferential in nature, *human beings will ever and anon, at all places and all times, prefer hanging out in the company of some people over hanging out in the company of others.* They will always form special groups, little groups and big groups, groups to which they feel a special connection, a special sense of belonging. They will always relate emotionally to these groups in the manner of concentric circles, loving the nearer rings more than they love the farther ones. They will always seek to perpetuate these familial, sociocultural, and possibly political entities for as long as they can. And they will always *distinguish* between their own special circles, and those that are special not to them—but to others.

Is this because human beings are small-minded, visionless creatures who can't appreciate the lustrous loveliness and messianic morality of universal oneness? *No*. It is because they are (thank God) supremely and congenitally motivated by preferential love, and special groups of this sort are the inexorable consequence and highest, most beautiful expression of such love. It is because loving in this way is the bread-and-butter of authentic human happiness. It is because if they didn't love in this way, human beings would have absolutely nothing left to live for. *Nothing.* This, to my mind, is the underlying meaning of the well-known talmudic determination: "*O hevruta, o mituta*" (loosely: Give me society, or give me death). Either you have around you a particular group of people that you especially love (a "*hevreh*," as modern Hebrew slang has it)—or you might as well be dead.

(Jesus knew this; he knew it full well. That's why he continually emphasized that "My kingdom is not of this earth." He didn't want to—or at least was aware that he was unable to—bring about the establishment of "universal love" *here in the mundane sphere*: It just wouldn't work. Perhaps he even believed it *shouldn't* work. So he decided to institute it in the "kingdom of heaven." That is ultimately the reason why he departed. That is also the reason why there is no parallel in Christianity to Judaism's 613 commandments and their hundreds of thousands of derivatives, which are all about how to live and act and get along right down here in this world. Jesus, on the other hand, specifically relegated unto *Caesar* all things terrestrial. Early Christianity, at least, was not interested in creating a system designed for living and loving in this world: It was interested in ushering in the *next* one.)

Do you know who nearly managed to pull off John Lennon's vision of no religions, no nations, no countries, one world—*right here on earth*? Do you know who almost succeeded—even if only within relative geographic and demographic microcosms—in bringing about that beautiful dream of universal love, no barriers, no walls, and no special or distinct human cliques or clans? How about these fine-feathered fellows: Stalin, Mao, Pol Pot. Any of *these* names ring a bell? Because the only way to stop people from loving preferentially and start them loving universally; the only way to see to it that they do not divide up—as people who love at all naturally do—into distinct sociocultural and sociopolitical communities and associations, is by *forcibly ensuring that they all dress, eat, sleep, talk, sing, dance, work, play, and think the same*—and killing them if they diverge. There's your "One World," John, with all the divisions and barriers erased, there's Ofer and Doron and Shira's magnificent, imploding, united utopia, where "all hearts are as one heart, all minds are as one mind, so that through the spirit of oneness you may heal the sickness of a divided community." Feast your eyes.

VI

My grandfather on my father's side was an Iranian Jew from a little town about 150 miles south of Teheran, called Kashan. He told me this story.

Once, in the time of *his* grandfather's grandfather, already in the previous century, a Jewish merchant from Kashan allegedly overcharged a local Muslim man of the cloth (oh, believe me, he *did* it). This complacent clergyman metamorphosed overnight into the Mad Mullah, and swore upon the Holy Qur'an that he'd have his revenge, and then some. He quickly assembled and whipped into a religious frenzy all the beturbaned ayatollahs in the entire province, and together they proceeded to the palace of the *qaim-maqam*, the regional governor. By hook or by crook they managed to prevail upon him to issue an official edict requiring the conversion of every single Jewish man, woman, and child to Islam by such-and-such a date, upon pain of death.

Well, the appointed deadline was fast approaching, and the Jewish community of Kashan province was in an absolute tizzy. What to do? With two weeks left, the various elders finally buried their long-standing differences and held a solemn conference at the house of Kashan's chief rabbi. Prayers were offered, psalms were intoned, supplications were... supplicated. But nobody really had any suggestions worth considering. It was agreed by all present that a delegation should be sent to the governor, but no one could figure out what exactly they should say to him. The meeting was about to disperse, when the rabbi's wife—who had, of course, been bringing in round after round of sweet, samovar-seethed tea for the assembled guests—dared to address the company she had been so dutifully serving. "You leave it to me and my sisters," she enjoined confidently. "Just come back when it's time to go to the governor."

Iranian families are *big*, and soon the sound of looms hard at weaving could be heard not just at the rabbi's house, but at most of the houses surrounding it. The seven sisters worked like devils through day and night, scarcely pausing to rest, and when the elders returned one week later—on their way to petition the governor to rescind the evil decree—the rabbi's wife laid two enormous, rolled-up Persian rugs, made of the finest Kashan silk, at their feet. "Now, when you are received in audience by the governor, here's what you will do…," she explained.

A few days later the delegation of venerable, white-bearded old men—weary from their long trek through the desert on camel- and donkey-back—stood trembling in His Excellency's august presence. "You have wasted your time in traveling all the way here," he chided them, right off the bat. "There is nothing that will make me change my mind. You will all be good Muslims in time for next Friday's public prayers in the mosque. Nevertheless, since you have come all this way, I will go through the motions of entertaining your petition. What have you to say?"

The elders approached the governor's divan and bowed low (*real* low). "Your Honor, before presenting our petition, we have brought you a gift, as a token of our gratitude for these many long years during which we have been privileged to live quietly and obediently under your powerful protection."

The governor liked gifts. Especially the kind one received from large delegations of rich and frightened Jewish merchants. "Enough of your pathetic truckling," said he. "What have you brought me?" The elders immediately had both of the carpets brought in and unfurled at the ruler's feet. "On behalf of the Jewish community of Kashan province, we beg leave to place these two humble offerings before His Excellency, and request that He choose *one* of them as our tribute."

Both carpets were broad, plush, tightly woven, and made out of the most exquisite material. The first one was covered with colorful curving calyxes and designs of gold and green and turquoise, intricately intertwined with whirling waves of purple petunias which spiraled ceaselessly and centripetally towards the median. Splendid silhouettes of every size, shape, and hue graced the corners, like an ornamental garnish surrounding and supporting a magnificent main course. The vast center was an alternately placid and surging sea of breathtaking royal blue, periodically punctuated by a cornucopia of gemlike little islands of the most elegant design, each embroidered in a different form and color and bordered by hundreds of finely interlaced, snow-white cilia swimming softly in agile and decorous understatement.

The second carpet was… red.

That's all it was. The whole rug was just one sprawling, solid red mat, from warp to woof, from end to end. "*What?*" cried the governor. "How *dare* you! I should have you all decapitated for such insolence! Do you take me for a fool? What kind of choice is this? Who in his right mind would *not* choose the first carpet—and who in full possession of his faculties *would* choose the second?"

The hoariest head of the Jewish delegation stepped forward from amongst his peers and looked the governor straight in the eye. "The silk rugs, my liege, are the territories under your benevolent sway—Kashan province. Today that province is filled with peoples of every imaginable culture and creed—Muslims, Christians, Zoroastrians, Manicheans, Azeris, Mandeans, Turkmen, Jews—and in this way it resembles the first carpet. Would Your Excellency, then, exchange the first carpet for the second?"

("This gimmick," my grandfather would conclude with a twinkle in his eye, "plus about 175,000 gold tomans placed discreetly in the governor's coffers, succeeded in averting the evil decree.")

You know I have to ask: Which rug would *you* want? Which *world* do you want? The world of "Imagine," where nothing of any significance separates us, where there are "no countries and no religions," and where everybody is concomitantly possessed of the same tastes, the same loves, the same mind? The chiliastic borgian paradise of Shira, Ofer, and Doron, where all human beings blend into one another like some kind of massive, flavorless, mud-colored milk shake?

Or would you rather the world you live in be the diametric opposite of these worlds? A world of dazzling diversity, of independent and self-respecting societies and communities that value, retain, and revel in their own uniqueness? Would you rather live in a world where real people unapologetically express real preferences for the company and society of particular persons with whom they have special cultural, historical, and emotional bonds?

O, *when* will we stop striving to be the same, when will we stop "ever searching for the *one*"? (You guessed it, the Spice Girls again.) We'll never get there anyway, but we'll destroy so incredibly much of what makes life interesting and mysterious and exciting and beautiful along the way. Consult your biology book. It is *mitosis* which is the engine of creation, it is the proliferation of internal *heterogeneity* which is the substance and process of human life, of *all* life. It is increasing variety and diversity that are the hallmark of growth, of evolution, of progress—not approaching ever nearer the great, all-encompassing *One*, but rather... *fleeing it headlong like the plague.*

Move over to psychology, and peruse your Piaget. This famous Swiss shrimp-shrink explained time and again how the deepening ability to distinguish between the self and others—and between others and others—is the most powerful indicant of infant maturation. In this manner, declared he, we go forward step by step, distancing ourselves further and further each day from our original, *non*-distinguishing, fetal disposition, that all-engulfing oneness which Freud dubbed "ocean consciousness."

So what is it? Is *regression* your thing? Is life so bad and growth so scary that you want to make 180-degree turn and head right back into the womb?

Divided we stand, my friends—united we fall.

VII

"Okay," you might say, "point taken, but it isn't exactly a *new* point. You're simply preaching multi-culturalism. A day doesn't go by when I don't have that concept shoved in my face." Me, too, and I support it with all my heart. And I think you will agree that in order to promote and maintain authentic, polychromatic, humanity-enriching multiculturalism, we simply have to preserve and cultivate multiple, coherent, and distinctive cultures the world over. There's only one thing that the vast majority of young, fiery, and so very often Jewish advocates of the modern multi-cultural approach almost always seem to forget: That one of the foremost examples of such cultures *is their own.*

What kind of sense does it make when (among others) college-age, Jewish-born intellectuals espouse the toleration, nay, *celebration* of the international cultural mosaic, while at the same time entirely ignoring and neglecting almost everything even remotely Mosaic? Is it not astounding—along similar lines—that the same Jewish post-modernist professors who have for three decades and more decried "Western Cultural Imperialism" of every type, are in the overwhelming majority of cases themselves the very personification of the unconditional surrender of what is perhaps the most ancient and enduring non-Western culture—their own Jewishness—at the feet of that very same "Western Cultural Imperialism"? What is going on in the hearts and heads of Jewish students who ostensibly support constructive dialogue and illuminating interaction among different ethnic, national, cultural, and religious groups—but identify only peripherally (if at all) with their own? How on earth can people be expected to tolerate, respect, and eventually learn from each other's sociocultural differences… *if they don't have any?*

The Global Village is getting me down. I buy an outrageously expensive airline ticket, board the plane in New York and squirm around uncomfortably in my chair for ten hours, the bird lands, I deplane and, lo and behold, *I'm right back where I started from*: The same English language plastered all over the storefronts, the same Calvin Klein jeans plastered on everybody's behind, the same rap music as back in the States issuing ever so rhythmically from the taxi driver's radio (though neither he nor his passengers could ever possibly decipher a word of it—which, by the way, makes them very lucky people, if you ask me). Why are so many people driven by this lukewarm, lemming-like, perennial search for sameness? Why don't they prefer being themselves—both individually *and* collectively?

Am I advocating that nations and cultures insulate themselves, that they dig in behind an ethnocentric and xenophobic fortress and erect all types of intellectual and ideological tariffs, the better to maintain their separate group identity, their "cultural purity" (to paraphrase Jimmy Carter)? Not on your life. *Au contraire!* I am specifically and passionately advocating that the various sociocultural units of the world interact and share, that they challenge, stimulate, edify, surprise, enlighten, influence, and *open the eyes* of one another.

But in order to share, you have to have *what* to share, you have to cultivate, and become knowledgeable about, and rejoice in, and build upon *your own unique, accumulated heritage*. You need to cherish and nourish specifically the *distinguishing traits* and characteristics that make you different and fascinating, and place you in possession of tantalizing and desirable gifts to bestow upon others—things they don't already have! (Who wants to bring home a Bruce Lee or Michael Jackson T-shirt as a souvenir from Morocco? And yet these were the only two examples of Moroccan fashion memorabilia available at the Abu'l Hadi and Sons souvenir shop in Fez in the summer of 1987.) If you sow rutabaga and I grow kumquats, we certainly have every impetus to trade with each another; if we both plant kidney beans—what's the point?

I guess like most people, my general ideas about "the way things should be" are to a large extent the product of my childhood. My suburban Philadelphia block was made up of about ten separate houses with ample space between, all of which formed the peripheral ring around this huge, green, common lawn in the middle. The families inhabiting these houses—the Ciartes, the Fitzgeralds, the Popowitches, the Hing-Yips, the Rosenbergs, the Sanchezes—were as incurably and pridefully diverse as the architecture of the houses themselves. Visiting each other, as we often did, was a mind-expanding *tour de force*: The unexpected smells, the strange conventions, the vastly different notions of decor (for years I begged my parents to paint the inside of our house pink and green like the Ciartes had).

Now, what if someone had taken all these families, and somehow convinced them that it was a waste of space, all these separate houses; a waste of crockery, all these diverse dishes; a waste of artistic effort, all these varying internal and external decors? Everybody should move into one big, humungous house and do all that stuff together, and uniformly. Then everything would be hunky-dory, and far more economical, and look how much closer and more unified everybody would be!

How would you like to live in *that* house?

We *need* our separate houses. It's the only way we can be good neighbors. It's the only way we can avoid *butchering* each other with chain-saws and Ginsu knives in a matter of two to three days, tops. And it's the only way that the interaction between us—nightly on the grassy knoll, or daily in the world of work—can bear any fruit and be any fun. Just as you no doubt live your personal life within a given community as an individual, self-confidently sporting your own singular and special trademark qualities, so nations and ethnic groups need to actively participate in and contribute to the world order and the totality of human civilization as proud, particular, peculiar, *unique* sociocultural entities, each boasting a brash and defiant attitude of "national individualism," each, as it were, building, decorating, and living in its own distinctive cultural home within the overall neighborhood of nations. Here is Woodrow Wilson's simple yet crucial insight: The need for "self-determination." Here is Samuel Coleridge's "most general definition of beauty—*Multeity in Unity*."

"Gotcha!" you say, a self-satisfied smirk spreading speedily across your visage. "All you've been pushing for pages now is the direct-ratio relationship between waxing heterogeneity and human progress, between expanding diversity and a life that's worth living—and now, you've thrown the loaded term 'individualism' into the pot, to boot. Very well. By your logic, then, we should none of us affiliate with *any* association or community or nation or even family. Rather, we should focus solely on our own, independent, individual selves—renouncing loyalty to or prejudicial affection for any one particular group—and thereby provide the world with the largest amount of variety and individualism possible! *Six billion* different and unique colors!"

This is indeed the conclusion which has been reached, consciously or unconsciously, by a great many members of what is often (correctly) referred to as "alienated Western society." But this approach is not one iota different from the universal "oneness-or-bust" frenzy we've been striving to dethrone and debunk so far. *If you love everybody you love nobody—and if you love nobody you love nobody.* It's a big circle, and you've come full 'round it. You're talking about eradicating preferential love again—or at least severely restricting its scope and outlets to yourself and perhaps a few intimate relatives and acquaintances (is that all the love you've got?). You are talking about opting out of that special community, the *hevreh*, which the Talmud rightly says it is not worth living without.

And consider, if you will, the humble Persian carpet from my grandfather's story. Suppose the elders of Kashan had unrolled before the governor not two rugs, but three: The first of elaborate and colorful design, as described; the second, just plain red; and the third, made up of literally tens of thousands of tiny pixels and knots, each dyed its own unique tint, and with no attempt at thematic organization or color coordination whatsoever. What would *that* rug look like? Dreck, that's what. Neither full-blown universalism nor full-blown individualism makes for a beautiful world. Only a world which is based on a conception and structure planted firmly *between* these two poles can ever be called truly beautiful.

For God's sake, *be* an individual—and an individualist! I for one certainly lay claim to such a title—with a vengeance. It is *because* I am an arrogant, uncompromising, incorrigible individualist, and I know like I know my own bedsheets that nobody can ever take my "me-ness" away from me without a sawed-off twelve-gauge shotgun or some such—it is *because* of this that it never occurred to me to be afraid that I would lose myself in a crowd; it is *because* of this that I am able and willing to provide myself with the incredible privilege of being an integral participant in that unparalleled, nearly impossible phenomenon... called the Jewish people.

(I guess I should stop here and say this, just for the record: The above generalizations about the position taken respectively by Christianity and Judaism on the issue of love of—and affiliation with—national, cultural, tribal, and familial collectives, are just that: generalizations. I have no doubt they could become the target of virulent and often justified assault, at least on some counts. Again, however, I don't think anyone knowledgeable about these issues would dare to deny that non-Jewish creeds from Bahai to Buddhism, from Islam to Secular Humanism, from Christianity to Communism, are at least far stronger supporters of universal love than Judaism ever was or ever will be. This, I think, everyone will grant. It is true if for no other reason than that none of the other faiths or doctrines mentioned above lays claim in any way to being the cultural-ideological constitution of a particular national or ethnic group. Indeed, such an imputation would be an insult and anathema to the most fundamental principles of every single one of them.

Judaism, on the other hand, makes specifically this claim, and the Jews have traditionally seen the Tora as their own, special, personal possession and guide (there are a few eschatological prognostications emanating from the mouths of the Prophets which might be construed as contradicting this, but even here, the daily Jewish expression of gratitude to "He who separated and distinguished us"—*hamavdil* or *asher bahar*—remains at all times the dominant motif). We Jews are and have always been not only adherents to a set of spiritual dogmas, but *members of an extended family*, of a nation, and of a "tribe" (as the appellative "Jew"—*yehudi*—most emphatically implies). We have never referred to ourselves anywhere in our sources as "*dat yisra'el*" (the Religion of Israel) or "*emunat yisra'el*" (the Faith of Israel). Rather, we have always denoted ourselves throughout our long history by the significant cognomens *"am yisra'el"* (the Nation of Israel), *"klal yisra'el"* (the Totality of Israel), *"knesset yisra'el"* (the Assembly of Israel), *"beit yisra'el"* (the House of Israel), and *"bnei yisra'el"* (the Children of Israel). You see where the emphasis lies, right?

The point is, however, that I promised that I would utilize the purported positions of these various religions and ideologies regarding questions of love and oneness, solely as a paradigm—and that, I hope you understand, is the only thing I am doing. If all the learned rabbis in the entire State of Israel were to assemble in my living room tomorrow and—prior to excoriating and excommunicating one another for various perceived heresies—prove to me chapter and verse that the attitude to love and oneness which I have outlined herein is completely foreign to Judaism, and that it is, say, specifically *Christianity* which happens to see such issues in that way (i.e., the opposite of the theory I am propounding)—this wouldn't matter even a *smidgen* to the argument on behalf of which I am so vehemently expostulating. I would *still* advocate the particular positions I am currently advocating, regardless of which theology or philosophy is privileged to be used or abused as the paradigm. It is the attitude *itself* (preferential love, sociocultural diversity) which I am pushing with all my might—*not* the religion.)

VIII

A few issues, however, may still be troubling you. For instance: Isn't the world I am asking for perforce a world forever doomed to incessant, desolating warfare between peoples, all of whom love "their own" with a passion and hate everybody else with the same?

For starters, even assuming the One-Worlders could ever bring us peace, which they most definitively cannot, it would only be at the price of a terrorist, totalitarian, socially engineered nightmare that would make George Orwell and Aldous Huxley wet their pants. That is the only possible, earth-bound consummation of the words: "Imagine all the people, living life in peace." (Stop humming.) If you've got no will, no emotions, no preferences, and no special ties left to speak of, I guess that'll take the fight out of you pretty good, all right.

Contrary to the immortal and oft-cited last utterance of the early Zionist hero Joseph Trumpeldor—"It is good to die for our country"—you would probably agree with me that there isn't the slightest thing good about dying for your country, your nation, your religious beliefs, or whatever. I don't wish this fate upon anybody (except maybe Saddam Hussein; I hope he is privileged to die for his country—soon). What I *do* wish, upon every single person still persevering through these pages, is that you do have things in your life that are dear enough to you that you would be *willing* to die for them, if it ever—God forbid—became absolutely necessary. Says John: "Nothing to kill or die for...." Says me: In that case, nothing much to live for, either.

There is another important subject to be addressed in this connection, however, a subject we left dangling more than ten pages ago. Back then we were trying to figure out the motives of R. Akiva for apparently contradicting himself by lauding the precept "Love your neighbor as yourself," while at the same time ruling elsewhere (in the case of the forgotten flask) that when it comes to choosing between your life and that of your neighbor—*your* life is paramount. We have tried to show that as a Judaic scholar, Akiva was reared on the principle of preferential love, and thus he was forced to rule as he did. But we still haven't resolved the glaring disagreement between his ruling and the explicit scriptural prescription he praises so highly. Let's try to do that now.

Last week I was sitting in this Yemenite restaurant in Jerusalem reading a book and munching my *malawah*. At 7:00 p.m., the air was shrilly pierced—as it is every hour on the hour—by those six long beeps that some sadistic socialist functionary from the early days of pre-state broadcasting decided was an appropriate way to introduce the news. After a run-of-the-mill item—some foreign dignitary's helicopter had been hovering on the brink of Israeli airspace for the last three hours and was about to plunge into the Mediterranean because officials of the Foreign and Defense Ministries were quarreling over whose prerogative it was to issue the entry permit—the anchorperson announced that 230 people had been killed in an airplane crash in Indonesia.

"That's terrible," I thought, and proceeded to cut myself another large, juicy morsel of *malawah*, drench it in my side dish of *humus*, and loft it lazily into my watering, hangar-like mouth. Yummmmm. "That's really *awful*—oh, there's a nice big piece of chicken smothered in delectable *harif* sauce, come to papa... mmmm, yummmm...."

And then I stopped. I was actually a little angry at myself for being unable to get sufficiently upset about those 230 Indonesians and their poor, grief-stricken, destroyed families to have it affect my appetite even for five seconds. So I tried an experiment. I took the headline I had just heard on the radio, and changed only one or two words. Now it read: Two Hundred Thirty Israeli Soldiers Die in Plane Crash over Negev.

"Oh, God. That really *hurts*. It physically *hurts*. As if someone punched me really hard in the stomach. Is that what it feels like? That much pain? I'm not thinking about my next bite of food anymore, that's for sure. I'm pretty close to being nauseous. So now I know. Now I have some inkling at least of what those crushed, devastated, wrecked, innocent families are experiencing right now, as the news reaches them one by one that everything they ever lived for is gone. Dear *God*...."

You may not believe this, but I actually got up and left without finishing my *malawah* (and there was at least a third still sitting there on the plate). I know, I know: My momentary abstinence really helped those Indonesian families. That's not my point. Let me give you another example.

A couple of years ago I was under Manhattan, riding the One Train downtown to South Ferry. Round about Sixty-Sixth Street, the door on the end of our car slid open, and a man with no legs came through, propelling himself with his arms and carrying a bucket in his teeth. He didn't say anything (obviously), wore no explanatory sign, but I guarantee you this: By the time he made it to the other end of the car, there was *easily* upwards of fifty more dollars in that bucket. Granted, people give for all types of reasons. But I know what made *me* at least reach for the paper and not the change. It wasn't "altruism," whatever that is. It was really a much simpler, more compelling deal: As I would imagine most other people did on that train, I looked at that indescribably miserable man and instinctively said to myself: "My God: What if that were *me*? What if that were my father, or my brother, or my son?"

Preferential love is the most powerful love there is, the only truly *motivating* love there is. It is by *means* of that love—the *special* love we harbor for those close to us—that we learn how to begin to love others, who are farther away. Genuine and galvanizing empathy for "the other" is acquired most effectively and lastingly through a process which involves, first and foremost, immersion in love of self, then of family, then of friends, then of community... and so on. It is via *emotional analogy* to these types of strong-bond affections that one becomes capable of executing a sort of "love leap," a hyper-space transference of the strength and immediacy of the feelings one retains for his favorite people, smack onto those who have no direct claim on such sentiments.

If you don't love your own best of all, we said, you really have no idea what *genuine* love is. If you have no idea what genuine love is, your chances of learning to love people in Indonesia or Syria or Tajikestan or Wyoming, your chances of learning to feel for people in faraway places or contexts (or on the other side of a tense border, or in the opposite camp of a *kulturkampf*), are pretty slim indeed.

Here, then, is (my guess at) R. Akiva's exegesis of the much-touted verse: "Love your neighbor as yourself." In his eyes, it doesn't signify "Love your neighbor *as much as* you love yourself"; R. Akiva doesn't believe in such artificial love, we know that from the flask story. To him it reads (and the Hebrew happens to support this, even though Akiva was not generally the type who cared): "Love your neighbor *in the same fashion* as you love yourself." Use the feelings you have toward yourself as a guide for how to feel about him. You will never love him *as much* as you love yourself—you *should* never love him as much as you love yourself—but you will learn to love him at all, in the first place, solely through your overwhelmingly powerful love of yourself and your own. It is to this process and no other that the Tora refers when it urges—in over twenty different versions of the same statement—"Love the stranger: For you were strangers in the land of Egypt." (Deuteronomy 10:19)

The world of preferential love and distinct sociocultural and political entities certainly need not be one of hatred and interminable warfare (what is Isaiah's vision? "*Nation* shall not lift up sword against *nation*, neither shall they learn war anymore." Isaiah 2:4). It may, in fact, be the only system available to the human race which will ever have a chance of breeding genuine global empathy and tolerance.

Imagine *that*.

IX

You are still not happy. "Okay," you might say, "I'll concede, for the moment, the following points: (1) I accept that the kind of love that means the most to me is preferential, distinguishing love: I want it, I need it, I can't live without it; (2) I'll give you that the world should optimally resemble a tapestry of distinctive families, or groups, or peoples, or nations; and (3) I'll even grant you that I personally, for the sake of my own happiness and for the general good of humanity, should connect myself in a vigorous and loving fashion to one of said groups. Fine. What you haven't really told me is... *why on earth should that group be the Jews?*"

Well said. After all, you might claim that you've had little or no exposure to Judaism or the Jewish community, so what's it to you; or you might claim that what meager exposure you did have was not exactly tantalizing, and you can't see much point in going back for seconds; or you might (finally) ask this extremely excellent question: Why shouldn't I adopt as my "special society" all the members of the intramural hockey league I play in? Or all the guys I go bowling with? Or all the fighting feminists of the world? Or everybody who digs Biz? Or all the people who live in the same city I do? Or all the people who live in the same country I do (I'm as good a patriot as the next fellow!)? Why not *these* groups as my first loves? After all, I probably have a great deal more in common with them than I do with your average Jewish person walking down the street.

I'll tell you (in the immortal words of Tevye the milkman):

...I don't know.

Because here we stand on the threshold of things that are not really rational: They are emotional (which, however, as we have been striving to argue, is a far more fundamental and powerful human motivation). It is very hard—indeed, well nigh impossible—to logically argue something that belongs not to the realm of logic, but to the kingdom of the heart. Nevertheless, I'll give it my best shot.

I could start by telling you how much *we* need *you*, and how much what you personally decide to do with your life has earth-shattering consequences and ramifications for your whole extended national clan, wherever they sleep and dream, wherever they wake and work, wherever they fight and fall. The Midrash tells this terse tale: There are twelve people in a boat. One guy, he starts drilling a hole under his seat. When everybody gapes at him in dismay and astonishment, he looks up and says: "What's it to ya? I'm only drilling under my *own* seat."

The idea is, of course, that we Jews are all in the same boat, so your particular actions or inactions naturally attract our interest and concern, whether you like it or not—because they are inextricably bound up with our collective prospects and welfare. Make no mistake about it: Whether you are aware of this or not, *the future of the Jewish people is as much up to you as it is up to Benjamin Netanyahu.* But this is too close to a Jewish guilt trip, and I'm just not into that. A very brilliant Zionist revolutionary by the name of Vladimir Jabotinsky always made it clear to his cohorts and disciples in the movement that if a Jew chooses to opt out of his nation's ongoing struggle and experience, there certainly is no effective or morally defensible way to force him back in. If he wants to go, let him go—more work for the rest of us.

I could also advance the proposition that you ought to join us with a passion and a fury for the following very simple reason: You are a Jew. You are a Jew, and another Jew (who was once upon a time *extremely* as-similated)—the heart that was huge enough to imagine the State of Israel and then bring that imagination to fruition, Dr. Theodor Herzl—once declared plainly: "The greatest happiness in life, is to be that which one is." I couldn't agree more. And if you *are* going to be who you are—a Jew—*then do it up.* Don't be a "by-default Jew," a "checkbook Jew," a "High-Holiday Jew," a "peripheral Jew" or a "marginal Jew." Be a "bold, breathless" Jew, be a "wild, wanton" Jew, be an "I'm going to milk this cultural identity thing for *everything it's got*" Jew—be a knowledgeable, thirsty, caring, daring, *actively involved* Jew.

This is not a bad argument, but neither is it without problems. Al-though I certainly don't intend anything of the sort—far from it!—it is possible that a certain tinge of traditionalism or conservatism could be read into a thesis which suggests: "Be what you are—because that is what you are." It could conceivably smack of an attack on human mobility—a concept as dear to me as it is dear (in my humble interpretation) to the Tora itself. Besides, you might easily parry by claiming that "being who you are" at this point in your life entails being a bowler, or a feminist, or a Bostonian, or an American or Canadian, far more than it does be-ing a Jew, which is "what you are" only due to an accident of birth. So this contention doesn't completely pass muster, either.

What of the oft-repeated apologetic asseveration that the Jewish legal and behavioral system is morally superior to that of any other religion, culture, and ideology? I personally happen to believe—after a respectable amount of round-robin investigation—that Judaism as a lifestyle and *weltanschauung* has a good deal more to recommend itself than many other ready-made systems available to people for the adopting and practicing—but that's just me. I also happen to think there are a lot of *less* than palatable provisions to be found in the dos and don'ts of Judaic jurisprudence, and besides: Who says we should conduct every aspect of our existence according to a prefabricated plan purveyed to us by our illustrious predecessors? We were given minds, I would venture, for the purpose of judging and evaluating each and every instance and episode in our lives independently, on a case-by-case basis—not so that we should know how and where to look up the proper response to every single stimulus in a book. So this argument goes down the tubes as well.

Let's try a different approach. Again, the gnawing question: "Why not choose my bowling buddies, or the people on my block, or the International Society of Vegans, or who knows what other coherent entity as my spiritual center and the object of my primary affections? Why is the Jewish people a better candidate for this exalted position in my thoughts and emotions than these previously named options?"

Let's hum along with Dr. Winston O'Boogie—Lennon's favorite nickname—once again: "Imagine all the people, living for today...." *Living for today.* Oh, John, my main *man*, what it *is*? Did you *think* about this wish before you made it? Granted, this line suffers a number of possible interpretations, but they all more or less connect to the problem I would like to raise here.

We have already discussed the ugliness and emptiness engendered by the modern Western ailment of exaggerated individualism and complete nonaffiliation. The symptoms of this disease are sequestration and isolation from a whole concentrically constructed solar system of potentially enriching relationships on the horizontal—or spatial—plane. In a word, this is the affliction of "living for yourself."

Well, one thing is for sure: Being Jewish cures *this* affliction, like no antidote I've ever seen. As a Jew, you literally have millions of people all around you, right this very second, throughout the world, with whom you share a secret, with whom you can exchange a knowing glance, at whom you can wink (use your judgment). These people are *your* people, they feel tied to you, they are pulling for you, they are *on your side* (travel tip: this does *not* mean you will not get ripped off by Israeli cab drivers—that's *their* way of saying, "I love you").

I don't know if this special relationship is a product of the historical and international uniqueness of the Jewish phenomenon—we are neither a "nation" like the French, nor a "religion" like the Christians—or whether it is because as a group, we are not too big (like the population of America) and not too small (like the tenants in your apartment building), but just the right size to elicit that super-family feel, that combination of transcendence *and* immanence, of greatness *and* closeness. Or maybe it is just because the rest of humanity has always been so kind to us. I don't know exactly *why* there is this powerful electricity constantly coursing and pulsating between Jews the world over—I just know it's there.

Just before my latest stint in the reserves, I was in New York blading with my brother down the lower West Side promenade hard by the Hudson, and we stopped to rest near the World Trade Center. This guy a few feet away from us was trying to pick up a young lady by aggressively and intimately massaging her dog, and Alex and I switched to Hebrew in order to comment upon his original methodology. As we were talking, this be-suited fellow sitting on the bench opposite—clearly taking a five-minute lunch break from an action-packed morning of corporate raiding—kept staring at us. Finally, he rose, walked over, and stood rather awkwardly dead center in front of our bench. I looked up at him, and he faltered, gestured, fumbled, hesitated, and then just stammered, "Um… uh… *Shalom!*" I extended my hand and he shook it warmly and smiled. Still flustered, he half-saluted us goodbye, and went back to merging and acquiring.

What he really wanted to say was: "Hey—I'm Jewish, too." What he really intended by "Um… uh… *Shalom,*" was: "I embrace you, my brother, member of my tribe from a faraway place. We share something tremendous and indescribable, something ancient and exalted, something wonderful and mysterious. We were soldered together, you and I, by the fires of hell on earth, and our bonds are since unsunderable. I'm glad you are in the world, and it gives me strength and pleasure to see you. Here: Have some genuine affection." He meant all this, and more. He wanted to momentarily close that circuit and tap into that energy flow.

The modern Western sickness of living solely for oneself, however—for which Jewish identity is such a powerful serum—is usually accompanied by *another* malady, which Lennon and so many others aspire to infect us all with: Living solely for today. This second disorder—let's call it "time hermitism," for lack of a better term (is there a *worse* term?)—emaciates our psyches by disconnecting us from a vast and fascinating potpourri of mind- and soul-expanding elements on the vertical—or temporal—plane. You can be alone in space, and you can be alone in time.

"Living for today"—an extremely pervasive slogan among so many people for so many years—means, essentially, *being alone in time*, alone historically speaking (a feat which can obviously be achieved even while surrounded in the present by a whole soccer stadium's worth of companions). Well, I suppose that's fine, if that's what you like. Living for the moment—and only for the moment—has certain genuine advantages. But I think that in the long run, you lose out *big* time. I mean, let's reason from the specific to the general again: Did you ever see that *Star Trek* where they strap Kirk down into a big, black, padded chair, and beam this memory-erasing light at his head, such that after a few minutes he would have been emptied of all recollection? Now suppose we strapped you into that chair, and erased your entire memory—everything you did, everything you felt, everything you learned, everything you treasured, everything you daily and constantly reference. What, do you suppose, would be left?

A turnip, that's what. "You" are the accumulation of your experiences throughout your life. Growing and living and enjoying and fulfilling is all about the interaction, combination, and application of those past experiences—which constitute the greater part (if not the whole) of your consciousness—to what it is you are thinking, feeling, and doing at the present instant. If all you know and all you feel is what you know and feel *today*—or this week, or this year—well, you aren't going to get invited to a lot of dinner parties, I can promise you that.

But along the same lines, "you" are—or should be—even more. Why settle, after all? You have the opportunity to extend your horizons further than any normal eye can see, further than any detached intellect can perceive, further than any untouched heart can feel. You can reach beyond your individual, birth-and-death-bound walls, and palpate immortality. You can draw on, you can *gorge* upon, the accumulated experience, knowledge, and inextinguishable fire of the manifold ascending centuries which preceded you. You can stand higher than Everest on the shoulders of a hundred generations, and thereby see light-years farther into the future than those who have grounded themselves at sea level, and cannot see past their noses in any direction. In a word: You can be HUGE.

How does one do all this? After all, *you personally* were born quite recently. You haven't existed, built, climbed, fallen, lost, won, wept, rejoiced, created, learned, argued, loved, and struggled for thousands of years. Nevertheless: You happen to have lucked out. As a Jew, you are a distinguished member of a nation which *has* done all these things, and then some. You have special eyes, eyes that can see for miles and miles. If you only will it—enough to work at it—you can extend your arms and touch the eons and the millennia, you can suck in the insights and bask in the glory and writhe in the pain and draw on the power emanating from every era and every episode and every experience of your indomitable, indestructible, obstinately everlasting people.

This is not an ability acquired solely through learning or reading (although this is a *major* ingredient, I hasten to emphasize); it is first and foremost a function of connection, of belonging, of powerful love. If you reach out and grasp your people's hands—*you were there*. You participated in what they did, in all places at all times, you fought their battles, felt their feelings and learned their lessons. You tended flocks with Rachel, and slaved in Potiphar's house with Joseph; you sang in the wilderness with Miriam, and toppled the walls of Jericho with Joshua; you carried first fruits to the Temple Mount, and were mesmerized by Elijah on the slopes of Carmel; you brought the house down on the Philistines with Samson, and bewailed your lost youth in the mountains with Jephthah's daughter; you fought the chariots of Hatzor under Deborah, and danced before the ascending Ark with David; you went into exile with the prophet Jeremiah, and hung your harp and wept by the rivers of Babylon; you defied the divinity of Nebuchadnezzar with the courage and cunning of Daniel, and vanquished the might of imperial Persia with the wisdom and beauty of Esther; you sought communion with the infinite with Shimon bar Yohai, and studied law and lore in the vineyards of Yavneh with Elazar ben Arach; you were with Judah the Maccabee at Modi'in, with the Zealots at Masada, with Akiva in the Roman torture chamber, and with Bar Kochba at Beitar; you devoted your life to Tora at Sura and Pumpedita, and philosophized by the Nile in Fustat with the circle of Maimonides; you were crucified for refusing the cross in the Crusades, and were turned into ashes for your stubbornness at the *autos-da-fé*; you were exiled from the shores of Spain by Isabella, and chased down and raped by the hordes of Khmelnitsky; you went out to Safed's fields to greet the Sabbath bride with Luria, and went in to Galicia's huts to seek the ecstasy of the fervent Ba'al Shem Tov; you fled the Black Hundreds across Russia's taiga, and were welcomed by Lazarus at the gates of Ellis Island; you filed into gas chambers at Bergen Belsen, and were hurled living into the flames at Matthausen and Sobibor; you parachuted into Hungary with Hanna Senesh, and fought back at Warsaw with Mordechai Anilewitz; you were shot with your family in the forests of Poland, and dug a mass grave and perished there at Babi Yar; you revived your dead language, you resurrected your sapped strength, you returned to yourself and renewed the lapsed covenant, you arose like a lion and hewed out your freedom on the plains and the mountains of your old-new land.

Throughout all this and so much more, *you were there with them*—and they are here with you. This is the thrust of the Passover Haggada when it exhorts: "In every generation, a person must see himself as if he *personally* left Egypt." This is the intention of the Talmud when it whispers—based upon a strongly suggestive biblical verse—that we were *all* present and accounted for at the foot of Mount Sinai in the desert, over three thousand years ago. This, I would venture, is the deepest symbolic meaning and ultimate emotional motivation behind the Jewish-originated concept of the Resurrection of the Dead in the end of days: You see, I think that in certain ways, we loved one another so damn much that we simply couldn't bear the notion that we wouldn't all—all of us, from every place and every Jewish generation throughout history—eventually have the opportunity and pleasure of meeting each other face-to-face, and just spending some quality time. Not to worry, crooned the rabbis of the Talmud (with the Supremes): *Someday, we'll be together....*

I am a Jew, and I am tied to teleology as well as to history. I live not just "for today," and not even just for all that has *led up* to today—I also live for a thousand tomorrows. I do not know what will be in ten centuries from now, but I know that Jews will be. How do I know? Because I will work for it, because I will see to it—and I believe in myself as much as I believe in my people. Yes, Jews there will be. And through them, *I* will be, and through them, I will *touch* what will be, and through them, I will *create* what will be. You and I are members of a unique, extended family, extended in *time* as well as in space, extended into the *future* as well as into the past. My noble ancestors will pardon me for the odious comparison, but it is like having access to a vast Internet of Existence, like being plugged-in and logged-on to forever (and believe it or not, at the highest and deepest levels, the connection is *interactive*). In the words of Leo Tolstoy (not that we need his approval or reinforcement, he just happens to be the world's most talented writer, and he put this—and everything else—rather nicely):

> The Jew is the emblem of eternity. He whom neither slaughter nor torture of thousands of years could destroy, he whom neither fire nor swords nor inquisition was able to wipe off the face of the earth, he who was the first to produce the oracles of God, he who has been for so long the guardian of prophecy, the pioneer of liberty and the creator of true civilization, and who transmitted all these to the rest of the world—such a nation cannot be destroyed. The Jew is as everlasting as eternity itself.

You need not, then, live the impoverished life of the "time hermit." You, my sister or brother, spiritual daughter or son of Sarah and Abraham, you are blessed with the opportunity to connect with and benefit from a sprawling, boundless, spatial, *and* temporal network, suffused with the deepest secrets of the ages, humming with the love of countless generations, a love that was always channeled directly and unhesitatingly at you.

By tying into all of this—while *fiercely* maintaining your own, stubborn individuality—you indeed achieve a great deal: You add innumerable new intellectual and emotional dimensions to your life, as you absorb, melt down, and re-fashion in your own image the fruits of untold centuries of evolving Jewish thought and churning Jewish tumult; you teach yourself the syntax and vocabulary of a timeless language, which you can use—as it were—to communicate with all that went into creating you, and all that you will one day create; you partake in a four-thousand-year-long journey of savage struggle and jubilant exultation, of unimaginable sacrifice and ineffable beauty, an adventure recently rekindled in a phoenix-like flash of incandescent splendor the likes of which human history has never seen; and eventually you burn, my brother and sister, you burn with the light and the fever and the strength and the passion of the magnificent and undying people of Israel, the bush that burns, but is never consumed.

Try getting that from bowling.

PART III

ZION AND HISTORY

MAKING HISTORY

DANIEL POLISAR

ISRAEL'S "NEW HISTORIANS" have come of age. It was scarcely a decade ago that books such as Benny Morris' *Birth of the Palestinian Refugee
Problem, 1947-1949* (1987) and Tom Segev's *The Seventh Million* (1991)
appeared, heralding the arrival of a cadre of young Israeli historians radically at odds with the way that previous scholars had recounted the story
of Zionism. In particular, the new historians painted a highly unflatter-
ing picture of Israel's founding, centered around the Zionist leadership's
mistreatment of the Arabs during and after the War of Independence
(Morris) and its errors of omission and commission towards the victims
and survivors of the Holocaust (Segev). At the time, the new perspective on Israel's past was generally dismissed as a fringe phenomenon, and
only a handful of names were associated with it. Since then, however,
scholars openly identified with the new history—and with the similar
treatment of Zionism in disciplines such as political science, sociology,
and philosophy—have grown appreciably in numbers and influence. Many
of them have earned coveted tenure-track positions at Israeli universities,
while their views have been widely disseminated by the Israeli media,
especially in the daily *Haaretz* (Israel's equivalent of the *New York Times*),

and most spectacularly in *Tekuma*, Israel Television's 1998 documentary miniseries on the Jewish state's first fifty years.

In the past year, however, the new historians have taken a quantum leap towards acceptance by the cultural mainstream. In July 1999, the Israel Defense Forces, through its History Division, cosponsored the publication of *The Struggle for Israel's Security*, a book which the daily *Yediot Aharonot* described as "shattering a number of the most splendid myths on which we were raised" (August 4, 1999), and which was particularly harsh in assessing Israel's security policy during the formative period of the 1950s. Two months later, the Ministry of Education introduced into ninth-grade classrooms across the country the first three textbooks about Israel that are part of a new curriculum aimed at teaching history from an expressly "universal" (as opposed to "nationalist") perspective. The most radical of these texts is *A World of Changes: History for Ninth Grade*, edited by Danny Ya'akobi and published by the Ministry's own Curriculum Division, which attributes the victory of Jewish forces over five Arab armies in the War of Independence to the Jews' organizational and logistical edge rather than to determined leadership, brilliant military tactics, or individual heroism, and suggests that Israel precipitated the Six Day War by acting aggressively against Syria in the months prior to the outbreak of fighting. The new history has captured the interest of a growing segment of the Israeli public as well: Tom Segev's *Days of the Anemones* (1999), an account of the Mandate period that credits the Arabs rather than the Jews with driving the British out of Palestine, has been on the *Haaretz* national best seller list for thirty-one weeks, and counting—a feat unparalleled by any historical work published in Israel in the last decade and a half.

At least as impressive has been the new historians' penetration of the American intellectual mainstream—which sets the trend for the way that Israel is viewed throughout the democratic world, and which until now has remained largely immune to the trends in Israeli academia. In September 1999, New York's prestigious Knopf publishing house released Benny Morris' *Righteous Victims: A History of the Zionist-Arab Conflict, 1881-1999*, a 750-page reinterpretation of Zionist history which suggests that Zionism was "tainted by a measure of moral dubiousness" from the outset, and argues that the Israeli leadership bears substantial responsibility for all the wars fought since 1948. The following month, W.W. Norton published *The Iron Wall: Israel and the Arab World Since*

1948, a 670-page tour of the last half-century authored by Avi Shlaim, an Israeli-born "new historian" who teaches at Oxford. Shlaim's conclusions, though presented in a less scholarly manner than those of Morris, are similar in substance. Many of America's leading opinion-making publications, including *The New York Times*, *The Wall Street Journal*, the *New Republic*, *Commentary*, *Foreign Affairs*, and *The Weekly Standard*, devoted lengthy reviews to these iconoclastic works, making them the most widely discussed books on Israel to appear in the English-speaking world in the past decade.

Clearly, the new historians can no longer be dismissed as a fringe group. Moreover, many of the facts they present concerning errors made by the Zionist movement cannot be denied by fair-minded readers. At the same time, however, their conclusions often seem tailor-made to undermine the very legitimacy of those Israeli leaders most centrally associated with the establishment of the Jewish state—especially Labor stalwarts like David Ben-Gurion, Moshe Dayan, Yigal Allon, and Golda Meir. And while the main targets of the new historians' animus are no longer alive, the assault on the legacy of Zionism poses a grave threat to Israel's future. No nation can retain its basic vitality if its entire historical narrative comes to be seen in the public mind as a long series of moral failings compounded by errors of judgment. And to this point, it is far from clear that Israeli intellectuals have succeeded in mounting an effective response to this challenge. How, then, should those who on balance have a favorable view of Zionism's first century respond to the new historians?

The first step is to recognize that the new historians' main contribution to the debate over Zionist history is not one of facts, but one of *perspective*. Of course, this is not the way they have sought to portray themselves. Since Benny Morris first coined the term "new historians" in an article that appeared in the November 1988 issue of *Tikkun*, he and his colleagues have claimed that what distinguishes them from their predecessors is the willingness and ability to unearth the inconvenient facts of Israeli history. They have argued that their authority to rewrite Zionist and Israeli history was based in large part on the opening of Israel's state archives (like other democracies, Israel follows a thirty-year rule for the declassification of documents, which means that most primary

sources on the 1948 War of Independence first began to be made available to the public in the late 1970s). And indeed, many of their more
impressive works have appeared in the wake of the declassification of
the relevant documents: The initial spate of publications about the War
of Independence was followed in turn by books and articles excoriating
what the new historians perceived as Israel's high-handed immigration
policies of the early 1950s, its aggressive cross-border raids of the early
and mid-1950s, its imperialist war with Egypt in 1956, and its discriminatory social policies of the early 1960s.

But while some of the sources presented by the new historians had
previously been untapped, the factual core on which they based their
findings was far from original. Avi Shlaim's *Collusion Across the Jordan*
(1988) covered material much of which had been familiar to Israeli historians for over a decade, and whose major components Dan Schueftan
had already explored in *A Jordanian Option* (1986). The depiction of
the Zionist leadership's response to the Holocaust in Segev's *The Seventh
Million* (1991) likewise added little to the research on which Dina Porat
had based her *Entangled Leadership* (1986). What made the new works
highly controversial was therefore not the facts they presented, but the
perspective from which they were written, which was characterized by a
markedly more negative evaluation of Zionist leaders than that reached
by previous Israeli historians. Shlaim, for example, took the well-known
story of contacts between Ben-Gurion and King Abdullah of Jordan before
and during Israel's War of Independence, embellished it with additional
material from the archives, and wrote a sensationalized account premised
on the notion that this strategic partnership was illicit "collusion."

In considering the impact of the new historians' perspective on their
scholarship, it is appropriate to begin with Benny Morris, if only because
his research and writing are often cited, with some justification, as being
of a higher quality than that of other partisans of the new history. In
1948 and After: Israel and the Palestinians (1994), Morris acknowledged
that his research agenda was shaped by political opinions that were at
variance with those held by earlier historians ("the political views of the
new historians and current political concerns were among the factors that
led these historians to research particular subjects"). His often extreme use
of language is likewise a reflection of perspective: In his November 1988
Tikkun article, Morris raised the possibility that Israel "was besmirched by
original sin" due to the manner in which the Jewish state had come into

being. Last year, he went even further, describing the Zionist leadership's treatment of the Palestinian Arabs during the War of Independence as "a variety of ethnic cleansing." (Roy Gutman and David Rieff, eds., *Crimes of War: What the Public Should Know*, 1999, pp. 28-37.)

These are not "facts" that one discovers in recently opened archives. They are indicative of profound moral evaluations, which may or may not have been shaped by some formative archival experience. It is such evaluations which have allowed Morris and others to write a sweeping new narrative of Zionist history that goes far beyond anything suggested by the revelations of recently declassified documents. Thus Morris' latest book, *Righteous Victims*, argues that Zionism was from the outset "a colonizing and expansionist ideology and movement," which was infected by "the European colonist's mental obliteration of the 'natives.'" It is this damning characterization that permits him to conclude that the Zionists reduced the Arabs to "objects to be utilized when necessary," rather than human beings with legitimate aspirations.

Needless to say, someone else examining the facts Morris presents might easily describe these matters differently. But once seen from such a perspective, the factual landscape of Israel's history—both the "new" facts and those that have been known for decades—immediately takes on an ugly slant that no amount of arguing over the facts can set aright.

Unfortunately, the response of Israel's mainstream cultural leadership has been less than inspiring. Efforts to take on the new historians have frequently missed their target, precisely because they have mistaken the broad assault on the Jewish nationalist perspective on history for an argument about facts. Typical of this problem is Efraim Karsh's *Fabricating Israeli History*, which was published in English in 1997 and first translated into Hebrew last year. While Karsh does succeed in showing that some of the claims put forward by new historians such as Morris and Shlaim are based on sloppy archival work, if not deliberate falsification of the sources, the points on which he goes to the mat with them are peripheral to their central theses. He takes Morris to task, for example, for distorting the evidence in trying to show that from the mid-1930s on, Ben-Gurion and the mainstream Labor-Zionist leadership favored the wholesale transfer of Arabs from the areas of Palestine slated for a Jewish state. Yet even if Karsh is right on this point—which he almost certainly is—Morris' main claims about Israeli actions during the War of Independence remain unaffected. Moreover, when Karsh presents his own interpretation, which seeks to vindicate the Zionist leaders, his elaboration of their motives is so implausible as to all but ruin his case. For example, Karsh insists on taking at face value speeches in which Ben-Gurion waxed poetic over his desire for idyllic relations with the Arabs—desires which may have been sincere in the abstract, but which were frequently at odds with the hard-nosed character of his policies.

To compete effectively, scholars who do not share the new historians' ideological predilections must set as their primary task the formulation of an appropriate perspective from which Israeli history can be understood. And this means, first and foremost, a clarification of the moral standards by which the actions undertaken by the Zionist leadership are to be judged. Underlying much of the work of the new historians is the unspoken premise that the wielding of power necessary to found and defend a state is morally problematic in general, and especially so in the case of Israel. This premise leads them to take a magnifying glass to those cases in which the Zionists' use of power led (or may have led) to the suffering of others—both Arab and Jew—while downplaying the circumstances that rendered those actions necessary. In responding, it is necessary to articulate and defend a competing set of premises, which more faithfully reflect the proper application of morality to politics: That the behavior of historical actors must be assessed in light of their obligation to wield power on behalf of the people whose interests they were bound to protect; that the establishment and preservation of a state for the Jewish people was not only legitimate but a moral imperative; and that Zionist leaders have generally been faced by international and local exigencies that have compelled them to make difficult choices. This, of course, does not mean accepting the idea that everything the Zionists did was right, or even reasonable. But it does make it possible to take historical facts that come to light and put them in their proper place within a narrative whose conclusions remain fundamentally sympathetic to Zionism.

We can take as an instructive example the research done by Benny Morris in *Birth of the Palestinian Refugee Problem*. Despite occasional inaccuracies, Morris' account of the subject is more detailed and accurate than anything that preceded it. If we consider the facts Morris presents, it is reasonably clear that the flight of much of the Arab population from the territory that became Israel stemmed from battles between Arab and Jewish forces, and from the fears of Arab civilians of getting caught in the fighting. The Zionist leadership, Morris' research shows, correctly understood the danger that the Palestinian Arabs posed to the nascent Jewish state, and therefore did little to prevent their departure, at times encouraging or even precipitating it through political or military actions. In fact, Morris' own research does much to disprove the claims of his recent writings that what happened during the War of Independence was "ethnic cleansing."

This is not to say that one cannot document cases of unjustified Jewish brutality. Recording and condemning such atrocities is the duty of a balanced history. But these do not necessarily warrant Morris' conclusion that from the outset, the Zionist enterprise was "tainted by a measure of moral dubiousness." The fact that Israeli troops at times used excessive force in retaliating against terror attacks in the 1950s does not, for example, prove that Israel's counterterrorism efforts of this period were unnecessary or immoral. On the contrary, when viewed in the context of the challenges that Israel faced, and in light of how other nations responded to comparable dangers, the Zionist record remains admirable. Likewise, the fact that Holocaust survivors and immigrants from Arab countries were not always received in Israel with appropriate dignity does not fundamentally alter the picture of a Zionist leadership deeply committed to the safety and well-being of these Jews.

Rather, what these and other errors demonstrate is that practice sometimes fell short of national ideals—a fact that should serve as a reminder of the responsibility that comes with statecraft, and of the vigilance that is needed in order to prevent the exigencies of power from leading to moral corruption. Only people who believe that the Jewish state should be held to standards of purity that are incompatible with the exercise of sovereign power, or who think that such errors are representative of Israel's entire past, need fear an honest stocktaking with regard to the nation's history.

At the same time, however, it is a mistake to respond to the challenge posed by the new historians in a purely reactive manner. Because of the perspective that guides their research, the new historians invariably focus on those topics that best lend themselves to uncovering evidence of

Zionism's sins, both real and imagined. If they are allowed to dictate the agenda for scholarly debate, public discourse about Israel's legacy will be reduced to a series of arguments concerning the precise degree of blame to be assigned the Jewish state in the most problematic chapters of its history. To mount a successful opposition, scholars of Zionist and Israeli history need to concentrate on producing original works that reflect the full range of significant events, and that employ a comparative perspective appropriate for describing the establishment and development of a state born under difficult circumstances. In doing so, they will necessarily give the most noble aspects of Zionism their due, without whitewashing the failures that are part of every major historic enterprise.

In describing the individuals who shaped this enterprise, there is no reason to try to cast great men and women as angels. Rather, they should be depicted as they were: As great men and women, faced with terrible choices, who took responsibility for the fate of their people, with all of the good—and ill—that this entails. One need only think of Anita Shapira's two-volume masterpiece *Berl* (1980), or Shabtai Teveth's three-volume *The Burning Ground* (1976, 1980, 1987)—monumental biographies of leading Zionist figures Berl Katznelson and David Ben-Gurion, respectively—to see how painstaking works of scholarship can also become a source of national pride. Though markedly different in their approach to the craft of writing history, these authors carried out exhaustive research, recorded the most problematic elements in the lives of their subjects, and still painted a picture that elevates the reader's respect for these leaders. It is in the hard labor of producing such works that scholars refine a perspective which is capable not only of destroying myths that lack a real basis, but of contributing to the creation of legends solidly grounded in truth. Though there doubtless are further skeletons waiting to be exhumed from the Zionist closet, there are also many stories marked by heroism and justice which await the appropriate chronicler. To be a Zionist historian is not to deny the existence of the former. It is to believe that—taken on the whole—it is the latter that dominate a fair and truthful retelling of the history of the Jewish state.

If the new historians spur scholars more sympathetic to the legacy of the Jewish state to re-tell the story of Zionism in a manner that is theoretically compelling, and which takes full advantage of newly available sources, they will have performed an invaluable service. Such an outcome, however, depends not on the new historians, but on those intellectuals whose assessment of the Zionist heritage is more positive. It is they who will have to display the creativity and diligence necessary to vindicate their nation's past in the eyes of scholars and the broad public alike. The future of the Jewish state may well depend on their success.

DISPERSION AND THE LONGING FOR ZION, 1240-1840

ARIE MORGENSTERN

IT HAS BECOME INCREASINGLY ACCEPTED in recent years that Zionism is a strictly modern nationalist movement, born just over a century ago, with the revolutionary aim of restoring Jewish sovereignty in the land of Israel. And indeed, Zionism was revolutionary in many ways: It rebelled against a tradition that in large part accepted the exile, and it attempted to bring to the Jewish people some of the nationalist ideas that were animating European civilization in the late nineteenth and early twentieth centuries. But Zionist leaders always stressed that their movement had deep historical roots, and that it drew its vitality from forces that had shaped the Jewish consciousness over thousands of years. One such force was the Jewish faith in a national redemption—the belief that the Jews would ultimately return to the homeland from which they had been uprooted.

This tension, between the modern and the traditional aspects of Zionism, has given rise to a contentious debate among scholars in Israel and elsewhere over the question of how the Zionist movement should be described. Was it basically a modern phenomenon, an imitation of the other nationalist movements of nineteenth-century Europe? If so, then its continuous reference to the traditional roots of Jewish nationalism was in reality a kind of facade, a bid to create an "imaginary community" by selling a revisionist collective memory as if it had been part of the Jewish historical consciousness all along. Or is it possible to accept the claim of the early Zionists, that at the heart of their movement stood far more ancient hopes—and that what ultimately drove the most remarkable national revival of modernity was an age-old messianic dream?

For many years, it was the latter belief that prevailed among historians of Zionism. Its leading proponent was Benzion Dinur, a central figure in what became known as the Jerusalem school of Jewish history. Dinur, a historian at the Hebrew University of Jerusalem who was also Israel's minister of education from 1951 to 1955, understood the relationship between the Jewish people and the land of Israel to be a basic element of Jewish consciousness, and believed that messianic longing had played a decisive role in *aliyot*, or waves of Jewish immigration to the land of Israel, throughout history. For Dinur, the driving force behind the *aliyot* of the medieval and early modern periods was the "messianic ferment" that cropped up in Jewish communities from time to time, precipitating widespread efforts to predict the exact date the messianic era would begin; the appearance of charismatic leaders in various Jewish communities, who were seen as heralding the end of days; and, most notably, efforts to organize groups of Jews who would go to live in the land of Israel in order to hasten the redemption. "These two phenomena," wrote Dinur, "messianic ferment and movements of immigration to the land of Israel, are among the basic phenomena of Jewish history throughout the generations...."[1]

Animated by this perspective, Dinur and his colleagues succeeded in uncovering much of the lineage of Jewish nationalism. Against the commonly held belief that Zionist activism was a rejoinder to the "passivity" of traditional Judaism, scholars of the Jerusalem school stressed the dynamic and activist quality of the messianic impulse in Jewish history. In every generation, it was shown, there were a great many Jews, including communal and spiritual leaders, who were not content with passively hoping for divine intervention, and who instead took action aimed at bringing it about. Of the means at their disposal, *aliya* was often seen as the most potent way to bring the redemption: For centuries, despite the danger and hardship involved in making the trip to Palestine, Jews from all over the Diaspora continuously attempted to re-establish the presence and even sovereignty of the Jews in the land of Israel—efforts that stemmed from a longing for Zion that had suffused the prayers and practices of Jews around the world. In Dinur's view, the Zionist awakening was not motivated primarily by modern European ideas, but by this same longing, which flowed from the deep springs of Jewish historical consciousness.

In recent years, however, this view of Jewish history has been subjected to relentless criticism. Dinur and his colleagues have been accused of allowing their Zionist ideology to inflate the importance they attributed to the land of Israel as a part of the Jewish consciousness, and as a goal for practical action. One of the most prominent critics of Dinur's approach is Jacob Barnai of the University of Haifa. In his study on nationalism and the land of Israel, *Historiography and Nationalism* (1995), Barnai argues that Dinur's belief in the centrality of *aliya* cannot be reconciled with the fact that Jews did not succeed in establishing an uninterrupted presence in Palestine. Moreover, those who did come were hardly the elites of the Jewish people whom Dinur had depicted—and therefore could not be said to reflect anything essential regarding the Jewish experience in exile. "The definition of the *Yishuv* as the elite of the Jewish people... was not subject to a clear analysis and definition in [Dinur's] thought, and contradicts what we know about the land of Israel at different times as the place where precisely the 'lower' elements of Jewish society were concentrated."[2]

The historian Amnon Raz-Krakotzkin has made a wider claim in his critique of Dinur and his colleagues, arguing that Zionist historiography erred in offering a portrayal of Jewish attitudes towards the land of Israel as being consistent and uniform. According to Raz-Krakotzkin, a distinction should be drawn between positive and even fervent Jewish attitudes towards redemption, on the one hand, and the minimal effect these attitudes had in encouraging a return to the land of Israel, on the other.[3] In building his case, he relies on Elhanan Reiner's study of *aliyot* in the Middle Ages, which depicted Jewish immigration to Palestine as having been inspired far more by Christian pilgrimages than by any Jewish messianic belief.[4] Raz-Krakotzkin argues that the time has come to "rea-ppropriate" the discussion of the Jewish relationship to the land of Israel and to remove it from its Zionist "framing narrative"; he sees Reiner's study as setting a new course for historians, who will no longer be constrained by what he calls the "principle of return" that characterizes the classic Zionist narrative.[5] According to this view, the Jewish conception of redemption related to the land of Israel only in abstract terms, as a spiritualized goal to be reached in a far-off time, whereas the classic Zionist assertion that Jews consistently and actively sought out the physical Palestine is simply wishful thinking.

Of course, this debate among scholars is of far more than academic interest. Scholars such as Raz-Krakotzkin, as well as the sociologists Uri Ram and David Myers, have placed the criticism of the Jerusalem school at the center of a broader critique of the Zionist movement it-self.[6] These scholars take it as self-evident that Zionism re-wrote Jewish historical memory, exaggerating the importance of the land of Israel in order to give its adherents the "false consciousness" needed to realize its colonialist goals. This critique of the Jerusalem school has been central to a larger effort in recent years to assail the foundations of the Zionist movement, and it is on the basis of these criticisms that some Israelis have in recent times come to question Zionism's founding beliefs, including the very justice of the enterprise. If it turns out that their criticisms are firmly based in the historical record, the implications may be far-reaching indeed.

Today, however, the evidence exists to resolve this historical debate—evidence that was available in only limited measure to Dinur and his colleagues, and that has largely been ignored by recent critics of the traditional Zionist historiography. Indeed, with the opening of archives in the former Soviet Union, and in the wake of archival discoveries in Western and Central Europe and in Israel, much that was a matter of speculation can now be addressed on the basis of well-documented sources.

On the basis of this evidence, it seems that Dinur was largely correct in his understanding of the centrality of the land of Israel and *aliyot* in the centuries preceding Zionism, while his critics erred. The work of scholars such as Joseph Hacker, Yisrael Yuval, Binyamin Ze'ev Kedar, David Tamar, Elhanan Reiner, and Avraham David, as well as my own research, indicates clearly that the land of Israel served as a focus not only of spiritual longing for the Jews in the exile, but also of continual organized *aliyot* from all over the Diaspora. These efforts brought thousands of Jews, including many important scholars and leaders, to settle in Palestine throughout the six centuries that preceded the appearance of Zionism.

Indeed, from the time of the Crusades until the nineteenth century, Jewish life was infused with a sense of messianic anticipation, which found expression, among other things, in *aliya*. This messianic anticipation was focused on specific dates, which were endowed with mystical significance. Starting with the year 5000 on the Jewish calendar (1240 C.E.), the beginning of each new century signaled for many the possibility of redemption, leading large groups of Jews to make the journey to Palestine as a necessary step in bringing it about. Some of these *aliyot* were unknown to us until recently; in other cases, recent research has added substantial detail to the historical record. The picture which emerges is one of a clear, recurrent trend of immigration to the land of Israel, which was by no means limited to the "lower" elements of society but took with it Jews from all walks of life. Indeed, in many cases, some of the outstanding Jewish figures of their day led the way. Although the number of Jews who succeeded in making the voyage and settling in Palestine never constituted more than a small portion of world Jewry, these messianic *aliyot* were of enduring significance, partly because of the renown of those who took part, partly because of their regular appearance over the centuries, and partly because of the variety of diaspora communities which participated. The messianic impulse which spawned these waves of immigration, and the belief in the centrality of the land of Israel upon which they depended, were in no way marginal to the Jewish tradition, but in fact became an axis of Jewish spiritual life. Indeed, the story of *aliya* from the thirteenth to the nineteenth centuries illustrates the depth and force of the Jewish people's connection to its ancestral homeland, a connection that was carried into the late nineteenth and twentieth centuries, when modern Zionism found a new way of giving it voice.

II

The key to understanding the recurrence of pre-Zionist *aliyot* is to be found in the intense messianic ferment that began to grip the Jewish people in the first half of the thirteenth century. This was expressed not only in spiritual revivals in many communities, but also, on a deeper level, in changes in the theological and mystical doctrines upon which Jewish messianism was based. These were to have a decisive influence on messianic awakenings throughout the sixth millennium of the Jewish calendar (beginning in 1240 C.E.), charging this period with hopes of imminent redemption, and prompting regular movements of immigration aimed at bringing it about.

These powerful drives were largely a product of the traditional Jewish view of human history, which is based on an analogy from the story of creation as presented in the book of Genesis. In this view, each "day" of creation is seen as corresponding to one thousand years of human history, a parallel which the rabbis of the Talmud derived from a verse in Psalms: "For a thousand years in your sight are but as yesterday when it is past."[7] Since God created the world in six days, they concluded, human history will span six thousand years. This period was divided into three ages, each lasting two thousand years.[8] During the first two thousand years, described in the first eleven chapters of Genesis, man had no knowledge of God, and corruption and licentiousness reigned. During the second period, the "age of Tora" that is likewise described in the Bible, the Israelites received the divine revelation and took upon themselves the belief in God and the yoke of his laws. This period came to an end when the chosen people, who had not been true to their faith and had not carried out God's commandments, suffered the destruction of their Temple and were exiled from their land.[9]

Since shortly after the beginning of the exile, human history has been in its third age, whose characteristics are discussed extensively in the Talmud, Midrash, and Kabbalistic literature. According to this tradition, this is the "age of the Messiah," during which all that was damaged during the second age will be "repaired" in preparation for the final redemption of the world. It is during this period that God will fulfill his promise of ending the exile, allowing the Jewish people to return to the land of their fathers and rebuild the independent Jewish kingdom "as in days of old."[10]

However, at the time when this "third age" was actually dawning (it formally began in the year 240 C.E.),[11] it was difficult to identify the signs of the "age of the Messiah" in the real world—a difficulty that did not go unnoticed by the talmudic sages. They were also well aware of the vagueness of the date when redemption was supposed to take place, as the Bible had provided only hints. The rabbis' difficulty with these problems was exemplified in their effort to interpret the prophet Isaiah's ambiguous statement regarding the time of redemption: "I am the Eternal; in its time I will hasten it."[12] In considering this verse, the rabbis asked whether the redemption would come at a fixed time, or would

depend on the repentance of the Jewish people.[13] "R. Alexander, son
of R. Yehoshua ben Levi, said: It is written, 'in its time,' but it is also
written, 'I will hasten it.' [How so?] If they are worthy, 'I will hasten
it.' If not, [the redemption will come] 'in its time.'" According to this
interpretation, the date of the redemption is fixed and predetermined; yet
if Israel repents, God will hasten its realization.[14] In other words, even
in the third age, the Messiah would not come automatically; rather, the
time of his coming would depend on the behavior of the Jewish people.
The same talmudic discussion quotes the opinion of R. Dosa, that the
delay may extend well into the sixth millennium, up to four hundred
years before the end of history (that is, until the year 1840).[15] R. Eliezer's
view is even more pessimistic, suggesting that it may last until forty years
before the end (2200).[16]

With the passage of centuries, the idea of a two-thousand-year-long
"age of the Messiah" disappeared from the Jewish sources. Instead, the
medieval rabbis tended to divide the third age into two smaller periods:
A thousand years of "exile" in the fifth millennium (240-1240) and a
thousand years of "redemption" in the sixth millennium (1240-2240).[17]
As the fifth millennium drew to a close, expectations grew throughout
the Jewish world, sharpened by the difficulties of exile in the medieval period. The longing for redemption became a powerful motivating
force—overcoming, for example, the belief in the talmudic parable stating
that God had imposed "three oaths," of which one was a commitment
not to retake the land of Israel by force.[18] One of the first thinkers who
rejected the strictures of the "three oaths" was R. Judah Halevi (1075-
1141), who asserted that mass immigration to the land of Israel was the
necessary first step towards redemption. This attitude is found both in
his poems of exile and redemption and in his major philosophical treatise, the *Kuzari*. In the latter, for example, he offers his interpretation
of a passage from Psalms: "You will surely arise and take pity on Zion,
for it is time to be gracious to her; the appointed time has come. Your
servants take delight in its stones, and cherish its dust."[19] According to
Halevi, the first verse relates to the ultimate goal, while the second adds a
precondition: "This means that Jerusalem can only be rebuilt when Israel
yearns for it to such an extent that they embrace her stones and dust."[20]
Halevi's words present a kind of messianic activism, one which re-surfaced
in Jewish thought throughout the sixth millennium, according to which

Jews must be prepared to take action to rebuild Zion. Passive yearning for redemption must give way to action, and in particular *aliya*.

The sense that the coming sixth millennium would bring with it the messianic era prompted many Kabbalists to intensify their efforts at "calculating the end." The mystical literature composed during this period is filled with eschatological calculations of one sort or another, many of which are based on astrology, the alphanumerical system of *gematria*, or acrostic interpretations of apocalyptic verses in the Bible such as those in the book of Daniel.[21] Even a rationalist like Maimonides, whose approach towards the redemption was largely naturalistic, took part in these efforts. In his *Epistle to Yemen*, written in 1169, he cites approvingly what was probably his own messianic calculation with regard to the end of the fifth millennium, which, in his opinion, would witness the return of prophecy to Israel: "But I have a wondrous tradition...," he wrote, "that prophecy will return to Israel in the year 4972 [1212]. And there is no doubt that the restoration of prophecy in Israel is one of the signs of the Messiah... and this is the truest of the 'ends' that have been told to us."[22]

Such "certified" predictions seemed to legitimize abrogation of the "three oaths," and to give sanction to practices aimed at bringing the Messiah, which were collectively referred to as "forcing the end." While these efforts became a constant feature of Jewish life, dramatic events such as wars, revolutions, expulsions, religious persecutions, and natural disasters intensified them. Jews tended to view such upheavals through an eschatological lens, as manifestations of divine providence that would bring about the cosmic "repair," a change in the nature of the world, and ultimately the redemption of Israel.

Most of these apocalyptic speculations had little impact on Jewish history, and their memory is preserved only in recondite manuscripts. However, those calculations which pointed to the turn of each century of the sixth millennium had a more lasting effect.[23] The *Zohar*, a book that was widely believed to have been written with divine inspiration, mentions several of these dates explicitly. Six dates in particular receive the most widespread attention in the mystical and homiletic literature of the medieval period—and it was these dates which resulted in intense messianic activity as they approached, including waves of *aliya*: (i) The year 1240 (5000 on the Hebrew calendar); (ii) the period leading up to 1440 (5200); (iii) the period between 1540 and 1575 (5300-5335); (iv) the period leading up to 1640 (5400); (v) the period between 1740 and 1781 (5500-5541); and (vi) the years before and after 1840 (5600), which the *Zohar* fixes as the final date of the redemption. The political, social, and economic conditions in and around Palestine had an important role in determining the scope and success of each *aliya*; however, in almost every century its occurrence correlates directly with a messianic awakening. In these movements, as we shall see in the coming sections, the central motivation was both spiritual and nationalistic in nature: The longing of the Jewish people to return to the land of their fathers, and in so doing to hasten the coming of the Messiah.

III

The messianic *aliya* that preceded the year 1240 took place in the wake of the collapse of the Crusader kingdom in Palestine and the subsequent improvement of the situation of the Jews there. In 1187 the Muslims reconquered Jerusalem, and the new rulers not only allowed Jews to settle in Jerusalem, which had been forbidden during the Crusader period, but even encouraged them to do so. In 1216, fewer than thirty years before the beginning of the sixth millennium on the Hebrew calendar, the poet Judah al-Harizi visited Jerusalem, and described the change in the status of the Jews:

> God is zealous for his name and has had mercy for his people.... In the year 4950 of the creation [1190], God awakened the spirit of the king of Ishmael, and he and all of his army went up from Egypt and laid siege to Jerusalem, and God delivered it into his hands.... And he bid a proclamation be made throughout the city... saying: Speak unto the heart of Jerusalem, that whoever from the seed of Ephraim wishes may go unto it....[24]

The Jews understood the Crusader defeat as a fulfillment of the divine promise that the land of Israel would not tolerate foreign conquerors, and that the struggle for the land between Christians and Muslims would ultimately pave the way for the Jews' "return to Zion." The new Muslim rulers were seen to be playing their part in the process.

Against this background we can understand a prediction dating from that time, which appeared in a letter sent to the Jews of Egypt, which was discovered among the findings of the Cairo Geniza in the nineteenth century. The letter cites a new "prophecy" according to which a series of messianic events—including the ingathering of the exiles, the coming of the Messiah, and the establishment of the kingdom of Israel—would begin some fourteen years before the end of the fifth millennium: "Letters have come from France... [saying] that there has arisen among them a prophet... who has said that in the year 4986 [1226] the great ingathering will begin, and our master Elijah, of blessed memory, will come.... And in the year 4993 [1233] the Messiah, son of David, will come... and kingship will return to the house of Jerusalem." On the basis of this prophecy, the author decided to move to Palestine and take an active part in the ingathering.[25]

The belief that the redemption would begin at this time prompted Jews from many lands to move to Palestine.[26] By 1211, groups of immigrants were already arriving, including a large number of the leading Tora scholars of France, England, North Africa, and Egypt. This movement, which historians refer to as the "*aliya* of the three hundred rabbis," was unusual in both size and composition. It included several key figures of the French school of the Tosafists, such as R. Samson of Schantz, one of the leading scholars in France, whose talmudic commentaries are studied in yeshivot to this day; and R. Jonathan Hacohen of Lunel, one of the outstanding scholars in Provence and a follower of Maimonides.

The messianic impulse behind this movement comes through clearly in an anonymous pamphlet written at the time, which was uncovered by the historian Yisrael Yuval. According to its author, the time for the coming of the Messiah had already arrived, "for the fifth millennium will not end until the King Messiah has come." The author calls upon the Jews of the Diaspora to go to the land of Israel, in order to prepare the Jewish settlement that would greet the Messiah.

> Let no one say that the King Messiah will be revealed in an impure land... and let no one make the mistake of saying that he will be revealed in the land of Israel among the Gentiles. Rather, the matter is clear: In the land of Israel there will be Tora scholars and pious men of good deeds from the four corners of the earth, a handful from every city and every family, and then the King Messiah will be revealed among them.[27]

The author insists that the messianic era will come as the result of a critical mass of *aliya* and the creation of an infrastructure of Jewish settlements in the land of Israel. The next stage in the redemption will involve a great awakening, including a mass immigration to the Holy Land—a mighty host of Jews which, under the leadership of the messianic king, will smite the resident Gentiles and expel them from the land. By Yuval's estimate, preparations for this multi-staged messianic movement were meant to begin about thirty years before the end of the fifth millennium, or around 1210—at just about the time of the "*aliya* of the three hundred rabbis." As he describes it, this messianic idea was a product of growing messianic expectations, which were amplified in the wake of the Crusades.[28] The efforts of Christians to wrest the Holy Land from the Muslims appear to have raised hopes in certain Jewish communities that they might follow in the footsteps of the Crusaders and organize their own sort of crusade, laying the groundwork for the establishment of the messianic kingdom.[29] Over time, this led to other daring ideas: In 1256, some Jewish writers were still meditating on radical measures, such as offering sacrifices on the Temple Mount in Jerusalem, to help bring about the redemption. The traveler R. Estori Hafarhi described this in the early fourteenth century, relating that R. Yehiel of Paris, one of the central figures among the French sages of the previous century, "said that one should go up to Jerusalem—and this was during the seventeenth year of the sixth millennium—and that one should offer sacrifices at this time."[30]

We know little about the fate of the three hundred rabbis and the community they established. Some settled in Jerusalem, but when the city again fell into the hands of the Crusaders in 1229, the majority of the immigrants and their families apparently were forced to move to the city of Acre. The bloody battles that took place in the area, and the shifts from Muslim rule to Crusader rule and back again, wore down the Jewish communities of Palestine and were, apparently, a major factor in preventing them from taking root in the country. Jerusalem's Jewish population withered and was not to flourish again for many years. Finally, after Acre fell into Muslim hands in 1291, the large Jewish community of that city, where the yeshiva of R. Yehiel of Paris had been established, was destroyed.

Evidently, the failure of the "*aliya* of the three hundred rabbis" and their descendants' return to Europe left their mark on the Jewish people, who did not make another similar effort for some time.[31] Nevertheless, this movement stood as a model for future messianic *aliyot*. Unlike the pilgrimage of isolated individuals that had preceded it, this was an organized effort, spearheaded by a large group of communal leaders and Tora scholars from all over the Diaspora. As we will see, this activist model marked the beginning of a new age in the history of the land of Israel, beginning a trend that was to repeat itself with increasing intensity in later centuries.

IV

Though we know nothing of messianic efforts to move Jews to the land of Israel around the date 1340 (5100 on the Jewish calendar), there is ample evidence that in the years leading up to the start of the next century, in 1440 (5200), intense messianic ferment culminated in a mass movement of *aliya* that lasted for decades, involving Jews from North Africa, Spain, France, Italy, and the German lands. As in similar cases where radical changes in the status of the Jews prompted messianic activity, the awakening that took place around 1440 followed a severe crisis in Jewish-Christian relations throughout Europe. Spain, a country in which the Jews had hoped to prosper, became the scene of waves of violent persecution for nearly fourteen years, beginning in 1391. A similar fate befell the Jews of Central Europe during this period: In 1389 the Jews of Prague suffered a pogrom; in 1391 the Jews were driven out of France; and in 1421 Austria expelled its Jews. During the years 1415-1431, a bloody war took place between a reformist religious group, the Hussites, and the Catholic Church in Bohemia. The Jews found themselves caught in the middle, suffering the depredations of the Catholic armies while the latter were pursuing their "crusade" against the Hussite heretics.

These grim events nourished hopes for redemption, and messianic calculations of various sorts flourished in the literature of the period.[32] One of the most prominent devotees of calculations of this sort was R. Yom-Tov Lipmann Mulhausen, a leading rabbi in Central Europe and the *dayan* (chief rabbinic judge) of Prague, who was not only a leading halachic authority but also a respected theologian and mystic. His calculations fixed the date of the redemption for the year 1410 (5170), and again, later on, for the year 1430 (5190).[33] Indications of messianic ferment at the time can also be found in the writings of R. Hasdai Crescas, one of the eminent Jewish philosophers of the Middle Ages. He recounts a prophetic revelation that took place in 1393, according to which the redemption would take place in the year 1396 (5156, the numerical value of the Hebrew word "Zion"). Crescas goes on to cite a testimony from Jerusalem, also of a prophetic character, which tells of a divine command directing the Muslims to transfer their rule over Jerusalem to the Jews. According to this testimony, a voice emerged from the site of the Temple and addressed the Muslims, calling to them, "Leave my house, and let my sons enter!" and the Muslims were filled with fear. Another story from Jerusalem told of three elders who appeared before one of the Muslim leaders of the city and said to him: "We are of the children of Israel. Now, go and tell the Ishmaelites to leave this place, for the time of their end has come."[34]

Testimonies of this type, like the widespread messianic calculations of that period, reflect a strong messianic sentiment. Alongside the reports of miraculous events, they also contain a clear political element: While some testimonies portrayed Muslim rule as the essential obstacle to the redemption, others cited it as the factor that would permit the Jews to return to their own soil, and even to rebuild the Temple under the aegis of the Mameluke regimes. Crescas himself, for instance, raised this possibility as early as 1406: "In the final analysis... perhaps the king of Egypt who now rules in the land of Israel would allow the Jews in the extremities of his kingdom to go up and build the Temple, on condition that they dwell under his rule...."[35] In light of this expectation, it is not surprising that Jews of the time portrayed the Ottomans' capture of Constantinople, the capital of eastern Christianity, which took place in 1453, as heralding the redemption. This change in the world order—Christianity's defeat at the hands of Islam—gave the Jews reason to hope for the victory of the true religion, Judaism, over these two leading competitors.

At about the same time, persistent rumors that the ten lost Israelite tribes had been discovered—an event that tradition considered a clear sign of the redemption—added fuel to the messianic fire. These rumors, which spread in 1404 and again in 1430, were precipitated by the new geographical discoveries that resulted from the voyages of explorers to China and India. Various interpretations of these discoveries captured the Jews' imagination. For example, rumors that the lost kingdom of the ten tribes had been discovered somewhere in distant Asia, on the Indian subcontinent, in a place where the nations of the world did not rule, made a powerful impression, and led to speculation about the possibility of re-uniting all the world's Jews.[36]

But the most explicit expression of messianic awakening during this period was a mass movement of *aliya* embracing thousands of Jews from Spain, Italy, North Africa, and Egypt. We find evidence of this movement in a contemporary edition of an anonymous historical text that had first appeared two centuries earlier, in 1240, and was re-copied in Rome in 1429, discussing the "*aliya* of the three hundred rabbis."[37] After quoting the original text, the copyist added an aside concerning the events of his day: "And now many people have awakened, and have decided to go to the land of Israel, and many think that we are close to the coming of the redeemer, seeing that the nations of the world weigh heavily upon Israel."[38]

In this movement, the Jews of Spain, among whom messianic visions and calculations were particularly widespread, played a central role.[39] The historian Binyamin Ze'ev Kedar has discovered an account of a Jewish voyage from Spain to the port of Jaffa in the early fifteenth century: "Old and young, women and youths and infants, they went up to Jerusalem and there built [houses]...." Kedar goes on to quote a contemporary witness, the learned Christian Thomas Gascoigne: "The Jews who are gathered there from various lands believe that they shall in the future be victorious over the Saracens, the pagans, and the Christians. And after the golden Jerusalem and the Temple of the Lord are built, they say that their messiah, that is, the Antichrist, will come to Jerusalem to his holy sanctuary."[40]

We can also judge the scope of the Spanish movement of Jews to Palestine from the opposition that it elicited within some Spanish Jewish communities, whose leaders occasionally took exception to what was viewed as a violation of the "three oaths." Such opposition appears, for example, in a letter that the Jews of Saragossa wrote to the community of Castile, in which they complain about the exodus of a large number of Jews from Spain to Palestine: "For God has created a new thing in the land: People of little quality and large numbers have set out, their children and families with them, infants and women, saying: Let us go to the land, unto its length and breadth, until we come to the mountain of the house of the Eternal, to the house of the God of Jacob...."[41] The authors call for bringing the movement to an immediate end, out of a fear that all of Jewry will suffer because of it: "We have come to beseech you, distinguished Tora scholars, that you take all possible measures to turn back all those who are going in this way, and let each man return to his tent in peace, and let them not hasten the end."[42] It is important to note in this regard that the Saragossans' denigration of the quality of the *olim* did not at all correspond to the reality. Joseph Hacker, who has studied the immigration from Spain, has demonstrated that it included not only "people of little quality" but also serious scholars who engaged in halachic discussion about *aliya*, and wrote passionate letters on the subject. Several of them went on to become leaders of the Jewish community of Jerusalem.[43]

Another large diaspora community, that of Italy, also experienced a messianic awakening at the time, as we learn from the case of R. Elijah of Ferrara, a leading rabbi who arrived in Palestine in 1435 and left an account of his journey. R. Elijah appears to have taken this trip in order to verify rumors that had reached Italy in 1419 about the discovery of the ten lost tribes.[44] His journey prompted many other Jews from the Italian communities to leave for Palestine to take part in the imminent redemption. The movement was substantial enough that the Italian authorities took action to stem it. In 1428, a papal order was issued prohibiting sea captains from carrying Jews to Palestine. Soon afterward, the Venetian government forbade the use of their city's port for this purpose, while Sicily issued a similar prohibition in 1455.[45]

The Vatican's concern about the growing strength of the Jewish settlement in Palestine was not without grounds. In 1427, for instance, the Jews of Jerusalem attempted to wrest control of the Tomb of David on Mount Zion from the members of the Franciscan order who held it, and to acquire ownership of the site from the Muslim authorities. As a result of the subsequent dispute, the Franciscans were removed from the holy site, but the Jews of Jerusalem also lost their hold on it. The audacity of Jerusalem's Jews, which elicited the anger of the Church against them, was certainly fueled by the messianic euphoria which had come to characterize Jewish life at the time. The Jews were energized not only in their bid for Mount Zion, but also in their success in expanding the area of their residence into a new quarter of the city: The "Street of the

Jews' Synagogue," today known as the Jewish Quarter of the Old City. Jews purchased extensive property in this area, as a Christian traveler reports in 1421.[46] The confidence of the Jews during this period led them to build a synagogue on the Street of the Jews—despite the strict prohibition in Omarite law against building new synagogues under the rule of Islam. A document from 1425, discovered recently in the archive of the Islamic court in Jerusalem, indicates that in exchange for payment, the authorities accepted a Jewish claim that a synagogue had already existed on the site in ancient times, and that it could therefore be left in Jewish hands.[47]

The assertiveness among the Jews of Jerusalem also stemmed from a major demographic boost they received from immigrants who had arrived in anticipation of 1440. One source from this period depicts worshippers in Jerusalem on the festival of Shavuot. According to the report, the community was overwhelmed with pilgrims and local Jews; the author was deeply moved by the display of devotion, which he describes as a miraculous sign of the approaching redemption: "At the time there gathered there on the festival of Shavuot more than three hundred celebrants, all of whom came in and could be seated comfortably, for it [Jerusalem] still retains its sanctity, and this is a sign of the third redemption."[48] Another testimony mentions that at this time there were as many as five hundred Jews residing permanently in Jerusalem; a later source places the number at 1,200.[49]

But the boom of the Jewish community in Jerusalem did not last long. A heavy increase in taxation forced many members of the community to sell their property in order to pay off debts.[50] The erosion of the economic power of the Jews played into the hands of their Muslim rivals in the city. After the Mameluke sultan and his court in Cairo rejected the demand of the Waqf to tear down the synagogue on the Street of the Jews, Muslim fanatics took matters into their own hands, destroying it in 1474. If not for the protection of the government in Egypt, they would have expelled all the Jews from the city as well. These and other events led to a waning of the Jews' hopes for imminent redemption.

Nonetheless, the *aliya* leading up to the year 1440 played an important role in setting the stage for future efforts to settle the land of Israel. Most importantly, it was much larger and more diverse than the "*aliya* of the three hundred rabbis" that preceded it, and included both ordinary Jews and intellectual elites. In this respect, it laid the foundation for the great messianic ingathering that was to take place during the first half of the next century.

V

Of all the messianic *aliyot* of the sixth millennium, the one that took place in the years leading up to 1540 (5300 on the Jewish calendar) is the best known, because of its formative impact on the development of Judaism and the Jewish world. During this period, a new wave of immigration sustained a material and spiritual flowering such as the Jewish community in Palestine had not enjoyed since the period of the Mishna. This relatively brief heyday, centering on the northern town of Safed, gave rise to some of the most important intellectual achievements of Jewish history—of which the most enduring were the *Shulhan Aruch* and *Beit Yosef* of R. Joseph Karo, which today remain two of the pillars of the Jewish legal tradition; and the Kabbalistic teachings of R. Isaac Luria, which revolutionized Jewish mysticism and later formed part of the doctrinal basis of hasidism.

Not surprisingly, this revival came in the wake of one of the most traumatic events in Jewish history. In 1492, after a century of persecution, the vast Jewish community of Spain was expelled. Messianic thought of the period was strongly influenced by this catastrophe: According to many rabbis at the time, the scope and severity of the persecutions were indicators of a divine hand behind them, aimed at spurring the Jewish people to realize the "return to Zion" and bring about the redemption. One of the leaders of Spanish Jewry, the noted Bible commentator R. Isaac Abravanel, found a proof in the book of Isaiah: "I will say to the north, Give; and to the south, Do not withhold; bring my sons from afar, and my daughters from the ends of the earth."[51] Abravanel interpreted this passage to mean that the expulsion from Spain was an act of God meant to push the Jews towards Zion:

> And in the year 5252 [1492], the Eternal roused the spirit of the kings
> of Spain to expel from their land all of the Jews, some three hundred

thousand souls, in such a manner that all of them would leave... and all of them would pass before the land of Israel, not only the Jews but also the Conversos [i.e., Jews who had converted to Christianity under the Spanish persecutions]... and in this way they would gather upon the holy soil.[52]

After the trauma of expulsion at the hands of the Christian rulers of Spain, the Jews viewed the Ottomans' conquest of Palestine in 1517 as a significant turn for the better. The Ottoman government's sympathetic attitude towards Jewish immigration raised messianic anticipations further, as did the religious upheavals in Christendom which accompanied the advent of Protestantism. In the words of the Kabbalist R. Abraham Halevi, who headed the Sephardi yeshiva in Jerusalem, "And now, there have recently arrived in Jerusalem faithful Jews from the lands of Ashkenaz and Bohemia... who tell of the man... named Martin Luther... who began in the year 5284 [1524] to reject the creed of the uncircumcised and to show them that their fathers had inherited a lie."[53]

At the same time, messianic longing found expression in the feverish efforts of David Reuveni and Solomon Molcho in Italy and Portugal. These two figures created a new model of Jewish leadership, characterized by a combination of messianic and political activism. Reuveni, who claimed to be a member of the lost tribe of Reuben and the king of a portion of the ten lost tribes, went so far as to visit Pope Clement VII and urge that he advise the king of Portugal to form a military alliance between the Christians and the Jews to wage war against the Muslims and wrest the Holy Land from Turkish rule. Reuveni's diplomatic efforts grew, in part, out of messianic calculations that placed redemption in the year 1540.[54] Reuveni's colleague, Solomon Molcho, was born into a Converso family and rose to the position of secretary of the Portuguese royal council. When Reuveni came to the Portuguese royal court in 1525, he convinced Molcho to return to Judaism—a decision which forced Molcho to flee to Salonika, where he met R. Joseph Karo and became deeply involved in esoteric studies and mystical rites aimed at bringing about the redemption. He believed that at the end of days, "all the secrets of the Tora which have been hidden from us due to our sins will be revealed, and then the teachings, laws, and testimonies, whose divine secrets we do not apprehend today, will be interpreted for us."[55] According to the scholar of mysticism Moshe Idel, Molcho saw 1540 as the date of the restoration of the Davidic dynasty: "The year 5300 will complete the appointed number of days, and over it will rule the house of David."[56] Reuveni's and Molcho's activity came to an end in Regensburg in the summer of 1532, when they were arrested by Charles V, emperor of the Holy Roman Empire and king of Spain and Germany. Molcho, the former Converso, was taken to Mantua, in Italy, where he was burned at the stake, while Reuveni was exiled to Spain, where his story, as far as we know, comes to an end.

As the year 5300 drew near, the messianic ferment intensified. R. Abraham Halevi, who immigrated to Jerusalem at that time, expressed this sentiment in describing what he considered to be clear signs of the coming redemption. He notes the troubles that have befallen the Jewish people in exile, and the special prayers that are recited in Jerusalem to arouse the mercies of heaven and bring the redemption; most importantly, he writes of the divine response to these prayers, in the form of a fire which he describes as having come down from heaven and damaged the Church of the Holy Sepulchre.[57] Further testimony appears in a letter that students from the yeshiva in Jerusalem sent to Italy in 1521, in which they describe vigils held in the city on Mondays and Thursdays for the recital of special prayers requesting divine intervention to hasten the redemption.[58] The authors of the letter also interpreted certain unusual events as a sign of divine response to their prayers:

> And on the day that we arranged the vigil, that night the sleep of the King of the World was disturbed, and he showed us a sign of redemption, and the Eternal thundered in the heavens, and his voice was heard from on high, and there was a driving rain and a great wind that broke up mountains and smashed rocks. And this was on the eleventh day of the *omer*, when rain in Jerusalem is a miracle, for rain does not fall there in the summer days, but only during the rainy season between Sukkot and Passover... and this was nothing if not a sign of redemption.[59]

In the last few years leading up to 1540, the movement to bring Jews to the land of Israel, which encompassed thousands of families, intensified. Jews from Poland and Lithuania took part, in addition to those who came from Western Europe in the wake of the expulsions. In 1539 the land registry of Horodno (Grodno) records the sale of homes by Jews who intended to go to Palestine. About the same time, Lithuanian King Zygmunt I sought to verify rumors that the Jews were taking with them to Palestine Christian children whom they had circumcised.[60] The historian Yitzhak Shefer attributes the messianic sentiment underlying this *aliya* from Central Europe to the appearance of Solomon Molcho in Prague and his meeting with Emperor Charles V.[61] Messianic enthusiasm may also have prompted R. Jacob Pollack, the rabbi from Prague and Krakow who is credited with having founded the world of Eastern European yeshivot and pioneering the method of talmudic study known as *pilpul*, to move to Jerusalem in 1530.[62]

The great majority of those who moved to Palestine at this time settled in the Galilee, particularly in Safed. The choice of this small town in the hills west of the Sea of Galilee had to do with a tradition that the Messiah would first make himself known in the Galilee,[63] and also with the fact that neither Muslims nor Christians had a religious center there. Moreover, the income that could be gained from the local textile industry added a further incentive to settle there.[64] The local authorities even commissioned some of the newly arrived merchants and businessmen to handle the collection of taxes and other state income, or to act as leaseholders in different areas. Safed and the Galilee were rapidly transformed into a flourishing economic center, which exported fruits and grain, sheep and wool, and woven goods. Merchandise was shipped abroad via the ports of Acre, Haifa, Beirut, Sidon, and Tripoli. A contemporary source describes the dramatic change that occurred in Safed within just ten years of the arrival of the first wave of Jewish immigrants: "Whoever saw Safed ten years ago, and sees it today, will find it remarkable, because more and more Jews are coming all the time, and the clothing industry grows daily.... Any man or woman who works in wool at any labor can earn his living comfortably."[65]

Safed's prosperity and the growth of its Jewish community were matched by the spiritual flowering that resulted from the arrival of a learned elite, which included such prominent scholars and Kabbalists as R. Jacob Berab, R. Joseph Karo, R. Solomon Alkabetz, and their followers. This vanguard added to the messianic spirit of the time, and sought to take an active role in bringing about the redemption. Within a very short time, the Safed community had transformed the city into one of the greatest spiritual centers of world Jewry since the redaction of the Talmud.

The period of Safed's intellectual renaissance began in 1524, with the arrival of R. Jacob Berab, one of the leading Spanish scholars of his generation. Berab, a man of great boldness and energy, sought to re-instate the ancient practice of rabbinic ordination known as *semicha*, and through this to enable the re-establishment of the ancient Jewish legislative-judicial body, the Sanhedrin. These efforts were of a plainly messianic character. The re-establishment of the Sanhedrin was universally accepted as a major step in the messianic process, since it represented the most concrete expression of Jewish sovereignty in the land of Israel; however, a requirement for membership in the Sanhedrin was ordination by *semicha*, which had been handed down through the generations of rabbinic leaders until around the fifth century C.E., at which time the chain of transmission was broken, and the tradition was lost. Berab's efforts to re-instate *semicha* were thus aimed at eventually re-establishing Judaism's sovereign legislative house, in preparation for the messianic era.[66] In 1538, in the presence of twenty-five of the greatest rabbis in Safed, Berab was ordained—creating the first link in what was meant to be a renewed chain of ordination. But the leading rabbi of Jerusalem, R. Levi ibn Habib, objected that the ordination did not satisfy one of the conditions stipulated by Maimonides without which the *semicha* could not be re-instated—namely, the agreement of all the sages in the land of Israel—and as a result had no halachic validity. The controversy between the two sides grew increasingly heated, to the point that Berab's opponents apparently reported on him to the authorities for disloyalty. Fearing imprisonment, Berab was forced to flee the country—but not before he had hurriedly ordained four of the great scholars of the generation living in the city, including R. Joseph Karo.

Following Berab's departure, Karo assumed leadership of the community in Safed. Karo was born in Portugal; because of the persecutions and expulsion there he emigrated, together with many other refugees, to Egypt, which was part of the Ottoman Empire. In 1536 he came to Palestine along with a group of Kabbalists headed by R. Solomon Alkabetz, and settled in Safed. The Kabbalists had an explicitly mystical motivation for moving to Palestine: Alkabetz had preached a sermon on Shavuot night, the eve of the group's *aliya*, in which he described how a *magid*, an emissary from God, had urged Karo to lead his disciples to the land of Israel because it was a time of grace: "Fortunate are you, my sons," the *magid* told him. "Return to your studies and do not interrupt them for even a moment, and ascend to the land of Israel, for not all times are equally [propitious].... Therefore make haste and go up... for it has already been said, 'the time of reaping the fruits has come,' and not all times are the same."[67]

Alkabetz, the third outstanding figure in the spiritual leadership of Safed, introduced special prayer customs and composed works of Kabala and many religious poems, which were suffused with a yearning for redemption (one of his best-known poems, *Lecha Dodi*, "Come, My Beloved," became part of the Sabbath eve service throughout the Jewish world). In one of his prayers, Alkabetz calls upon the Almighty to redeem the Jewish people, arguing that by going up to the land of their fathers, he and his colleagues had proven their devotion and were worthy of divine assistance:

> And now their spirit has led them to go up to Mount Zion, the Mountain of the Eternal, to please its stones and to re-establish the dust of its ruins; they all are gathered and come unto you; they have put their lives in their own hands, setting their path upon the sea. They were lighter than eagles, stronger than lions, to go up and to worship before you upon this land. And they abandoned their property and their houses of pleasure, silver and gold were of no account to them, to come to the land. And the land is abandoned, ruined and desolate before them, and its inhabitants are gentiles who rule over it, and they are wicked and sinful. And every day your servants are beaten, and your servants go up to it. Shall not the Eternal remember and save us from these things? Have you had contempt for them, is your soul disgusted by such a nation?[68]

Another major religious figure who left his imprint on Safed was R. Isaac Luria, also known as the "Ari." Luria was born in Jerusalem and attended the yeshiva of R. Betzalel Ashkenazi in Cairo, where he studied the *Zohar*. By his account, the prophet Elijah appeared to him and commanded him to go back to the land of Israel in order to attain the highest holiness, an understanding of the divine wisdom, and a knowledge of the secrets of the Tora. Inspired by this revelation, he returned to Palestine and settled with his disciples in Safed, where he played an unparalleled role in the development of Jewish mysticism. His doctrines concerning creation and redemption, and the Kabbalistic school that formed around them, were crucial not only for the development of Kabbala in subsequent generations, but also in the emergence of the Hasidic movement in the eighteenth century.

The Messiah did not materialize in 1540, but this did not discourage those who had built their vision of the future around that date. A number of mystics tried to resurrect messianic hopes by pushing the date back to 5335 (1575), based on their reading of a verse in the book of Daniel.[69] However, the messianic anticipations for the later date paled in comparison to those that had preceded the year 5300. An aborted plan to rebuild the city of Tiberias raised hopes among Italian Jews during this intermediary period (according to several midrashic traditions, the first step in the process of redemption is to take place there),[70] but these were quickly dashed and did not trigger any serious movement of *aliya*.[71] Luria died three years before the second date posited for redemption, in 1572, at the age of 38; and Karo's death followed in 1575—the very year that he had hoped to see the Messiah.

As the messianic ferment subsided, Safed itself declined. One main cause was the severe economic crisis that struck the country and damaged most of the city's wool industry. Government authorities also grew more hostile to the Jews, and in 1576 even attempted to expel about one thousand Jewish families from Palestine to Cyprus. Religious persecution of the Jews of Safed—on the pretext that they had built synagogues without permission—brought an end to the community. R. Moses Alsheich's lamentation, modeled on the book of Lamentations, which Jews read every year on Tisha B'av, depicts the end of this crucial chapter in the history of Jewish settlement in Palestine: "And who is the man who has seen the city, which has been called the acme of beauty, the joy of all the world, a great city of scholars and scribes...? How has its blossom been plundered like a wilderness.... Many are its enemies and those who destroy it."[72]

VI

Despite these crises in the Jewish community in Palestine towards the end of the sixteenth century, and especially in Safed, a new movement of immigration to the land of Israel started up only a few decades later. This time, the messianic ferment was based on a passage from the *Zohar*, which concluded that in the year 5408 (1648), the dead would be resurrected, an event which the tradition describes as one of the later stages in the process of redemption.[73] In the words of the *Zohar*:

In the sixth millennium, in the 408th year, all those who dwell in the dust will rise.... And the verse calls them "the children of Heth," because they shall arise in the year 408,[74] as it is written, "In *this* jubilee year each of you shall return to his property." And when "*this*" is completed, which is 5,408,[75] each man will return to his property, to his soul, which is his property and his inheritance.[76]

Dozens of leading rabbinic sages and their families came to Palestine in the years before 1648. Most of them were Kabbalists of the school of R. Moses Cordovero and R. Isaac Luria, who believed that by studying and disseminating esoteric doctrines they were fulfilling one of the important conditions for the coming of the Messiah. These included R. Abraham Azulai from Morocco, author of the important Kabbalistic treatise *Hesed Le'avraham*; R. Jacob Tzemah from Portugal, who edited the writings of R. Haim Vital, the renowned disciple of Luria; and R. Nathan Shapira of Krakow, author of the well-known work *Tuv Ha'aretz* which deals with the sanctity of the Holy Land according to the Kabbala.

But perhaps the most illustrious figure who came to Palestine at this time was R. Isaiah Horowitz, author of *Shnei Luhot Habrit* and known as the "Shelah," after the acronym of the title of this work. Around 1620, Horowitz, who had served as chief rabbi in Dubno, Ostraha, Frankfurt am Main, and Prague, decided to move to Palestine. Prior to that, Horowitz had argued strenuously for the existence of a natural link between settling the land and the coming of the redemption, and it upset him deeply that the masses of Jews did not go to the land of Israel. "For my heart burned continually," he wrote, "when I saw the children of Israel building houses like princely fortresses, making permanent homes in this world in an impure land... which seems, heaven forbid, as if they were turning their minds away from the redemption."[77] Horowitz saw his own *aliya* as a necessary step in bringing about the redemption that was expected with the turn of the fifth century of the millennium.[78]

Horowitz arrived early in 1622, staying for a short time in Safed. From there he went to Jerusalem, where he made his home. He had several reasons for re-locating to Jerusalem, the most important of which was his belief that Israel's historic capital, and not Safed, would come first in the process of redemption, and he wanted to focus his efforts on rebuilding it: "Our rabbis also said... 'I will not come to the Jerusalem above until I come to the Jerusalem below.' The simple meaning of this is that the Jerusalem below is the Jerusalem that is here, in the land,

whose rebuilding we anticipate speedily in our days...."[79] The growth
of the Jewish community in the city during that period, driven by an
influx of immigrants from various countries, also encouraged the move.
In a letter he wrote while still in Safed, he observed: "For, thank God,
it has become crowded in Jerusalem. For the Ashkenazi community in
Jerusalem is already twice that of Safed; may it be speedily rebuilt in
our days, for every day it increases.... Also the Sephardim in Jerusalem
increase greatly, to literally hundreds [of families]." Horowitz particularly
praised the quality of the *aliya*, noting that "the Ashkenazi community
includes quite a few important people, great scholars of the Tora." This
being the case, he cherished the hope that the number of immigrants
would swell further in the wake of his own arrival: "And in a short time,
God willing, we will hear that the Ashkenazi community has become
inspiring in its grandeur, for I know that, praise God, many will come
there and wish to attach themselves to me."[80]

The enthusiasm Horowitz expressed over his expected move to Jerusalem did not subside after he settled in the city. In a letter from
Jerusalem, which was recently uncovered by Avraham David, he again
asserts that the city has changed profoundly, emphasizing its sanctity no
less than the great improvement in the physical conditions that he found
there.[81] Whereas the praise in his earlier letter had been based on hear-
say, now he extols Jerusalem on the basis of direct experience, and even
compares its scope to that of the major cities of Eastern Europe: "And
know... that it is a large city like Krakow, and every day large buildings are added to it and it is filled with people, whether of the nations
of the world without number or limit, or of the children of Israel."[82]
The rapid growth convinced Horowitz that the time of the Messiah was
drawing close. "We consider all this a sign of the approaching redemption
quickly in our days, amen," he wrote. "Every day we see the ingathering
of the exiles. Day by day they come. Wander about the courtyards of
Jerusalem: All of them, praise God, are filled with Jews, may their Rock
and Redeemer protect them, and with houses of study and schools filled
with small children."[83]

Horowitz's attempts to discover the manuscripts of R. Isaac Luria
also reflected his messianic enthusiasm. He was convinced that the works
attributed to Luria that were circulating in the Diaspora were not authentic, since Luria's disciple, R. Haim Vital, had forbidden his master's
writings to be copied or removed from the land of Israel. In one of his

letters, Horowitz mentions that when he arrived in Damascus on his way to Palestine, local Jews allowed him to inspect the writings of Vital. He expressed the hope that after arriving in Jerusalem he would continue to study the Lurianic Kabbala from Palestinian manuscripts, identify and confirm the authenticity of its mystical doctrines, and succeed in annulling the ban on their dissemination and publication:

> For I desire and yearn for this wisdom. And there are many great sages here, and all of them have the treatises of his [Vital's] disciples that have become widespread. And we have found and seen that they differ regarding many matters.... But we hope to the Eternal that the time may come when the holy book of that godly man [Luria] will be revealed, for there is a time and season to every purpose. And if God sees our merit as I have hoped, then surely the vow will be nullified, that is, the earlier ban.... And we are certain that with God's mercies we shall quickly merit it, and the secret things will be revealed to us....[84]

Horowitz's quest to uncover Luria's original manuscripts was not motivated by intellectual curiosity alone. Vital had taught that the discovery of Luria's true, original writings would be a sign of the coming of the Messiah: "In these generations it is a commandment and a great joy before the Holy One that this wisdom be revealed, for by its merit the Messiah shall come."[85] The hope expressed by Horowitz—"But we hope to the Eternal that the time may come when the holy book of that godly man will be revealed, for there is a time and season to every purpose"—indicates his faith that the dissemination of Luria's true teaching would assure the redemption.[86]

Horowitz's impassioned letters reflect the pervasive messianic ferment in the Jewish community of Palestine in the years before 1640 (5400). But, as at many times in the history of the Jews in the land of Israel, this period of success came to an end. In 1625, Jerusalem came under the control of the Ibn Farukh family. The family, which had purchased control over the city from the Ottoman government, saw themselves as free to oppress the city's inhabitants and embitter the lives of anyone too poor to pay a sufficient levy. Most of all they targeted the city's Jews, who were politically powerless and could be exploited by taking the financial support they received from the Diaspora.[87] Within a two-year period, from 1625 to the end of 1627, the position of the Jewish community in Jerusalem was completely undermined. The governor,

Muhammad ibn Farukh, persecuted the Jews of the whole country, issued various edicts against them, restricted their numbers arbitrarily,
and extorted enormous sums of money.[88] When they were unable to
pay their debts, they were summarily jailed and tortured. The new regime destroyed the Jews' sacred objects; placed their synagogues in lien
against debts and shut them down;[89] interrupted their prayer services;
desecrated their Tora scrolls, tearing and stealing them to make clothing and bags; closed their religious courts and dispersed the judges;
and shut down Jewish schools and sent the children away. Many Jews
starved. Those with means fled far from the reach of Muhammad ibn
Farukh. Among the refugees was Horowitz, who succeeded in escaping
to Safed. Of the 2,500 to 3,000 Jews who lived in Jerusalem in 1624,
on the eve of Ibn Farukh's rise to power, only a few hundred remained
by the end of his rule in 1627.[90]

Nevertheless, the messianic excitement that had characterized the
period prior to Ibn Farukh did not dissipate. The Christian traveler Eugene Roger, who visited Palestine between 1629 and 1634, was witness
to persistent efforts by the Jews to greet the Messiah. Roger recounts
two occasions on which he saw more than two thousand Jews awaiting
the coming of the Messiah—on Shavuot of the year 1630, and again in
1633: "The gathering of the Jews took place in the city of Safed in the
Galilee, because they think, as several of their rabbis have taught them,
that in this city of Safed the Messiah whom they await will come."[91] A
mood of optimism also suffuses an anonymous testimony of the time,
entitled *The Ruins of Jerusalem*, printed in Venice in 1631, which describes
the persecution of the Jews of Jerusalem, with all its horrors, as having
been temporary in nature. The author expresses the hope that the Jews
of the land of Israel will again prosper as in the past, as befitting the
age of the "footsteps of the Messiah." He thus begins his survey with a
description of the settlement of the Jews in Jerusalem that preceded the
arrival of the Ibn Farukh regime: "And the city of our God was settled
by members of our people, more than it had been since the day that
Israel was exiled from its land, for from day to day more Jews came to
dwell there.... And many of them bought fields and houses and rebuilt
the ruins, and old men and women settled in the streets of Jerusalem,
and the streets of the city were filled with little boys and girls."[92] Further on, the author rejects the complaints of the Jews who remained
in Jerusalem and regretted that they had not fled. He argues that with

the passing of the danger, it is crucial to remain strong, to act so as to realize the hopes for redemption, and to settle the land of Israel, and especially Jerusalem:

> For from the day the Temple was destroyed, did God not take an oath—and he will not go back on it—that he will not enter the heavenly Jerusalem until he enters the earthly Jerusalem? And before the coming of Ibn Farukh, children from the four corners of the earth fluttered like birds in their eagerness to settle in Jerusalem. And to us, this was an evident sign of the beginning of the ingathering of the exiles.... All the more so, now that God has remembered his people and his land and expelled before our eyes the enemy Ibn Farukh; they hover like an eagle, and the children will return to their borders.[93]

According to the author of *The Ruins of Jerusalem*, the sufferings endured by the Jews during the two years under Ibn Farukh's rule were essentially "birth pangs of the Messiah" that served to purge Israel of its sins before the redemption: "Reason suggests that God is testing us like one who smelts and purifies... [in order] to cleanse us and whiten us in the purifying fire that has passed over us, that he may relieve us of these birth pangs of the Messiah."[94]

But instead of the long-awaited redemption, 1648 [5408], the very year cited by the *Zohar* as heralding the resurrection of the dead, brought with it one of the worst tragedies in the history of the Jewish people. In the course of an uprising against the Polish government, Cossacks under the leadership of Bogdan Khmelnitsky killed tens of thousands of Jews. They sowed ruin and desolation, destroying about three hundred Jewish communities. One of the great rabbinic figures of that time, R. Shabtai Hacohen (also known as the "Shach," after his major halachic commentary, *Siftei Kohen*), expressed the widespread bitterness among the Jews: "In the year 5408, which I had thought would reflect the verse '*Thus* shall Aaron come into the holy place,' to the innermost sanctum, instead my harp was turned to mourning and my joy to anguish."[95] The chronicler R. Joseph Sambari similarly writes: "And in the year 5408... the Eternal's anger flared up against his people... for they thought that it would be a year of redemption, in '*this*' year, as is written in the *Zohar*... 'In the year of "the sons of Heth"'; and now it is turned into *thistles*."[96] (The numerical values for "thus," "this," "Heth," and "thistles" in the foregoing all add up to 5,408 or 408.)[97]

But despite the disillusionment brought about by tragedy where there had been hope for redemption, the Jewish longing for the Messiah did not take long to re-surface. A new messianic fervor came to the fore less than twenty years later, focused on the renowned false messiah Shabtai Tzvi. Despite his peculiar behavior, which was later explained by some scholars as manifestations of mental illness,[98] his messianic claims fell on eager ears. After an extended tour through various Jewish communities and a brief stay in Palestine, his proclamation in 1665 that he was the Messiah met with substantial support among rabbis and Kabbalists, which increased in subsequent months as the messianic fever spread. His pronouncements caused great excitement among the masses, who were instilled with a renewed belief in imminent redemption. His followers began to take up ascetic practices and to engage in mystical acts of repentance (tikunei teshuva); some of them sold their property, packed their belongings, and made ready to move to Palestine. Certain communities even attempted, with the help of their wealthy members, to rent ships that would carry them en masse to the Holy Land. In 1666, the new movement came to a sudden end, when Shabtai Tzvi converted to Islam under threat from the sultan.

Unlike other messianic movements among the Jews, Sabbateanism did not see aliya as a precondition for redemption, since the Messiah himself had ostensibly been revealed already. Moreover, Sabbatean messianism distanced itself from political, earthly activism, focusing instead on spiritual-mystical activity directed heavenward.[99] Nevertheless, it did not take long before a new messianic movement arose, bringing many hundreds of Jews to Palestine in a new mass aliya. At the center of this movement was the itinerant preacher R. Judah Hasid and his circle, who went to Palestine from Europe in 1700 with the aim of bringing about the redemption.[100] It is known that a number of Shabtai Tzvi's followers, believing that their messiah would have a second coming in the year 1706, took part in the movement surrounding R. Judah.[101] Several scholars have even attributed Sabbatean tendencies to the movement as a whole.[102] However, there is no indication that R. Judah himself, or the majority of those who came with him, were Sabbateans.[103] Either way, at some point after 1706 passed without Shabtai Tzvi's having revealed himself a second time, hopes for imminent redemption subsided.

VII

In the aftermath of the Sabbatean apostasy, messianic expectations began to focus on the next likely date for the redemption: The year 1740, or 5500 on the Jewish calendar.[104] Indeed, the crisis occasioned by the appearance and downfall of a false messiah did not detract from the force of the next awakening. Though they were approaching the five hundredth year of the sixth millennium without the footsteps of the Messiah being heard, the spirits of those Jews who longed for redemption remained unbroken. Now their hopes were pinned on a theory of messianic history that had emerged in the early eighteenth century, according to which the sixth millennium was to be divided into halves. The first five hundred years, from 1240 to 1740, was the period of "night," symbolizing the darkness of exile; the second half-millennium, beginning with 1740, would be the period of "day," during which the redemption would occur.[105]

One of the most influential advocates of this view was the Italian Kabbalist R. Immanuel Hai Ricchi, better known as the author of *Mishnat Hasidim*, who in the eighteenth century was considered the most authoritative interpreter of Luria's Kabbalistic works. Rather than pointing to one specific year as the time for redemption, Ricchi spread his estimate over forty years, from 1740 (5500) until the middle of 1781 (5541), a prediction which became widely accepted among Eastern European Jewry.[106] The acceptance of this understanding of the coming of the messianic period may have had something to do with the events in Eastern Europe during the second half of the eighteenth century. In 1768, Jews in the Ukraine suffered persecutions; in the years 1768-1774, Russia fought and won a war with the Ottoman Empire; and in 1772 Poland was partitioned. In the eyes of many Jews, these events had eschatological significance and were interpreted as signs of the Messiah's approach onto the stage of world history.

Recently discovered historical sources from the period indicate that the messianic expectations that preceded the year 1740 sparked a mass immigration to Palestine lasting many years. These immigrants, whose numbers reached several thousand within a decade, arrived in Palestine from all over the Diaspora, and particularly from within the Ottoman Empire and Italy. They settled mostly in Tiberias and Jerusalem, two cities that the talmudic tradition had singled out for a central role in the redemption.

The year 1740 indeed brought good news to the Jewish settlement in Tiberias. At that time, the Ottoman authorities invited the renowned Kabbalist R. Haim Abulafia, the rabbi of Izmir, to come to Palestine and rebuild Tiberias, which had lain desolate for some time. The Ottoman authorities wanted the city rebuilt for economic reasons, but the Jews considered Abulafia's mission a sign of the approaching fulfillment of their messianic hopes. Abulafia personally encouraged these hopes, according to the rare testimony of an Arab of Tiberias, who reports that Abulafia "told the Jews who lived there that the Messiah would soon come."[107]

At the same time, the Jews of Jerusalem also enjoyed a resurgence. The Jewish immigrants significantly boosted their numbers, prompting complaints from their neighbors: "[The Muslims] stood like a wall when they saw that [the Jews] were a great host, and that they added dwelling places in the courtyards of Jerusalem, and they took counsel together, saying, 'Behold the people of the children of Israel are too numerous to count, and there are ten thousand Jewish men.'"[108] Sources indicate that the stream of immigrants arriving in the city during this period increased the demand for housing and drove up food prices dramatically. The impressive growth of the community was also reflected in its spiritual and educational needs: Within a short time, eight new yeshivot were founded; synagogues were repaired and expanded, and new ones were built.[109]

Among the immigrants during this period were several spiritual leaders of the first rank. Particularly notable were R. Moses Haim Luzzatto, renowned author of *Mesilat Yesharim*; the Kabbalist R. Haim ben Atar, author of *Or Hahaim*, one of the central mystical texts in Jewish tradition;[110] R. Elazar Rokeah, chief rabbi of Brody and Amsterdam; R. Gershon of Kutow; as well as R. Gedaliah Hayun and R. Shalom Sharabi (known as Rashash), who served as heads of the Kabbala-oriented Beit El Yeshiva in Jerusalem. A Hasidic tradition, which until recently could not be documented, refers to attempts by the founder of Hasidism, R. Israel Ba'al Shem Tov, to move to Palestine at this time. According to this tradition, the Ba'al Shem Tov sought to meet with R. Haim ben Atar in the land of Israel, so that together they might bring about the redemption through a joint mystical effort. Evidence recently uncovered by Adam Teller confirms this tradition: It seems that during a visit he paid in 1733 to a wealthy Jewish family in Slutsk, the Ba'al Shem Tov asked for financial support for his intended move to the Holy Land.[111]

And indeed, a number of the Ba'al Shem Tov's closest friends and disciples in fact undertook the move between the years 1740-1781. The largest group of these hasidic immigrants, numbering about three hundred and led by R. Menahem Mendel of Vitebsk (a disciple of R. Dov Baer of Mezrich, the "Magid of Mezrich"), arrived in Palestine in 1777, four years before the end of the messianic period outlined by R. Immanuel Hai Ricchi. Opinions are divided regarding the motivation for the *aliya* of the disciples of the Ba'al Shem Tov—which included a significant number of simple Jews who attached themselves to the group during the course of their travels. Some scholars have suggested that perhaps it was the hostility of the mitnagdim in Lithuania which compelled them to flee; others have claimed that the hasidim wanted to achieve sanctification and mystical elevation, or to set up a new center for the Hasidic movement in Israel.[112] However, from a contemporary source which I recently discovered in an archive in St. Petersburg, we may be able to conclude that this great hasidic *aliya* was endowed with a messianic purpose. This source quotes a Karaite who had spoken with the immigrants shortly before their arrival:

> May it be remembered by the later generations what happened in the year 5537 [1777], how a rumor came about that the Messiah son of David had come. Then the rabbis living abroad began to go up to the city of Jerusalem, may it speedily be rebuilt.... And the reason they believed that the Messiah son of David had come was that at that time the evil nation of Moscow [Russia], that bitter people, a people whose language has not been heard, stretched its hand over the entire world, so that there was no place left that was not caught in war. And they thought that this was the time of the end of days, as promised by the prophets.[113]

This testimony helps to confirm Benzion Dinur's speculation that the movement of the Ba'al Shem Tov's disciples was of a messianic nature; it reveals that at the beginning of hasidism, a significant portion of its leadership wished to bring the redemption closer by moving to the land of Israel.

But it was not only hasidim who undertook messianic *aliyot* at this time. R. Elijah of Vilna, the "Vilna Gaon," also set off for Palestine, but his attempt did not succeed, and upon arriving in Holland he was forced to turn back.[114] From his son's writings we learn that the Gaon had intended to compose in the land of Israel a "new *Shulhan Aruch*":

> Two things I heard from his holy and pure mouth, to which his Crea-
> tor did not consent, and which he did not do. Towards his old age
> I asked him many times why he did not complete his journey to the
> Holy Land, and he did not answer me…. And he also promised me
> that he would make [a collection of] halachic rulings from the *Arba'a
> Turim* [upon which Karo's *Shulhan Aruch* was based], using decisive
> reasoning to write the one opinion that was correct in his wise eyes,
> with strong and powerful proofs that could not be rejected.[115]

The Gaon's desire to compose a standard, unifying halachic code in the land of Israel was an echo of R. Joseph Karo's immensely influential halachic efforts more than two hundred years earlier—efforts that had clear messianic overtones: A grand unification of Jewish law was widely seen as a first step in the re-establishment of the Sanhedrin, and therefore could serve as a catalyst in the redemptive process.

For a number of reasons, Jewish messianic activity in Palestine declined towards the end of the eighteenth century. The economic restrictions the Ottoman authorities and the local Muslim establishment imposed upon the Jews in Jerusalem, violent persecutions by the local Arab population, and bitter controversies within the Jewish leadership led to a severe de-terioration of Jewish life in the land of Israel. A significant number of Jews left Palestine; those who remained suffered harsh poverty. Neverthe-less, the Jewish community continued to hold together, enjoying a rich spiritual life alongside its economic hardship. The Tora was studied by some three thousand Jews who continued to live in Jerusalem; the rab-bis preached on Sabbaths and festivals and wrote halachic responsa. The presses of Western Europe and the Ottoman Empire published the output of this intellectual center—dozens of books of commentary, homiletics, halacha, and Kabbala. The Jewish community in Palestine maintained contact with the communities of the Diaspora, which provided them, whenever possible, with economic and diplomatic support. As the eight-eenth century drew to a close, Jewish life in Palestine, fueled largely by a messianic devotion to the land of Israel that was shared not only by the members of the *Yishuv* but also by their brethren abroad, continued despite difficult conditions, laying the groundwork for the great influx of Jewish immigrants that was soon to come.

VIII

In the late eighteenth and early nineteenth centuries, a great many Jews took part in the movement known as the Haskala, or Jewish Enlightenment. Among the movement's goals was to enable the Jews to assimilate into European society and culture, which necessarily would mean abandoning their traditional expectations of imminent national and political redemption in the Holy Land. But despite the efforts of the *maskilim*, a large portion of the Jewish world continued to believe in the centrality of the land of Israel.[116] In the years leading up to 1840 (5600), messianic fervor again spread throughout traditional Jewry in the West and East and inspired a mass movement of *aliya*. In strictly numerical terms, this movement was more successful than all those which had preceded it: Over the ensuing decades, tens of thousands of Jews arrived in Palestine, radically changing the demography of the Jewish community there; by the time the first of the Zionist immigrants began arriving towards the end of the nineteenth century, the land of Israel was already host to its largest and most vibrant Jewish community in many centuries.

The textual source behind much of the messianic ferment in the nineteenth century was R. Dosa's prediction in the Talmud, according to which the messianic age would begin in the last four hundred years of the sixth millennium—that is, starting around 1840.[117] A statement in the *Zohar* lent support to this belief:

> When the sixth millennium comes, in the six hundredth year of the sixth millennium, the gates of wisdom shall be opened above, and founts of wisdom below.... And the Holy One shall raise up the congregation of Israel from the dust of exile, and remember it.[118]

A great many sources of the early nineteenth century cite the *Zohar*'s prediction. Thus, R. Yaakov Tzvi Yalish of Dinov writes: "In the *Zohar* there are several different times suggested for the end of days, and the last of them is the year six hundred of the sixth millennium, and it seems that later than this it will not tarry. Thus we find that when 5,600 years have been completed, everything will be clarified, and our righteous Messiah will come."[119]

Until recently, historians did not attribute real importance to these mystical texts, and saw no connection between them and the awakening of widespread messianic activism. Sources uncovered in recent years have revised these evaluations, demonstrating that faith in the Messiah's coming in 1840 was responsible for the *aliya* of thousands of people. Thousands of letters in the archive of the Officers and Administrators of Amsterdam, from officials who maintained close contact with the leadership of the Jewish community in Palestine, provide ample evidence of the messianic sentiment that prevailed. In one letter, dated 1831, R. Tzvi Hirsch Lehren, head of that organization, writes:

> But the simple and imminent salvation for which we have longed is the coming of our Messiah, and we shall express our hope to the Holy One that salvation is not far off. Many pious people have said that it will be no later than the year 5600, may it come upon us for the good.[120]

Diaries of the Anglican missionaries who were active among the Jews in Palestine and throughout the world during that time also mention this sentiment. Missionary reports from Russia in 1812 state that between 1809 and 1811, hundreds of Jewish families immigrated to Palestine. When asked the purpose of their journey, these Jews replied that they "hope that the words of the prophets will soon be realized, that God will gather his dispersed people from all corners of the earth.... [They] therefore wish to see the appearance of the Messiah in the land of Israel."[121]

Among the *olim* of this period, the disciples of the Vilna Gaon particularly stand out. Together with their families, they numbered about five hundred souls; but their organization, their ideological motivation, and their standing as Tora scholars of the first rank lent them a degree of influence far beyond their numbers. This group adopted an ideology of "natural redemption" that translated the messianic faith into practical activity. In this spirit, the Gaon's disciples sought to advance the redemption by rebuilding Jerusalem. Their involvement in rebuilding the ruins of the "Court of the Ashkenazim," a complex of buildings where the Ashkenazi community lived, worked, and studied, was to them a realization of the call to build the "earthly Jerusalem"—a condition for the redemption. In 1820, R. Menahem Mendel of Shklov, a disciple of the Gaon, wrote from Jerusalem to donors in Europe, describing the building of the courtyard as the beginning of redemption:

> And you should understand fully that the lowly situation of our group in general, and regarding the ruin in particular, which we needed to… redeem from the hands of cruel foreigners…. And we rely upon responsive people like yourselves, who pursue righteousness… to greet our words with rejoicing, for, thank God, in our day we are witnessing the beginning of the redemption….[122]

The documents of the Gaon's disciples echo this same sentiment some twenty years later, when the group finally received the long-awaited permission to rebuild the ruin: "And now our horn is raised up to the Eternal our God, to honor and establish our Temple, and to build synagogues on the holy mountain of Jerusalem…. This is a good sign of the beginning of redemption…."[123] Once they had received permission to build, the Gaon's disciples initiated changes in the Jerusalemite order of prayer, including the removal of the verse "Arise, shake off the dust, arise" from the Friday night liturgical poem *Lecha Dodi*—since, in their mind, the divine Presence had already risen from the dust.[124]

Some members of this group sought to further the redemption by re-instating the Sanhedrin, and the institution of *semicha* upon which it depended. To this end, they were forced to contend with the halachic problems that had led to the failure of the previous attempt, hundreds of years earlier in Safed. In particular, they had to deal with Maimonides' ruling that once the chain of ordination had been broken, its renewal required the agreement of all the sages in the land of Israel. To circumvent this objection, R. Israel of Shklov, the leader of the Gaon's disciples in Safed, sent an emissary to the deserts of Yemen in order to locate the ten lost tribes; according to tradition, the tribes still preserved the institution of *semicha*, and might be enlisted to renew the ancient ordination for the Jewish world. In a letter carried by the envoy, R. Israel wrote to the ten tribes as follows: "It is a well-known principle… that before our righteous Messiah may come, there needs to be a great court of ordained judges…. In your mercy for all of the people of the Eternal, please choose several of your ordained sages, and please come to the land of Israel, the inheritance of our fathers, and let them ordain the great scholars so that there may be an ordained court in the land of Israel, upon which the beginning of the redemption depends."[125]

The disciples of the Gaon also purchased agricultural lands in order to carry out those commandments of the Tora that were applicable only in the land of Israel. They believed that the flourishing of the harvest would serve as proof of God's renewed love for his people, as per a well-known talmudic interpretation of a verse in Ezekiel: "'But you, O mountains of Israel, shall shoot forth your branches, and yield your fruit to my people Israel'—there is no better sign of the End than this."[126] R. Haim ben Tuvia Katz, who had been a leading rabbi in Vilna, gave voice to this belief in 1810, when he wrote from Safed: "Regarding the matter of the contributions that were sent for the fulfillment of the commandments dependent upon the land, we have already purchased lands in accordance with the view of my dear friend, the true great and pious one, our teacher R. Haim of Volozhin... and it seems that we shall yet buy lands that shall become available according to the time and place...."[127] The immense significance that the Jews in Palestine attributed to agriculture also emerges from a letter sent by the leaders of the community in Jerusalem—both Sephardim and Ashkenazim—to the philanthropist Moses Montefiore in 1839, when they learned of his intention to purchase lands for rural Jewish settlement:

> And his mercies were aroused and his pure heart offered to establish pillars and stands... by giving them a hold in the holy soil, the soil of Israel, to plow and sow and reap in joy.... And all of us take this thing upon ourselves with love.... We await and anticipate the divine salvation through Moses, the faithful one of his house, to say when he shall begin this beginning of the redemption.[128]

In 1836, R. Tzvi Hirsch Kalischer proposed an even more far-reaching project to Baron Anshel Rothschild: The latter would purchase the Temple Mount from the Egyptian ruler Muhammad Ali, in order to renew the sacrificial service. In a letter to the baron, Kalischer writes:

> And particularly at a time like this, when the province of the land of Israel is not under the rule of a powerful regime as it was in former times... he may well sell you the city of Jerusalem and its surroundings. From this too there will spring forth a horn of salvation, if we have the power and authority to seek the place of the altar and to offer

acceptable burnt offerings to the God of Eternity, and from this may Judah be delivered in an eternal deliverance.[129]

Kalischer's idea was explicitly messianic; like R. Yehiel of Paris six centuries earlier, he planned, by the renewal of sacrifices at the Temple Mount, to quicken the redemption and to hasten the coming of the Messiah.[130]

The messianic expectations of the Jews of Palestine were sorely tested, however, by the tragic events that they faced in the years leading up to 1840. The plagues that raged throughout the region, the earthquake of 1837 that killed more than two thousand Jews in the Galilee, and particularly the systematic attacks by the Muslim authorities and the local Arab population, threatened to make Jewish existence there intolerable. Anti-Jewish violence reached its height during the rebellion of the Arab farm workers that broke out in 1834 against the rule of Muhammad Ali. In the course of these riots, the rebels also attacked the Jews living in major cities. Over a period of several weeks, they rampaged against the Jews of Safed, looting their property, destroying their homes, desecrating their synagogues and study houses, and raping, beating, and in many cases killing Jews. R. Shmuel Heller of Safed reported:

> For forty days, day after day, from the Sunday following Shavuot, all of the people of our holy city, men, women, and children, have been like refuse upon the field. Hungry, thirsty, naked, barefoot, wandering to and fro in fear and confusion like lambs led to the slaughter.... They [the Arab marauders] removed all the Tora scrolls and thrust them contemptuously to the ground, and they ravished the daughters of Israel—woe to the ears that hear it—and the great study house they burned to its foundations.... And the entire city was destroyed and laid ruin, they did not leave a single wall whole; they dug and sought treasures, and the city stood ruined and desolate without a single person....[131]

These events took a heavy toll in lives on the Jews in Palestine, causing many to leave. But in spite of it all, most Jews did not leave Palestine. Those who stayed enjoyed the protection and active support of Jewish groups and institutions throughout the world, as well as the aid of such philanthropists as Moses Montefiore and the Rothschild family; and, especially, the protection of the representatives of European powers, including the consuls in the coastal cities of Syria, Egypt, and Palestine, who protected the Jewish settlement and demanded compensation from the authorities for the damage caused by the 1834 riots. In many ways, Jews in the land of Israel were less vulnerable than in earlier periods.

Even the failure of the Messiah to appear in 1840 had only a minor impact on the lot of the Jewish community in Palestine, though it was accompanied by a period of crisis and a brief decline in the spirit of the Jews living there. Most importantly, the flow of Jewish immigrants did not stop, as the successes of the messianic *aliya* of the first half of the nineteenth century laid the groundwork for a large wave of Jewish immigrants in the following decades, most of whom came due to other, nonmessianic motives: Most were pious, traditional Jews who sought refuge from the influences of the Haskala, the Emancipation, and the Reform movement, which at that time were spreading throughout Europe. As a result of this continuing wave of immigration, the number of Jews in Palestine increased dramatically: By the 1870s, the Jewish population in Jerusalem was already greater than that of the Muslims and Christians combined. For the first time since the destruction of the Temple, Jews formed a majority in the city.[132]

And indeed, from a broader perspective, the Jewish community in Palestine advanced a great deal during the course of the nineteenth century. If early in the century the number of Jews there stood at a few thousand and their situation was anything but stable, by the second half of the century tens of thousands of Jews lived in Jerusalem alone, and they enjoyed the political and economic protection of representatives of the great powers, as well as support from Jewish communities in the Diaspora. These developments allowed the continuation of settlement in distinctly agricultural areas as well, and facilitated the immigrations of tens of thousands of additional Jews during the 1880s—the "First Aliya," which opened an entirely new chapter in the history of Jewish settlement in the land of Israel.

IX

Until the appearance of Zionism, it is difficult to find more conclusive evidence for a deep, abiding historical connection between the Jewish people and the land of Israel than the messianic *aliyot* of the sixth millennium. Over a period lasting more than six centuries, the traditional longing of the Jews for their homeland found concrete expression in repeated efforts to realize the dream of return. From the practical viewpoint, these messianic waves of immigration, which began early in the thirteenth century, represented a quantum leap in scope and energy above the efforts of individuals and groups who had gone to Palestine previously. First, they were more communal in nature, numbering hundreds and at times even thousands. Second, the *aliyot* drew on Jewish communities from different countries, rather than the more localized efforts that had characterized earlier pilgrimages. Third, they comprised Jews of all classes: Alongside the common folk, they included communal leaders and Tora scholars of the first magnitude. One can only imagine the effect that the re-location of such central figures in the Jewish world to the land of Israel had on the diaspora communities they left behind. Even if the majority of Jews did not dare to make the journey, there can be no doubt that the departure of so many of their luminaries to the Holy Land, and in a context of messianic hope, left a profound impression.

Fourth, the messianic *aliyot* of the sixth millennium were characterized by a spiritual and ethical vigor the likes of which had not been seen before. The new immigrants were called upon to repent, to develop their character, and to act according to a strict moral code. In some of these movements, the demand for character improvement attended the mystical activity of Kabbalists or other individuals who took it upon themselves to catalyze the messianic redemption. Among the concrete projects for hastening the redemption, one finds attempts to find the ten lost tribes, to renew the ancient rabbinic ordination (*semicha*) and the institution of the Sanhedrin, to summarize the halacha so that a uniform code would be accepted by all of Israel, to uncover the "secrets of Tora" and hidden Kabbalistic writings, and even to renew the sacrificial service of the Temple in Jerusalem.

The activism of the messianic immigrant movements also demonstrates that long before the advent of modern Zionism, Jews did not limit themselves to spiritual yearning and symbolic remembrance of the land of Israel. Inspired by messianic anticipation, many Jews regarded a return to the Promised Land as a practical goal. True, the overwhelming majority of Jews did not go to Palestine. Considering the numerous hardships entailed by such a journey, the uncertainty of arriving in peace, finding a livelihood, and dwelling securely in the land, this is hardly surprising. Nonetheless, during the sixth millennium, the land of Israel was no longer an abstract, inaccessible ideal; no longer only a subject of dreams, whose name was mentioned mainly in prayers. It was a real place, absorbing waves of Jewish immigrants from many countries, sustaining a full-fledged Jewish community that preserved its unique identity throughout the generations.

Of course, there were major, substantive differences between the messianic *aliyot* and the Zionist awakening which followed. The nationalist ideology which revived the Jewish people in the late nineteenth and twentieth centuries was indeed modern in many ways, not the least of which was its rejection of the traditionalist worldview that had characterized the messianic movements. Nevertheless, the deep longing for their ancestral homeland and the profound faith in the possibility of national redemption, which ultimately drove the waves of Jewish immigration to Palestine in the sixth millennium, were also at the heart of the Zionist return. The widespread belief in the Jewish right to the land of Israel, the Zionist vision of the spiritual and physical redemption of the land, and the immense efforts of so many Jews to turn the dream into reality, could never have taken root without these prior beliefs. In this sense at least, one may see the period of messianic immigration to the land of Israel and the Zionist revolution as milestones on the same historical path, different chapters in an ongoing national story.

NOTES

1. Benzion Dinur, "The Messianic Fermentation and Immigration to the Land of Israel from the Crusades Until the Black Death, and Their Ideological Roots," in Benzion Dinur, *Historical Writings* (Jerusalem: Mosad Bialik, 1975), vol. ii, p. 238. [Hebrew]

2. Jacob Barnai, *Historiography and Nationalism: Trends in the Research of Palestine and Its Jewish Population, 634-1881* (Jerusalem: Magnes, 1995), p. 39. [Hebrew]

3. Amnon Raz-Krakotzkin, *The Nationalist Portrayal of the Exile, Zionist Historiography, and Medieval Jewry*, doctoral dissertation, Tel Aviv University, 1996, p. 331. [Hebrew]

4. Elhanan Reiner, *Pilgrims and Pilgrimage to the Land of Israel, 1099-1517*, doctoral dissertation, Hebrew University of Jerusalem, 1988. [Hebrew]

5. Raz-Krakotzkin, *Nationalist Portrayal*, pp. 333-334.

6. See David N. Myers, *Reinventing the Jewish Past: European Jewish Intellectuals and the Zionist Return to History* (New York: Oxford, 1995); Uri Ram, "Zionist Historiography and the Invention of Modern Jewish Nationhood: The Case of Benzion Dinur," *History and Memory* 7:1 (1995), pp. 91-124. For a critique of Dinur that does not tend towards a critique of Zionism as a whole, see Jacob Katz, *Jewish Nationalism: Essays and Studies* (Jerusalem: Zionist Library, 1979), pp. 230-238. [Hebrew]

7. Psalms 90:4.

8. "It was taught in the school of Eliyahu: The world will exist for six thousand years: Two thousand years of chaos; two thousand years of Tora; two thousand years of the age of the Messiah." Sanhedrin 97a.

9. The destruction of the Temple took place around the year 68 C.E., which was close to the end of the fourth millennium of Creation, in the year 3828.

10. See Joseph Dan, *Apocalypse Then and Now* (Tel Aviv: Yediot Aharonot, 2000), pp. 49-68. [Hebrew]

11. The Jewish year begins in the fall; therefore every Jewish year overlaps two years of the Christian calendar, and vice versa. For simplicity's sake, however, Christian years in this article are identified with the Jewish year with which they overlap for nine out of twelve months, that is, from January through September.

12. Isaiah 60:22.

13. Reference is made in the book of Daniel to three enigmatic dates for the end of days, which are not conditional upon repentance. Even Daniel himself, according to his own words, did not understand what they were. The three periods are expressed in obscure language: "Time, times, and half a time," "1,090 days," and "1,335 days." Daniel 12:1-13. The assumption throughout is that the end of days will come at a fixed time, without room for human influence.

14. Sanhedrin 97a. We will not enter here into the details of the debate cited in the Talmud, but it is worth noting that according to the rabbis, when the patriarch Jacob wished to reveal to his sons the time of the end of days, this referred to the end that would come about "in its time."

15. Sanhedrin 97a. This approach also appears in the *Zohar*, Genesis 117.

16. Sanhedrin 97a.

17. *Genesis Rabbati*, a midrashic collection compiled at the beginning of the sixth century, states: "The entire subjugation is during the fifth millennium, and

during its course, morning will come for Israel, when they shall be redeemed." Hanoch Albeck, ed., *Genesis Rabbati* (Jerusalem: Mekitzei Nirdamim, 1940), p. 16. [Hebrew] R. Judah Barceloni likewise states that "we are to be speedily redeemed at the end of the fifth millennium; thus has it been conveyed at all times to Israel." See his commentary in J.Z. Halberstamm, ed., *Sefer Yetzira* (Berlin, 1895), p. 239. [Hebrew] Among the earlier practitioners of messianic calculations, some placed the time of the redemption well before the sixth millennium; they argued that since the destruction of the land and of the Temple occurred in the year 3828 [68 C.E.], the current era would end one thousand years later, in 4828 [1068 C.E.], at which time the age of redemption would commence. But generally speaking, practitioners of messianic calculation identified the sixth millennium as the time of the redemption.

18. The source of these prohibitions is found in the Song of Songs, where the formula "I adjure you, O maidens of Jerusalem..." is repeated with minor variations. Cf. Ketubot 111a.

19. Psalms 102:14-15.

20. Judah Halevi, *The Kuzari: An Argument for the Faith of Israel*, trans. Hartwig Hirschfeld (New York: Schocken, 1964), 5:27, p. 295.

21. The book of Daniel posits the dates for the end of days in relation to some unidentified starting point. In every generation there were attempts to decipher the apocalyptic dates with reference to various events in Jewish history, such as the Exodus, the entrance into the land of Israel, the building of the First and Second Temples, and the Babylonian exile.

22. Maimonides, *Epistles of Maimonides*, ed. Yitzhak Shilat (Jerusalem: Ma'aliyot, 1987), vol. i, p. 153. [Hebrew] *The Epistle to Yemen* was composed about 1172.

23. Arie Morgenstern, *Mysticism and Messianism* (Jerusalem: Ma'or, 1999), p. 305. [Hebrew]

24. Avraham Ya'ari, *Travels in the Land of Israel* (Tel Aviv: Gazit, 1946), p. 67. [Hebrew]

25. Aaron Ze'ev Aescoly, *Jewish Messianic Movements* (Jerusalem: Bialik, 1988), p. 188. [Hebrew]

26. Yisrael Yuval, "Between Political Messianism and Utopian Messianism in the Middle Ages," in S.N. Eisenstadt and M. Lissak, eds., *Zionism and the Return to History* (Jerusalem: Yad Ben-Zvi, 1999), p. 84 n. 10. [Hebrew]

27. Yuval, "Political Messianism," pp. 85-86. A short passage from this manuscript is quoted in another anonymous travel journal of around the same time, *Totza'ot Eretz Yisrael*. See Ya'ari, *Travels*, p. 98.

28. Regarding the expectations of redemption, see Maimonides' calculation for the renewal of prophecy in 1212, mentioned above. On the reaction to the Crusades, see Yuval, "Political Messianism," p. 87.

29. Parallel to the messianic activism that found expression in the "*aliya* of the three hundred rabbis," the opposite tendency, a lowering of the profile of messianic expectations, could also be found among the Jews of Central Europe. Unlike the Jews of France, the latter were worried about the possibility of a Christian backlash to any Jewish messianic ferment, and tended to be resistant towards any activity aimed at bringing the redemption closer. The spiritual leaders of this community focused their efforts on mass repentance, and refrained from expressing their messianic hopes. Concerns about persecution were exacerbated by the Mongol invasion that was menacing Europe at the time. Christians identified the Mongols with the ten tribes, and subjected the Jews to reprisals as "partners" of the invaders. R. Moses of Coucy, author of *Sefer Mitzvot Gadol*, conducted a campaign for repentance in 1236, four years before the decisive Hebrew date of 5000. According to him, Jews were to refrain from any efforts of a political nature to hasten the coming of the Messiah. The only activity capable of bringing the redemption in his view was mass repentance. Yuval, "Political Messianism," p. 87.

30. Estori Hafarhi, *Kaftor Vaferah* (Berlin: Julii Sittenfeld, 1852), p. 15. See Reiner, *Pilgrims and Pilgrimage*, p. 79; and cf. Yisrael Ta-Shema, "Land of Israel Studies," *Shalem* 1 (1974), pp. 82-84 [Hebrew]; Arie Morgenstern, *Redemption Through Return: The Vilna Gaon's Disciples in the Land of Israel* (Jerusalem: Ma'or, 1997), pp. 182-185. [Hebrew]

31. Avraham Grossman, "A Letter of Vision and Rebuke from Fourteenth-Century Ashkenaz," *Katedra* 4 (1977), pp. 190-195.

32. And indeed, a series of messianic calculations from around the year 1440 deals with the different stages of the anticipated redemption: The beginning of the ingathering of exiles, the discovery of the ten lost tribes, the return of prophecy, the restoration of the Sanhedrin, the appearance of the Messiah, and the building of the Temple. The calculations closest to the year 1440 are based on astrological calculations of the "system of the stars," and are directed towards the years 1444 (5204 on the Hebrew calendar) and 1464 (5224), and towards the year equal to the numerical value of the Hebrew word for "the end" (*haketz*), which came out to 5190 on the Hebrew calendar, or 1430 C.E. Earlier calculations from this period were based on similar methods of *notarikon* and *gematria*. One of them, drawing on the verse in Habakkuk 2:3, "for still the vision awaits its time," was understood as referring to the year 1391 (5151). See Joseph Hacker, "The *Aliyot* and Attitudes Towards the Land of Israel Among Spanish Jews, 1391-1492," *Katedra* 36 (1985), p. 22 n. 83.

33. About 1400, Mulhausen stated: "And many among the multitude agree that the coming of the Messiah and the building of the Temple will be no later

than the year 170 of the sixth millennium [1410]." See Yom-Tov Lipmann Mulhausen, *Sefer Hanitzahon* (Jerusalem: Dinur, 1984), par. 335, p. 187.

34. Aescoly, *Jewish Messianic Movements*, p. 223.

35. I.F. Baer, *A History of the Jews in Christian Spain* (Tel Aviv: Am Oved, 1965), p. 320. [Hebrew] Based upon Crescas' *Or Hashem*, part iii, 8:2.

36. Avraham Gross, "The Ten Tribes and the Kingdom of Prester John: Rumors and Investigations Before and After the Expulsion from Spain," *Pe'amim* 48 (1991), pp. 5-38.

37. The primary source is the Darmstadt manuscript. See Yisrael Yuval, *Two Nations in Your Womb: Perceptions of Jews and Christians* (Tel Aviv: Am Oved, 2000), p. 276 n. 27. [Hebrew] By contrast, the manuscript copied in 1429 was the Rome manuscript, cited by Reiner, *Pilgrims and Pilgrimage*, p. 115 n. 232. My thanks to Yisrael Yuval, who allowed me to compare the manuscript in his possession with the Rome manuscript and to discover that the section beginning "And now many people have awakened..." appears only in the latter.

38. Reiner, *Pilgrims and Pilgrimage*, pp. 114-115 n. 232.

39. Baer, *History of the Jews*, pp. 318-319.

40. Binyamin Ze'ev Kedar, "Notes on the History of the Jews of Palestine in the Middle Ages," *Tarbitz* 42 (1973), pp. 413-416. Kedar ignores the connection between the messianic expectations expressed here and the *aliyot* originating in various countries. As a result, he does not see in messianism a motivation for *aliya*, and can only wonder why the latter took place at all, just when the situation of the Jews in Spain was improving, while the situation in Palestine had worsened.

41. Benzion Dinur, "The Emigration from Spain to the Land of Israel After the Decree of 1391," *Tzion* 32 (1967), p. 162.

42. Dinur, "Emigration," p. 163.

43. According to one testimony of the time, "And now, of late, people have come, great sages and elders together with their disciples... and have continued to settle and to increase the study of Tora far more." Quoted in Hacker, "*Aliyot* and Attitudes," p. 28 n. 107.

44. Joseph Hacker, "R. Elijah of Massa Lombarda in Jerusalem," *Tzion* 50 (1985), pp. 253-256.

45. Moshe Schulwas quotes historical sources indicating that the inhabitants of Malta captured Jews who were on their way to Palestine. See Moshe Schulwas, "On the Immigration of German Jews to Palestine in the Fifteenth Century," *Tzion* 3 (1938), pp. 86-87.

46. Elhanan Reiner, "'For Do Not Jerusalem and Zion Stand Apart?': The Jewish Quarter of Jerusalem in the Post-Crusade Period (Thirteenth to Fifteenth Centuries)," in Yossi Ben-Artzi, Israel Bartal, and Elhanan Reiner, eds., *A View of His Homeland: Studies in Geography and History in Honor of Yehoshua Ben-Aryeh* (Jerusalem: Magnes, 2000), pp. 314-315. [Hebrew] The discovery that the Jewish settlement in the center of the Old City dates only from the beginning of the fifteenth century is consistent with Reiner's conclusion that the Nahmanides Synagogue was near Mount Zion, where the Jewish neighborhood was located after the Crusader period, and not as the folk tradition has it, near the Court of the Ashkenazim. See Reiner, "The Jewish Quarter," pp. 277-279.

47. Reiner, "The Jewish Quarter," p. 306 n. 106. Around 1452, the Jews of Jerusalem were compelled to give money to the rulers of the city, and the community was forced to sell much of its land. Three hundred Tora scrolls, ancient books, and precious ritual objects that had been brought to the country by the immigrants around the year 1440 were also sold. These findings suggest an *aliya* of wealthy people during this period. See Avraham Ya'ari, ed., *Letters from the Land of Israel* (Ramat Gan: Masada, 1971), pp. 129-130. [Hebrew]

48. Hacker, "*Aliyot* and Attitudes," p. 12.

49. Hacker, "*Aliyot* and Attitudes," p. 32.

50. Michael Ish Shalom, *In the Shadow of Foreign Rule: The History of the Jews in the Land of Israel* (Tel Aviv: Karni, 1975), p. 312. [Hebrew]

51. Isaiah 43:6.

52. Abravanel's commentary on Isaiah 43:6.

53. Aescoly, *Jewish Messianic Movements*, p. 331. R. Abraham ben Eliezer Halevi wrote several works of a messianic character and engaged in messianic calculations concerning the Jewish year 5300. According to Moshe Idel, there is no connection between his messianic calculations and the expulsion from Spain, as his interest in the problem of the end of days had already begun in his youth, that is, before the expulsion. Moshe Idel, introduction to Aescoly, *Jewish Messianic Movements*, pp. 24-26. Messianic calculations thus were not prompted by historical events alone; these events only heightened the mystics' faith in an imminent redemption.

54. Idel, introduction, pp. 24-34.

55. Moshe Idel, "Solomon Molcho as Magician," *Sefunot* 18 (1985), p. 215.

56. Moshe Idel, introduction to Aaron Ze'ev Aescoly, *The Story of David Hareuveni* (Jerusalem: Mosad Bialik, 1993), p. 33. [Hebrew]

57. According to R. Abraham Halevi, "The things said in the midrash of the *Zohar* about the great troubles and destruction that will herald the time of

the Messiah are very frightening.... Only repentance annuls everything. And in regard to the instructions about the year of visitation, which is the year 5284 [1524], it is fitting that every man take to heart the great wonder that was done in Jerusalem.... For when, gentlemen, the sages gathered together and set vigils... to plead for mercy for themselves and their brethren in the exile... when they said, 'And a redeemer shall come to Zion'—at that moment fire descended from heaven upon the abomination in Jerusalem, and made it into a great ruin, and this was a sign and symbol of the redemption." See Aescoly, *Jewish Messianic Movements*, p. 329.

58. Ya'ari, *Letters*, p. 165.

59. Ya'ari, *Letters*, p. 165. To emphasize that God acts in order to hasten the redemption, the authors open with a literary allusion to a passage in the book of Esther that they consider an instance of divine intervention for the sake of the Jews: "On that night the sleep of the king was disturbed" (Esther 6:1; according to rabbinic interpretation, the "king" referred to is God).

60. Dov Rabin, "The History of the Jews in Grodno," in *Encyclopedia of the Jewish Diaspora* (Jerusalem: Encyclopedia of the Jewish Diaspora, 1977), vol. ix, p. 43. [Hebrew]

61. Ignacy Schipper, *Polish-Lithuanian Jews in Palestine* (Wieden: Moriah, 1917), p. 10. [Polish]

62. Tuvia Preschel, "R. Jacob Pollack's *Aliya* to Jerusalem," in Shaul Israeli, Norman Lamm, and Yitzhak Raphael, eds., *Jubilee Volume in Honor of Our Teacher Rabbi Joseph B. Soloveitchik* (Jerusalem: Mosad Harav Kook, 1984), vol. ii, pp. 1124-1129. [Hebrew]

63. Thus, according to the *Zohar*: "In 66 the King Messiah will be revealed in the land of the Galilee." *Zohar*, Vayera 478.

64. Many of the immigrants from Spain who came to Safed had been weavers and dyers. They saw Safed, located near water sources in the Galilee, as a suitable place to continue in their professions, as it was relatively close to their contacts in the Salonikan clothing trade and was safer than other places in Palestine, including Jerusalem. The Ottoman army protected the city from attacks by the surrounding Bedouin tribes, and in 1549 the authorities added to the city's security by building a wall around it.

65. Ya'ari, *Letters*, p. 184.

66. Apart from R. Jacob Berab's principal reasons for renewing the *semicha*, restoring the Sanhedrin was meant to solve a practical halachic problem that fell within the jurisdiction of the Sanhedrin alone. The inhabitants of Safed included a number of forced converts from Spain and Portugal, who wished to atone for their past as Conversos. This atonement could be accomplished only by administering the punishment of lashes, which the Sanhedrin alone could dispense.

67. R. Isaiah Horowitz, *Shnei Luhot Habrit* (Haifa: Mechon Yad Rama, 1992), vol. 2, pp. 250-251. [Hebrew] The verse cited is Song of Songs 2:12.

68. R.J. Zwi Werblowsky, "R. Solomon Halevi Alkabetz's *Tikun Tefilot*," *Sefunot* 6 (1962), pp. 152-155.

69. They based their calculations mainly on a verse in the book of Daniel that alludes to the time of the end of days: "Fortunate is he who waits and reaches 1,335 days" (Daniel 12:11); and on the talmudic statement attributing messianic significance to the *notarikon* of Jacob's blessing to his sons: "The scepter shall not depart from Judah, nor the ruler's staff from between his feet, until Shiloh comes, and the homage of the peoples be his" (Genesis 49:10). According to the messianic calculations, these two sources point towards the 335th year of the sixth millennium—the numerical value of "Shiloh." On messianic expectations for the year 1575 (5335), see David Tamar, "The Messianic Expectations in Italy for the Year 1575," *Sefunot* 2 (1958), pp. 61-85.

70. According to the tradition, the order of redemption will parallel in reverse the order of exile. Hence, since on the eve of the destruction of the Temple the Sanhedrin was removed from its place there, and subsequently reconvened at various locations until it reached its final seat in Tiberias, the redemption is destined to begin in Tiberias. From there, it will progressively expand until it reaches Jerusalem and the Temple is rebuilt: "And we have a tradition that it shall first return in Tiberias, and from there they shall be re-located to the Temple." Maimonides, *Mishneh Tora*, Laws of Sanhedrin 14:12.

71. Tamar, "Messianic Expectations," pp. 63-65.

72. Mordechai Pachter, *From Safed's Hidden Treasures* (Jerusalem: Zalman Shazar, 1994), pp. 103-105. [Hebrew] Cf. Uriel Hed, "Turkish Documents from Ottoman Archives Concerning Safed Jews in the Sixteenth Century," *Mehkerei Eretz Yisrael* 2 (1955), pp. 169, 174-175.

73. Later sources repeat this prediction. Thus, for example, the Kabbalist R. Naftali Bachrach, author of *Emek Hamelech*, stated that in 1647 Ishmael's rights over the land of Israel, which he had enjoyed for observing the commandment of circumcision, would come to an end. From this point on, the rights of the Jewish people would be acknowledged, and would be realized by the Messiah at the end of days: "And even today we await God, and he shall pour his spirit upon us from above... and the land of Israel will be taken from the Ishmaelites, as it is written, 'I will multiply him exceedingly... and I will make him a great nation,' which [referring to the word *asimenu*, 'I will make him'] is numerically equivalent to 407. That is, until that time of 'I will make him,' he [Ishmael] will be a great nation. And he shall be paid for the merit of the commandment of circumcision... and in the year 5408 [1648], the Messiah will take the kingship from him.... And this is the secret of 'This [*zot*] is my resting place forever' [Psalms 132:14]." See Naftali Bachrach, *Emek Hamelech*

(Amsterdam: Immanuel Benvenisti, 1648), p. 33b; and regarding the year 5408, see ibid., pp. 68a, 79c.

74. The numerical value of the word "Heth" is 408.

75. The word for "this" is *hazot*, of which the numerical value is 5,408.

76. *Zohar*, Toldot 139. The passage is found in the earliest manuscript of the *Zohar*, from the fourteenth century. See Gershom Scholem, *Sabbatai Sevi: The Mystical Messiah 1626-1676* (Princeton: Princeton, 1973), p. 88. The verses quoted in the above passage are Genesis 23:3 and Leviticus 25:13.

77. Horowitz, *Shnei Luhot Habrit*, 65, vol. 2, pp. 478-479.

78. Horowitz, *Shnei Luhot Habrit*, 261, vol. 1, p. 86. It is surprising that scholars of Horowitz have not at all noticed this source and do not attribute messianic significance to his *aliya*.

79. Horowitz, *Shnei Luhot Habrit*, 291, vol. 1, p. 97. It follows from this that Horowitz wrote these words when he was already living in Jerusalem.

80. Ya'ari, *Letters*, p. 216. We do not have exact figures for the Sephardi population of Jerusalem, but in his letter Horowitz mentions that in Jerusalem there were more than five hundred "important Sephardi householders, and every day their number grows, thank God." If Horowitz is referring only to wealthy family heads, then one is speaking here of at least 2,000 members of the Sephardi elite, apart from the numerous poor people from this community who lived in Jerusalem. Regarding the Ashkenazi population, no figures exist. Ya'ari, *Letters*, p. 220.

81. Horowitz sent this letter to his wife's relative, R. Shmuel ben Meshullam Feibusch, chief rabbi of the Krakow community. An important discussion of this letter was related at a lecture by the historian Avraham David at Bar-Ilan University on December 31, 2000; the lecture is soon to be published. My thanks to David for allowing me to use his article prior to publication. In this paper, David does not deal with the connection between messianic expectations for the year 5408 and Horowitz's *aliya*.

82. Avraham David, "R. Isaiah Horowitz's Letter from Jerusalem After the Year 5538," unpublished. [Hebrew]

83. David, "Horowitz's Letter."

84. See David, "Horowitz's Letter." This section of the full letter was published in its day by Joseph Solomon Delmedigo of Candia in the introduction to his book *Novlot Hochma* (1631).

85. See R. Haim Vital, *Etz Haim* (Jerusalem, 1973), introduction to *Sha'ar Hahakdamot*.

86. According to Jacob Elbaum and Elliot Wolfson, the main reason for Horowitz's *aliya* was his wish to study the teachings of Lurianic Kabbala more deeply, without the limitations that were placed on its study outside of the land of Israel. See Jacob Elbaum, "The Land of Israel in Isaiah Horowitz's *Shnei Luhot Habrit*," in Aviezer Ravitzky, ed., *The Land of Israel in Modern Jewish Thought* (Jerusalem: Yad Ben-Zvi, 1998), p. 94; cf. Elliot R. Wolfson, "The Influence of Luria on the *Shelah*," *Jerusalem Studies in Jewish Thought* 10 (1992), p. 430. However, it seems that this activity too was directed towards a messianic purpose: The realization of the redemption in the year 5400, which Horowitz wished to ensure by uncovering Luria's writings.

87. The amount of money extracted from the Jews by the local rulers during the period of Ottoman rule was unparalleled in any other place of Jewish settlement during that period. R. Samuel de Ozida wrote: "What we have in our day is that of all the places under the rule of the king... there is no country in which there are so many taxes and levies on the Jews as in the land of Israel, and particularly Jerusalem. And if money were not being sent from all over the Diaspora to pay off the taxes and levies, the Jews would be unable to live there because of the abundance of taxes." R. Samuel de Ozida, *Lehem Dim'a* (Venice: Daniel Zenitti, 1600), commentary on Lamentations 1:1.

88. Presumably, the rapid growth of the Jewish population in Jerusalem after 1620 upset the Muslims. Eventually they restricted the number of Jewish inhabitants in the city, and to this end even ordered the expulsion from Jerusalem of Jews who were already living there. "What the rulers demanded of the inhabitants of Jerusalem was that whoever had come to live there during the past three years should leave. And they again [later] said that whoever had come during the past ten years [should leave]." Eliezer Rivlin, ed., *The Ruins of Jerusalem* (Jerusalem: Salomon, 1928), p. 45. [Hebrew] According to the author of *The Ruins of Jerusalem*, the Muslims' fear of the return of the Jews to Jerusalem was one of the main reasons for the persecution and expulsion of the Jews of the city: "When a man rose against us who gathered together empty and impudent people... and they took counsel together to cut off the name of Israel from the holy city.... When they saw the ingathering of the exiles of our brethren from East and West, from North and South, going up to Jerusalem...." Rivlin, *Ruins*, p. 49.

89. Among other things, they denounced the Jews for violating the prohibition against building synagogues. In return for not razing the synagogues, the Muslims demanded ever-higher "penalties" to be paid by the Jewish community. Rivlin, *Ruins*, p. 51.

90. Rivlin, *Ruins*, p. 14.

91. See Michael Ish Shalom, *Christian Travels in the Holy Land* (Tel Aviv: Am Oved, 1979), pp. 333, 341. [Hebrew]

354 ARIE MORGENSTERN

92. Minna Rozen, ed., *The Ruins of Jerusalem* (Tel Aviv: Tel Aviv University, 1981), p. 87. [Hebrew] The quotations are a combination of verses of consolation from Jeremiah 32:15 and Zechariah 8:5.

93. Rozen, *Ruins*, pp. 81-82.

94. Rozen, *Ruins*, pp. 82-83.

95. Simon Bernfeld, *The Book of Tears* (Berlin: Eshkol, 1925), vol. iii, p. 140. [Hebrew] The verse cited is Leviticus 16:3.

96. Avraham Neubauer, *Seder Hahachamim Vekorot Hayamim* (Oxford: Clarendon, 1888), p. 149. On the expectations for the year 5400, see also Joseph Hacker, "Despair of the Redemption and Messianic Hopes in the Writings of R. Solomon Halevi of Salonika," *Tarbitz* 39 (1970), pp. 195-213.

97. The word for "thus" is *zot*; for "thorns," *dardar*. Both have a numerical value of 408, as does "Heth." The word for "this," *hazot*, can be readily understood as having a value of 5,408.

98. Scholem, *Sabbatai Sevi*, pp. 103-198.

99. Yehuda Liebes, "Sabbatean Messianism," *Pe'amim* 40 (1989), pp. 4-20.

100. Benzion Dinur attributed great importance to this *aliya*, because in his opinion it marked the beginning of the period of "realistic" *aliyot*, which constituted the basis for the new Jewish presence in the land of Israel. See Dinur, *Historical Writings*, vol. i, pp. 19-68.

101. Meir Benayahu, "The 'Holy Brotherhood' of R. Judah Hasid and Their Settlement in Jerusalem," *Sefunot* 3-4 (1959-1960), pp. 131-182.

102. In the wake of Shabtai Tzvi's conversion to Islam, some of his followers developed the idea that his apostasy was meant to elevate the "holy sparks" within Islam, as only the descent of the Messiah himself to the "shells" would be able to lift up the "sparks." After the Messiah had fulfilled this purpose he would be revealed again, forty years after his conversion; that is, in the year 1706.

103. The disciples of R. Elijah of Vilna, the "Vilna Gaon," who came up to Jerusalem a century later, refer in their writing in a very positive way to R. Judah Hasid, using extraordinary terms of honor. The disciples of the Gaon were aware of the fact that some of the immigrants during this period were Sabbateans. See "The Appointments of Emissaries from the Ashkenazic Community in Jerusalem for the Building of the Hurvah from 1837," in Pinhas Ben-Tzvi Grayevski, ed., *From the Archives of Jerusalem* (Jerusalem: Tzion, 1930), vol. 2. [Hebrew]

104. It may be that R. Judah's circle of immigrants to Palestine had seen 5500 as the date of redemption from the outset, and not only retrospectively. Even such a confirmed Sabbatean as Gedaliah Hayun stated that: "You shall surely know that our rabbis said, 'All the day he laments'—that the exile was

the entire fifth millennium. And when we come to the sixth millennium, the first five hundred years are called night... and the latter five hundred years are called day... and the redemption is the morning." See Zalman Shazar, *The Messianic Hope for the Year 5500* (Jerusalem: Magnes, 1970), p. 29 [Hebrew]; Shazar cites Nehemiah Hayun, *Divrei Nehemia* 9a. I will discuss this issue at greater length elsewhere, on the basis of new documents that I have uncovered in the archive of the community of Livorno, in Italy.

105. R. Haim ben Atar, *Or Hahaim*, commentary on Leviticus 6:2.

106. Immanuel Hai Ricchi writes concerning this: "According to the words of R. Shimon bar Yohai [the putative author of the *Zohar*], in 5541 and two-thirds, the mountain of the house of the Eternal will have been established." See Immanuel Hai Ricchi, *Yosher Levav* (Amsterdam, 1742), p. 37b. The composition of the manuscript itself was completed in Aram-Zovah, in modern Syria, in 1737.

107. Morgenstern, *Mysticism and Messianism*, p. 64 n. 76.

108. Morgenstern, *Mysticism and Messianism*, p. 39.

109. Jewish officials of Istanbul wrote in a letter early in 5501 (late 1740): "Praise to his great name, several benches have been added and several new yeshivot established in the holy city; such a thing has not been since the day of the exile from the land.... Everyone is ascending to the land of Israel, and the multitude of the people has been the reason for the doubling and re-doubling of the expenses. Due to the large numbers of homes in the holy city, whose like has not been since the day of the exile from the land... sustenance has become expensive in the holy city...." Morgenstern: *Mysticism and Messianism*, p. 40 nn. 8-9.

110. In Jerusalem in 1742, R. Haim ben Atar established Yeshivat Kneset Yisrael, whose students engaged in, among other things, the study of esoteric teachings and mystical practices.

111. Adam Teller, "The Tradition from Slutsk Concerning the Early Days of the Ba'al Shem Tov," in David Assaf, Joseph Dan, and Immanuel Etkes, eds., *Studies in Hasidism* (Jerusalem: Mosad Bialik, 1999), pp. 15-38. [Hebrew]

112. Morgenstern, *Mysticism and Messianism*, p. 180. On the messianic motivations for *aliya* and mystical activity of R. Yehiel Michel "Magid" of Zloczow, on Shavuot 5537 [1777], see Mor Altshuler, *R. Meshullam Feibusch Heller and His Place in Early Hasidism*, doctoral dissertation, Hebrew University of Jerusalem, 1994. [Hebrew] Cf. also Arie Morgenstern, "An Attempt to Hasten the Redemption," *Jewish Action* 58:1 (1997), pp. 38-44.

113. Morgenstern, *Mysticism and Messianism*, p. 182.

114. Morgenstern, *Mysticism and Messianism*, pp. 263-274.

115. Introduction of R. Elijah's sons to *Shulhan Aruch: Orah Haim* (Shklov, 1803); cf. Morgenstern, *Mysticism and Messianism*, pp. 275-306.

116. Arie Morgenstern, *Messianism and the Settlement of the Land of Israel* (Jerusalem: Yad Ben-Zvi, 1985). [Hebrew]

117. Sanhedrin 99a. Cf. Morgenstern, *Messianism*, p. 38.

118. *Zohar*, Vayera 445-449, and *Sulam* ad loc.

119. Morgenstern, *Messianism*, p. 55 n. 92.

120. Morgenstern, *Messianism*, p. 58 n. 104.

121. Morgenstern, *Messianism*, p. 75 n. 39, and pp. 66-83.

122. The letter is in the archive of Manfred Lehmann of New York. I am grateful to the family for permission to publish this excerpt.

123. Morgenstern, *Messianism*, p. 133.

124. Morgenstern, *Messianism*, pp. 156-159. In Kabbalistic terminology, "the rising of the divine Presence from the dust" refers to activity of messianic preparation and is symbolic of the redemption.

125. Ya'ari, *Letters*, pp. 353-354. See also Arie Morgenstern, "Messianic Concepts and Settlement in the Land of Israel," in Marc Saperstein, ed., *Essential Papers on Messianic Movements and Personalities in Jewish History* (New York: New York University, 1992), pp. 433-455; and Arie Morgenstern, "Symposium: Messianic Concepts and Settlement in the Land of Israel," in Richard I. Cohen, ed., *Vision and Conflict in the Holy Land* (Jerusalem: Yad Ben-Zvi, 1985), pp. 141-189.

126. Sanhedrin 98a. The verse cited is Ezekiel 36:8.

127. Ya'ari, *Letters*, p. 341.

128. Morgenstern, *Messianism*, p. 193 n. 179.

129. Yisrael Klausner, *Zionist Writings of Rabbi Kalischer* (Jerusalem: Mosad Harav Kook, 1947), p. 13. [Hebrew] Cf. Morgenstern, *Redemption Through Return*, pp. 182-185.

130. Jacob Katz, "The Historical Image of R. Tzvi Hirsch Kalischer," *Shivat Tzion* 2-3 (1951-1952), p. 28; cf. Morgenstern, *Redemption Through Return*, pp. 182-185.

131. Tzvi Karagila, "R. Samuel ben R. Israel Peretz Heller Describes the Sack of Safed, 1834," *Katedra* 27 (1983), pp. 112-114.

132. Yehoshua Ben-Aryeh, *A City Reflected in Time: Jerusalem in the Nineteenth Century* (Jerusalem: Yad Ben-Zvi, 1977), vol. i, p. 395. [Hebrew]

DID HERZL WANT A
JEWISH STATE?

YORAM HAZONY

THE CENTENNIAL OF THEODOR HERZL'S 1897 founding of the Zionist Organization (ZO) met with hardly a tremor of public recognition in Israel,[1] and in general it would be safe to say that Herzl's works and ideas are of not much interest to contemporary Israeli intellectuals and culture makers. Yet there is one point in the vast corpus of his writings that has become a recurring theme in public discourse: Leading Israeli intellectuals have, in the last fifteen years, been increasingly insistent that Herzl's small book *Der Judenstaat* (1896)—traditionally known in English by the title *The Jewish State*—was not intended to inspire the establishment of anything like a "Jewish state." Instead, it is claimed, Herzl has been misunderstood. What he really meant was to give his book the name *The State of the Jews*—a term intended to suggest a state with a Jewish majority, but which would otherwise not have any particularly "Jewish" characteristics.

Now, this issue would probably not be worth discussing were it not a subject of great ideological significance for many of those propagating this claim, and if their ranks did not include some of Israel's most important legal scholars, academics, educators, and civil rights activists—precisely those individuals with the inclination and ability to apply their reading of Herzl to the transformation of contemporary Israel's national character. Consider, for example, the following assertions made by such prominent Israelis.

Former Education Minister and civil rights leader Shulamit Aloni:

> I do not accept the idea of a "Jewish state." It is a "state of the Jews," to be exact. Herzl wrote a book called *The State of the Jews*.[2]

Hebrew University historian and chairman of a key Education Ministry committee on history textbooks, Moshe Zimmermann:

> In Israel... the Herzlian concept of a "state of the Jews" is developing in the direction of a blatantly ethnocentric "Jewish state"....[3]

The novelist Amos Oz:

> Herzl's book was called *The State of the Jews* and not *The Jewish State*: A state cannot be Jewish, any more than a chair or a bus can be Jewish....

And this view has been repeated by a remarkable number of other leading intellectuals as well.[4]

Obviously, arguments over nomenclature do not receive this kind of attention unless the semantic question is merely a stand-in for a much larger struggle over history and culture. And this case is no exception. For partisans of a "state of the Jews" are deliberately seeking to replace a term—"Jewish state" (Heb., *medina yehudit*)—which until recently was a matter of virtually wall-to-wall consensus, a synonym for the State of Israel. In fact, the expression "Jewish state" had been in common use by Zionists all over the world, including the Jews of Palestine, for decades prior to the establishment of Israel. And when Jewish independence was finally declared by David Ben-Gurion on May 14, 1948, the term "Jewish state" was so unequivocally associated with the Jews' political aspirations that it was inserted no fewer than five times into the Israeli Declaration of Independence—which was signed by every Jewish political party in Palestine, from the Communists to the ultra-Orthodox Agudat Israel.[5] (In fact, the Declaration explicitly attributed the term to "Theodor Herzl, progenitor of the vision of *the Jewish state*."[6])

Not only was the concept of Israel as a "Jewish state" a matter of consensus at the time of Israel's establishment; this concept had by that time become part of a political tradition so authoritative that it

commanded the support of the overwhelming majority of Jews everywhere for decades. Indeed, as late as 1988, even a political radical such
as Yeshayahu Leibowitz—who may have agreed with Ben-Gurion on
nothing else—could still define the term precisely as it had been used
by the Israeli founders four decades earlier:

> A Jewish state... [is one that] directs the best part of its resources to
> dealing with the problems of the Jewish people, within the state and
> in the Diaspora: To its social, sectoral, educational, and economic prob-
> lems; to the relationship of the state with the Jewish Diaspora; to the
> relationship of the state to Judaism; and so forth.[7]

That is, the Jewish state is a state that is *intrinsically* Jewish in that the
purpose it serves is to direct the powers of the state to "dealing with
the problems of the Jewish people." In practice, this principle meant the
promulgation of a vast array of particularistic "Jewish" laws and policies,
including the Law of Return granting the right of free Jewish immigration to Israel; the State Education Law mandating the inculcation of "the
values of Jewish culture" and "loyalty to the Jewish people"; the involvement of the Israeli armed forces and security services in rescue operations
of non-Israeli Jews in foreign countries; the use of Israeli courts to try
and punish Nazi war criminals for "crimes against the Jewish people";
laws mandating the state's adoption of Jewish symbols, as well as the
Jewish holidays and Sabbath; and many others. Of course, one could
argue about the specifics of any of these particular "Jewish" policies. But
virtually all Jews embraced the idea that Israel had been established as
a "Jewish state," not only in terms of its demographics, but also in its
purpose, values, policies, and institutions.

The present effort to propagate the new concept of a "state of the
Jews"—and to read it back into Zionist history beginning with Herzl—
therefore represents a conscious choice to break with the most central
concept in the Israeli political tradition, and to replace it with something
else. As the historian Mordechai Bar-On of Yad Yitzhak Ben-Zvi has
described this movement recently:

> In the debate over the Jewishness of Israel... [many] prefer to refrain
> from calling Israel a "Jewish state." They prefer to use the more neutral
> term "the state of the Jews." This preference implies that... Israel is best
> described factually as a state in which Jews are a majority....[8]

As Bar-On explains, the term "Jewish state" is being rejected by leading Israeli intellectuals and public figures due to a growing ideological
discomfort with the normative implications of a state that is "Jewish" in
its essential purpose. The term "state of the Jews," on the other hand, is
descriptive, relating almost exclusively to the fact that Israel is "a state
in which Jews are a majority." Although adherents of the term do not
all use it in precisely the same way, the common denominator among
them is that they are opposed to, or uncertain about, the idea that the
State of Israel should be principally concerned with the interests and
aspirations of the Jewish people. They prefer to understand Israel's purpose as being identical to that of "all other states"—namely, providing
for the welfare of the individuals living within its borders. As Amos
Oz puts it: "The state is a tool... and this tool has to belong to all its
citizens—Jews, Muslims, Christians.... The concept of a 'Jewish state' is
nothing other than a snare."[9]

It is this contemporary dissent from the political concept of Israel as
a "Jewish state" that is in large part driving the insistence that Theodor
Herzl never wanted such a state—and that his *Judenstaat* was supposed
to be a "state of the Jews." For if Herzl, as the founder of the Zionist
Organization, never intended to establish anything other than a "state
of the Jews"—a neutral state that would contain a majority of Jews, but
would in other respects be an essentially *non-Jewish* state—then today's
"state of the Jews" partisans can portray themselves as advocates of the
real Zionist tradition on which Israel's public life rests. In other words,
the claim that Herzl might have opposed the idea of a Jewish state is
becoming a weapon in the struggle against the explicit intention of
David Ben-Gurion and the signers of the Declaration of Independence
to establish Israel as a "Jewish state."

Obviously, one cannot argue that the movement to uproot the traditional concept of Israel as the Jewish state is illegitimate. But there is
little to be said for enlisting Herzl in this struggle. For much as today's
"state of the Jews" activists may wish it, Herzl was not one of them. He
named his book *The Jewish State* because he believed that this term accurately described the state he sought to establish. In order to establish this
claim, I will consider three questions. First, I will examine the semantic
issue of whether Herzl did or did not intend the title of his book to be
The Jewish State. Second, I will ask whether, in terms of political ideals,
the state that Herzl proposed in his book was in a significant sense an

intrinsically "Jewish" state. And third, since many who have jumped on the "state of the Jews" bandwagon have linked this term with Herzl's supposed belief in a "separation" of Jewish religion from the state, I will inquire whether the author of *The Jewish State* did in fact embrace such a doctrine. Once these various aspects are taken into consideration, I believe it will be possible to conclude that the argument that Herzl's *Judenstaat* was intended to be a neutral "state of the Jews" is without merit.

II

Let us begin with the semantic question. Did Herzl intend, as has been frequently claimed, that the term *Judenstaat* in the title of his book be understood to mean a "state of the Jews"—and *not* a Jewish state?

Theodor Herzl wrote *Der Judenstaat* during the course of 1895, originally intending to deliver it in the form of an oral presentation to bankers and other powerful Jewish personalities in Western Europe, who he hoped would take the lead in negotiating with the imperial powers for the establishment of an independent Jewish state. In November of that year, Herzl brought his *Judenstaat* scheme before a group of influential English Jews called the Maccabean Society. As a result of this lecture, he was asked to submit an article for publication in English in the London *Jewish Chronicle*. Appearing on January 17, 1896 under the title "A Solution of the Jewish Question" this article was in fact the public debut of Herzl's idea. It briefly summarized the main points of his pamphlet, and, significantly, used the term "Jewish state" to describe the independent state he wished to establish for the Jewish people.

On January 19, after the appearance of the English-language article, Herzl signed an agreement for the publication of the full-length version of the book, noting in his diary that he planned to replace its awkward title with the far simpler *Der Judenstaat*.[10] The German edition was published on February 14, 1896. At the same time, Herzl also brought out French and English editions, for which he paid from his own pocket.[11] For the title of his French edition, Herzl used *L'État Juif* ("The Jewish State"), while he gave his English edition the title *A Jewish State*.[12]

It can hardly be claimed that the titles Herzl chose in the latter two languages were an accident. Herzl's French was fluent, and his English,

although mediocre, was certainly good enough so that he could understand the meaning of the words "Jewish state." Moreover, the English and
French editions of the pamphlet were central to Herzl's political aims.
The leading Jews behind Jewish resettlement efforts in Palestine and other
lands—whom Herzl fervently hoped to attract to his cause—were French
speakers, and their most important organization, the Jewish Colonization
Association, was based in Paris. It was in England, on the other hand,
that Herzl intended to base his own organization, and *Der Judenstaat*
was explicitly written with the assumption that the English Jews would
be the backbone of his project.[13] Thus neither in the French nor in the
English editions does it seem likely that Herzl would have been willing
to misrepresent his political intentions by using a title that he considered
ideologically problematic. Similarly, when Herzl approved the publication of a Yiddish edition in 1899, it too bore a title that as a speaker
of German he was certainly capable of understanding: It was called *Die
Yudische Medineh* ("The Jewish State").[14]

Thus in every language with which Herzl was familiar, the title of his
booklet was translated as *The Jewish State*, and not *The State of the Jews*.[15]
Moreover, Herzl remained consistent in his usage of the term "Jewish state"
in the years that followed, not only in referring to his book, but also
in describing the state he was seeking to found. This fact is particularly
striking when one examines Herzl's correspondence, which he generally
wrote in German or French: When writing in German, he continued to
use the word *Judenstaat*, yet in French-language letters written more or
less concurrently, he always referred to the state he wanted to found as
an *état juif*.[16] From this it is evident that Herzl believed that the term
"Jewish state" served quite well as a translation of the word *Judenstaat*.
Indeed, it was as a result of Herzl's consistent usage of the term "Jewish state" in English and French that this term became so remarkably
successful. For over a hundred years after Herzl first used it, statesmen
the world over continued to speak in favor of, or against, the idea of a
"Jewish state"—including the 1937 British Royal Commission which for
the first time recommended Jewish independence in Palestine, as well as
the 1947 United Nations partition resolution which gave international
sanction to this idea.

The claim of "state of the Jews" activists today is that all of this was
a mistake. Those who use the term "Jewish state" in referring to Herzl's
Judenstaat, they argue, do not realize that the German prefix *Juden-* means

"Jews," whereas the word for "Jewish" in German is *juedisch*. Herzl's real intention can be learned only from the German title of his book: It was a *Judenstaat*, not a *juedischer Staat*. If he had really been proposing a Jewish state, he would have given his book the title *Der Juedische Staat*.

This entire argument, however, is based on a misunderstanding of the way the prefix *Juden-* ("Jews") was used in Herzl's German. An examination of Herzl's writings reveals that they are replete with words using this prefix, where the reference is clearly to something "Jewish." Thus, for instance, Herzl writes *Judenblatt* in referring to a "Jewish paper" (or, rather, a "Jewish rag"), and *Judenroman* in speaking of a "Jewish novel" he hoped to write. Similarly, he writes *Judenkinder* for "Jewish children" and *Judenkongress* for "Jewish Congress." One would hardly expect these words to be translated as "children of the Jews" or "congress of the Jews," "rag of the Jews" or "novel of the Jews." The clearest way of rendering such terms into English is to use the word "Jewish": Jewish children, Jewish congress, Jewish rag, Jewish novel. Similarly, the term "Jewish state" (or *état juif*) is the best available translation of the word *Judenstaat*.

But even if "Jewish state" was a reasonable translation of the word *Judenstaat* into English, perhaps it is the German term that nevertheless reveals his *true* intentions? Perhaps Herzl chose to use the prefix *Juden-* ("Jews") over the word *juedisch* ("Jewish") because he felt that, in German at least, the second option had a distinct, and less desirable, meaning?

Yet this possibility, too, is refuted by the evidence. In fact, Herzl used the terms *Juden-* and *juedisch* more or less interchangeably. Thus, for example, when writing about the "Jewish question," he would use both *Judenfrage* and *juedische Frage*; for "Jewish community," he used both *Judengemeinde* and *juedische Gemeinde*; and for the "Jewish spirit," he wrote both *Judengeist* and *juedischer Geist*. Similarly, the famous newspaper term *Judenblatt* ("Jewish rag") also appears in Herzl's diaries as a *juedisches Blatt*. Moreover, Herzl did not have any hesitation about using the word *juedisch* to describe organs of the Zionist movement; when he established a bank in London whose purpose was to provide financial services to back up his diplomatic activities, he named it the *Juedische Colonialbank* ("Jewish Colonial Bank"). The fact is that for Herzl, the German prefix *Juden-* was basically synonymous with the word *juedisch*. The terms *Judenstaat* and *juedischer Staat* were essentially synonyms.

Herzl did, of course, have to choose between these terms. One can only give a book one title, and he knew that whichever term he chose would become a slogan and a symbol that would be used for years or perhaps centuries. Thus just as he was always careful to use only the term "Jewish state" in English, he was just as careful to use only the term *Judenstaat* in German. If *Judenstaat* and *juedischer Staat* were for Herzl essentially synonyms, how did he come to choose the former over the latter?

Although it cannot be confirmed conclusively on the basis of his writings, it would appear that Herzl's grounds for making these decisions were literary. One cannot ignore the fact that *Judenstaat* is the shorter and less cumbersome of the two German options—just as "Jewish state" and *état juif* are the shorter and less cumbersome options in English and French. Moreover, there is also a strong possibility that Herzl was attracted to the word *Judenstaat* because of its value as an ideologically loaded play on words. We can see such considerations operating in Herzl's choice of a title for his subsequent novel *Altneuland* ("Old-New Land"), which painted a utopian portrait of a future Palestine. As is well known, the title of the novel is just such a pun, being a conscious reference to Prague's famous synagogue, the Altneuschul ("Old-New Synagogue").[17] This title was intended to be amusing, but it also sought to make an important ideological point: The Jews of Central Europe had for six hundred years seen the Altneuschul as their spiritual center, and Herzl was gently calling on them to give up on their Old-New synagogue and replace it with something much more spectacular—their Old-New land, Palestine. It is precisely this playful pun and its deeper, deadly serious meaning that Herzl believed would make for a successful title for the book. In his diary, he wrote of the term *Altneuland*: "It will become a famous word."[18]

Herzl may very well have had the same thing in mind in coining the term *Judenstaat*. The Jews in a given city often lived in a particular district, which was sometimes referred to as the *Judenstadt* ("Jew Town"). Indeed, the Altneuschul itself was situated in Prague's *Judenstadt*. By calling his book *Der Judenstaat*, Herzl thus employed another pun to get across precisely the same central ideological point that he made later with the title of his novel. Jews were called upon to leave their town, their Jewish district, and exchange it for something that sounded similar, but which was in reality far greater: The Jewish state.

In sum, the claim that Herzl intended the word *Judenstaat* to mean "the state of the Jews," and *not* "Jewish state," is simply mistaken. Herzl was himself the inventor of the term "Jewish state," and he was perfectly comfortable and consistent in using this term throughout the years that he led the Zionist movement.

There remains, of course, the problem of the Hebrew edition of Herzl's book, which has been called *Medinat Hayehudim* ("The State of the Jews") since it was first translated in 1896 at the initiative of the Tushia publishing house in Warsaw. It is this Hebrew-language title which has, of course, been the single greatest factor in persuading Israelis that Herzl was opposed to the term "Jewish state." But in light of the fact that Herzl himself saw no difficulty in using the term "Jewish state," it seems unlikely that the choice of the Hebrew title was actually of real significance. Much more plausible is that Herzl—who knew almost no Hebrew—did not delve too deeply into the matter of the Hebrew title; or that he simply asked his translator, the Viennese Hebraist Michael Berkowicz, which option sounded better.

Moreover, one need only read Berkowicz's edition in order to realize that the translator did not feel the need to be too consistent about using the expression *medinat hayehudim* ("state of the Jews") as the "correct" translation of the German word *Judenstaat.* On the contrary, Berkowicz's translation used a number of different expressions to render this word into Hebrew—one of which was the term *medina yehudit* ("Jewish state").[19]

III

To this point, I have considered the semantic evidence that Herzl believed the expression "Jewish state" to be the best available translation of the word *Judenstaat.* But this does not answer the substantive argument that has been advanced concerning Herzl's intention in publishing his book. For even if Herzl did prefer the term "Jewish state," as I have suggested, it is still theoretically possible that what he meant by this term was what is today being referred to as the "state of the Jews": An essentially neutral state much like the one envisioned in Rousseau's *On the Social Contract,* which, although it would have a majority of Jews, would otherwise not be constituted as a Jewish state in any way. An even more extreme possibility—which is likewise popular among Israeli intellectuals—is that even the Jews *themselves,* once they were living in Herzl's "state of the

Jews," were not intended to remain distinctively Jewish in a significant cultural sense, but would merely be assimilated Jews (or former Jews), living free of anti-Semitism in a new and more comfortable location. It goes without saying that if this were the case, and the Jews of the Jewish state were to lose their unique Jewish character and ideals, it would not be long before the state would cease to be Jewish in any way as well.

It is therefore worth turning first to the argument that the Jews of Herzl's *Judenstaat* were not themselves intended to be distinctively Jewish. Thereafter, I will return to the issue of the intrinsically Jewish character of their state.

The idea that Herzl was a proponent of creating a "non-Jewish" state comprised of thoroughly assimilated Jews is almost as old as the Zionist movement itself, going all the way back to Ahad Ha'am's blistering attacks on Herzl and his lieutenant Max Nordau, whom he accused of wanting to establish a "state of Germans or Frenchmen of the Jewish race."[20] And similar claims continue to be made down to our own day. Consider, for example, the description of Herzl by Amnon Rubinstein in his book *The Zionist Dream Revisited: From Herzl to Gush Emunim and Back*. According to Rubinstein, Herzl was a "cosmopolitan," whose dedication to the idea of a Jewish state "was neither motivated, nor accompanied, by a return to Judaism." What Herzl really wanted was a state where the Jews would be free to be "Europeans":

> His attachment to Judaism was minimal; his knowledge of things Jewish nebulous.... He was driven to the idea of a Jewish state [by anti-Semitism]. Yet, his very philosophy remained European, secular, liberal.... There was precious little Jewishness in Herzl's writings. The new Maccabees who would inhabit the utopian future state were not really different from the cultivated European....[21]

Or, as Israeli Justice Minister Yossi Beilin wrote recently concerning Herzl:

> If the world had been willing to accept the Jews as human beings, and if, as a result, the Jews had given up their Jewishness, no one would have been happier than he.... Herzl's real dream was the American dream: Give the Jews the chance to live as human beings—and to assimilate because they have it so good. In many respects, he was the prophet of Jewish life in America much more than he was the prophet of the Jewish state....[22]

Nor is this kind of reading of Herzl limited to Rubinstein and Beilin. Similar views are expressed frequently by Israeli cultural figures.[23]

Yet it is important to recognize that the claim that Herzl wished to found a "state of Germans or Frenchmen of the Jewish race" did not originate with Herzl. He himself never made statements to this effect. To find such a description of his aims, one must go to the writings of his most unrelenting political rival, Ahad Ha'am, whose purpose in making such claims was to discredit Herzl among the traditional Russian Jews who were the largest constituency in Herzl's Zionist Organization.[24] This does not mean that those who repeat this argument today do so out of improper motives. But since Ahad Ha'am outlived Herzl by twenty-three years—eventually moving to Palestine when it came under British rule—it is nevertheless true that much of what is said today about Herzl's Jewishness is based on what was originally a politically motivated and not necessarily fair rendering of him. To take just one glaring example, no one who knew Herzl's thought reasonably well could have accused him of desiring a state comprised of members of the "Jewish race"—for the simple reason that Herzl consistently rejected the idea that the Jews were a race.[25] Instead, he believed that Jews were united *only by a common heritage and culture*, and it was this Jewish cultural identity that he saw as the cornerstone of Jewish nationalism.

To understand Herzl's views on this subject, one must begin with what he himself referred to as his own "return to Judaism."[26] As everyone knows, Herzl began his Zionist career as a thoroughly assimilated Jew. Nonetheless, this characterization is often used to imply, incorrectly, that he had no Jewish roots. In fact, Herzl went to a Jewish elementary school, and his father took him to Friday night services as a child. His grandfather, from whom Herzl may have absorbed the idea of the restoration of the Jewish people to their ancient independence, was an observant Jew, and a follower of R. Yehuda Alkalai, one of the leading Jewish nationalists of the mid-nineteenth century. But it is nonetheless clear from Herzl's diaries and other sources that, before his embrace of Jewish nationalism at the age of thirty-five, he had become extremely distanced from almost anything distinctively "Jewish." It suffices to recall that on Christmas Eve 1895—*after* Herzl had spent months badgering Vienna's chief rabbi Moritz Guedemann about the idea of establishing a Jewish state—the rabbi walked into Herzl's living room to discover him lighting a Christmas tree. As Herzl writes in his diary:

I was just lighting the Christmas tree for my children when Guedemann arrived. He seemed upset by the "Christian" custom. Well, I will
not let myself be pressured. But I don't mind if they call it a Hanuka
tree—or the winter solstice.[27]

The desire not to be "pressured" by rabbis was characteristic of Herzl's
personal and political outlook. Yet at the same time, Herzl's growing attachment to the traditions of the Jewish people rapidly outstripped his
wariness of rabbis. "I am taking up once again the torn thread of the
tradition of our people," he noted in his diary,[28] and the more he pulled
on this thread, the more sympathetic he became to Jewish custom. Indeed, two years after the incident with Guedemann, he published an essay
entitled "The Menora," in which he described the joy he felt at turning
his back on Christmas, and for the first time lighting the traditional
Hanuka candelabrum with his children. In this essay, Herzl described
an unnamed German-Jewish intellectual—quite obviously Herzl—as
someone who had "long since ceased to care about his Jewish origin or
about the faith of his fathers." Yet despite this distance, he wrote, he
had always been "a man who deep in his soul felt the need to be a Jew."
And when he witnessed the rising tide of anti-Semitism around him, this
need began to force its way to the surface. As he described the process
of change in "The Menora":

> Gradually his soul became one bleeding wound. Now this secret psychic
> torment had the effect of steering him to its source, namely, his Jew-
> ishness, with the result that he experienced a change that might never
> have taken place in better days.... He began to love Judaism with a
> great fervor. At first he did not fully acknowledge this... but finally
> it grew so powerful... that there was only one way out... namely, to
> return to Judaism.[29]

Herzl describes how he struggled with himself, in the end realizing that
even though he was distant from things Jewish, he at least had the opportunity to give his children a Jewish education. And this education
was to begin with Hanuka, the festival of the Maccabees:

> In previous years, he had let the festival... pass unobserved. Now, how-
> ever, he used it as an occasion to provide his children with a beautiful
> memory for the future.... A menora was acquired.... The very sound
> of the name, which he now pronounced in front of the children every

evening, gave him pleasure. Its sound was especially lovely when it came from the mouth of a child.

The first candle was lit and the origin of the holiday was retold: The miracle of the little lamp… as well as the story of the return from the Babylonian exile, of the Second Temple, of the Maccabees. Our friend told his children all he knew. It was not much, but for them it was enough. When the second candle was lit, they repeated what he had told them, and although they had learned it all from him, it seemed to him quite new and beautiful. In the days that followed, he could hardly wait for the evenings, which became ever brighter….

There came the eighth day, on which the entire row of lights is kindled…. A great radiance shone forth from the menora. The eyes of the children sparkled. For our friend, the occasion became a parable for the kindling of a whole nation. First one candle… then another, and yet another…. When all the candles are ablaze, everyone must stop in amazement and rejoice at what has been wrought.[30]

This is not a tale told by a man who is opposed to the Jewish character of the Jews. On the contrary, the "return to Judaism" which was at the basis of Zionism was for Herzl a "great radiance," and he was steadfast in his belief that "the greatest triumph of Zionism is having led a youth that already was lost to his people back to Judaism."[31]

Moreover, Herzl's diaries show that this positive inclination towards the heritage of his people was by no means limited to the lighting of the Hanuka candelabrum. He similarly reports the respect—and sometimes the delight—with which he participated in other Jewish customs: Friday night services, being called up to read from the Tora, the traditional grace after meals, the Passover Seder, his children's recitation of a bedtime prayer in Hebrew.[32] He wrote sympathetically about the Jewish Sabbath, and emphatically about the symbolism of the Star of David.[33] He cited the Bible as the basis of the Jewish claim to Palestine.[34] His skepticism concerning the possibility of reviving Hebrew similarly gave way to enthusiasm, and he not only took lessons in Hebrew, but had his children tutored in the ancient language of the Jews.[35]

Nor was Herzl an atheist—as is frequently claimed—and early on his diaries begin to reflect his struggles to explain why the idea of God should be retained, criticizing Spinoza's deity as being too "inert":

I want to bring up my children with what might be called the historical God…. I can conceive of an omnipresent will, for I see it at work in the physical world. I see it as I can see the functioning of a muscle. The world is the body and God is the functioning of it. The ultimate purpose I do not and need not know. For me it is enough that it is something higher....[36]

Indeed, Herzl's diaries, in which he scrupulously recorded his evolving feelings, often refer to God. And although these references are erratic, uncertain, and generally embarrassed, they are sometimes also straight-forward in the belief they express:

> By means of our state, we can educate our people for tasks which still lie beyond our horizon. For God would not have preserved our people for so long if we did not have another destiny in the history of mankind.[37]

Obviously, none of this means that Herzl became an Orthodox Jew, either in his observance or in his beliefs. Until his death at the age of forty-four, Herzl's understanding of the Jewish faith remained fiercely independent of all movements. But his need to struggle with the Jewish tradition rather than to reject it outright rendered Herzl's attitude to being a Jew so very different from the facile anti-Jewish views that are attributed to him. Certainly, he did not find Jewish customs and tradi-tions and ideas *easy* to accept, but he was far from being an opponent of such traditions. On the contrary, he believed that his overexposure to non-Jewish culture had robbed him of the "spiritual counterpoise which our strong forefathers had possessed"—and this was an error he would not repeat with his own children. As he wrote in "The Menora":

> He had absorbed ineradicable elements from the cultures of the nations among which his intellectual pursuits had taken him.... This gave rise to many doubts.... Perhaps the generation that had grown up under the influence of other cultures was no longer capable of that return [to Judaism] which he had discovered as the solution. But the next genera-tion, provided it were given the right guidance early enough, would be able to do so. He therefore tried to make sure that his own children, at least, would be shown the right way. He was going to give them a Jewish education from the very beginning.[38]

A man who considers it important that his children be "shown the right way" by receiving the Jewish education he himself had not received may be many things, but he is not a man attempting to bring up a family of "Germans or Frenchmen of the Jewish race." No, Herzl believed that his children must be raised as Jews, so that they would not suffer the distress that comes of an over-rootedness in "non-Jewish customs."

And far from seeing this as a personal matter for his family, Herzl understood that the raising of a nation of Jewish children, who would develop a *unique* Jewish character, was one of the essential reasons for founding a Jewish state. As he wrote in an essay called "Judaism," which he published not long after the appearance of *The Jewish State*, the only path to the development of such a unique Jewish character was to regain the inner security possessed by past generations of Jews:

> The atrocities of the Middle Ages were unprecedented, and the people who withstood those tortures must have had some great strength, an inner unity which we have lost. A generation which has grown apart from Judaism does not have this unity. It can neither rely upon our past nor look to our future. That is why we shall once more retreat into Judaism and never again permit ourselves to be thrown out of this fortress.... We shall thereby regain our lost inner wholeness and along with it a little character—our own character. Not a Marrano-like, borrowed, untruthful character, but our own.[39]

These words were written at the very beginning of Herzl's career as a Jewish public figure. In 1903, a year before his death, the Zionist leader returned to this subject in a letter in which he scored Jewish life in the Western countries as being blighted not because of anti-Semitism, but because the possibility of developing a unique character and contributing to the world *as Jews* had been eradicated. As he wrote:

> What political, social, material, or moral influence do the Jews have on... the European peoples?... It may happen that people of Jewish descent exert a certain influence.... However, they do this only as individuals who deny any connection with their real national traditions. The Jews of today... strive for no greater aim than to live *unrecognized* among the other peoples.... They are better Anglo-Saxons than the English, more Gallic than the French, more German than the Germans. Only my comrades, the Zionists, wish to be Jewish Jews.[40]

IV

As is evident from his writings, Herzl hoped for the "return" of Western Jews to their heritage, "first one candle then another," until this revival became a "great radiance." But unlike Ahad Ha'am, Herzl did not see himself as the man who would dictate the exact content of this Jewish revival. On the contrary, Herzl consistently emphasized that both "free-thinkers" and the most traditional Orthodox Jews had a place within the Jewish national movement.[41] In order to make this possible, he resisted every effort to determine precisely what the "Jewishness" of the Jewish state would look like. Such premature determinations, he argued, would only serve to alienate one segment of Jewry or another.

This is among the reasons that *The Jewish State*, which is so rich in detail on political and economic subjects, is starkly lacking in particulars concerning the way in which the return to the Jewish heritage would express itself once the state had been established. Even where Herzl had something important to say about the Jewish culture of the state, he speaks only in the vaguest terms so as to avoid unnecessary controversy. For example, when, in *The Jewish State*, he turns to the issue of establishing great Jewish religious centers to meet the "deep religious needs of our people," he only mentions the crucial role of Mecca in the Islamic world, but is careful not to go further with the analogy. "I do not wish to offend anyone's religious sensibilities with words that might be mis-interpreted," he writes.[42] Yet we know from his diaries that when Herzl later visited Jerusalem, he was still intent on making the city a powerful religious center that would be for the Jews what the city of Mecca was for Muslims.[43]

But Herzl's reticence in painting detailed pictures of what the Jew-ish culture of the state would look like did not prevent him from ar-guing for the Jewish particularism of the state *in principle*. Indeed, in *The Jewish State*, Herzl explicitly rejects Rousseau's universally applicable citizens' state (what is today referred to as a "state of its citizens"), ar-guing that no state actually receives its political mandate from a social contract among all its citizens of the type Rousseau envisioned. In fact, argued Herzl, the political guardianship of a people always comes into being when individuals motivated by "higher necessity" step forward to attempt to protect their people's welfare.[44] In the case of the Jews, he proposed assembling a "Society of Jews," to consist of influential Jewish leaders, which would undertake to negotiate with the European states for the creation of a new Jewish polity. In Herzl's view, it was this Society of Jews that would itself become the sovereign Jewish state:

> The Jews who espouse our idea of a state will rally around the Society of Jews. Thereby, they will give it the authority to speak in the name of the Jews and negotiate with governments on their behalf. To put it in the terminology of international law, the Society will be recognized as a state-creating power, and this in itself will mean the formation of the state.[45]

And this new sovereign state, the Jewish state, would not be a "neutral" regime such as that envisioned by Rousseau. On the contrary, the Jewish state would be established with a particular purpose:

> At present, the Jewish people is prevented by its dispersion from conducting its own political affairs. Yet it is in a condition of more or less severe distress in a number of places. It needs, above all things, a guardian.... And that is the Society of Jews... from which the public institutions of the Jewish state are to develop....[46]

Thus, Herzl's new state was to be characterized by a specific and intrinsically Jewish mission: Serving as the guardian of the Jews. Of course, such a state could come to be characterized by various "Jewish" cultural attributes; for example, it might work to build up Jerusalem as a center of Jewish religious pilgrimage, as Herzl advocated. But such particularist characteristics were not the essence of what would make the state "Jewish." They would merely be *consequences* of the one central principle—that the Jewish state was to serve as the guardian of the Jewish people.

For an example of how this principle of Jewish guardianship would work, one can look to Herzl's formal testimony before the British Royal Commission on Alien Immigration in London in July 1902. The commission was considering the imposition of restrictions on Russian-Jewish immigration—restrictions that Herzl believed would mean a resounding defeat for Jewish interests, signaling to the world that even a liberal country such as England could not tolerate more than a certain number of Jews.[47] He therefore testified that Britain could avoid the need to enact such anti-Jewish legislation by assisting in the creation of a self-governing Jewish colony, whose policies would make it "naturally" attractive to Jews, "for they would arrive there as citizens just because they are Jews, and not as aliens."[48] Although the Zionist Organization, the real-life version of the "Society of Jews," had not yet acquired a foothold in Palestine, Herzl was already acting as guardian of the interests of the Jewish people. By publicizing his desire to grant automatic citizenship for immigrant Jews, he was demonstrating how his embryonic Jewish state could do much more than serve as a safe haven for Jews fleeing persecution. It could also assist Jewry in Britain and other countries by reducing the pressure for radical anti-Jewish "solutions" by their respective governments; and at the same time, those Russian Jews who truly wished to go to England rather than to the Jewish state might be able to keep the right to do so. Herzl's intercession with Britain thus served as an example of how the Jewish state would be able to pursue policies that would benefit Jews the world over, whether they chose to immigrate to this state or not.

The workings of the principle of Jewish guardianship were also evident in documents that Herzl and his colleagues prepared as the basis of negotiations with the imperial powers. Almost from the establishment of the Zionist Organization, Herzl was active in developing various versions of what was in those days called a "charter"—essentially a constitutional document describing the aims and powers of a government operating in a given territory with the sanction of Britain or one of the other European powers. On the basis of such a charter, Herzl expected to found a Jewish colony or settlement as a prelude to full Jewish independence. Since these drafts described the actual terms under which the Zionists hoped to establish a Jewish state, they are among the more compelling indicators that we have of the kind of state Herzl wanted to establish.

Of these, the most significant is the proposed charter submitted by Herzl to the British government on July 13, 1903, which led to the offer by the British Foreign Office to negotiate over the establishment of a Jewish colony in British East Africa. (The Zionists had been hoping to persuade the British to allow them to establish the settlement in the British-controlled Sinai Peninsula, but this option had fallen through two months earlier.) Prepared by the English Zionist leaders Leopold Greenberg, Joseph Cowen, and Israel Zangwill, together with the British lawyer and parliamentarian David Lloyd George—later the prime minister who would actually establish Palestine as the Jewish national home—this draft charter provided that:

1. A "Jewish settlement" would be established which would permit "the settling of Jews under conditions favorable to their retention and encouragement of the Jewish national idea."

2. The Jewish settlement would be "founded under laws and regulations adopted for the well-being of the Jewish people."

3. The Jewish settlement would have a "popular government... which shall be Jewish in character and with a Jewish governor...."

4. It would follow English law except where the colony made "alteration and amendments therein based upon Jewish law."

5. The settlement would have a Jewish name and a Jewish flag.[49]

Thus the colony that Herzl envisioned as eventually gaining independence was not to be a neutral non-Jewish polity that happened to have a majority of Jews. On the contrary, it would have Jewish purposes—the advancement of the "Jewish national idea" and the "well-being of the Jewish people" as a whole. To this end it would have Jewish leaders, a governmental form Jewish in character, and the ability to adopt the provisions of Jewish law. And these Jewish characteristics would be represented by particularist symbols such as a Jewish flag. As Herzl wrote to Max Nordau a few days after this draft charter was submitted to the British government: "We colonize on a national basis, with a flag... and with self-government. The draft charter that we submit today on July 13 on Downing Street contains these demands... and the Jewish nation is there."[50] (Although the British government did not commit itself to the details of the plan, the Foreign Office responded favorably to the plan in principle, agreeing to entertain favorably proposals for a "Jewish colony or settlement" whose purpose would be to enable Jews "to observe their national customs." A Jewish governor and Jewish legislation in "religious and purely domestic matters" were also accepted as reasonable.[51] Due to opposition within the ZO to any negotiations with Britain over settlements outside of Palestine, these discussions with the British were suspended until 1914 when it became evident that Britain might invade Palestine.)

In sum, Herzl's Jewish state was one whose purpose was to serve as the legal and political guardian of the interests of the Jewish people, and it was this purpose that made the theoretical state he envisioned a "Jewish" one. Nor did Herzl pursue a different course in practice: It was the principle of Jewish guardianship that dictated the policies of the Zionist Organization, the Jewish "government in exile"; and it was this principle that characterized the proposed charter the Zionists submitted to Britain, which envisioned a government that would be "Jewish in character" and that would promulgate "laws and regulations adopted for the well-being of the Jewish people."

On the other hand, a "state of the Jews" that would have been "neutral"—which is to say, *non-Jewish*—with regard to the character of its government and the purposes of its policies, would not have served Herzl's purposes at all. In fact, it is fair to say that it would have been worthless to him.

V

As evidence that Herzl was an advocate of a neutral "state of the Jews," Israeli intellectuals invariably point to his argument in *The Jewish State*, to the effect that the Jews have no intention of establishing a theocracy. Through endless repetition, this passage has surely become the best known in Herzl's writings, and it is constantly being pressed into service as proof that Herzl did not want a Jewish state; or else that he wanted to see a complete "separation" between the state and the Jewish religion; or that he was opposed to the involvement of rabbis in politics. But *none* of these claims have a basis in Herzl's thought, and none of them can reasonably be read into the passage in question.

The famous "theocracy" passage reads as follows:

> Shall we, then, end up by having a theocracy? No!… We shall permit no theocratic inclinations on the part of our clergy to raise their heads. We shall know how to restrict them to their temples, just as we shall restrict our professional soldiers to their barracks. The army and the clergy shall be honored to the extent that their noble functions require and deserve it. But they will have no privileged voice in the state… for otherwise they might cause trouble externally and internally.[52]

Herzl here compares the rabbinate to the officers of the military, argu-ing that both have "noble" functions within the state, but that neither should be permitted to extend their authority beyond its proper sphere. It does not take too much effort, however, to recognize that this passage in no way advocates a "separation of religion and state." No state in Europe had attempted a separation of "military and state," of course, and if the rabbinate were to have a place in the Jewish state similar to that of the military, then Herzl was in fact arguing for the opposite of such a separation: He was assuming a government such as that familiar from Britain, Germany, and Austria of his own day, in which religion, like the military, was politically subordinated to the government of the state, but was nevertheless an integral part of it.[53] The actual meaning of this passage is that the sphere of state policy belongs to the elected authorities, and that those fulfilling other functions in the state—including generals and chief rabbis—should be firmly prevented from usurping the authority to make such policy.

What, then, did Herzl actually believe concerning the role of the Jewish religion and its representatives in the Jewish state?

One cannot answer this question without first recognizing the place of Judaism in Herzl's understanding of the Jewish people. As presented in *The Jewish State* and elsewhere, Herzl's theory of nationality was based on the belief that peoples appear within history as the result of adversity.[54] That is, it is the struggle against a common enemy that fuses a great mass of individuals into a people. This view has often been criticized as being exclusively "negative," but it is really nothing of the sort. On the contrary, as is evident from his essay "The Menora," Herzl believed that this adversity is to an important extent the catalyst for the creation of the *positive* content of civilizations—the struggle of the Maccabees and the Hanuka festival being an example of precisely this phenomenon.

An important concomitant of Herzl's theory of nationality is that if peoples are created in the struggle against adversity, then there is no simple formula—neither land, nor language, nor race, nor even a combination of these—that will exhaustively describe the unifying characteristics of all peoples. That is, not every people would necessarily have the same kind of positive elements at the basis of its civilization. Indeed, a people such as the Germans might be divided religiously and geographically, and its essence might be best expressed in the German language. The Swiss, on the other hand, lacked a common language, but were nevertheless united by history and territory. And the centerpiece of the positive Jewish civilization that unites the Jewish people, according to Herzl, is not language or territory, but *religion*—"We recognize ourselves as a nation by our faith."[55]

This is not to say that Herzl opposed efforts to forge Jewish culture beyond the bounds of religion—the revival of the Hebrew language, Jewish art, Jewish literature, and a Jewish academia. Herzl supported them all, and he wished to contribute to the Jewish cultural revival himself.[56] He hoped to write a biblical drama, to be entitled *Moses*,[57] and he spoke to his colleagues about his dream of establishing a "neo-Jewish" style in architecture in the Jewish state, even drawing sketches for them so that they could see what he had in mind.[58] But unlike Ahad Ha'am, who believed he could change the core content of the Jewish people by overthrowing the Jewish religion and replacing it with a "modernist" Jewish culture, Herzl adopted as a political principle the idea that Zionism must "hold tradition sacred."[59] (Or, as he liked to say, "I am not planning anything harmful to religion, *but just the opposite....*"[60]) Every individual could make his own contribution to Jewish civilization, but it was not neo-Jewish architecture that was going to be at the heart of the Jewish national identity. It would be Judaism.

The significance of this idea could easily be seen after the founding of the Zionist Organization in 1897. Herzl established the ZO as a democratic movement with a mass membership and annual elections. The Zionist Organization granted women the vote—at a time when virtually no democratic state had yet done so[61]—and Herzl's support for other liberal principles, especially freedom of conscience, is well known. As he wrote in *The Jewish State*, individuals belonging to other peoples or faiths would find themselves welcome and well treated in his state: "Should it happen that men of other creeds and other nationalities come to live among us, we will accord them honorable protection and equality before the law."[62]

And yet despite this concern for the welfare of the stranger, Herzl was from his first steps as a Jewish nationalist unwilling to accommodate Jews who had converted to Christianity, whom he considered to have betrayed not only the Jewish faith, but the Jewish *people*.[63] Thus while he was adamant that the Zionist Organization and the Jewish state would be willing to take *every* Jew—"all beggars, all peddlers"[64]—he was overtly hostile to Jews who had betrayed the faith of their fathers:

> Let the cowardly, assimilated, baptized Jews remain.... We faithful Jews, however, will once again become great.[65]

Nor was this just rhetoric. It was policy. The Zionist Organization would not accept baptized Jews as members.[66] Despite having been established on a democratic basis, it nonetheless retained this crucial element of the aristocratic republic that Herzl had wished to found: The ZO was the political guardian of the Jews, and would one day become the government of the Jewish state.[67] And a person could hardly be expected to serve as guardian of the Jews if he could not understand that in apostasy he had betrayed his people.

Thus for Herzl, loyalty to the Jewish religion was at the heart of Jewish nationalism. And it was this fact, so central to his thought and his politics, which dictated the place he envisioned for organized Judaism in the Jewish state. Indeed, far from being removed from politics, Herzl expected the rabbis of all persuasions ("I want to work with the rabbis, all rabbis," he wrote)[68] to be *central* to the Jewish state, both in the effort to bring about the immigration of Jewry, and in the subsequent effort to build the Jewish homeland. As he wrote in his diary,

> The rabbis will be pillars of my organization, and I shall honor them for it. They will arouse the people, instruct them... and enlighten them....[69]

He envisioned the rabbis—whom he referred to hopefully as "our spiritual leaders," and even as "the leaders of the Jewish people"[70]— playing a critical political role, with immigration being conducted on the basis of "local groups," each one centered around a rabbi who would serve as the chairman of the committee organized to lead the local group. The rabbis would be the leaders of every Jewish community, spreading word of the great event of the return to Palestine from their pulpits:

> The appeal [to emigrate] will be included in the religious service, and properly so. We recognize our historic unity only by the faith of our fathers.... The rabbis will then regularly receive the announcements of the Society [of Jews]... and they will share them with and explain them to their congregations. Israel will pray for us....[71]

Similarly, prayer services would be an important part of preparing the Jewish immigrants on the journey to Palestine.[72] Moreover, he hoped that rabbis would use their influence to apply pressure on recalcitrant wealthy Jews to choose the right path and return to their homeland with their people.[73]

Established religion was also meant to have a role in the Jewish state itself. Herzl's theory of religious centers, mentioned earlier, was part of a greater picture. As he wrote in *The Jewish State*: "We shall not give up our cherished customs. We shall find them again."[74] And in Herzl's estimation, the Jewish state should do what it could to assist in this process. Thus his diaries repeatedly reveal his intention for the state to appoint leading rabbinic figures as the rabbis of cities or regions, and he noted that these would receive a salary from the state.[75] Similarly, each town would have its synagogue, which would be built by the Jewish authorities so that "the synagogue will be visible from afar, for the old faith is the only thing that has kept us together."[76] The great Temple in Jerusalem would also be restored.[77] Up until his death, Herzl continued to take an interest in other efforts that might similarly enrich the religious drawing power of the new state, including archaeological efforts to find the biblical ark of the covenant.[78]

Nor was Herzl's pro-religious orientation contradicted in any way by his politics as the leader of the Zionist Organization. Much to the consternation of young radicals such as Chaim Weizmann and Martin Buber, Herzl's political strategy was characterized by an alliance with Jewish religion and with religious Jews from his earliest days at the head of the ZO—an alliance that expressed itself, for example, in his speech before the Third Zionist Congress, in which he argued that the poor Jews of the Russian empire would be "the best Zionists, because among them the old national tradition is still unforgotten, [and] because they have strong religious feelings...."[79] He was even involved in the founding of the Mizrahi, the Zionist Orthodox party, which he hoped would serve as a counterweight to the growing strength of Ahad Ha'am's followers.[80]

In short, the claim that Herzl's *Der Judenstaat* aimed at separating Jewish religion from the state is without basis in fact. Herzl did not see himself as a religious man, but his belief in the crucial role played by religion in the state—and especially his belief in the importance of Judaism for the Jewish state—made him an ally of the Jewish faith throughout his political career. And while his firm belief in freedom of conscience would likely have made him a supporter of substantial pluralism among rabbinical functionaries of the state, this does not alter the fact that Herzl believed in Judaism as the established religion of the Jewish state.

VI

The claim that Herzl never intended to establish a Jewish state, but only a neutral "state of the Jews," is far from being just an academic question. It is an important part of the ideological and political efforts to delegitimize the concept of the Jewish state today. Obviously, this does not mean that everyone who is propagating the idea that Herzl sought a "state of the Jews" has signed on to all of the ideological implications that have been hitched to this supposed historical fact. Indeed, this idea has gone so far that by now even those who wish to see Israel remain a Jewish state are found repeating the fallacy of Herzl's "state of the Jews," thus becoming unwitting accomplices in the effort to discard the political ideal they support.

For example, Claude Klein, a professor of law at the Hebrew University, has become so convinced that Herzl wished to establish a "state of the Jews"—and that the world must understand this—that in 1990 he went so far as to release a new French-language edition of the book in Paris, in which he changed the title from the one that Herzl gave it to a title of his own devising. Thus after ninety-four years of being published under the title of *L'État Juif* ("The Jewish State"), one can now buy the Claude Klein edition, which sports the title *L'État des Juifs* ("The State of the Jews"). Klein does not offer any new historical research to demonstrate that Herzl was unsatisfied with the original French title. Indeed, the only evidence Klein brings in support of changing the title is the famous theocracy section, in which Herzl compares the role of the rabbis in the state to that of the army. "There can be no doubt," concludes Klein. "It is definitely about a state of the Jews, not about a Jewish state."[81]

Since then, Klein's innovation has been picked up by an American publisher as well, and as of 1996, one can for the first time buy an English-language edition of Herzl's *Der Judenstaat*, under the newly invented title *The Jews' State*.[82]

This meddlesome re-touching of Zionist history may have been conducted out of pure motives. But in the end it serves only one purpose: It renders a not-insignificant service to the ongoing war to discredit the idea of the Jewish state. Obviously, those who wish to see the State of Israel change its course have every right to express their political preferences, and to work for a new non-Jewish Israel that will be more to their liking. But an honest appraisal of Herzl's ideas leaves little room to involve his name in this effort. Not only did the founder of political Zionism create this term, using it as the title of his book by that name. He also spent the last years of his life working to popularize this expression throughout the world. And this was not merely a semantic choice. For Herzl was also unequivocally committed to the establishment of an intrinsically Jewish state: One that would not only have a Jewish majority, but that would be Jewish in its purposes, government, and constitution, as well as in its relationship to the Jewish people and the Jewish faith. Indeed, when examined in the context of Herzl's writings and political activities, it becomes clear that the ideal of the Jewish state, as advocated by David Ben-Gurion and the mainstream of the Zionist movement, and as expressed in Israel's Declaration of Independence, is perfectly in keeping with Herzl's vision of a Jewish state.

NOTES

This article was written with the assistance of Evelyne Geurtz.

In the notes that follow, I have endeavored to refer the reader to English-language sources wherever these are available. In cases where the English translation was not adequate, I have supplied the foreign-language citation first, and the material available in English second.

1. The Israeli government felt no need to mark this, the decisive event on the road to Jewish national independence, nor did it bother to send a representative to the commemorative events in Basel (where Herzl's Zionist Congresses were held) which had been organized by the Swiss. The Canton of Basel and the University of Basel, on the other hand, were at the forefront of organizing several days of events with the participation of the Jewish Agency. *Maariv*, August 28, 1997. See also *Jerusalem Post*, August 26, 1997; Calev Ben-David, "Zionism, R.I.P.," *Jerusalem Post* Magazine, August 29, 1997; Israel Harel, "Prophet of Truth," *Haaretz*, August 29, 1997; Aharon Papo, "The Great Lost Opportunity," *Maariv*, September 11, 1997; Yoram Hazony, "*The Jewish State* at 100," *Azure* 2 (Spring 1997), pp. 17-46.

2. Shulamit Aloni in "Zionism Here and Now," a film produced by the Diaspora Museum, 1997. [Hebrew]

3. Moshe Zimmermann, "The Historians' Debate: The German Experiment and the Israeli Experience," *Theory and Criticism* 8 (Summer 1996), p. 102. [Hebrew]

4. Amos Oz, "A Loaded Wagon and an Empty Wagon? Thoughts on the Culture of Israel," *Yahadut Hofshit*, October 1997, p. 5. [Hebrew]

For other, similar arguments, see David Kretzmer, "A Jewish and Democratic State: Between Paradox and Harmony," *Ravgoni* 2 (July 1998), p. 22 [Hebrew]; David Vital, "A Prince of the Jews," *Times Literary Supplement*, June 7, 1996; David Vital, "Zionism as Revolution? Zionism as Rebellion?" *Modern Judaism*, October 1998, p. 206; comments by Ruth Gavison in Ron Margolin, ed., *The State of Israel as a Jewish and Democratic State* (Jerusalem: World Union of Jewish Studies, 1999), p. 46 [Hebrew]; Gideon Shimoni, *The Zionist Ideology* (Hanover: Brandeis, 1995), pp. 93-95; Michael Harsegor, "Has the Zionist Revolution Failed?" *Al Hamishmar*, December 4, 1987; Claude Klein's introduction to Theodor Herzl, *L'État des Juifs*, ed. Claude Klein (Paris: Editions de la Decouverte, 1990), pp. 10-11 [French]; Aviad Kleinberg, "A Nostalgic Glance into the Future," *Haaretz*, June 2, 1999.

In some cases, these authors attempt to describe Herzl's overall view of the state through a combined reading of Herzl's practical program in *The Jewish State* along with the society depicted in Herzl's utopian novel *Altneuland*. The assumption that one can read the two books as being of a piece is not, however, sustainable. Herzl's this-worldly "Jewish state" is radically different from the end-of-days vision of a "New Society" in *Altneuland*, which is not even a "state" in any sense in which we are familiar with the term.

5. In fact, the identity of the term "Jewish state" with Israel was so self-evident that the Declaration used the term as though it were the very definition of the new state: "We herewith declare the establishment of a *Jewish state* in the land of Israel, which is the State of Israel…. The People's Administration will constitute the provisional government of *the Jewish state*, which will be called by the name Israel." Similarly striking was the speech of Meir Wilner, representative of the Communist Party, at the assembly that ratified the text of the Declaration of Independence. As Wilner said: "All of us are united in our appreciation of this great day for the Jewish settlement and for the Jewish people—the day of the termination of the Mandate and the declaration of the independent *Jewish state*." Emphasis added. Third meeting of the People's Council, May 14, 1948, in Minutes of the People's Council, vol. 1, pp. 13-15. [Hebrew]

6. Emphasis added. In addition, the Declaration uses variations on the term "state of the Jewish people" (*medinato shel ha'am hayehudi*). Like the term "Jewish state," the concept of Israel as the "state of the Jewish people" is today

understood as representing the intrinsically Jewish character of the state, since it suggests a particularistic link with one specific people.

7. Yeshayahu Leibowitz, "At the End of Forty Years," *Politika*, Fall 1988. [Hebrew] See also Jacob Talmon, "Herzl's *The Jewish State* after Seventy Years," in *The Age of Violence* (Tel Aviv: Am Oved, 1974), pp. 143-184. [Hebrew]

8. Mordechai Bar-On, "Zionism into Its Second Century: A Stock-Taking," in Keith Kyle and Joel Peters, eds., *Whither Israel? The Domestic Challenges* (New York: Royal Institute of International Affairs and I.B. Tauris, 1993), p. 34. On Bar-On's reading, the "state of the Jews" does, however, include retaining the Law of Return, which is understood as related to maintaining a Jewish majority.

9. Amos Oz, "A Loaded Wagon," p. 5. For a more general discussion of the decay of the ideal of the "Jewish state" in Israeli culture, see Yoram Hazony, *The Jewish State: The Struggle for Israel's Soul* (New York: Basic Books, 2000).

10. Diary entry, January 19, 1896. Theodor Herzl, *The Complete Diaries of Theodor Herzl*, ed. Raphael Patai, trans. Harry Zohn (New York: Herzl Press, 1960), p. 286 (hereafter "Herzl diary").

11. Herzl diary, July 10 and 27, 1896, pp. 414, 443.

12. Later editions of the English version were changed to *The Jewish State* to match the specific form of the German and French.

13. The principal backers of Jewish settlement activity whom Herzl wished to attract were Baron Maurice de Hirsch and Baron Edmond de Rothschild, both of Paris. For the centrality of English Jews, see Theodor Herzl, *The Jewish State*, trans. Harry Zohn (New York: Herzl Press, 1970), p. 94.

14. Only in 1915, eleven years after Herzl's death, was the Yiddish title adjusted to match the German, and thus became *Der Yiddenstot*.

15. During Herzl's lifetime, there were also three other editions of the book: Russian, Romanian, and Bulgarian—*Yevreyskoye gosudarstvo* (Russian; 1896); *Statul evreilor* (Romanian; trans. Martin Spinner, 1896); *Evreyska drzhava* (Bulgarian; trans. Joshua Caleb and Karl Herbst, 1896). The Russian and Bulgarian translations are entitled "The Jewish State"; the Romanian title means "The State of the Jews."

16. See, for example, Herzl to Solomon Joseph Solomon, May 12, 1896; and Herzl to Wilhelm Gross, September 18, 1896, p. 139. Both in the new German-language edition of Herzl's letters and diaries. Theodor Herzl, *Briefe und Tagebuecher* [Letters and Diaries] (Berlin: Propylaeen, 1983-1996), vol. 4, pp. 103, 139.

17. Herzl diary, August 30, 1899, p. 869.

18. Herzl diary, August 30, 1899, p. 869.

19. Theodor Herzl, *The Jewish State*, trans. Michael Berkowicz (Warsaw: Tushia, 1896), p. 67. [Hebrew]

20. Ahad Ha'am, "The Jewish State and the Jewish Problem," in Ahad Ha'am, *Ten Essays on Zionism and Judaism*, trans. Leon Simon (London: Routledge, 1922), pp. 45-47.

21. Rubinstein, *The Zionist Dream Revisited*, pp. 8-10.

22. Yossi Beilin, *The Death of the American Uncle: Jews in the Twenty-First Century* (Tel Aviv: Yediot Aharonot, 1999), pp. 45-48. [Hebrew] Herzl explicitly says that he does not desire assimilation for the Jews because "our national character is too famous in history... and too noble to make its decline desirable." Herzl, *The Jewish State*, p. 48.

23. For similar presentations of Herzl, see Tom Segev, "The First Post-Zionist," in *Haaretz*, April 3, 1996; Rachel Elbaum-Dror interviewed in *Kol Ha'ir*, March 22, 1996.

24. Scholars who have studied Ahad Ha'am's attacks on Herzl carefully have found it difficult not to notice the effects of his political aims on his judgments of Herzl. See Steven J. Zipperstein, *Elusive Prophet: Ahad Ha'am and the Origins of Zionism* (Berkeley: University of California, 1993), pp. 128f; Yosef Goldstein, *Ahad Ha'am: A Biography* (Jerusalem: Keter, 1992), pp. 243f. [Hebrew]

25. Herzl diary, November 21, 1895, p. 276.

26. In Herzl's speech before the First Zionist Congress, he famously said that "Zionism is a return to Judaism even before there is a return to the Jewish land." Minutes of the First Zionist Congress in Basel, August 29-31, 1897 (Prague: Barissa, 1911). [German] Cf. Theodor Herzl, *Zionist Writings: Essays and Addresses*, trans. Harry Zohn (New York: Herzl Press, 1973), vol. 1, p. 133. The German word translated here as "Judaism" is *Judentum*, which can also be translated as "Jewishness." As is clear from my discussion below, Herzl would not likely have distinguished between the two terms.

27. Herzl diary, December 24, 1895, p. 285.

28. Herzl diary, June 10, 1895, p. 64.

29. Herzl, "The Menora," *Die Welt*, December 31, 1897. Cf. Herzl, *Zionist Writings*, vol. 1, p. 203.

30. Herzl, "Menora." Cf. Herzl, *Zionist Writings*, vol. 1, pp. 204-206.

31. Herzl to Chaim S. Schor, January 30, 1900. Herzl, *Briefe und Tagebuecher*, vol. 5, pp. 302-303.

32. Herzl diary, June 2, 1895, November 23, 1895, March 29, 1896, September 6, 1897, January 10, 1901, pp. 11, 278, 317, 588, 1040.

33. Theodor Herzl, "The Congress," *Die Welt*, August 26, 1898, translated in Herzl, *Zionist Writings*, vol. 2, p. 13; Herzl to the Zionists of America, July 5, 1901, in Herzl, *Briefe und Tagebuecher*, vol. 6, pp. 241-242.

34. Theodor Herzl, "For a Jewish State," *The Jewish Chronicle*, July 6, 1896, translated in Herzl, *Zionist Writings*, vol. 1, p. 38; address before the Second Zionist Congress, August 28, 1898, translated in Herzl, *Zionist Writings*, vol. 2, p. 19; address before the Fourth Zionist Congress, August 13, 1900, translated in Herzl, *Zionist Writings*, vol. 2, p. 153. Cf. Herzl's description of the return of the Jews to Palestine as a "holy moment." Herzl to the Zionists of America, July 5, 1901, in Herzl, *Briefe und Tagebuecher*, vol. 6, pp. 241-242. See also his treatment of the position of women in traditional Judaism, in an address before a Vienna women's group on January 12, 1901. Translated as "Women and Zionism," in Herzl, *Zionist Writings*, vol. 2, p. 160.

35. Michael Berkowicz, "Herzl and Hebrew," in Meyer Weisgal, ed., *Theodor Herzl: A Memorial* (New York: The New Palestine, 1929), p. 74; Shlomo Haramati, "Next Year in Hebrew," *Haaretz*, March 26, 1996.

36. Herzl, *Briefe und Tagebuecher*, vol. 2, p. 241. Cf. Herzl diary, August 18, 1895, p. 231. Herzl's diaries frequently refer to God, although it is clear that he is self-conscious about this. The first time that he speaks of the consequences of Zionism being "a gift of God," he immediately stops himself to explain: "When I say God, I don't mean to offend the freethinkers. As far as I am concerned, they can use World Spirit...." Herzl, *Briefe und Tagebuecher*, vol. 2, p. 124. Cf. Herzl diary, June 12, 1895, p. 96.

37. Herzl, *Briefe und Tagebuecher*, vol. 2, pp. 128-129. Cf. Herzl diary, June 14, 1895, p. 101. See also June 15, 1895, pp. 165, 183. On the other hand, in his political activities, he emphasized that he was not "a religious man," but a "freethinker." See Herzl to Guedemann, July 21, 1895, p. 205; Herzl diary, November 26, 1895, p. 283.

38. Herzl, "Menora." Cf. Herzl, *Zionist Writings*, vol. 1, p. 204.

39. Theodor Herzl, "Judaism," *Oesterreichische Wochenschrift*, November 13, 1896. Cf. Herzl, *Zionist Writings*, vol. 1, pp. 57-58.

40. Emphasis added. Herzl to unknown, June 9, 1903. Herzl, *Briefe und Tagebuecher*, vol. 7, pp. 148-149. Similarly, see Herzl's statement before the British Royal Commission on Alien Immigration, July 7, 1902, in which he testified, regarding the Jews of the proposed Jewish national territory, that, "I am convinced they would develop a distinct Jewish cult[ure]—national characteristics and national aspirations...." Reprinted in *Zionist Writings*, vol. 2, p. 186.

41. Herzl, *The Jewish State*, p. 88.

42. Herzl, *The Jewish State*, pp. 87-88. See also Herzl diary, June 15, 1895, p. 155. In a letter, Herzl explains that he decided not to elaborate on this point

in *The Jewish State* after a rabbi had told him that further discussion might give offense to the pious. See Herzl to Ahron Marcus, May 8, 1896. *Briefe und Tagebuecher*, vol. 7, pp. 607-608.

43. Herzl diary, October 31, 1898, p. 747.

44. Herzl, *The Jewish State*, pp. 91f; Theodor Herzl, "A Solution of the Jewish Question," in *The Jewish Chronicle*, January 17, 1896. See also Herzl diary, June 7 and 11, 1895, pp. 41, 80.

45. Herzl, *The Jewish State*, p. 51. The flag of the Society of Jews would likewise become the flag of the new state. Herzl diary, June 12, 1895, p. 91.

46. Theodor Herzl, *Der Judenstaat* (Vienna: Breitenstein, 1896), pp. 69-71. Cf. Herzl, *The Jewish State*, pp. 94-95.

47. In retrospect, we know that Herzl's instincts were right; the imposition of immigration restrictions by England marked the beginning of a general policy shift in the West that was to culminate in the failure to provide a haven for Jews during the Holocaust.

48. See Herzl's opening statement before the Royal Commission on Alien Immigration, July 7, 1902. Reprinted in *Zionist Writings*, vol. 2, p. 186.

49. See Oskar K. Rabinowicz, "New Light on the East Africa Scheme," in Israel Cohen, ed., *The Rebirth of Israel: A Memorial Tribute to Paul Goodman* (London: Goldstein and Sons, 1952), pp. 81-91. Almost all of the Jewish provisions in the draft charter submitted to the British government on July 13 had been included in draft charters that Herzl and his colleagues had been working on for months. See, for example, Greenberg's draft charter for a Jewish settlement in Sinai, dated February 10, 1903. Central Zionist Archives, H/842. Cf. Herzl diary, April 2, 1903, p. 1460.

50. Herzl to Nordau, July 13, 1903. Herzl, *Briefe und Tagebuecher*, vol. 7, p. 208.

51. Sir Clement Hill to Leopold Greenberg, August 14, 1903. Michael Heymann, ed., *The Uganda Controversy* (Jerusalem: Hasifria Hatzionit, 1997), vol. 2, p. 124. [Hebrew]

52. Herzl, *Der Judenstaat*, p. 75. Cf. Herzl, *The Jewish State*, p. 100.

53. See Herzl diary, June 15, 1895, p. 104.

54. Herzl, *The Jewish State*, p. 49.

55. Herzl diary, June 9, 1895, p. 56.

56. "If I should live so long…," Herzl wrote, "I would like to begin work on this spiritual regeneration…." Herzl to Carl Friedrich Heman, October 11, 1899. Herzl, *Briefe und Tagebuecher*, vol. 5, pp. 226-227. See also Herzl to Emil Eisner, September 25, 1900, in Herzl, *Briefe und Tagebuecher*, vol. 6, p. 46.

57. Herzl diary, March 26, 1898, pp. 623-624. Herzl also mentions a "neo-Jewish" style in theater. See entry of April 25, 1897, p. 538.

58. Herzl diary, June 8, 1895 and July 10, 1898, pp. 45, 645.

59. Herzl diary, June 11 and 14, 1895, pp. 72, 149.

60. Emphasis added. Herzl, *Briefe und Tagebuecher*, vol. 2, p. 135. Cf. Herzl diary, June 16, 1895, p. 109.

61. Minutes of the Second Zionist Congress in Basel, August 28-31, 1898 (Vienna: Industrie, 1898), p. 239. [German]

62. Herzl, *The Jewish State*, p. 100; Herzl diary, June 15, 1895, p. 171. Similarly: "Make your state in such a way that the stranger will feel comfortable among you." Herzl diary, August 26, 1899, p. 856.

63. See, for example, Herzl diary, August 10, 1895, pp. 227-228.

64. Herzl diary, June 8, 1895, p. 44. See also Herzl diary, June 6, 7, 9, 13, and 15, 1895, pp. 35, 38, 55, 135, 160.

65. Herzl diary, June 7, 1895, p. 36.

66. Max I. Bodenheimer, *Prelude to Israel*, trans. Israel Cohen (New York: Thomas Yoseloff, 1963), p. 140.

67. As he told the assembled delegates at the Zionist Congress: "Our Congress must live forever, not only until we are redeemed from our age-old sufferings, but even more so afterwards." Speech before the First Zionist Congress, August 29, 1897, p. 19. Minutes of the First Zionist Congress, p. 19. Cf. Herzl, *Zionist Writings*, vol. 1, p. 138.

68. Herzl, *Briefe und Tagebuecher*, vol. 2, p. 135. Cf. Herzl diary, June 16, 1895, p. 109.

69. Herzl diary, June 15, 1895, p. 104.

70. Herzl, *The Jewish State*, p. 81; Herzl diary, June 14, 1895, p. 151; Herzl to the Theological Society of the Students of the Israelite Theological Educational Establishment of Vienna, December 7, 1901, in Herzl, *Briefe und Tagebuecher*, vol. 6, p. 379.

71. Herzl, *The Jewish State*, p. 81; Herzl diary, June 14, 1895, p. 151.

72. Herzl, *The Jewish State*, p. 71.

73. Herzl diary, June 15, 1895, p. 103.

74. Herzl, *The Jewish State*, p. 39.

75. Herzl diary, June 6 and 15, 1895, pp. 34, 37, 171.

76. Herzl, *The Jewish State*, p. 59.

77. Herzl, "A 'Solution of the Jewish Question,'" in *The Jewish Chronicle*, January 17, 1896, in *Zionist Writings*, vol. 1, p. 27; Theodor Herzl, "Zionism," in *Zionist Writings*, vol. 2, p. 116. The article was originally written for publication in *North American Review*, but was never published. It was then published in Leon Kellner's German edition of Herzl's writings in 1934. Leon Kellner, *Theodor Herzl: Gesammelte Zionistische Werke* (Tel Aviv: Hotza'a Ivrit, 1934). [German]

78. Ernst Pawel, *The Labyrinth of Exile: A Life of Theodor Herzl* (London: Collins Harvill, 1989), p. 361.

79. Speech before the Third Zionist Congress, August 15, 1899. Minutes of the Third Zionist Congress in Basel, August 15-18, 1899 (Vienna: Eretz Israel Organization, 1899), p. 8. [German] Cf. Herzl, *Zionist Writings*, vol. 2, p. 107. For a discussion of Herzl's alliance with religious Jewry, see Ehud Luz, *Parallels Meet: Religion and Nationalism in the Early Zionist Movement (1882-1904)* (Philadelphia: The Jewish Publication Society, 1988), pp. 141-142; Michael Berkowitz, *Zionist Culture and West European Jewry Before the First World War* (Chapel Hill: University of North Carolina, 1996), p. 15.

80. Joseph Adler, "Religion and Herzl: Fact and Fable," in *Herzl Year Book* 4 (New York: Herzl Press, 1961-1962), pp. 298-300; Pawel, *Labyrinth*, p. 453.

81. Herzl, *L'État des Juifs*, pp. 10-11.

82. Theodor Herzl, *The Jews' State*, ed. Henk Overberg (Northvale, N.J.: Jason Aronson, 1997).

ORDE WINGATE:
FATHER OF THE IDF

MICHAEL B. OREN

WHILE CONDUCTING RESEARCH in Washington recently, I took a break and looked up an old friend. A cab brought me to his "neighborhood"—the Arlington National Cemetery—where the information center provided me with his exact address: Section 12, grave number 288. This was the final resting place of Maj.-Gen. Orde Wingate, a British officer widely regarded as the father of modern guerilla warfare. A brilliant tactician and a daring innovator, Wingate was credited by many with turning the tide against Axis forces in Ethiopia and Burma during World War II. Winston Churchill hailed him as "a man of genius who might well have become also a man of destiny."[1] Yet Wingate had his share of detractors, as well; if some admired him as a hero and a visionary, others denigrated him as an egotist, an eccentric, even a madman.

On one point all his observers agree: Wingate was a Zionist. An implacable advocate for Jewish statehood in the late 1930s, when the British had all but abandoned their promise to create a homeland for the Jews, he formed and led the Special Night Squads (SNS), a Jewish fighting force that saved dozens of settlements from destruction during the Arab Revolt (1936-1939) and trained military leaders such as Yigal Allon and Moshe Dayan, who would later form the core of the Israel

Defense Forces. Wingate dreamed of one day commanding the first Jewish army in two thousand years, and of leading the fight to establish an independent Jewish state in the land of Israel.

A vivid literature has grown up around Wingate. The earliest books about him were penned by war correspondents and comrades-in-arms, mostly those who served with him during the campaigns in Burma and Ethiopia. Slender works by Charles Rolo, Bernard Fergusson, Wilfred Burchett, Leonard Mosley, and many others told of Wingate's dash and endurance, his coolness under fire, and his unflagging leadership.[2] But for every favorable account of Wingate, another emerged assailing him. Particularly censorious were Britain's official military historians, I.S.O. Playfair and Woodburn Kirby.[3] Though bound by tradition to be dispassionate and fair, these writers went out of their way to denounce Wingate as solipsistic, unstable, and impudent.

So contrasting were these portraits that additional works were later written—most notably Peter Mead's *Orde Wingate and the Historians* and David Rooney's *Wingate and the Chindits*—to reconcile them. A more nuanced Wingate also emerged from a number of biographies, which went beyond specific military campaigns to cover his entire life. *Orde Wingate* by Christopher Sykes highlighted the pivotal place that Zionism held in Wingate's thinking. Exhaustive in its details, scrupulously balanced, the book remained ambivalent about its subject, much as Sykes was about Zionism in general. Wingate becomes more categorical and sympathetic in Trevor Royle's biography, *Orde Wingate: Irregular Soldier*, published in 1995. Though Royle provides few additional facts beyond those put forth by Sykes, by adopting a less academic tone he makes Wingate more accessible.[4]

These biographies continued what was essentially an internal British debate. In Israel, on the other hand, history books and school texts have always lauded Wingate as a heroic, larger-than-life figure to whom the Jewish people owed a deep and enduring debt. Israel Carmi, who had fought under Wingate in the SNS, portrayed his contribution to the Zionist effort in glowing terms in a memoir, *In the Path of Fighters*, while Avraham Akavia, another SNS veteran, sympathetically depicted his commander's full career in *Orde Wingate: His Life and Works*.[5]

In recent years, however, as the heroes of the Zionist movement have been increasingly criticized by Israel's "new historians," the figure of Wingate has come under fire in the Jewish state. Taking the lead has been the journalist-historian and best-selling author Tom Segev. In March 1999, in reviewing Yigal Eyal's *The First Intifada*, a study of the Arab Revolt, Segev described Wingate as "quite mad, and perhaps a sadist, too," and reproved Eyal for "turn[ing] a blind eye to the war crimes committed by Orde Wingate and his men."[6] In his own book published a few months later, *Days of the Anemones: Palestine During the Mandatory Period*, Segev portrays Wingate as delusional and homicidal, "a madman" who "employed terror against terror." Though he does cite praise for Wingate from David Ben-Gurion, Chaim Weizmann, and Moshe Sharett, Segev refuses to grant him any redeeming qualities, even as a military commander.[7]

One might have expected the wholesale disparagement of a man who had until now been universally revered by Israelis to spark a wave of criticism. Instead, Segev's revisionist view has hardly been noticed by the Israeli press. One prominent exception was Gideon Levy, a columnist for the daily *Haaretz*, who wrote an article in July 1999 praising Segev's exposure of Wingate as "an oddball with sadistic tendencies" and a "villain" who "tortured Arabs." Segev has performed an invaluable service by exposing "the dark sides" of the Wingate myth, Levy wrote, and called for the inclusion of those "dark sides" in the public school curriculum.[8] So successful was Segev in re-casting Wingate's image that a month later, in reviewing a new biography of Israel's first Sephardi chief rabbi for *Haaretz*, Yehiam Padan noted regretfully that Wingate "was, until this year, considered a friend of Israel."[9] Though calls to change the way Israelis are taught about Wingate have not yet been heeded—most textbooks continue to portray him glowingly—the Education Ministry's recently published history text, *A World of Changes* (1999), is the first government-sponsored textbook covering this period to ignore Wingate's contributions to Zionism entirely.[10]

It is significant, then, that just as Wingate has come under fire in Israel, a new biography by British authors has appeared casting him in a positive light. *Fire in the Night: Wingate of Burma, Ethiopia, and Zion*, by John Bierman and Colin Smith, is the most comprehensive biography to date. Here, Wingate appears in his full complexity, his pugnaciousness and peculiarities, his brilliance and courage. It is a book that must be read by anyone who wishes to understand this influential Zionist figure.

Journalists stationed in Cyprus, Bierman and Smith have extensive experience covering the Middle East, and show no particular affection for Israel. On the contrary, their text bristles with barbs against the

Jewish state ("not quite the 'light unto nations'" that Wingate intended) and its army (a tool of "territorial expansion," demolishing Arab houses "*con brio* on the occupied West Bank and Gaza Strip").[11] But despite their feelings for Israel, and despite their failure to consult the wealth of Hebrew-language sources about Wingate—surely the book's greatest flaw—*Fire in the Night* captures the nature of Wingate's Zionism, and the impact it had on his actions in Palestine. Wingate, the authors realize, saw Jewish independence in the land of Israel as more than just a historical imperative. It was the driving force of his life.

Charles Orde Wingate was born in 1903, one of seven children in a strict Protestant family. "On Sundays," write Bierman and Smith, "the entire family dressed in black, attended... prayer meetings... in the morning, and devoted the rest of the day to Bible studies and other 'improving' pastimes."[12] Both his father and grandfather were army officers who became missionaries, and were devoted, among other pursuits, to converting the Jews. Though often poor, the Wingates came from distinguished Norman and Scottish stock, and among Orde's prominent cousins were Sir Reginald Wingate, the governor of Sudan, and T.E. Lawrence, who gained fame for his exploits in Arabia during World War I.

As a student, Wingate proved to be unexceptional, disinterested in sports, and socially inept. Though often discouraged and depressed, Wingate harbored a strong sense of his own destiny, a conviction that he was fated to do great things, lead armies, liberate nations. After graduating from military academy in 1923, he mastered Arabic at London's School of Oriental Studies and secured a post with the Sudan Defense Force. Fighting bandits, he developed the hit-and-run and night-fighting tactics he would later use, to such devastating effect, in much larger battles. "A most successful expedition conducted with great dash and judgment," the force's commander commented on one long-range patrol which Wingate commanded.[13] Yet Wingate also experienced prolonged bouts of depression—"nervous attacks," he called them, which he was able to endure only by ceaseless repetition of the phrase "God is good"—and began exhibiting some of the eccentricity that later became his trademark: Eating raw onions, steeping tea through his socks, greeting guests in the nude.

In the Sudan in 1933 Wingate became fascinated, as were many explorers at the time, by the prospects of finding the mythic oasis of

Zerzura. Planning an expedition to locate it, he corresponded with Count Laudislaus Almasy, the renowned Hungarian archaeologist who would later serve as the model for *The English Patient*. Though Wingate never found Zerzura, he conducted pioneering cartographic research that was hailed by the Royal Geographic Society. En route to present his findings in London, he met a beautiful, independent-minded, and outspoken young woman, Lorna Patterson, whom he married soon afterward.

In September 1936, Wingate was assigned to an intelligence post with the British Mandatory forces in Palestine, and given the rank of captain. Previously, he had had no close relations with Jews and no direct knowledge of Zionism. This would change radically, as would the course of his life, over the following weeks. Though his linguistic training and military experience predisposed him to accept the pro-Arab views of most British officials, Wingate began to read intensively about the history of Palestine and the *Yishuv* (the pre-state Jewish community) and emerged a committed Zionist. He visited Jewish settlements around the country, taught himself Hebrew, and earned the trust and friendship of Zionist leaders Chaim Weizmann and Moshe Sharett. Critiquing British policy in Palestine in a letter to his cousin Reginald, Wingate wrote:

> The Jews are loyal to the empire. The Jews are men of their word—they have always been so—in fact it is the gentile's main complaint against them. There are fifteen million Jews in the world. Palestine will take over a million within seven years. You can have no idea of what they have already done here. You would be amazed to see the desert blossom like a rose; intensive horticulture everywhere—such energy, faith, ability, and inventiveness as the world has not seen. I have seen the young Jews in the *kvutzot* [kibbutzim]. I tell you that the Jews will provide soldiery better than ours. We have only to train it. They will equip it.[14]

Wingate urged Britain to "advance the foundation of an autonomous Jewish community with all the means in its power," adding portentously: "For pity's sake, let us do something just and honorable before it [world war] comes. Let us redeem our promises to Jewry and shame the devil of Nazism, Fascism, and our own prejudices."[15]

Wingate was eager to dedicate his talents to this cause, and he did not have far to look. The grand mufti of Jerusalem had recently launched a coordinated military and economic rebellion aimed at ousting the British from Palestine and bringing the Zionist enterprise to an end. This insurrection was then at its apogee, with Jewish settlements cut off and thrown on the defensive. Wingate proposed to create units of swift-moving, hard-hitting commandos who would take the initiative and strike Arab guerillas in the villages that hosted them. The notion of arming Jews against the Arabs appalled the British authorities, but Wingate outflanked them, taking his plan to the commander of Britain's Middle East forces, Gen. Archibald Wavell, who would remain his mentor throughout the campaigns of Palestine, Ethiopia, and Burma.

With Wavell's approval, Wingate set up the Special Night Squads, a mixed force of British officers and Jewish supernumeraries. Headquartered at Kibbutz Ein Harod in the Jezreel Valley, close to the spring where the biblical Gideon—Wingate's hero—had his camp, the SNS succeeded in all but ending Arab attacks in the north. An entire generation of future IDF commanders would learn their tactics from Wingate, adopt his disregard for rank and protocol, and accept his demand that officers set an example by leading their men into battle—the origin of the legendary IDF battle cry *aharai* ("after me"). "You are the first soldiers of the Jewish army," he would remind his men before embarking on a mission, and he would declaim to them passages from the Bible describing the country they would pass through and prophesying their victory.[16] For them, Wingate was never Orde, or even "commander," but simply *hayedid*—the friend.

Wingate's comrades and subordinates, Christians and Jews alike, would remember him as a man of unlimited stamina, with an uncanny sense of direction and a total absence of fear. "A most extraordinary man," said Lt. Rex King-Clark. Capt. John Hackett painted him as a "puritanical, fire-eating, dedicated, Round Head–type Cromwellian soldier with a Bible in one hand and an alarm clock in the other." "We were amazed," recalled SNS veteran Tzvi Brenner, describing his first patrol with Wingate. "Only he was capable of leading us in such territory and with such confidence."[17] In a skirmish at Dabburiya in July 1938, Wingate was struck by a number of bullets early on and was bleeding profusely, but continued to give orders until his men had won the battle—an act of heroism for which the British army awarded him one of its highest honors, the Distinguished Service Order.

But there was also a less heroic side to Wingate: An irascible, moody, mercurial side. He was known to strike soldiers who disappointed him, and to employ collective punishment against Arab villagers suspected of aiding guerillas. Bierman and Smith describe how, after learning of the murder of his close friend, Ein Harod leader Haim Sturmann ("A great Jew," Wingate eulogized him, "a friend of the Arabs, who was killed by the Arabs"[18]), the commander of the SNS led his men in a rampage in the Arab section of Beit Shean, the rebels' suspected base. During the raid, Wingate's forces damaged property and wounded several people—a number of them mortally, according to some accounts.[19]

For the British army, though, it was not Wingate's excesses that proved insufferable but his advocacy of, and success with, the Jews. Thus, when Wingate requested home leave to London a few weeks after he was wounded at Dabburiya (and in the wake of narrowly escaping assassination at the hands of Arab assailants), his superiors were only too happy to comply. It was October 1938, the time of the Munich Conference and Britain's sellout of Czechoslovakia, and of the beginning of Britain's final retreat from the promises of the Balfour Declaration. Wingate took advantage of his time in London to lobby tirelessly for the Zionist cause. He urged the Zionist leadership to present Britain with an ultimatum—either honor its pledges or forfeit the Jews' loyalty—and argued the Zionist case in the press and before Colonial Secretary Malcolm MacDonald. Returning to Palestine in December, he found himself barred from further contact with the SNS, which was disbanded soon thereafter, and transferred back to Britain.

In May 1939, the notorious White Paper was issued, imposing crippling restrictions on Jewish immigration and land purchases in Palestine. Wingate, however, remained undeterred. With the outbreak of World War II, he campaigned for the immediate creation of a Jewish state in Palestine and a Jewish army, which he saw as "a necessity of the moral strategy of this war... for human justice and freedom."[20] He nearly fell out with the Zionist leadership, which he found insufficiently aggressive in pressing these demands. Further friction was averted when Wavell ordered Wingate to Ethiopia, there to apply his guerilla tactics to defeating the Italian fascists.

Wingate's efforts in Ethiopia were crowned with success. With a meager assemblage of British officers and mountain tribesmen—Gideon Force, he called it—Wingate, now a lieutenant colonel, succeeded in tricking an enemy column fourteen thousand strong into surrendering, and then rode a white horse into newly liberated Addis Ababa.

Willing though he was to die for it, Ethiopia was for Wingate merely a means of returning to Palestine with a higher rank and greater influence in the army. Throughout the campaign, he insisted on keeping an SNS veteran, Avraham Akavia, as his aide-de-camp, and on using doctors from Jewish Palestine to treat his wounded. On Passover, Wingate held a field Seder for his Jewish troops, delivering what Akavia called "a moving Zionist speech."[21]

As in Palestine, Wingate alienated his superiors in Ethiopia with his arrogance, his disdain for hierarchy, and his support for the country's independence from all empires, whether Italian or British. "To give the black races of Africa a chance to realize a free civilization," he wrote at the height of the battles there, "is a worthy cause for which to die and more worthy than a mere defense of one's own midden."[22] And while Wingate was again commended for bravery for his efforts in Ethiopia, the army leadership never forgave him for his insolence and his support for native independence. Posted to Cairo to await re-assignment, Wingate languished there for months while the battle for North Africa raged. Idle, depressed, and suffering from severe malaria, he took a knife to his own throat one night in July 1941. He survived the attempt, and during his long and painful convalescence, shunned by fellow officers, he received a long line of visitors from Palestine, including David Ben-Gurion.

Wingate's saga might have ended there had Wavell not again intervened. Now commander of the Far East Theater, the general accepted Wingate's plan for a "long-range penetration unit" to work behind enemy lines in Burma. The Japanese, whom the British believed to be invincible in the jungle, were at the time poised to invade India. Wingate's raiders—"Chindits," he later called them, after the mythic Burmese lion—were something of a last hope. Though the army continued to resist his efforts, Wingate managed to construct his force and, in January 1943, march it across the Chinese Himalayas into Burma.

The fighting was brutal. A third of Wingate's men were lost, and most of the remainder rendered unfit for service. Yet the Chindits succeeded in thwarting Japan's invasion plans, and in shattering the myth of Japanese supremacy. Wingate returned to find himself a celebrity and a favorite of Prime Minister Churchill, who took him and Lorna to meet

President Roosevelt at the Allied summit in Quebec. There, before the leaders of the free world, he presented his plan for using light, mobile forces to defeat the Japanese in Burma, and it was accepted. After years of vilification by his superiors in the army, Wingate was at last vindicated. But for him, the impact of his success was to be measured not in Burma but in Palestine. His dream remained to return to "Eretz Israel," as he referred to it, and to farm the soil until called upon to lead the Jewish army to victory and independence. In one of his last letters to Lorna, who was no less ardent a Zionist, Wingate wrote a transliteration of the Hebrew verse "If I forget thee, Jerusalem, let my right hand lose its strength," adding his prayer that "our lot takes us there together, to the place and the work we love."[23]

By early 1944, Wingate, now a major general, commanded a Chindit force four times as large as the first. He led his men back into Burma, but on March 24, while flying to a forward position, the Mitchell bomber carrying him crashed in the jungle. No identifiable remains of Wingate were ever found, save for his trademark pith helmet. Charges of foul play were later raised and never conclusively settled. Since five out of the nine men aboard the Mitchell bomber were Americans, their common remains—several pounds of bones—were interred at Arlington National Cemetery, far from the places in which Wingate was revered as a hero.

Orde Wingate, who had just turned forty-one when he was killed, never saw his son Jonathan who was born two months later, nor did he see the birth of the Jewish state he so longed for. That state would memorialize him, though, in the Wingate sports village near Netanya and the Yemin Orde immigrants' school near Haifa, and in the names of dozens of streets and squares throughout the country.

The Wingate of *Fire in the Night* is an astounding, quirky, and poignantly human figure, who stands in utter contrast to the cold and one-dimensional killer depicted by Tom Segev in *Days of the Anemones*. It is tempting to explain the difference on the grounds that Segev had access to material from Hebrew-speaking soldiers and politicians who presumably observed Wingate's defects up close. Yet the Hebrew sources are overwhelmingly flattering to Wingate. The answer lies, rather, in the perspective that Segev brought to his writing, and in the way he used these sources.

For example, one of Segev's principal aims is to demonstrate that opposition to Wingate came not only from British higher-ups, but also from the Jewish leadership in Palestine. To this end, he quotes a senior *Yishuv* leader, Moshe Shertok (later Sharett), telling the Jewish Agency Executive that Wingate's SNS efforts had encountered "serious obstacles from some of our best people," who claimed that operations of this sort "are not appropriate for us." Segev then paraphrases Shertok, writing: "They feared that it would spoil forever any chance of coexistence with the Arabs."[24] But what Shertok really said was:

> They [the operations] will invariably spoil relations with the neighboring Arab villages. These operations, they believe, can only be carried out by an army, and not by our settlements. The reason is that in many cases these operations do not receive the necessary support, not in their initial pioneering phases and not even later, when the operations are approved by the authorities.[25]

In other words, the reason "some of our best people" opposed the SNS was not, as Segev claims, because they threatened Arab-Jewish harmony, but because the British were unwilling to back up the operations with sufficient firepower, leaving the settlements exposed. The problem was not that the SNS were too strong, but that they were not strong enough. Segev also chooses to omit Shertok's call, made in the same speech, for "expanding the range of operation and enhancing the offensive element in our defense power," as well as his depiction of Wingate as "that officer so committed to us in heart and soul."[26]

Similarly, Segev claims that Wingate's Jewish soldiers in the SNS accused him of being insane: "Behind his back, they said he was crazy," Segev writes.[27] A footnote to that assertion leads the reader to the testimony in the Central Zionist Archives of Haim Levkov, a member of the SNS who reported that another SNS fighter, Israel Carmi, had on one occasion referred to Wingate as "crazy" after an argument.[28] As it turns out, "they" did not call Wingate crazy behind his back. Only a single man did so, once, and that man, Israel Carmi, later became one of Wingate's most devoted followers, even writing a book filled with praise for his former commander.

Indeed, an inspection of the sources on which Segev draws to show that Wingate's men disapproved of their commander reveals repeated expressions of admiration for Wingate from those who served under him.

Thus, Segev quotes from Zion Cohen's *From Teheran and Back* to but-
tress his allegations about Wingate's cruelty,[29] but he sidesteps Cohen's
praise of Wingate as "a great and loyal friend of the Jewish people and
of the Jewish *Yishuv*... [who] laid the foundations of the Israel Defense
Forces...."[30] Nor is Segev interested in Haim Levkov's testimony when he
speaks in admiration of Wingate: "Everything about his demeanor—his
ability to advance without scouts, without fear—instilled in me a sense
of confidence, that we were marching with a man who knew what lay
ahead."[31] Segev cites the testimony of another SNS member, identified
only as "Efraim," to show that Wingate occasionally concocted harebrained
battle plans that he never carried out,[32] yet ignored Efraim's observations
about Wingate when they were positive, including the following:

> It is difficult to gauge the impact of his [i.e., Wingate's] deeds and op-
> erations for the sake of our security, for the benefits he brought to our
> enterprise were great in such a short life. There is no real expression
> that can convey our feelings and respect for the man and his actions.
> All we can say, in our humble way, is that his example and his faith
> will stand before us forever, and that by their light we will continue
> to build and defend this land.[33]

Segev likewise goes to extreme lengths to prove that Wingate was ruthless
and cruel. One passage has Wingate storming into the Arab village of
Danna, ordering the adult males to strip, and then whipping them. "It
was a horrifying sight," recalls an SNS veteran in a testimony cited by
Segev and filed in the Central Zionist Archives.[34] Yet a look at the file
reveals that the SNS veteran never attributes these actions to Wingate,
but rather to an unnamed "British officer." He describes the cold and
rainy conditions in Danna that day, which would hardly accord with the
two operations Wingate did conduct in the village, both in the summer.
Finally, the testimony places the whipping incident at a time after October
1938, when Wingate was no longer in command of the SNS.[35]

This is not to say that Wingate was incapable of committing excesses.
The Arab Revolt was a particularly brutal conflict in which it was rarely
possible to distinguish combatants from civilians, and atrocities were
commonplace on both sides. Indeed, one of the rampages Segev attributes to Wingate occurred immediately after the slaughter of nineteen
Jews in Tiberias, eleven of whom were children burned to death in their
beds. Moreover, as depicted in *Fire in the Night*, Wingate himself was

continually tormented by the moral implications of his military actions, and sought to prevent innocent people from being harmed whenever possible. "Wingate had always stressed that the squads must not mistreat Arab prisoners or civilians," Bierman and Smith write, even if he "did not always practice what he preached."[36] The authors quote Tzvi Brenner, who worked closely under Wingate in the SNS, as observing:

> The problem of punishment and… the morality of battle was something which concerned Wingate greatly. On the one hand, he demanded that the innocent not be harmed. On the other hand, he knew that he faced a dilemma: Can one observe this rule in battle against gangs which receive assistance from the residents of the villages?[37]

This, of course, has been a central moral question facing military officers around the world, including in Israel, from Wingate's time until today: How is one to fight an enemy bent on blurring the lines between the military and civilian, and using that ambiguity to its advantage? To dismiss all operations on what appear to be "civilian" targets as morally indefensible, as Segev appears to do, is as unfair as it is simplistic in the context of a vicious guerilla war such as the one in which Wingate was engaged.

Yet even if one grants that Wingate's behavior occasionally crossed the line of what was morally appropriate, there is still something misguided about placing these errors, as Segev and others do, at the heart of an overall assessment of the man's life and work. A clear example is a letter to the editor written by Tel Aviv University historian and geographer Dan Yahav, in reaction to a balanced and judicious review of *Fire in the Night* in February of this year by Benny Landau of *Haaretz*.[38] Yahav accused Landau of underemphasizing Wingate's negative features, and denounced Wingate as a man who "viewed reality through the sight of a gun," who "dealt in collective punishments, in harming innocent people, in looting, in arbitrary killing… and in unrestrained degradation."[39]

Such critics of Wingate ignore the fact that the British commander devoted himself to bringing independence to the Jews at a time when the use of force was an indispensable part of achieving this goal—and when virtually no one else was willing or able to give Palestinian Jewry the assistance they needed to achieve it. It is not as if there were dozens of brilliant British military men who, after the rise of Hitler, extended a hand to the Jews to help them. In fact, there was only one.

Viewed in this context, it is clear that Wingate's contribution to the cause of the Jewish state was decisive and enduring. Indeed, in spite of the criticism now being leveled against him, supporters of Zionism the world over continue to view Wingate much as he is portrayed in *Fire in the Night*: A complex figure, but one deserving of respect and gratitude.

That esteem was evident during my visit to the Arlington National Cemetery. Locating a particular grave among the endless and indistinguishable rows can prove daunting, but I was able to find Wingate's easily. His tomb, alone, was adorned with a number of the small stones that Jews traditionally leave after visiting a gravesite. And under one of those stones, I found a handwritten note. Crumpled, washed out by rain, only a single word of it was still legible. *Layedid*, it said in Hebrew. *To the Friend.*

NOTES

1. John Bierman and Colin Smith, *Fire in the Night: Wingate of Burma, Ethiopia, and Zion* (New York: Random House, 1999).

2. Charles Rolo, *Wingate's Raiders* (London: Harrap, 1944); Bernard Fergusson, *Beyond the Chindwin* (London: Collins, 1945); Bernard Fergusson, *The Wild Green Earth* (London: Collins, 1946); Wilfred G. Burchett, *Wingate's Phantom Army* (Bombay: Thacker, 1944); Leonard Mosley, *Gideon Goes to War* (London: Barker, 1955).

3. I.S.O. Playfair, ed., *The Mediterranean and the Middle East* (London: H.M. Stationery Office, 1954), vol. i; S. Woodburn Kirby, ed., *The War Against Japan* (London: H.M. Stationery Office, 1957).

4. Peter Mead, *Orde Wingate and the Historians* (Braunton: Merlin, 1987); David Rooney, *Wingate and the Chindits: Redressing the Balance* (London: Arms and Armour, 1994); Christopher Sykes, *Orde Wingate* (London: Collins, 1959); Trevor Royle, *Orde Wingate: Irregular Soldier* (London: Weidenfeld and Nicolson, 1995).

5. Israel Carmi, *In the Path of Fighters* (Tel Aviv: Ministry of Defense, 1960) [Hebrew]; Avraham Akavia, *Orde Wingate: His Life and Works* (Tel Aviv: Ministry of Defense, 1993). [Hebrew]

6. Tom Segev, "When the High Commissioner Had a Toothache," *Haaretz*, March 13, 1999.

7. Tom Segev, *Days of the Anemones: Palestine During the Mandatory Period* (Jerusalem: Keter, 1999), pp. 348-349, 387. [Hebrew]

8. Gideon Levy, "When Will They Teach It in School?" *Haaretz*, June 27, 1999.

9. Yehiam Padan, "The Rabbi, the Grandson, and the Angel," *Haaretz*, August 18, 1999.

10. *A World of Changes* (Jerusalem: Ministry of Education, Culture, and Sport and Ma'alot Publishers, 1999). [Hebrew]

11. Bierman and Smith, *Fire in the Night*, pp. 379, 388, 76.

12. Bierman and Smith, *Fire in the Night*, p. 11.

13. Bierman and Smith, *Fire in the Night*, p. 41.

14. Royle, *Irregular Soldier*, p. 105.

15. Bierman and Smith, *Fire in the Night*, p. 66.

16. Bierman and Smith, *Fire in the Night*, p. 113.

17. Bierman and Smith, *Fire in the Night*, pp. 102, 109, 93.

18. Bierman and Smith, *Fire in the Night*, p. 115.

19. Bierman and Smith, *Fire in the Night*, pp. 115-116.

20. Bierman and Smith, *Fire in the Night*, p. 138.

21. Bierman and Smith, *Fire in the Night*, p. 208.

22. Bierman and Smith, *Fire in the Night*, p. 190.

23. Akavia, *Wingate*, p. 240.

24. Segev, *Days of the Anemones*, p. 350.

25. Moshe Sharett, *Political Diary: 1938* (Tel Aviv: Am Oved, 1972), vol. iii, p. 202. [Hebrew]

26. Sharett, *Political Diary*, p. 202.

27. Segev, *Days of the Anemones*, p. 348.

28. Central Zionist Archives (hereafter "CZA"), S25/10685, Haim Levkov's testimony, p. 2.

29. Segev, *Days of the Anemones*, p. 349.

30. Zion Cohen, *From Teheran and Back* (Tel Aviv: Ministry of Defense, 1995), p. 56. [Hebrew]

31. CZA, S25/10685, Haim Levkov's testimony, p. 2.

32. Segev, *Days of the Anemones*, p. 349.

33. CZA, S25/10685, Efraim's testimony, p. 4.

34. Segev, *Days of the Anemones*, p. 349.

35. CZA, S25/10685, Jonathan's testimony, p. 3.

36. Bierman and Smith, *Fire in the Night*, p. 115.

37. Bierman and Smith, *Fire in the Night*, p. 115.

38. Benny Landau, "Regards from a Friend," *Haaretz*, February 25, 2000.

39. *Haaretz*, March 10, 2000.

BEN-GURION AND THE RETURN TO JEWISH POWER

MICHAEL B. OREN

OVER THE PAST FEW YEARS, as the Israeli army has become the world's foremost anti-terrorist fighting force, great numbers of American servicemen and servicewomen have come to Israel to learn from our experience and to apply it in America's own war on terror. It has been my privilege to host many of these officers at my home in Jerusalem—people from Oklahoma and Arkansas and other exotic places, individuals with no prior experience in the Middle East. It is always fascinating to hear their impressions of the area and their analyses of both the conflicts in the Middle East and the nature of Middle Eastern societies.

Invariably they home in on one characteristic—the refusal of many Arab leaders, whether they be Palestinians, Iraqis, Saudis, or Syrians, to take responsibility for their own failures and foibles. Whenever something goes wrong in Arab societies, these Americans observe, it is never these societies' fault, but instead the fault of the United States or the West or, most commonly, of Israel and the Jews. And this refusal to accept responsibility is the largest single obstacle to America's efforts to foster democracy in the Middle East—so these officers tell me—because the essence of democracy, of sovereignty and freedom, is the willingness to take responsibility for one's actions and decisions.

I listen to them, and I cannot help but agree, but I also cannot help wondering whether Israelis and Jews don't face similar difficulties in shouldering the burdens of statehood. Inevitably, I find myself thinking back to the eve of Israel's independence, to May 14, 1948, when one man had to grapple with the question of whether the Jews, after generations of powerlessness, could learn to act as sovereigns in their own state—whether they could live up to the challenges of independence.

That man was the leader of the Zionist movement, the soon-to-be prime minister, David Ben-Gurion. On that day, Ben-Gurion sat in his living room and watched while outside in the street, the Jews of Palestine were dancing. They were dancing because they were about to realize what was one of the most remarkable and inspiring achievements in human history: A people which had been exiled from its homeland two thousand years before, which had endured countless pogroms, expulsions, and persecutions, but which had refused to relinquish its identity—which had, on the contrary, substantially strengthened that identity; a people which only a few years before had been the victim of mankind's largest single act of mass murder, killing a third of the world's Jews, that people was returning home as sovereign citizens in their own independent state.

And so they danced, filling the streets; but Ben-Gurion wasn't dancing. Instead he sat alone and wrote in his diary about his fears, confiding doubts about the Jews' ability to withstand the onslaught of the combined Arab armies, and about the world's willingness to accept a permanent Jewish state. He wondered whether the Zionist vision of a normal state, a state like all others, could be reconciled with a Jewish state that aspired to be a light unto the nations. Most disconcertingly, he questioned whether a people so long accustomed to being the victims of sovereign power could suddenly turn around and judiciously wield it—whether they could, in fact, take responsibility for themselves.

Formerly David Green, Ben-Gurion, like many Zionist leaders of his generation—Levi Eshkol, Golda Meir, Moshe Dayan—had Hebraized his name in order to establish a direct link between the dynamic Zionist present and Israel's heroic past, skipping over the millennia of Jewish powerlessness. Yet he knew that such leapfrogging was not really possible. The Jews, Ben-Gurion knew, had problems with power.

Those problems are already discernible in the Bible—with the serious reservations regarding kingship raised by the Prophets, and with the unstable and often violent relationships between monarchs and priests during the period of the Temples. The problems multiplied a thousandfold, however, with the destruction of the Second Temple and the annihilation of the Jewish commonwealth in biblical Israel.

Shorn of sovereignty, the Jews developed a cult of powerlessness, which many deemed a form of divine punishment for their sins and which developed, in time, into an actual *repugnance* toward power. If the Bible was clear about whom it considered the hero—Joshua conquering Canaanite cities, Gideon smiting Midianites, Samson wielding a jawbone like an axe—the Talmud, written mostly by Jews lacking sovereign political power, was far less categorical. "Who is the hero?" asks the Mishna. Not King David dancing as he escorts the ark to liberated Jerusalem, not Judah Maccabee and the Hasmoneans defeating the Greeks and rededicating the Temple; no, the hero is "the man who conquers his own passions." Losing sovereignty, the Jews fled inward from the fields of politics and battle—into their communities, into their synagogues, and into themselves.

To be sure, this retreat had its ameliorative rewards, enabling Jews to attain a heightened sense of spirituality and morality. But doing so came at the price of increasing alienation from temporal matters—from responsibility for themselves not only as individuals but also as a nation. True, Jews might provide shelter to banished coreligionists, or pay their ransoms—"*kol yisrael arevim zeh lazeh*—all Jews are responsible for one another," the famous rabbinic teaching has it—but how often did those Jews build a city and elect officials to govern it? How often could they, or would they, make the most basic sovereign decision to defend themselves? In much of rabbinic thinking, political power is profane, mundane, and dangerous. May God bless and keep the czar far away from us, Tevye prays.

In its most extreme form, the Jewish revulsion *towards* power becomes a total prohibition *of* power, and any attempted exercise of sovereignty becomes in effect a challenge to God's omnipotence—in other words, blasphemy. Blasphemy, desecration, *hilul*, are precisely the words applied by parts of the ultra-Orthodox Haredi world to Zionism, which in its view is an abominable attempt to arrogate God's exclusive purview—to end Jewish exile and reinvest the Jewish people with power. Even Rabbi Abraham Isaac Kook, the most influential figure in religious Zionism, questioned whether Jews could or should act as wolves, for states, Kook said, were by nature wolf-like.

In modernity, however, the ever-inventive Jewish people came up with another answer to the problem of power: Not turning inward, but—as soon as the Emancipation and the fall of the ghetto walls allowed it—by bursting out through assimilation. Thus, beginning in the nineteenth century, Jews could become powerful—they could become a Benjamin Disraeli or a Ferdinand Lassalle—but as Englishmen and Germans, not as Jews; in spite of their Jewishness, and usually at its expense.

It has often been remarked that perhaps the one thing ultra-Orthodox and assimilated Jews agreed upon early in the last century was a staunch opposition to Zionism: The Orthodox because it claimed that Zionism aspired to play God and redeem the Jewish nation; the highly assimilated Jews because they denied that the Jews were a nation at all. Ultra-Orthodox and assimilated Jews would reunite tragically on the train to Auschwitz, the final destination on the 2,000-year-long path of Jewish powerlessness. The Nazis sent them there claiming, paradoxically, that Jews wielded too much power.

Though American Jewry would later explain the Holocaust as the product of an absence of toleration and universal values, the Zionist interpretation of the Holocaust has always been that six million Jews died because they lacked an army, a state—power.

But for the 600,000 Jews in Israel in 1948, facing six Arab armies preparing to invade the nascent state, the question of whether Jewish power was necessary was moot. Without power, the citizens of the new state would die—not only spiritually, but physically.

Yet, as Ben-Gurion realized, knowing this and acting on it were not synonymous. He understood that the transformation from a people recoiling from power to a people capable of embracing it would be the single greatest challenge facing Israel. "We must adopt a new approach, new habits of mind," he told listeners shortly before the state's founding. "We must learn to think like a state."

He even coined a Hebrew word for that challenge, *mamlachtiyut*, a neologism which eludes English equivalents but which roughly translates as "acting in a sovereign-like manner." By *mamlachtiyut*, Ben-Gurion meant the Jews' ability to handle power—military power as well as democratic and political power—effectively, justly, responsibly. The Jews of Israel, Ben-Gurion knew, might succeed in repelling Arab armies, in absorbing many times their number of new immigrants, and in creating world-class governmental and cultural institutions, but without *mamlachtiyut*, without the ability to deal with power and take responsibility for its ramifications, they could not ultimately survive.

The newborn state did in fact repel the invaders and establish its independence. Yet not all of the threats to Israel's existence emanated from the Arabs. In the summer of 1948, at the height of the fighting, Ben-Gurion faced a challenge from the Revisionist Zionists, led by Menachem Begin, who balked at following orders from the provisional authorities. Ben-Gurion told Begin that a sovereign state has one government and one army, and when Begin tried to bring a ship, the *Altalena*, into Israel bearing arms for his own militia, Ben-Gurion ordered the vessel sunk. Later, Ben-Gurion would also meet a challenge to his democratically endowed authority from the Left, from the kibbutz-based military force known as the Palmah, which he ordered disbanded.

Israel had established its independence, but some of the greatest challenges to its sovereignty lay ahead. In 1956, Ben-Gurion demonstrated what he meant by *mamlachtiyut* by going to war against Egyptian President Gamal Abdel Nasser and his Soviet-supplied army. The decision was roundly condemned by most of the world, including by the United States, but Ben-Gurion's position was that no state, and certainly not the Jewish state, was obliged to sit idly while an army sworn to its destruction massed on its borders.

Ben-Gurion also exercised *mamlachtiyut* by building what became the greatest physical manifestation of Jewish power ever, the Dimona nuclear facility. Just over a decade after Jews were herded by the millions into Nazi death camps, an independent Jewish state possessed the power enjoyed by only a handful of nations.

Yet, for all its successful displays of *mamlachtiyut*, Israel sometimes displayed a frightening inability to understand the rudiments of sovereignty. In May 1967, for example, while Nasser's troops again gathered on Israel's border, Israel's leadership was torn between the generals who wanted to go to war immediately, and the ministers, who insisted on first proving—to the United States, especially—that Israel had done everything possible to avoid bloodshed. The ministers won out, and in June 1967 Israel defeated at least three major Arab armies, almost quadrupling its territorial size.

But the Six Day victory precipitated a different kind of power complex in Israel—an over-reliance on tanks and planes and paratroopers, a fetishizing of the Israel Defense Forces, and the near apotheosis of its generals. The edifice would come crashing down, suddenly, at 2 p.m. on October 6, 1973, when the armies of Egypt and Syria simultaneously attacked Israel, catching it off guard and killing 2,600 of its soldiers. Though the IDF managed to turn the tide and to achieve a stunning victory which would in time pacify Israel's two most threatening borders, the shock of that initial attack would remain a national nightmare. Come Yom Kippur time every year—and this year was no exception—much of the country engages in a paroxysm of pain and an all-out assault on the very notion of power. Since 1973, virtually every Israeli resort to armed force—the 1976 Entebbe raid and the 1981 attack on the Osirak nuclear reactor in Iraq are notable exceptions—has been the focus of profound controversy not only in the world, but more keenly, within Israel itself.

The Yom Kippur trauma would give rise to two new, mutually incompatible movements: First, Shalom Achshav (Peace Now), a leftist organization, recoiled from an over-reliance on power and instead sought a mediated solution in which Israeli sovereignty would dissolve into a borderless New Middle East—essentially the old assimilationist vision revisited. Second, Gush Emunim (the Bloc of the Faithful), championed by parts of the Right and many religious settlers of Judea, Samaria, and Gaza, revered power as the panacea for Israel's security problems. These are the poles between which Israel has been torn for the last thirty years, and the dividing issue is not race or economics, but power.

It goes without saying that this struggle does not occur in a vacuum. Israel is situated in the midst of the Arab world, in the historic Islamic heartland, a region that also has a problem with power, but one that is diametrically opposed to Israel's. Unlike normative Judaism, a product of powerlessness, Islam developed during a period when Muslims ruled most of the civilized world. Power is integral to Islam. There is no medieval manual on how to run a Jewish state, but thousands of such texts exist on how to run an Islamic state. Islam, therefore, harbors no misgivings regarding power. It is the tool by which God fulfills his will for the world, and, as such, the attainment of power is incumbent on every individual Muslim.

Arab Muslims thus have a problem with a palpably powerful Jewish state, and in recent years they hit upon the ideal solution. Terrorism not only requires little by way of technical sophistication or capital outlays, but it forces Israel to fight back in densely populated areas, imposing roadblocks and curfews. By drawing international wrath toward Israeli policies, it thrusts to the fore the deepest Jewish ambivalence toward power. Though it patently failed in its goal of destroying Israel's economy and unraveling its civil society, terror did succeed in exacerbating the Jewish confusion over sovereignty, over *mamlachtiyut*.

Part of the Israeli population, for example, reacted by building unauthorized settlements in the territories—essentially subverting the democratic process—while another part tried to negotiate a European-funded peace treaty with Palestinian officials behind the Israeli government's back. Some Israelis wanted to drive the Palestinians out entirely—an extreme abuse of power—while others advocated the creation of a binational state—the final abdication of power. Both are classic examples of what Ben-Gurion would call a breakdown of *mamlachtiyut*.

Mamlachtiyut, in fact, was what drew me to Israel in the first place. I grew up just about the only Jewish kid on the block, and the almost daily trouncing I took from the neighborhood gang taught me a great deal about power and the hazards of lacking it.

But what really convinced me was a coin. I was a fanatical numismatic, collecting coins from around the world. I was especially keen on ancient Jewish coins of the Second Temple period. One day—I must have been about nine—a distant cousin of mine from Israel gave me a coin that was an exact replica of a Second Temple coin, only it wasn't ancient. It was shiny and clean and the letters emblazoned on it were identical to those I was just then learning in Hebrew school. Though not a particularly precocious nine-year-old, I knew that modern coins came from existing countries and Hebrew from Jews and quickly completed the syllogism: There was a Jewish state. From that epiphanous moment on, I was hooked.

There followed the Six Day War—the only event in history in which Jews have been powerful and appreciated for it. I was fascinated by the notion of Jews taking responsibility for themselves as Jews—for their taxes and their sewers and their lampposts. My Zionism was less Herzlian than Schwartzian—as in the beat generation poet Delmore Schwartz. If Herzl said, "If you will it, it is no dream," then Schwartz said (as the title of his 1937 short story put it), "In dreams begin responsibilities." I wanted the responsibility.

So I moved to Israel, became a citizen, and joined the army. I put on those red paratrooper boots the first time and was overwhelmed by the realization that I was a member of the first Jewish fighting force in 2,000 years, a Jew from New Jersey lucky enough to live at a time when I could serve a sovereign Jewish state.

What a privilege—and what a responsibility. Its weight became apparent to me fighting in Lebanon and in the territories. It also became clear later, when I had removed those boots and, a civilian again, was working for the government at a time when its prime minister was, in a despicable misuse of power and an egregious failure of *mamlachtiyut*, assassinated.

Today, as an Israeli, I must confront questions that derive from having power. I had to decide, for instance, whether to support the construction of a fence which may provide greater security against terrorist attacks, but which evokes the very ghetto walls that Zionism aspired to topple. During the last two years, when two of my children were serving in the IDF—one of whom was wounded in action fighting against Hamas in Hebron—I had to decide whether to favor a pullout of Israeli forces from Palestinian cities and perhaps give a jump-start to peace, or whether, by doing so, I'd be giving encouragement to terror, jeopardizing my third child, who took a bus to and from school every day in Jerusalem. Last August, when I, together with a group of Israeli officers, broke into a synagogue in a Jewish settlement in Gaza and confronted a hundred men, women, and children lying on the floor, wailing and screaming out to God, I had to decide whether evicting these people from that synagogue and from their homes would strengthen the Israeli state or shatter the Israeli people. There was no escaping that decision; the responsibility was mine.

An American journalist once asked me to react to a charge made by a settler leader to the effect that the problem with the IDF is that it is a Western army, and not a biblical army, capable of exacting eye-for-an-eye revenge. The problem with the IDF, I replied, is that it is not Western enough. I said that the Palestinians should thank Allah daily that they are grappling with roadblocks and curfews, and not, say, with the American or French armies, which would have pulverized their cities long ago. The problem with the IDF, I said, is that it is too Jewish.

I remembered that when Lebanese Christian militiamen, sent by Defense Minister Ariel Sharon into the refugee camps of Beirut, killed 800 Palestinians, hundreds of thousands of Israelis took to the streets to protest Sharon's action. But in 2002, when President Bush sent the Northern Alliance into Taliban villages in Afghanistan, killing many thousands, scarcely an American voice rose in protest. I recalled that when U.S. forces believed that Saddam Hussein was hiding in a certain neighborhood in Baghdad, U.S. planes flattened the neighborhood, but that when the IDF learned that the entire leadership of Hamas was in a single building in Gaza, it chose a bomb too small to eliminate them for fear of harming nearby civilians.

Israeli soldiers go into the homes of terror suspects, risking their own lives and often sacrificing them in order to reduce civilian casualties, where another army might simply call in an air strike or an artillery barrage. Israel devotes but a single day each year to acknowledging its army—not an armed forces day, or flag day, or veterans' day—but Yom Hazikaron, Memorial Day, a day commemorated not with military parades and old men in uniform, but with songs and poems about the horrors of war and the holiness of peace. Here is a country that has been in the throes of a vicious war for more than four years—a war in which Israel has suffered as many casualties, per capita, as the United States in Vietnam—but which has yet to give that war a name.

Israel today faces challenges every bit as existential as those Ben-Gurion confronted in 1948. Terrorists still try to blow themselves up in public places within Israel, and vast forces, many armed with long-range missiles and unconventional weapons, assemble around it. As evidenced recently by Iranian President Mahmoud Ahmadinejad's call for Israel to be "wiped off the map," many of the world's 1.3 billion Muslims would not weep over the disappearance of the Jewish state, nor would they be too selective with respect to the manner in which that elimination would be implemented. Many Western Europeans, meanwhile, are indifferent and even hostile to Israel's fate. And even in America—in its universities in particular—Israel is increasingly vilified, delegitimized, and branded an anachronism at best, and a fascist regime at worst.

Yet, in spite of the immense forces arrayed against it, Israel has not only stood up to the test of power. Far more than that, it has presented to the world a model of balance between the requirements of justice and morality and the requisites of power. The IDF is generally regarded as one of the strongest and most sophisticated armies in the world, yet it does not use even a fraction of its potential strength against the people who, if *they* held such power, would hesitate not a moment to direct it at Israel's destruction. Israel does not evict a people that threatens its existence—and the last century is rife with such expulsions, especially in the West—but rather offers that people an opportunity to live with it side by side, even offering large parts of its own historical and spiritual homeland.

Israel's soldiers go into battle armed not only with guns and grenades but with pocket-size, laminated cards containing the IDF code of ethics, which reminds them that it is their solemn duty to make every effort to avoid causing civilian casualties and to use their weapons solely for the purposes of self- and national defense. Israelis fight, asking themselves at every stage whether in fact they are doing the right thing, the moral thing, the Jewish thing. Classical Judaism may not provide us with a detailed model of what a Jewish state should look like, but Israel has provided the world with a model of how a state threatened with terror and missiles and the hatred of millions can act justly.

The model is, admittedly, incomplete—a work in progress. We in Israel will continue to debate what acts are and are not permissible for the Jewish state to take in order to assure its survival, and to discuss the requirements of *mamlachtiyut*.

Our responsibility today is to prove to ourselves, and the world, that the phrase "Jewish state" is not in fact a contradiction in terms. Let us remain cognizant not only of our great achievements—the Nobel Prizes our scientists are awarded or the European championships our basketball players win—but also of the weighty responsibilities we bear: The responsibilities of reconciling our heritage with our sovereignty, our strength with our compassion, and our will to survive with our desire to inspire others.

ABOUT THE AUTHORS

EYAL CHOWERS is a senior lecturer and chairman of the department of political science at Tel Aviv University. He is the author of *The Modern Self in the Labyrinth: Politics and the Entrapment Imagination* (Harvard, 2004).

RUTH GAVISON is the Haim Cohn Professor for Human Rights at the Hebrew University Faculty of Law. Since January 2005 she has served as a senior adviser on the constitutional drafting process for the Knesset Committee on Constitution, Law, and Justice. She is the author of eight books in Hebrew on law, constitutional issues, and human rights.

OFIR HAIVRY is an Associate Fellow at the Shalem Center in Jerusalem. He has served as the Editor-in-Chief of *Azure* and the editor of the Leviathan Series of Shalem Press. He was also formerly the foreign affairs editor for the weekly newspaper *Haolam Hazeh*.

DAVID HAZONY is the Editor-in-Chief of *Azure*. He is the editor of *Essential Essays on Judaism* (Shalem Press, 2002), a collection of articles by Rabbi Eliezer Berkovits.

YORAM HAZONY is a Senior Fellow at the Shalem Center in Jerusalem. He is the author of *The Jewish State: The Struggle for Israel's Soul* (Basic Books/New Republic, 2000) and *The Dawn: Political Teachings of the Book of Esther* (Shalem Press, 2000).

ANNA ISAKOVA is a doctor, journalist, and author. From 1999 to 2001 she served as the prime minister's adviser on integration.

ZE'EV MAGHEN is a senior lecturer in Middle Eastern and Islamic history at Bar-Ilan University.

ARIE MORGENSTERN is a Senior Fellow at the Shalem Center in Jerusalem and the former supervisor of history instruction for Israel's Ministry of Education. He is the author of *Hastening Redemption: Messianism and the Resettlement of the Land of Israel* (Oxford, 2006).

MICHAEL B. OREN is a Senior Fellow at the Shalem Center in Jerusalem. He is the author of *The Origins of the Second Arab-Israeli War: Egypt, Israel, and the Great Powers, 1952-1956* (Frank Cass, 1992) and *Six Days of War: June 1967 and the Making of the Modern Middle East* (Oxford, 2002), which received the National Jewish Book Award and the *Los Angeles Times* Book Prize in History. Dr. Oren was a visiting faculty member at Harvard and Yale universities in 2006. His forthcoming book, *Power, Faith, and Fantasy: America in the Middle East from 1776 to the Present*, is due to be published by Norton Press in January 2007.

DANIEL POLISAR is President of the Shalem Center in Jerusalem. He is co-editor of *Choosing Freedom: Economic Policy for Israel, 1997-2000* (with Yitzhak Klein (The Shalem Center, 1997) and has written on the failure of democratization in the Palestinian Authority. Currently Dr. Polisar is the head of an initiative for drafting a constitution for the State of Israel.

AMNON RUBINSTEIN is the President of the Interdisciplinary Center in Herzliya and a recipient of the Israel Prize for the study of law. He was a member of Knesset from 1977 to 2003 and has served as Minister of Communication; Minister of Education, Culture, and Sport; and Minister of Science and Technology. Professor Rubinstein has published numerous books in the fields of jurisprudence and modern Jewish history, including *From Herzl to Rabin: The Changing Image of Zionism* (Holmes & Meier, 2000) and *Jurisdiction and Illegality: A Study in Public Law* (Clarendon, 1965).

ASSAF SAGIV is a Senior Editor of *Azure*.

NATAN SHARANSKY, the author of *Fear No Evil* (Random House, 1992) and *The Case for Democracy* (PublicAffairs, 2004), was a Prisoner of Zion and dissident in the former Soviet Union. In honor of his brave struggle against tyranny he was awarded the Congressional Gold Medal. In 1996, ten years after immigrating to Israel, he was elected to serve in the Knesset, and since then he has held ministerial posts in several administrations and has served as Deputy Prime Minister.

SOURCES

Ruth Gavison, "The Jewish State: A Justification," appeared as "The Jews' Right to Statehood: A Defense" in *Azure* 15 (Summer 2003), pp. 70-108.

Yoram Hazony, "The Guardian of the Jews," appeared in *Azure* 13 (Summer 2002), pp. 133-165.

Ofir Haivry, "On Zion: A Reality That Fashions Imagination," appeared as "Act and Comprehend" in *Azure* 1 (Summer 1996), pp. 5-42.

Natan Sharansky, "The Political Legacy of Theodor Herzl," appeared in *Azure* 21 (Summer 2005), pp. 83-99.

Amnon Rubinstein, "Zionism: A Deviant Nationalism?" appeared as "Zionism's Compatriots" in *Azure* 16 (Winter 2004), pp. 111-122.

Eyal Chowers, "The Zionist Revolution in Time," appeared as "Time in Zionism: The Life and Afterlife of a Temporal Revolution," in *Political Theory* 26:5 (October 1998), pp. 652-685.

David Hazony, "Zion and Moral Vision," appeared as "Eliezer Berkovits, Theologian of Zionism" in *Azure* 17 (Spring 2004), pp. 88-119.

Assaf Sagiv, "Dionysus in Zion," appeared in *Azure* 9 (Spring 2000), pp. 155-178.

Anna Isakova, "The Goldfish and the Jewish Problem," appeared in *Alpayim* 16 (1998), pp. 192-213. [Hebrew]

Ze'ev Maghen, "Imagine: On Love and Lennon," appeared in *Azure* 7 (Spring 1999), pp. 119-166.

Daniel Polisar, "Making History," appeared in *Azure* 9 (Spring 2000), pp. 14-22.

Arie Morgenstern, "Dispersion and the Longing for Zion, 1240-1840," appeared in *Azure* 12 (Winter 2002), pp. 71-132.

Yoram Hazony, "Did Herzl Want a Jewish State?" appeared in *Azure* 9 (Spring 2000), pp. 37-73.

Michael Oren, "Orde Wingate: Father of the IDF," appeared as "Orde Wingate: Friend Under Fire" in *Azure* 10 (Winter 2001), pp. 33-49.

Michael B. Oren, "Ben-Gurion and the Return to Jewish Power," appeared as "Jews and the Challenge of Sovereignty" in *Azure* 23 (Winter 2006), pp. 27-38.

INDEX

1948 and After: Israel and the Palestinians (Morris)   298

Abdullah (king of Jordan)   298
Abraham   70, 169, 262, 292
Abravanel, Isaac   320
Abulafia, Haim   334
Acre   314, 323
Addis Ababa   397
Afghanistan   413
Africa   109, 202, 313, 315, 317, 374, 397
Afula   92, 93
Agnon, Shmuel Yosef   59
Agudat Israel   viii, 358
Ahad Ha'am   55, 58-59, 83, 106, 144-145, 366-367, 372, 378
Aharonson, Shlomo   xii
Ahmadinejad, Mahmoud   414
Akavia, Avraham   391, 397
Akiva, R.   57, 68, 267-268, 270, 282, 284, 290
Albania   52, 120
Alexander, R.   310
Al-Harizi, Judah   312
Alkabetz, Solomon   323-325
Alkalai, Yehuda   367
Allenby, Edmund   58, 209
Allon, Yigal   110, 297, 390, 392
Almasy, Laudislaus   394
Allon Plan   87

Aloni, Shulamit   358
Alsheich, Moses   326
Altalena   409
Altneuland (Herzl)   107-108, 364
Altneuland   251
America   viii, 12, 47-49, 59, 107, 169, 208, 212, 288, 297, 366, 405, 414
Amsterdam   199-200, 213, 334, 338
Anilewitz, Mordechai   291
anti-Semitism   viii, xi, 8-9, 45, 101-104, 106, 135, 148, 227, 229, 234, 239, 262, 366, 368, 371
Apollo   75, 203
Arab-Israeli conflict   x
Arab Israelis   9-11, 17-18, 20-22, 24-27, 123
Arab Revolt   13, 392, 400
Arabs   13-15, 154
Arba'a Turim (R. Jacob ben Asher)   336
Arendt, Hannah   156
Argentina   12, 46
Ariel-Amir, Tal   209
Aristotle   155
Arkansas   405
Arlington National Cemetery   390, 398, 402
Armenia   119
Ashkelon   94
Ashkenazi, Betzalel   325

Ashkenazim   240, 246, 340
Asia   109, 317
Assyria   67
Astral Projection   210
Auschwitz   408
Austria   viii, 41, 120, 315, 377
Avineri, Shlomo   xii
Azeris   275
Azulai, Abraham   327
Azure   171, 416, 418

Ba'al Shem Tov, Israel   81, 290,
   334-335
Babel, Isaac   238
Babi Yar   291
Babylonia   53, 67, 69, 72, 290
Babylonians   70
Bacchae (Euripides)   202
Bacchanalia   200, 203, 206
Bacchus   200
Bacon, Francis   52
Baghdad   251
Bahai   280
Balfour Declaration   13, 396
Bar Kochba   72, 76, 78, 109, 290
Bar-Kosiba, Shimon *see* Bar Kochba
Bar-Menashe, Yehuda   78
Barnai, Jacob   306
Bar-On, Mordechai   359-360
Basel   116
Basques   118
Bataille, Georges   201
Bauer, Otto   136
BBC   232
Beatles   263, 266
Bedouin   240, 249
Beersheva   vii, 254
Begin, Benny   240
Begin, Menachem   101, 409
Beilin, Yossi   x, 366-367
Beirut   323, 413
Beit Shean   396

Beit Shemesh   240
Beit Yosef   320
Beitar   78, 290
Belgium   118
Ben Arach, Elazar   290
Ben Atar, Haim   334
Ben-Ba'aya, Yehonatan   78
Ben-Dov, Yoav   209-210
Ben-Gurion, David   viii, xii, 41,
   51, 84-85, 108-110, 112, 116,
   146, 154, 297-300, 302, 358-
   360, 382, 392, 397, 406, 408-
   409, 411
Ben-Petura   268-269
Berab, Jacob   323-324
Berdyczewski, Micha Josef   142-
   147, 151
Bergen Belsen   291
Berkovits, Eliezer   xii, 168-195
Berkowicz, Michael   365
Berl (Shapira)   302
Berlin   x, 184, 199-200, 213, 251
Bernstein, Eduard   136
Beth-El (yeshiva)   334
Bhagavad-Gita   254
Bialik, Haim Nahman   59
Bible   49-51, 60, 70, 76, 79, 109,
   177, 186, 267, 309, 311, 320,
   369, 393, 395, 407
Bierman, John   392-393, 396, 401
*Birth of the Palestinian Refugee Problem,
   1947-1949* (Morris)   295,
   300
*Birth of Tragedy Out of the Spirit of
   Music* (Nietzsche)   201, 203
Black Panthers   110
Bohemia   315, 321
Borjia, Caesare   94
Borochov, Dov Ber   143, 147-149,
   150-151, 156
Borowitz, Eugene B.   169, 176-177
Boston   225
Brenner, Tzvi   395, 401

Britain 39-40, 42-43, 154, 205, 208, 210, 232, 296, 373-377, 391, 394-396

British Royal Commission on Alien Immigration 362, 373

Britons 40

Brody 334

Buber, Martin 83, 175-176, 182, 204, 380

Buddhism 66, 258, 280

Bulgaria 52, 120, 246

Burchett, Wilfred 391

Burke, Edmund 39-42

Burma 390-391, 395, 397-398

Burning Ground (Teveth) 302

Bush, George W. 413

Cairo 325, 397

Camp David 16

Carmel 290

Carmi, Israel 391, 399

Carter, Jimmy 277

Castile 317

Catalans 118

Catholic Church 203, 315

Caucasus 245

Central Zionist Archives 399-400

Chagall, Marc 238

Chakra (musician) 210

Charles V (Holy Roman Emperor) 322, 323

China 38, 316

Chindits 397, 398

Christianity 66, 69, 75-77, 90, 144, 170, 258, 268-269, 272, 275, 280-281, 287, 312, 314, 316-317, 321, 323, 342, 360, 378

Church of the Holy Sepulchre 322

Churchill, Winston 42, 390, 397

CIS (Commonwealth of Independent States) 243, 247

Clement VII 321

Cohen, Hermann 44-45, 175-177, 182, 183-189

Cohen, Zion 400

Cold War x

Coleridge, Samuel 279

Collusion Across the Jordan (Shlaim) 298

Commentary 297

Communism 280

Confucianism 66

Constantinople 316

Content of the Form (White) 65

Cordovero, Moses 327

Corsicans 118

Council of Europe 118, 121

Coupland, Douglas 207

Cowen, Joseph 374

Crescas, Hasdai 316

Crimes of War: What the Public Should Know (Gutman and Rieff, eds.) 299

Crisis and Faith (Berkovits) 186-187

Crisis of Judaism in the Jewish State (Berkovits) 190

Critique of Judgment (Kant) 133

Croatia 120

Croce 260

Crusades 12, 312, 314

Cunaeus, Petrus 51

Cyprus 326, 392

Cyrus 76

Czechoslovakia 396

Dabburiya 395-396

Damascus 90, 329

Daniel 290

Daniel, book of 311, 326

Danna 400

Dante Alighieri 86

Darwin, Charles 263

David 76, 262, 290, 407

David, Avraham 307, 328

Dayan, Moshe 110, 297, 390, 406

Days of the Anemones: Palestine During the Mandatory Period (Segev) 296, 392, 398
Dead Sea 78
Deborah 290
Decalogue 73
Declaration of Independence, Israeli xii, 358, 360, 382
Denmark xi
Der Judenstaat (Herzl) 130, 357, 361-362, 380-381
Deuteronomy 262, 284
Diana (Princess) 250
Diderot, Denis 260
Die Yudische Medineh (Herzl) 362
Dimona 409
Dinov 337
Dinur, Benzion 59, 305-307, 335
Dionysian 200-209, 211-216
Dispirited Rebellion: Essays on Contemporary Israeli Culture (Taub) 212
Disraeli, Benjamin 408
Divine Comedy (Dante) 86
Doobie Brothers 267
Dosa, R. 310, 337
Dov Baer of Mezrich 335
Dovrat Commission 113
Downing Street 375
Dreyfus, Alfred 80
Druid 258
Druze 240, 249
Dubno 327
Dubnov, Simon 224
Dumas, Alexandre the Elder 227

Ecstasy 199, 205-206, 209, 218-219
Egypt 14-16, 67, 69, 107, 284, 291, 298, 312-313, 317, 319, 324, 341, 409-410
Eichmann, Adolf 47
Ein Harod 395, 396

Either/Or (Kierkegaard) 207
Elazar Rokeah 334
Eli 92
Eliade, Mircea 201-202
Eliezer, R. 310
Elijah 290, 313, 325
Elijah of Ferrara 318
Elijah of Vilna ("Vilna Gaon") 81, 336, 338-340
Elizabeth I 52
Ellis Island 290
Emancipation 342
Emile (Rousseau) 53
Engels, Friedrich 260
England viii, x, 12, 38, 45, 48-49, 148, 313, 362, 371, 373-374
English Patient (Ondaatje) 394
Enlightenment 51, 130, 134-135
Entangled Leadership (Porat) 298
Entebbe 46, 105, 410
Ephraim 312
Epistle to Yemen (Maimonides) 311
Eppie Zorea 152
Eren-Frucht, Leora 211
Eretz Yisrael 129, 184, 398
Erenburg, Ilya 238
Eshel, Amit 210
Eshkol, Levi 406
Esther 290
Esther, book of 79-80, 82
Estonians 119
Ethiopia 46, 390-391, 395-397
Euripides 202
Europe viii-xi, 25, 40-45, 51, 84, 103, 109, 117-124, 127, 134, 137, 139, 142, 144, 148-149, 184, 188-189, 203, 212, 234, 242-243, 304, 307, 314-315, 322-323, 328, 332-333, 336, 339, 342, 361, 364, 377
European Court of Human Rights 118
European Union 118

Exodus 67, 177
Ezekiel 340
Ezra 80

Fabricating Israeli History (Karsh) 299
Faith After the Holocaust (Berkovits) 178
Falk, Robert 238
Fascism 394
Fergusson, Bernard 391
Feuerbach, Ludwig Andreas von 260
Fez 278
Fichte, Johann Gottlieb 260
Fire in the Night: Wingate of Burma, Ethiopia, and Zion (Bierman and Smith) 392-393, 398, 400-402
First Intifada (Yigal Eyal) 392
Foreign Affairs 297
France viii, x, 41, 45, 48, 80, 118-119, 148, 313, 315, 371
Franciscan order 318
Frankfurt am Main 327
Freedom Station 232
Freud, Sigmund 76, 276
Freundlich, Sharon (DJ Choopy) 212
Frieling, Tuvia xii
Frisch, Felix 209
From Teheran and Back (Cohen) 400
Funkenstein, Amos 132
Fustat 290

Galilee 73, 323, 330, 341
Garibaldi, Giussepe 260
Gascoigne, Thomas 317
Gaza ix, 15, 92, 393, 410, 412-413
Gediminas Castle 225
Gefen, Assaf 214

Gefen, Aviv 212
Geiger, Abraham 135
Genesis 73, 309
Georgians 245
Germanism and Judaism (Cohen) 44
Germany viii, x, 41-45, 48, 59, 65, 184-185, 210, 225-226, 232, 239, 322, 371, 377
Gershon of Kutow 334
Gesher Theater 111
Gideon 395, 407
Gideon Force 396
Goa 201, 209
God 49, 51, 67-68, 70, 73-77, 132, 141, 151, 172, 175-176, 178, 181-184, 186-187, 189, 201, 292, 309-310, 312, 317-318, 320, 324, 328-331, 338, 340-341, 369-370, 393, 407, 412
God, Man and History (Berkovits) 171, 173
Golan Heights 15-16, 89, 262
Gordon, A.D. 87
Gorny, Yosef xii
Government Companies Law 123
Great Britain 119
Greece 68-69, 119-120, 200
Greek 71, 202-203
Greeks 407
Greenberg, Leopold 374
Grotius, Hugo 51
Guedemann, Moritz 367-368
Gulf War 213
Gush Emunim 410
Gush Etzion 92
Gutman, Roy 299

Haaretz 215, 295-296, 392, 401
Ha'ir (weekly) 210
Hacker, Joseph 307, 318
Hackett, John 395
Hacohen, Shabtai 331
Hadassa 79-80

Hadera   92, 93
Hafarhi, Estori   314
Hahartzufim   240
Haifa   vii, 94, 222, 323, 398
Haifa, University of   306
Haim of Volozhin   340
Haivry, Ofir   xii
halacha   9, 132, 169, 174, 186
Halevi, Abraham   321-322
Halevi, Judah   66, 80, 310
Haman   257
Hamas   412-413
Hamlet   208
Har Homa   154
Hare Krishna   252, 271
Haskala   337, 342
Hasmoneans   72, 407
Hatzor   290
Hayun, Gedaliah   334
Hazony, David   xii
Hebrew   6, 8-9, 59-60, 82, 108, 111,
    113, 129, 139, 154, 234, 236,
    240-241, 250, 369, 378, 394
Hebrew University of Jerusalem   305-
    306, 381
Hebron   92, 94, 412
Hegel, Georg Wilhelm Friedrich 138-
    140, 260
Heller, Shmuel   341
Hemingway, Ernest   234
Herder, Johann Gottfried von   137-
    138, 140, 260
Herzl, Theodor   viii, xii, 38, 40-41,
    44, 80-83, 101-104, 106-110,
    112, 114, 116, 130, 142, 157,
    191, 251, 286, 357
Hesed Le'avraham (Azulai)   327
Hess, Moses   51, 136
Heth   331
Hezbollah   213
Hillel   57, 71-76
Himalayas   397
Histories (Tacitus)   74

Hitler, Adolf   402
Hobbes, Thomas   51
Hohfeld, Wesley Newcomb   11-12
Holland   x, 39-40, 210, 336
Holocaust   viii-ix, 44, 47-48, 51,
    101, 169, 181, 229, 237, 295,
    298, 301, 408
Holy Roman Empire   322
Horev   67, 70
Horodno (Grodno)   322
Horowitz, Isaiah   327-330
Hume, David   260
Hungary   120-121, 291
Hussites   315
Huxley, Aldous   281

Ibiza   209
Ibn Farukh, Muhammad   330-331
Ibn Habib, Levi   324
Idel, Moshe   321
IDF   21, 113, 395-296, 400, 410,
    412-414
"Imagine" (Lennon)   264, 275
Imperial Gazette   40
In the Path of Fighters (Carmi)   391
Inbari, Assaf   xii
India   210, 316, 397
Indonesia   282, 284
Intifada   208, 213
Iran   414
Ireland   119
*Iron Wall: Israel and the Arab World
    Since 1948* (Shlaim)   296-297
Isaac   262
Isabella   290
Isaiah, book of   284, 320
Isakova, Anna   xii
Ishmaelites   316
Islam   66, 280, 316, 319, 332, 411
Israel   ix-xiii, 4-8, 10, 14, 16-20,
    22, 24-29, 38, 46, 49, 52, 57,
    59-60, 71-72, 77-78, 82, 84,
    86-87, 89-94, 102-106, 108-

111, 113-114, 117, 122-123, 130-131, 147, 154-155, 169-170, 176, 181, 186, 190, 201, 209-216, 221, 223, 226-227, 230-231, 235, 239-244, 250-251, 261-262, 280, 295-302, 304, 307, 311, 327, 357- 360, 382, 391-393, 406-414

Israel Lands Authority 124

Israel of Shklov 339

Israelis 254

Italy x, 86, 120

Izmir 334

Jabotinsky, Ze'ev 116, 123, 286

Jackson, Michael 277

Jacob 182, 262, 318

Jaffa 317

Japan 208, 215, 397-398

Jefferson, Thomas 260

Jephthah's daughter 290

Jeremiah 290

Jericho 152, 290

Jerusalem vii, xi, 15-16, 70, 73, 79, 105, 154, 188, 191, 232, 282, 307, 310, 312-314, 316-319, 321-325, 327-331, 333-334, 338-340, 342-343, 373, 380, 394, 398, 405, 407

Jerusalem Post 211

Jerusalem school of Jewish history 305, 307

Jesus 73, 77, 267-269, 272

Jewish Agency 123, 399

Jewish Chronicle 361

Jewish Colonization Association 362

Jewish people 83-84, 91, 94, 183, 242, 250

Jewish Quarter 319

Jewish State (Herzl) 44, 102, 106-107, 357, 360-361, 371-372, 376, 378, 380

Jewish state vii, ix-x, xii, 37, 39, 42-

44, 46-47, 101-102, 113, 154, 169, 171, 184, 190, 201, 237-238, 248, 296, 299, 302-303, 391, 412, 414-415

Jews vii-xi, xiii, 4, 6-8, 11-25, 27, 40-45, 47-49, 51-54, 59-60, 79-80, 82, 102-106, 110, 112, 116, 119, 122, 124, 132, 135-137, 139-150, 153-154, 168-169, 173-174, 181, 185, 187-189, 190-191, 225-231, 236, 239-240, 248-249, 254, 258, 260-262, 271, 275-276, 280, 286, 288, 290-292, 304-305, 308, 311-313, 315-322, 326-328, 330-333, 337, 340-343, 359-360, 364, 366-367, 369, 371-375, 378-381, 390, 394-395, 402, 406-408, 412

Jezreel Valley 395

Joel, Billy 263

Joint Distribution Committee 224

Jonathan Hacohen of Lunel 313

Jordan 14-16, 28, 298

Jordan River 13, 16, 18

Jordanian Option (Schueftan) 298

Joseph 290

Joshua 146, 231, 290

Joyce, James 234

Judah Hasid 332

Judah Maccabee 290, 407

Judaism 3, 50, 57, 67-72, 74-75, 78, 81, 83, 85-87, 90-91, 105, 108, 112-113, 131-132, 136, 144, 168, 170-174, 176-179, 181-182, 184-192, 230, 238, 259, 270, 280, 285-286, 320-321, 359, 368-371, 379-380, 410, 414

Judea 191, 410

Judenstaat 38, 360-366

Jupiter 75

Kabbala 69, 325, 327, 329, 334, 336

Kafka, Franz   251
Kalischer, Tzvi Hirsch   340
Kant, Immanuel   133-135, 170, 172, 260
Karo, Joseph   320-321, 323-326, 336
Karsh, Efraim   299-300
Kashan   273-275, 279
Katz, Haim ben Tuvia   340
Katznelson, Berl   302
Kautsky, Karl   136
Kedar, Binyamin Ze'ev   307, 317
Khayatauskas, Benyumen   237
Khmelnitsky, Bogdan   225, 290, 331
Kierkegaard, Sören Aabye   207-208, 260
King-Clark, Rex   395
Kirby, Woodburn   391
Kirk, James T. (television character) 289
Kiryat Arbiya   78
Klein, Calvin   277
Klein, Claude   381
Knesset   4, 123, 226
Kol Yisrael   232
Kook, Abraham Isaac   59, 180-181, 191, 408
Kook, Tzvi Yehuda   180-181, 191
Koselleck, Reinhart   138
Krakow   323, 327
Krishna   255, 256
Krochmal, Nahman   140-141
Kung-Fiu (Confucius)   93
Kurds   123
Kuzari (Halevi)   66, 80, 310

Lacedaemonia   38
Ladino   84
land of Israel   5-6, 10-12, 15-16, 70, 72, 78-79, 82, 101, 304-308, 310, 313-317, 322, 324, 328-331, 334-340, 342-344, 391, 393
Landau, Benny   401
Lapid, Yair   214
Lassalle, Ferdinand   260, 408
Latvians   119
Law of Return   x, 24-25, 123, 359
Lawrence, Thomas Edward   393
LAX (Los Angeles International Airport)   252
Lazarus, Emma   290
Leah   262
Leary, Timothy   204
Lebanon   ix, 93, 213
Lecha Dodi   325, 339
Lee, Bruce   277
Lehren, Tzvi Hirsch   338
Leibowitz, Yeshayahu   359
Lenin, Vladimir Ilyich   260
Lennon, John   263-265, 272-273, 282, 287-288
L'État Juif (Herzl)   361, 381
Levi-Strauss, Claude   76
Levkov, Haim   399-400
Levy, Gideon   392
Lieberman, Avigdor   240
Lifshitz, Nehama   237
Likud   154
Lissak, Moshe   xii
Lithuania   105, 225-226, 322, 335
Lithuanians   120
Lloyd George, David   374
Lombroso, Cesare   76
London   213, 232, 361, 363, 373, 396
London's School of Oriental Studies 393
Los Angeles   256
Love Parade   199, 200
LSD   204
Luke, Gospel of   269
Luria, Isaac   290, 320, 325-329

Luther, Martin 321
Luzzatto, Moses Haim 334

M*A*S*H 254
Maariv 199, 209, 214
Maccabean Society 361
Maccabees 262, 368-369, 377
MacDonald, Malcolm 396
Macedonians 123
Maghen, Ze'ev xii, 263
Magyar Law 120-121
Maimonides, Moses 51, 77, 109-
   110, 132, 188, 290, 311, 313,
   324, 339
Mamelukes 316, 319
Mandeans 275
Mandelstam, Osip 238
Manhattan 283
Manicheans 275
Mantua 322
Mao Zedong 272
Marinetti, Filippo Tommaso Emilio
   260
Marrakech 251
Marseilles 38
Marx, Karl 76, 135, 148, 260
Marxism 69
Masada 146, 290
Masbala 78
Matthausen 291
Matthew, Gospel of 269
Mazuz, Manny 113
Mazzini, Giuseppe 260
Mead, Peter 391
Mecca 372
Mediterranean 16, 18, 28, 52, 199,
   282
Meged, Aharon xii
Megilla 257
Meir, Golda 297, 406
Menahem Mendel of Shklov 339
Menahem Mendel of Vitebsk 335

Mendelssohn, Moses 134
"Menora" (Herzl) 377
Meras, Yitzhak 237, 238
Meretz 211
Meridor, Dan 240
Mesilat Yesharim (Luzzatto) 334
Micah 182
Middle East xi, 10, 27, 114, 201,
   239, 256
Midrash 186, 285, 309
Mikhoels, Solomon 238
Mill, John Stuart 54
Milton, John 51
Minsk Conference 59
Miriam 290
Mishna 174, 320, 407
Mishnat Hasidim (Ricchi) 333
Mizrahi 181, 191, 380
Modi'in 290
Molcho, Solomon 321-323
Montefiore, Moses 340, 341
Montenegro 52
Montesquieu, Charles-Louis de Secondat
   38, 43, 49
Mordechai 79-80
Moria 70
Morocco 327
Morris, Benny 295-301
Moscow 111, 238, 335
Moses 262
Mosley, Leonard 391
Mount Sinai 291
Mount Zion 318
Muhammad Ali 340-341
Mulhausen, Yom-Tov Lipmann 315
Munich Conference 396
Muslims 275, 312, 314, 316, 318-
   319, 321, 323, 334, 341-342,
   360, 372, 411
Myers, David 307

Nasser, Gamal Abdel 409

Nazism   41, 43, 169, 359, 394, 408-409

Nebuchadnezzar   290

Negev   231, 283

Nehemia   80

Netanya   398

Netanyahu, Benjamin   286

Netzarim   92

Neue Freie Presse   116

New Historians   131, 295, 391

New Jersey   412

new Middle East   45, 89, 249

New Republic   297

New Testament   45, 89, 268

New York   119, 199-200, 263, 277-288, 296

New York Times   210, 295, 297

Newcombe, Russell   206

Newton, Isaac   51

Nietzsche, Friedrich Wilhelm   144-145, 201, 203, 206, 208, 260

Nile   290

Nini, Itzik   209

Nordau, Max   82, 366, 375

North America   ix, 239

Norway   xi

Oforia (Ofer Dikovsky, musician)   210

Oklahoma   405

Old City   319

On the Social Contract (Rousseau)   51, 365

Ono, Yoko   263

Ophir, Adi   ix

Or Hahaim (Haim ben Atar)   334

Orde Wingate (Sykes)   391

Orde Wingate and the Historians (Mead)   391

Orde Wingate: His Life and Works (Akavia)   391

Orde Wingate: Irregular Soldier (Royle)   391

Origin of the Species (Darwin)   263

Orwell, George   281

Oslo process   86, 90, 92, 154

Ostraha   327

Ottoman Empire   316, 321, 324, 333, 336

"Our Platform" (Borochov)   149

Ovid   200

Oz, Amos   358, 360

Padan, Yehiam   392

Paglia, Camille   205

Palestine   viii, 10-13, 16, 40-42, 58-59, 119, 129, 152-153, 296, 305-308, 312-314, 317-318, 320-321, 323-327, 329-330, 332-338, 340-344, 358, 362, 364, 367, 369, 374-375, 379, 393-399, 406

Palestinian Authority   xi

Palestinian National Covenant   14

Palestinians   5, 8, 10, 14-18, 20, 24, 28, 299, 411, 413

Palmah   238, 409

Palmerston (Lord)   40

Paris   x, 107, 314, 362, 381

Pascal, Blaise   213

Passover Haggada   291

Patterson, Lorna   394, 397-398

Peace Now   410

Pentateuch   254

Peres, Shimon   78, 90

Persia   67, 76, 290

Petah Tikva   240

Philadelphia   278

Philistines   94, 290

Piaget, Jean   276

Playfair, Ian Stanley Ord   391

Plekhanov, Georgi Valentinovich   260

PLO   14, 92

Pol Pot   272

Poland   viii, 38, 41, 291, 322

Poles   225, 246
Politics (Aristotle)   155
Pollack, Jacob   323
Ponary   226
Pop, Iggy   208
Porat, Dina   298
Porat, Hanan   94
Porath, Yehoshua   xii, 296
Poraz, Avraham   211
Portugal   321, 324, 327
Potiphar   290
Prague   315, 323, 327, 364
Prayer (Berkovits)   174
Protestantism   128, 321
Provence   313
Psalms   309-310
Pumpedita   290

Quebec   398
Qur'an   273

Rabin, Yitzhak   86, 89, 110, 214
Rachel   262, 290
Ram, Uri   307
Rama   257
Ramat Hasharon   253-254
Rand, Ayn   260
Raz-Krakotzkin, Amnon   306
Rebecca   262
Regensburg   322
Rehovot   93
Reines, Isaac Jacob   181
Religion of Reason Out of the Sources of Judaism (Cohen)   176
Renewing the Covenant (Borowitz)   169, 176
Renner, Karl   149
"Report on the Preferential Treatment of National Minorities by Their Kin State"   121
Reuveni, David   321-322
Rhodians   38

Ricchi, Immanuel Hai   333, 335
Rieff, David   299
Righteous Victims: A History of the Zionist-Arab Conflict (Morris)   296, 299
Rig-Veda   255
Robin Hood   254
Roger, Eugene   330
Rohde, Erwin   200
Rolling Stone   264
Rolo, Charles   391
Romania   120, 121
Romanians   246
Romans   94, 146, 203
Rome   38, 69, 74, 317
Rome and Jerusalem (Hess)   51
Ronald, Tzvi Trotush   206
Rooney, David   391
Roosevelt, Franklin Delano   398
Rosenzweig, Franz   52, 175-176, 182-184
Rosh Pina   231
Rotenstreich, Natan   xi
Rothschild family   341
Rothschild, Baron Anshel   340
Rousseau, Jean-Jacques   51, 53-54, 59, 260, 365, 372-373
Royal Geographic Society   394
Royle, Trevor   391
Rubinstein, Amnon   xii, 366-367
Ruins of Jerusalem (anonymous)   330, 331
Russell, Bertrand   260
Russia   41, 45-46, 48, 107, 120, 225, 228, 230, 232-233, 236-239, 243, 247-248, 290, 333, 335, 338
Russian empire   380
Russians   226, 231, 237, 239-241, 245-246

Saddam Hussein   281, 413
Safed   323-328, 330, 339-341

Salonika   251, 321
Samaria   92, 191, 410
Sambari, Joseph   331
Samson   146, 290, 407
Samson of Schantz   313
Sana'a   251
Sandman (Itzik Levi, musician)   210
Sanhedrin   188, 324
Saragossa   317
Sarah   262
Sarid, Yossi   92
Satan   148, 203
Saul (Paul) of Tarsus   75-76, 90
Scholem, Gershom   59, 131-132
Schönau Castle   224
Schueftan, Dan   298
Schwartz, Delmore   412
Schweid, Eliezer   xi
Sea of Galilee   323
Second Lebanon War   xi
Segev, Tom   295-296, 298, 392, 398-401
Selden, John   51
Senesh, Hanna   291
Sephardim   240, 328, 340
Serbia   120
Seventh Million (Segev)   295, 298
Shabtai Tzvi   77, 133, 332
Shakespeare, William   52
Shamai   57, 71-74, 92-93
Shamir, Moshe   xii, 109
Shapira, Anita   xii, 302
Shapira, Nathan   327
Sharabi, Shalom   334
Sharett, Moshe   392, 394, 399
Sharon, Ariel   413
Shas   110
Shavit, Ari   215
Shefer, Yitzhak   323
Shiloh   94
Shimon bar Yohai   290
Shlaim, Avi   297-298

Shnei Luhot Habrit (Horowitz)   327
Shoham, Shlomo Giora   202
Shulhan Aruch (Karo)   320, 336
Siberia   105, 202, 228
Sidon   323
Siftei Kohen (Shabtai Hacohen)   331
Sinai   15-16, 68, 93-94, 169, 184
Six Day War   15-16, 46, 181, 296, 412
Slovakia   120-121
Slovenia   120
Slutsk   335
Smith, Adam   260
Smith, Anthony D.   119
Smith, Colin   392-393, 396, 401
SNS (Special Night Squads)   390-391, 395-397, 399-401
Sobibor   291
Soloveitchik, Joseph Ber (Yosef Dov)   xii, 169
South Africa   107
Soviet Union   ix-x, 25, 104, 110-111, 120, 223, 227, 230-234, 237, 243-244, 246, 307
Spain   12, 53, 118, 290, 315, 317-318, 320-322
Spice Girls   266, 276
Spinoza, Benedictus de   260, 369
Sri Krishna   255
St. Petersburg   335
Stalin   272
Star of Redemption (Rosenzweig)   183
Star Trek   289
State Education Law   123
State of Israel   vii, 4, 14-15, 23, 27, 85, 93, 143, 152, 169, 191, 224, 226, 229, 233, 238, 248-249, 360, 381
Strasbourg   118
Sturmann, Haim   396
Sudan   393
Sudan Defense Force   393

Sumer 67
Supreme Court 124
Sura 290
Switzerland 107, 377
Sykes, Christopher 391
Syria 15, 284, 296, 341, 410

Tacitus, Cornelius 74
Tajikestan 284
Taliban 413
Talmud 28, 51, 72, 143, 173, 186-187, 267, 279, 291, 309, 323, 337, 407
Tamar, David 307
Tami 110
Tan-Brink, Yaron 205, 208-209
Taoism 66
Taub, Gadi 212
Teheran 273, 400, 404
Tekuma 296
Tel Aviv vii, xi, 94, 117, 199, 201, 209-211, 253, 257
Tel Aviv (weekly) 205-206, 209
Tel Aviv University ix, 209-210, 401
Tel Hashomer Hospital 231, 233
Teller, Adam 334
Temple Mount 105, 290, 314, 340-341
Teveth, Shabtai xii, 302
Tevye the milkman 285, 407
Thailand 209
Thales 68
Tiberias 326, 333-334, 400
Tikkun 297-298
Tocqueville, Alexis de 49
Tolstoy, Leo 291
Tomb of David 318
Tora 68, 70-73, 77-78, 87, 95, 182, 186-188, 192, 254, 257, 268, 280, 284, 290, 313, 315, 318, 321, 325, 330, 336, 340, 343

Towards Historic Judaism (Berkovits) 184, 189, 190
Tripoli 323
Trumpeldor, Joseph 281
Turkmen 275
Turks 154
Tuv Ha'aretz (Shapira) 327
Tzameret, Tzvi xii
Tzemah, Jacob 327

Uganda 12, 130
Ukraine 120, 333
Ukrainians 105, 225, 245
UN General Assembly 13
United Nations viii, xi, 14-15, 25, 43
United Nations partition decision 13, 362
United States x, 42-43, 117, 224, 230, 234, 237, 242-243, 252, 409-410, 413
Unity in Judaism (Berkovits) 175
Upanishads 253
Urals 105
Uzbekistan 245

Valera, Eamon de 119
Valjean, Jean 266
Venice 318, 330
Venice Commission 121-122
Vienna 223, 367
Vietnam 413
Vilna 251
Vilnius 225-226
Vital, Haim 327-329
Vitebsk 251, 335
Voice of America 232

Wall Street Journal 297
War of Independence 14, 295-296, 298-299
Warsaw 251, 291, 365
Washington 390

Wavell, Archibald　395
Weber, Max　127-128
Weekly Standard　297
Weizmann, Chaim　380, 392, 394
West Bank　ix, 15-16, 295-296,
　　298, 299
White Paper　396
White, Hayden　65
Wilson, Woodrow　278
Winfrey, Oprah　259
Wingate and the Chindits (Rooney)
　　391
Wingate, Orde　390-404
Wingate, Sir Reginald　393-394
Wissenschaft des Judentums　135
World of Changes (Ya'akobi, ed.)　296,
　　392
World War I　393
World War II　viii, 65, 390, 396
World Zionist Organization　123
Wyoming　284

Ya'akobi, Danny　296
Yad Vashem　227
Yad Yitzhak Ben-Zvi　359
Yahav, Dan　401
Yakobson, Alex　xii
Yalish, Yaakov Tzvi　337
Yamit　94
Yavneh　290
Yediot Aharonot　296
Yehiel of Paris　314, 341
Yehoshua ben Levi　310
Yemen　339

Yiddish　82, 84, 111, 237, 362
Yishmael, R.　57
Yisrael Ba'aliya　110
Yisrael Beiteinu (Israel Our Home)
　　240
Yizhar, S. (Yizhar Smilansky)　215
Yohanan ben Zakai　187
Yom Kippur War　x
Yuval, Yisrael　307, 313-314

Zangwill, Israel　374
Zimmermann, Moshe　358
Zionism　viii-ix, xi-xiii, 5, 7-10, 12-
　　13, 15, 24, 40, 81-85, 87, 89,
　　104-106, 108, 111, 114, 116-
　　117, 119, 128-133, 136-137,
　　141-142, 145-148, 150-155,
　　168-171, 178, 180-182, 184,
　　190-191, 213, 216, 228-229,
　　232, 244, 248, 262, 295, 297,
　　299-300, 302, 304-305, 307-
　　308, 342-343, 363, 365-366,
　　369, 378, 380, 382, 390-391,
　　394, 402, 406-408, 412
Zionist Congress　106, 380
*Zionist Dream Revisited: From Herzl
　　to Gush Emunim and Back*
　　(Rubinstein)　366
Zionist Organization　viii, 40, 191,
　　357, 360, 367, 374-376, 378-
　　380
Zohar　311-312, 325-326, 331, 337
Zoroastrians　275
Zucker, Dedi　211
Zygmunt I　322